BASIC STATISTICAL CONCEPTS

FOURTH EDITION

BASIC STATISTICAL CONCEPTS

Albert E. Bartz
Concordia College
Moorhead, Minnesota

Merrill
an imprint of Prentice Hall
Upper Saddle River, New Jersey   Columbus, Ohio

Library of Congress Cataloging-in-Publication Data

Bartz, Albert E.
    Basic statistical concepts / Albert E. Bartz. — 4th ed.
       p.   cm.
    Includes bibliographical references and index.
    ISBN 0–13–737180–2
    1. Mathematical statistics.   I. Title
    QA276.12.B37   1999
    519.5—dc21   98–11398
                                               CIP

Cover Art: Karen Guzak, KG Inc.
Editor: Kevin M. Davis
Developmental Editor: Gianna Marsella
Production Editor: Julie Anderson Peters
Production Coordination: Betsy Keefer
Text Designer: Betsy Keefer
Design Coordinator: Karrie M. Converse
Cover Designer: Linda Fares, L. Design
Production Manager: Laura Messerly
Illustrations: The Clarinda Company
Director of Marketing: Kevin Flanagan
Marketing Manager: Suzanne Stanton
Advertising/Marketing Coordinator: Krista Groshong

This book was set in Garamond ITC Light by The Clarinda Company and was printed and bound by Courier. The cover was printed by Phoenix Color Corp.

© 1999 by Prentice-Hall, Inc.
A Pearson Education Company
Upper Saddle River, NJ 07458

Earlier edition © 1988 by Macmillan Publishing Company.

Printed in the United States of America

10 9 8 7 6 5 4 3 2

ISBN 0-13-737180-2

Prentice-Hall International (UK) Limited,London
Prentice-Hall of Australia Pty. Limited, Sydney
Prentice-Hall Canada Inc., Toronto
Prentice-Hall Hispanoamericana, S.A., Mexico
Prentice-Hall of India Private Limited, New Delhi
Prentice-Hall of Japan, Inc., Tokyo
Pearson Education Asia Pte. Ltd., Singapore
Editora Prentice-Hall do Brasil, Ltda., Rio de Janeiro

To Sally
who has always been significantly different

FOREWORD

There is an unmistakable look of gloom on the face of a student who has just been told by an advisor to take a quantitative methods or statistics course during the next semester. Fortunately for those of us who are given the opportunity to instruct these "dreaded" classes, we have an ally in Albert Bartz and an outstanding resource in the fourth edition of his text, *Basic Statistical Concepts*.

I have used Bartz's book to teach basic statistics for the past nine years for a number of important reasons, three of which seem most significant. First, the text effectively presents a wide range of the major concepts that constitute descriptive and inferential statistics. The amount of material is more than substantial for a semester's worth of work and it is presented in a thoughtful and judicious manner. Further, these significant areas of statistical study are sequenced appropriately and reasonably aligned.

Second, I find that when students read this text they do not become entangled in a web of mathematical complexity, but are led to understand the various statistical techniques as they relate to realistic data. The author has mastered the art of presenting difficult material in a form that is very clear and almost conversational in style. Many former students of mine report they frequently refer to the Bartz text for a clear description of some statistical procedure or technique they encounter in subsequent schooling or career activities. With good conscience, I tell my students that if they are only going to keep one text they buy for a class, it should definitely be the Bartz book.

The third reason that I am so drawn to *Basic Statistical Concepts* is that the text does not represent statistics as some detached form of mathematical exercise, but relates the quantitative methods to real research. Students are shown the usefulness of various techniques and are given examples of research contexts in which specific procedures are applicable. As a result, Bartz's approach makes statistics more meaningful as a necessary tool in the research process.

With the newest edition of *Basic Statistical Concepts* come several other significant features that make the text well worth adopting. Along with the outstanding characteristics of the book offered above, the fourth edition includes computer-oriented applications and problems, a reorganization of some basic concepts that makes the overall presentation even more concise, and a greater focus on contemporary research topics and questions.

Without hesitation, I can say the Bartz text is indeed one of the most usable, readable, and understandable basic statistics books available.

Kenneth D. Witmer, Jr., Ph.D
Associate Professor
Frostburg State University

PREFACE

PHILOSOPHY AND APPROACH

If a textbook is fortunate to make it to a fourth edition, the author should be warned to proceed with caution when deciding what text materials to omit, add, or delete. Some changes have been made in this edition to reflect accurately the current state of the discipline. But three primary concerns of the first edition remain as important as ever:

1. *A student-centered approach.* A deliberate effort has been made to develop techniques that will assist the student in grasping statistical concepts. A series of Notes set off by colored rules call the student's attention to helpful hints that will aid him or her in understanding concepts, avoiding errors, developing computational skills, or discovering the historical significance of statistical events. By isolating selected subject matter in this way, the student is able to associate these smaller bits of information with the larger whole, and more easily remember the connection between the two. Another learning aid is a Sample Problem that appears at the end of each chapter. Each one shows collected data, decision steps, calculations, and conclusions that can be drawn from the results. These techniques—in addition to the step-by-step progression from simpler to more complex material, the attempt to combine an intuitive approach with the usual mathematical development, and the Study Questions and Exercises for each chapter—should provide the learner with ample exposure to the conceptualizations and calculations necessary for proficiency in statistical techniques. And if any students feel the need for a review of basic mathematics and wish to upgrade their arithmetic and algebra skills, the Basic Mathematics Refresher is in Appendix 2.

2. *Selection and presentation of topics.* A 10-year-old girl, returning a book on penguins to the public library, remarked to the librarian, "This book told

me more about penguins than I really want to know." Many textbooks have included much more material than can reasonably be covered in a typical one-semester or two-quarter course in introductory statistics. The topics chosen for this book are concepts that form the foundation for measurement in education and the behavioral sciences. However, each instructor may have individual preferences, and a different order of topics may be used or some of the later topics may be omitted or abbreviated at the instructor's discretion. Most of the chapters here are organized to include an introduction to the concept with several familiar illustrations, progressing to formulas that define or demonstrate the concept, and concluding with computational formulas, worked examples, and applications and limitations of the concept.

3. *Simplified language.* In talking with other statistics instructors, I have found that much class time is spent on explaining what students didn't understand in reading their textbook assignment. In planning each chapter, I have tried to simplify the descriptions and applications for the chapter's concepts. Although it is one thing to discuss the meaning of percentiles or measures of central tendency and an entirely different thing to describe a two-way ANOVA, I have attempted to present both kinds of material in an uncomplicated, narrative style, with a profusion of lucid examples. A considerable portion of the material may seem redundant to the mathematically sophisticated student, but, in teaching the introductory statistics course for more than 30 years, I have found that a certain amount of redundancy is not only desirable but essential for realizing optimum gain as the student progresses through the material. There is a difference between a "watered-down" approach and one that attempts to be rigorous yet readable. I have attempted to present the traditionally difficult and more complex material in the same manner as the easier concepts.

NEW TO THIS EDITION

One major change from the previous editions is the inclusion of *research scenarios* at the beginning of each chapter. These introductory scenarios allow the student to see that the statistical methods and techniques introduced in each chapter have an immediate reason for being studied. In most cases more examples of the research scenario are presented later in the chapter, illustrating how the particular technique is used in applied settings.

Other changes that will be obvious to users of the previous edition include *a new chapter on power and effect size,* the omission of previous Chapters 4 and 14 on educational assessment, and *a change to the "N − 1" version of the standard deviation.* The last change was thought necessary because most computer statistical packages use the $N - 1$ formula. This change, of course, required alterations in several related formulas throughout the text.

In an increasing number of statistics courses, computer software packages are used to augment students' understanding of traditional statistical concepts. In response to this trend, this edition incorporates *the use of computers* to assist students with calculation and data analysis. For example, I have included computer examples (SPSS) with the Sample Problems at the end of the chapters. In addition, a computer data bank is described and presented in Appendix 4, and computer exercises are included at the end of most chapters. These exercises and the data bank, of course, will be appropriate for whichever statistical package is used.

A "SIGNIFICANT" NOTE

As most of you know, significance testing has become a controversial issue, and the American Psychological Association has appointed the Task Force on Statistical Inference to study the issue. Their initial report left intact the familiar null hypothesis and significance testing in general, so I have continued the approach found in most professional literature in education and the behavioral sciences. However, some instructors may wish to alter the explanations and approaches in the several chapters where significance tests are presented. Footnotes in those chapters inform the students about the controversy—a natural lead-in for the instructor pursuing other strategies.

ACKNOWLEDGMENTS

I thank Robert Barcikowski, Ohio University; Susan M. Brookhart, Duquesne University; Joe Cornett, Texas Tech University; Eric W. Corty, Pennsylvania State University; William L. Curlette, Georgia State University; Kenneth Duckworth, University of Louisville; Bryan W. Griffin, Georgia Southern University; and Diane Kraut, Oklahoma State University for their critical reviews. Their suggestions were very helpful; however, I must bear the responsibility for the finished product. A special note of gratitude is also due to Dr. Ken Witmer of Frostburg State University for carefully checking a thousand details and providing solutions for the usual glitches found when we try to combine words and numbers. And a sincere thank you is due Kevin Davis, senior editor, for his much appreciated efforts in bringing this project to completion.

I am grateful to Dr. Julie Legler of the National Cancer Institute for her Basic Mathematics Refresher in Appendix 2. I especially thank Marisa Asmus and Carla Locken for providing a new set of end-of-chapter exercises and answers for this edition. I am grateful to my wife, Sal, for providing ideas for research applications in the fields of school psychology and special education and patiently awaiting the completed revision. Finally, I thank the many students who have consented to serve as guinea pigs while different teaching methods and techniques were evaluated. Their willing participation in efforts to improve the teaching and learning of statistical methods is greatly appreciated.

Albert E. Bartz

TO THE STUDENT

Most of you have heard of "math anxiety" or "test anxiety" (or the new term, "evaluation apprehension"), and some of you may wonder if there is such a thing as "statistics anxiety." If you are feeling a bit apprehensive about this course, you are not alone. A fair number of students who confidently tackle such diverse college courses as archaeology, music theory, and transpersonal psychology are uneasy when approaching an upcoming course in statistics. For many, a weakness in mathematics is often given as an excuse, and this would be a legitimate reaction to a course that stressed the mathematical theory underlying each concept and the derivation of all formulas for a given statistic. However, this textbook for your current statistics course assumes no mathematical training beyond your first high school algebra course. Also, when it is necessary to manipulate some mathematical symbols, each step is shown and carefully explained.

But there is no denying the fact that a first course in statistics can be difficult, simply because the subject matter is new to most of you. As a result, this book has been organized deliberately to facilitate the understanding of each new concept. The beginning chapters contain the simpler material, and succeeding chapters become progressively more complex. However, there is a logical progression from one chapter to the next, so even the more complex concepts will not prove too difficult if you make certain that you completely understand the material in each chapter before going on.

Teaching by example has been shown to be an effective educational tool, so plan to spend time looking over each example and coordinating it with the text narrative. Each chapter begins with a brief summary of a research project that utilizes the chapter's concepts, and serves to show how statistics can help in understanding the research process. The *Study Questions* at the end of the chapter will help you to focus your reading on the important concepts in each chapter. The *Sample Problem* at the end of each chapter should help tie together the concepts presented, and there is an ample supply of *Exercises* that will sharpen your skills on the various concepts in each chapter. The answers to the odd-numbered exercises are given at the end of the book.

Because the material in the earlier chapters is somewhat simpler, you may have a natural tendency to devote less time to these chapters and to neglect the exercises. This could be a serious mistake, since it is the most frequent reason given by students for failing or dropping the course. Because the later chapters will require more time and effort, it is essential not to fall behind in your work at any time in the course. If you keep up with the daily assignments on both the reading and the problems, you will find that the material will be less difficult to learn and much easier to remember.

BRIEF CONTENTS

CONTENTS

CHAPTER 4

CHAPTER 5

CHAPTER 6

CHAPTER 8

CHAPTER 9

CHAPTER 1

Some Thoughts on Measurement

Whatever exists at all exists in some
amount . . . and whatever exists in some
amount can be measured.
                                        —*Thorndike*

There are three kinds of lies: lies, damned
lies, and statistics.
                                        —*Disraeli*

These two views of measurement certainly must represent the absolute opposite ends of the optimism–pessimism spectrum! As educators or social and behavioral scientists, we would hope that the view of the renowned psychologist Edward Thorndike would prevail, and that we could put some faith in the numbers (data) that we gather.

On the other hand, we also know of too many incidents where the comment by the British Prime Minister Benjamin Disraeli might be closer to the truth. It, of course, implies that part of a statistician's duties is to bend the data in some way or another to prove whatever point needs proving. Even if you were not acquainted with Disraeli's pessimistic viewpoint, you have at least heard statements such as "You can prove anything with statistics" or "Figures don't lie, but liars can figure."

It is not surprising, then, that the average person has less than complete confidence in statistics and statisticians. In Figure 1.1 we note that even Charlie Brown is not immune from the attitudes of the lay public toward statisticians.

Figure 1.1
Even the comics reflect the public's attitude about statistics. (*Source:* PEANUTS ©
United Feature Syndicate. Reprinted by permission.)

THE NEED FOR STATISTICS

It is hoped that a first course in statistics will clear up some of the misconceptions about statistics mentioned in the opening paragraphs. There are three general objectives that you should hope to achieve through this introductory course. It is expected that you will (1) be able to read the professional literature in your field of study, (2) appreciate the fact that statistics is a necessary tool for research, and (3) develop an increased ability to identify situations where statistics are used in an inappropriate or misleading manner. Let us examine these three objectives in detail.

Professional Literature

As your course of study progresses, you are in the process of becoming a professional in your chosen field, and you will be expected to read the professional literature in books and journals. Since statistics are used to communicate results of surveys, experiments, and tests, you must be able to understand what an author is saying by means of graphs, averages, correlation coefficients, *t* tests, and the like. You can no longer "skip the hard places," as you might have done back in grade school, but will have to be able to read—and understand what you are reading—to be a professional. And since statistics permits the most concise and exact way of describing data, you can expect that the majority of your professional reading will use a statistical analysis of some sort.

Research Tool

Statistics is a necessary tool for all research, where *research* is broadly defined. Whether you are a classroom teacher, guidance counselor, social caseworker, physiological psychologist, or personnel manager, a rudimentary knowledge of statistics is a prerequisite for analyzing data. As education and the behavioral sciences move increasingly toward a quantitative approach, the results of research studies of all kinds become the basic diet for everyone in the field. The days of armchair speculation are numbered, and more and more hard-nosed research results will be demanded as evidence for a particular point of view.

Misleading Statistics

Although we are all rather suspicious of claims using such statistics as "Three out of four doctors recommend . . ." or ". . . dissolves 50% more stomach acid than . . .," there are times when data manipulation is not so obvious. One candidate for ease of misinterpretation is the graphical method; examples are shown in Figures 1.2 and 1.3.

Figure 1.2 shows the familiar *pictogram*, where the height of the figures represents the amount of the quantity being graphed—in this case, the number of members of several church denominations in one small midwestern state. On first examination of the graph you would probably conclude that denomination A has anywhere from 6 to 10 times as many members as either B or C. The graph is misleading because you are being influenced not by the *height* of the figures alone but by the proportionate *space* they occupy. Actually, the height of the figure representing denomination A is correct. The figure is just over 4 times taller (representing 78,426 members) than either B (18,192 members) or C (17,513 members).

Two graphs representing unemployment figures for the last four months of a year are shown in Figure 1.3. Both graphs are constructed from the same basic data, but they differ with respect to the units of measurement on the vertical axis.

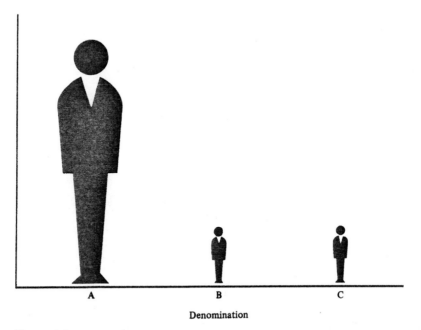

Denomination

Figure 1.2
Pictogram for church membership among three religious denominations.

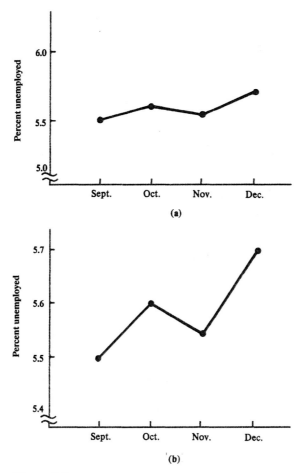

Figure 1.3
Unemployment figures graphed with different units.

Someone who wished to demonstrate that there is no cause for alarm might represent the data by Figure 1.3a. Since the units in this graph are large, an increase from 5.5 to 5.7 percent causes little change from September to December. On the other hand, someone who wished to exaggerate the increase in unemployment would demonstrate that point by means of Figure 1.3b, where the smaller units magnify the change from 5.5 to 5.7 percent.

These examples of inappropriate use of graphical methods demonstrate only one way in which statistics can be misleading. As you develop expertise with the statistical concepts to be presented in the following chapters, you will become familiar with the appropriate applications for each statistic and will be sensitized to possible uses and abuses in the presentation of data.

THE IMPORTANCE OF MEASUREMENT

The growth in importance of the physical sciences in the last few decades has been in part due to increased precision of measurement. The different teams of astronauts could not have explored the surface of the moon were it not for the ability of scientists to measure time, space, and matter with extreme precision. A visit to any facility for research in biology, medicine, or any other scientific discipline would show a large amount of floor and counter space devoted to precision measuring devices of one kind or another.

Although we do not claim the same degree of precision as the natural sciences, measurement is of supreme importance in education and the behavioral sciences as well. The use of statistical methods enables us to make *quantitative* statements about data that could not be formulated by any other means. The football coach who says he has a "big" team is making a less precise statement than one who states that the average weight of his defensive line is 250 pounds. To say that John is older than Lisa is not as informative as saying that John is about a year older than Lisa. And saying that John is 11 months and 3 days older than Lisa would give us information of even greater precision. Similarly, we make quantitative statements about Greg's IQ test score, Sheri's reading readiness score, Ryan's anxiety level, and Sue's college grade-point average.

So far we have been using the term *statistics* in several different ways, and at this point it might be helpful to sort out exactly what we mean. An acquaintance of mine informs her classes that "We calculate statistics from statistics by statistics." A good way to begin this course would be to clear up this apparent confusion.

1. "We calculate statistics . . ." What she means here are the results of a computation: the graphs and percentiles and correlation coefficients. These are the final figures that tell us what a particular batch of data means.
2. ". . . from statistics . . ." The term here refers to the data, the collection of numbers that constitutes the raw material we work with. They may be test scores, reaction times, frequency of divorces, or number of migraine headaches, or what have you.
3. ". . . by statistics." The last use of the term is the process or method that we use to get our averages, percentiles, or the like. Formulas have been derived and methods have been developed so that we follow a certain procedure and perform the necessary calculations to obtain the desired result.

The emphasis in this book will be on the first and third uses of the term. As the concepts are introduced in the following chapters, we will study the *method* or *process* that is appropriate for the desired results and learn how the *end product* tells what we need to know about our data. Viewed in this way, the task of statistics *is to reduce large masses of data to some meaningful values*. Whether we are working with 20 algebra test scores, 200 freshmen entrance exam scores, or

Figure 1.4
Statisticians and computer programmers can suffer from the same malady. (*Source:* FRANK & ERNEST © United Feature Syndicate.)

200,000 automobile driver records, our objective is the same: to come up with some meaningful values that tell us something about our set of data.

The second use of the term, the statistics as *raw data* or *scores,* will not be discussed at any great length in the chapters to follow. Since this book is written to cover broadly the concepts applied to education and the behavioral sciences, it must be left to each individual discipline to define the kinds of data that characterize its own peculiar domain. It must be emphasized that the statistical process yielding a statistical result will never be any better than the raw material on which it is based. Figure 1.4 illustrates the computer programmer's lament, "Garbage in, garbage out." It is a cliché to be remembered. An average or a correlation coefficient or any other statistic will never give respectability to a group of raw data that is essentially inaccurate.

From time to time we will take a look at some general considerations that may tend to bias the raw data and thus influence the accuracy of the final results. We will devote several of the remaining sections in this chapter to this problem, as well as noting the limitations of each statistic in the following chapters.

THE DESCRIPTIVE AND INFERENTIAL APPROACHES

The field of statistics has traditionally been divided into two broad categories—descriptive and inferential (sampling) statistics. After you have completed this first course, you will see that these two categories are not mutually exclusive and that there is a great deal of overlap in what may be labeled *descriptive* and what may be labeled *inferential.* However, it is useful at this point to distinguish these two concepts.

Descriptive Statistics

We noted earlier that the task of statistics in general was to reduce large masses of data to some meaningful values. In terms of descriptive statistics this statement would mean that these meaningful values *describe* the results of a particular sample of behavior. We might use statistics to describe the distribution of scores on a ninth-grade algebra exam, the distribution of weights of the entire football squad at a local high school, or the incidence of Asian flu among all college students at a particular university. Your grade-point average, checking account balance (sometimes a little too descriptive), and rank in high school graduating class are also descriptive statistics. The purpose of a descriptive statistic, as you can see, is to tell us something about a particular group of observations.

Inferential Statistics

In the study of inferential statistics we find our attention shifting from describing a limited group of observations to making *inferences* about the population. We will define *sample* and *population* precisely and in more detail in later chapters, but for now let us say that a sample is a smaller group of observations drawn from the larger group of observations, the population. For example, if we are conducting a poll on voting preferences, we might choose 100 voters out of a certain neighborhood. In this case the 100 voters would constitute our sample, while *all* possible voters in that neighborhood would make up the population. The task, then, of inferential statistics is to draw inferences or make predictions concerning the population on the basis of data from a smaller sample. In the case of the poll of voters, we are not particularly interested in the 100 voters but rather in making a prediction of how *all* the eligible voters in that neighborhood would vote. Similarly, if a research project is conducted by an automobile manufacturer to determine which of two designs of rear turning signals is easier to see, a sample of 500 drivers might be tested on their reaction time to the two types of lights. The engineers are not concerned only with the sample of 500 drivers but with how these results can be used to predict how *all* drivers will react.

Whether a given statistic is descriptive or inferential depends on the *purpose* for which it is intended. If a group of observations (heights, IQ scores, birth rates) is used merely to describe an event, the statistics calculated from these observations would be *descriptive*. If, on the other hand, a sample is selected (hence the term *sampling statistics*) with the intent of predicting what the larger population is like, the statistics would be *inferential*.

This book was designed to present both the descriptive and inferential approaches. Descriptive statistics, for example, would be found in measuring classroom performance (achievement tests), stock market trends, baseball records, and vital statistics. But as much a part of our life as these statistics are, I guess we would have to say that we are most often interested in the inferential approach.

We are rarely content as students of behavior merely to *measure* some characteristic but would rather use a single observation or a small number of observations to make statements about the world in general. We may measure Cathy's IQ,

Jim's grade-point average, and Tony's sociability, and, using these as descriptors, put them to good use in advisement or counseling. But quite often we go beyond a mere description and contemplate such things as how Cathy's low socioeconomic level has affected her IQ test performance, how Jim's grade-point average is related to his father's achievement motivation, and what effect Tony's being an only child has on his introversion–extroversion score. It is the inferential approach that can help us answer questions such as these, and the majority of the chapters to follow will describe techniques designed to measure these variables.

MEASUREMENT AND SCALES

Ever since our early childhood years we have been bombarded by numbers. We probably began by learning to count our fingers, graduated to toes, and continued into elementary school, sharpening our skills in the marvelous numerical system. We've reached a point now where we feel relatively comfortable with numbers because we have been adding and subtracting and multiplying and dividing for years.

Occasionally, the numbers that we worked with represented something concrete like ducks or money or people, but more often than not we worked with just simple rows or columns of digits. This approach bothered us not at all, and we performed arithmetic operations on acres of numbers with the sole objective of getting the right answer.

We would now like to apply our quantitative skills to observations of behavior, but before we perform arithmetic manipulations on numbers that represent something (e.g., test scores) we have to be aware of the properties that these numbers have. We cannot blindly manipulate a set of numbers without knowing something about their properties and what the numbers represent. Somewhere back in your arithmetic training a teacher no doubt said you couldn't add apples and oranges together. This warning probably didn't make much of an impact on you at the time (other than the fact that you have successfully avoided adding apples and oranges), but the statement could not be more true than in the field of measurement. We must be sensitive to precisely what the numbers represent.

Measurement is formally defined as the *assignment of numbers to objects or events according to certain prescribed rules.* Once this has been done, the numbers have certain properties of which we must be fully aware as we perform the arithmetic operations. We treat these numbers differently and with varying degrees of precision, depending upon what they represent. The number 9 representing the hardness of a rock sample is different from a glove size of 9 or nine items correct on a short geography quiz.

A very convenient way of looking at the properties that a given number may have is to examine four kinds of scales that describe different levels of precision in treating numbers. These are called, in increasing order of precision, *nominal, ordinal, interval,* and *ratio* scales. Each type of scale represents a way of assigning numbers to objects or events, and the description of each type that follows shows the rules that were applied.

Nominal Scale

The simplest and most elementary type of measurement uses the nominal scale. Numbers are assigned for the sole purpose of differentiating one object from another. Steve has a book locker labeled 80, Tonya wears basketball jersey number 22, and Dave is taking his motorbike for a trip on U.S. Highway 40. The nominal scale has only the property of differentiating one object or event from another.

In fact, it would not be necessary to use *numbers* to differentiate the categories. We could just as easily use letters of the alphabet, nouns, or proper names. When we categorize groups as male/female or freshman/sophomore/junior/senior, for example, we are categorizing according to a nominal scale.

When numbers are used in a nominal scale, we would not dream of adding them together or trying to calculate an average, because this scale does not have the necessary properties to enable us to do so. People would start avoiding you if you went around stating that the average basketball jersey number at the NCAA tournament was 37.63 or that the sum of the U.S. Interstate Highway numbers traveled on your vacation last summer was 208! In a similar vein book locker number 80 is not twice as large as book locker 40, and Tonya's basketball jersey number 22 does not mean she is only half as good as her teammate wearing jersey number 44.

Such examples may seem to be belaboring the obvious, but these extreme situations are used to make you fully aware of the single property of the nominal scale—that of differentiating one object or event from another. Crude as it may be, this scale is still a form of measurement and will be useful in certain statistical techniques.

Ordinal Scale

As the term implies, measurements in an ordinal scale have the property of *order*. Not only can we differentiate one object from another as in the nominal scale, but we can specify the *direction of the difference*. We can now make statements using "more than" or "less than," since our measuring system has the property of order, and the objects or events can be placed on a continuum in terms of some measurable characteristic.

The *ranking* of objects or events would be a good example of an ordinal scale. A third-grade teacher, for example, might rank Ann, Beth, and Cindy as 1, 2, and 3, respectively, on the trait of sociability. As a result of the teacher's ranking, we know that Ann is more sociable than Beth and Beth is more sociable than Cindy. This is a definite improvement over the nominal scale, where no indication of the *direction* of the difference could be made. Under a nominal scale, all we could say is that Ann, Beth, and Cindy are different in sociability.

But note that our scale still does not permit us to say *how much* of a difference exists between two or more objects or events. Ann may be just slightly more sociable than Beth, while Cindy may be considerably less sociable than either. Yet the ranks of 1, 2, and 3 do not communicate this information. In this example, there would be hardly any difference between ranks 1 and 2, while there would be a large difference between ranks 2 and 3.

As another example, consider an art critic ranking three paintings in terms of their realism. He could conceivably give the most realistic a rank of 1, the next most realistic a rank of 2, and so on. According to the critic, the paintings may have been very reliably put into their proper order in terms of realism, but there is no way to assess the *amount* of realism or to say that one is twice as realistic as another. This is an example of an ordinal scale.

Interval Scale

The most important characteristic of an interval scale is equality of units. This means that there are equal distances between observation points on the scale. Not only can we specify the direction of the difference, as we did in the ordinal scale, but we can indicate the amount of the difference as well. A very common example of an interval scale is our familiar Fahrenheit temperature scale. There are equal intervals between the points on the scale, and the difference between 30° and 34° is the same as the difference between 72° and 76°. We can also say that an increase from 50° to 70° is twice as much as an increase from 30° to 40°. With the interval scale we can now assess the *amount* of the difference between two or more objects or events, something we could not do with the ordinal scale.

Many of the measurements that characterize education and the behavioral sciences are of the interval type. For example, most test scores (in terms of number of items correct) are treated as if they were based on interval measures.

Ratio Scale

The ratio scale has all the characteristics of the interval scale plus an *absolute zero*. With an absolute zero point we can make statements involving ratios of two observations, such as "twice as long" or "half as fast."

In the Fahrenheit temperature scale discussed in the preceding section, we *cannot* say, for example, that a temperature of 80° is twice as warm as one of 40°. This limitation is due to the fact that the Fahrenheit temperature scale has only an arbitrary zero, not an absolute zero. A ratio scale must have a meaningful absolute zero. If Carla can jog 2 miles in 12 minutes, but it takes Lisa 24 minutes, we know that Carla can run twice as fast. But in intelligence testing, for example, we cannot say that a person with an IQ of 100 is twice as intelligent as someone with an IQ of 50. We cannot do so because zero intelligence cannot be defined, and thus there is no absolute zero point. Most physical scales such as time, length, and weight are ratio scales, but very few behavioral measures are of this type.

Comparing the Four Scales

Table 1.1 is a summary of the characteristics of the four types of scales, and, as you can see, each successive scale possesses the characteristics of the preceding scales.

It is easy to get the impression that the ideal measurement would be in a ratio scale and that measurements in the other three scales are something to be avoided if at all possible. Although this may be the theoretical goal or ideal of measurement purists, we are faced with the fact that most behavioral measures miss this ideal by a significant amount, and practical considerations require our making the most of the precision that we do have. As was stated earlier, many of the measurements that we deal with in education and the behavioral sciences are treated as interval measures. However, a good part of our data is of the ordinal type, and even the nominal scale serves us very well. If a teacher ranks his students on "social participation," or a poll taker asks her respondents to indicate their preferences of political candidates' views on some national issue, or a football coach judges his wide receiver candidates on their proficiency, all are making use of ordinal measures. And any study involving categorization according to some attribute (men/women, freshman/senior, alcoholic/social drinker/teetotaler) would involve the nominal scale.

As the various statistical methods are covered in the chapters to follow, you will notice very soon that a lot of information can be obtained from measurements that do not meet the theoretical ideal of a ratio scale. The important thing is that you must be aware of what sort of scale a given body of measurements represents and use the statistical procedures that are appropriate for that scale. After you have done this, the statistics that you do obtain can provide a wealth of meaning about

Table 1.1
Characteristics of measurement scales

Scale	Properties
Nominal	Indicates a difference
Ordinal	Indicates a difference
	Indicates the direction of the difference
	(e.g., more than or less than)
Interval	Indicates a difference
	Indicates the direction of the difference
	Indicates the amount of the difference
	(in equal intervals)
Ratio	Indicates a difference
	Indicates the direction of the difference
	Indicates the amount of the difference
	Indicates an absolute zero

a given set of measurements, whether they are nominal, ordinal, interval, or ratio in nature.

SOME STATISTICAL SHORTHAND

Statistics, like many other disciplines, has developed its own set of symbols or notation to help summarize or condense words and statements in an efficient manner. As the different statistical concepts are presented in the chapters to follow, each abbreviation or symbol will be defined and will continue to be used throughout the book. One set of symbols is so common that it might be a good idea to spend a little time at this point covering them in some detail, because they will be appearing in almost every chapter. These symbols are collectively called *summation notation,* and they are simply a way of expressing some simple mathematical operations in a very efficient way. Those of you with a mathematics background that included summation notation may skip this section.

Variables

Table 1.2 shows a group of test scores made by a number of students. The test score is the *variable* (so called because the scores *vary* from student to student) and is denoted by the letter X. Each test score in the column is one of the values of the variable X.

In order to identify *which* value of X we are considering, we give a tag or label to each value by attaching a *subscript* to X that corresponds to its position in the column (Table 1.2). The symbol X_1 is the value of the test score in the *first* row, and student No. 1 received a score of 72, so we say that $X_1 = 72$. Similarly, X_3 is the score of student No. 3, so $X_3 = 83$. In order to be able to express the *general* case of any student's score, we use the subscript i. Thus X_i (read "X sub i") means *any* value of the variable, and it corresponds to a score made by *any* student who has the general number designated by i. So X_i could be the score made by the 5th student, the 23rd student, or the 99th student. If you have trouble visualizing the ith student, just picture the values of X as belonging to particular people. Then your values of X could be X_{Mary}, X_{Pete}, and so on, while X_i would be X_{Someone}!

The last row in a set of numbers always contains the final observation. This row is denoted as N, and the corresponding score is X_N. So the score of the Nth student in Table 1.2 is X_N. If there were a total of 50 students, N would be 50, and the score of the 50th student would be X_{50}.

Since N is always the last row containing an observation, the symbol N is also used to denote the number of observations. If there is a group of 75 scores, we say that $N = 75$, or if 29 rats are run in a maze-learning experiment, $N = 29$. It is a convenient way of expressing the *size* of the group.

The letter X is usually used to express a variable quantity (test scores, IQs, heights, etc.), but theoretically we could use A, B, J, K, or any uppercase letter to stand for the variable. Traditionally, the letters X, Y, and Z have been used in sta-

Table 1.2
Summation notation

Student Number	X (Test Score)
1	72
2	31
3	83
4	42
5	57
6	91
7	42
8	31
⋮	⋮
i	X_i
⋮	⋮
N	X_N

Adding all values: $(X_1 + X_2 + X_3 + \cdots + X_N) = \sum\limits_{i=1}^{N} X_i$

Adding the first five values: $(X_1 + X_2 + X_3 + X_4 + X_5) = \sum\limits_{i=1}^{5} X_i$

Adding the third through the sixth: $(X_3 + X_4 + X_5 + X_6) = \sum\limits_{i=3}^{6} X_i$

tistics to express a variable, with the letter X being the most common. In a later chapter we will have occasion to use both X and Y when we need to identify two variables that are being studied simultaneously—such as height and weight or grade-point average and socioeconomic level.

Summation Notation

Many statistical techniques require the *addition* of columns or rows of numbers, so it is worthwhile to examine a shorthand way of expressing addition. This shorthand method is called *summation notation.*

The Greek letter sigma (Σ) is used to signify the addition of a group of quantities, and it means "sum of." Thus ΣX means "sum of the X values." If the X values are 5, 17, 22, and 25, $\Sigma X = 69$. It is just a shorthand way of saying, "The sum of the X values is 69."

It is often convenient to express quantities in *general,* so that the terms apply to any group of numbers. It is for this reason that it is necessary to define summation notation a little more precisely. Let us consider the case where we have a *single* column (or row) of numbers such as is shown in Table 1.2.

The symbol for adding any row or column of X values is $\sum\limits_{i=1}^{N} X_i$.

This rather imposing little set of symbols simply says, "Add up the values of X, starting with the first and stopping with the one called N." Note that the subscript of X is i. The $i = 1$ under the sigma symbol is the *starting* point for the addition. It is, in effect, telling you to start adding with the first value of X (when $i = 1$), go on to the next, and continue adding each value to the total. The *stopping* point is the value at the top of the sigma symbol. Since N is the stopping point, you are to keep adding the column until you get to the last value, or N.

In other words, when you see $\sum_{i=1}^{N} X_i$, it is saying, "Take the value X_1, then X_2, and add the two. Then take X_3, and add it to the previous two. Then take X_4, and add it to the total, and so on, until you come to the value labeled X_N. You add X_N to the total and then you stop." You have then completed the operation that $\sum_{i=1}^{N} X_i$ calls for.

Suppose that you want the sum of the first five values. You would then want to begin with $i = 1$ as usual and end with the fifth value, so your summation sign would be $\sum_{i=1}^{5} X_i$. If this were applied to Table 1.2, you would take $X_1 = 72$ and add $X_2 = 31$, $X_3 = 83$, $X_4 = 42$, and stop with $X_5 = 57$. So the value of $\sum_{i=1}^{5} X_i$ would be 72 + 31 + 83 + 42 + 57, or $\sum_{i=1}^{5} X_i = 285$. In a similar fashion $\sum_{i=3}^{6} X_i$ would start with $X_3 = 83$ and would sum all values through $X_6 = 91$, so $\sum_{i=3}^{6} X_i = 273$.

In an introductory textbook such as this, most of the uses of the operation of addition will involve adding *all* the numbers in a *single* column, so there is little need to specify the starting and stopping points in a summation operation. If you are going to add *all* the numbers, the starting point will always be $i = 1$ and the stopping point will always be N. For that reason it is customary to omit the limits from the summation symbol and use only Σ, since what is to be added is understood. For example, when ΣX is called for, it simply means that you are to add all the X values. Since ΣX is easier to write and less confusing to read than $\sum_{i=1}^{N} X_i$, we will use the abbreviated form throughout the text except for one occasion in Chapter 11. However, this one occasion will be very important, so it was essential to present the elements of summation at this point.

Summation Rules

There will be times when we will have to manipulate several formulas during the course of the remaining chapters, so it is essential to cover some rules governing the operation of summation. Three rules are presented here along with several examples. Make sure you understand the basic concepts involved in these rules, for they will be helpful in the coming chapters.

RULE 1.   The sum of a constant times a variable is equal to the constant times the sum of the variable. $\Sigma CX = C\Sigma X$.

Arithmetic Example:
Given the following four numbers added together:

$$7 + 3 + 4 + 8 = 22$$

let the constant C be equal to 5 and multiply each number in the preceding equation by the constant:

$$(5)7 + (5)3 + (5)4 + (5)8 =$$
$$35 + 15 + 20 + 40 = 110$$

But you can get the same result by multiplying the original sum by the constant 5:

$$22 \times 5 = 110$$

Algebraic Proof:
The sum of a constant times a variable X would be

$$\Sigma CX = CX_1 + CX_2 + CX_3 + \cdots + CX_N$$

But collecting terms and factoring would give

$$\Sigma CX = C(X_1 + X_2 + X_3 + \cdots + X_N) = C\Sigma X$$

So the sum of a constant times a variable (ΣCX) is equal to the constant times the sum of the variable ($C\Sigma X$), or $\Sigma CX = C\Sigma X$.

RULE 2.   The sum of a constant is equal to N times the constant, where N is the number of things added. $\Sigma C = NC$.

Arithmetic Example:
Let the constant C be equal again to 5 and be added six times:

$$5 + 5 + 5 + 5 + 5 + 5 = 30$$

But collecting and noting that the constant was added six times ($N = 6$):

$$6 \times 5 = 30$$

Algebraic Proof:
All values of C are the same, and they are added N times, so

$$\Sigma C = C + C + C + \cdots + C = NC$$

RULE 3.   The summation sign operates like a multiplier on quantities within parentheses. $\Sigma(X - Y) = \Sigma X - \Sigma Y$.

Arithmetic Example:

Given a number of pairs of X and Y values, subtract each Y from its paired X value and add the columns:

X	Y	$X - Y$
6	3	3
7	2	5
9	2	7
4	2	2
26	9	17

Then note that the sum of $X - Y$ is equal to 17, which is the same result as the sum of $X(26)$ minus the sum of $Y(9)$.

Algebraic Proof:

Given a number of $X - Y$ pairs, add them together:

$$\Sigma(X - Y) = (X_1 - Y_1) + (X_2 - Y_2) + (X_3 - Y_3) + \cdots + (X_N - Y_N)$$

Collect the common terms:

$$\Sigma(X - Y) = (X_1 + X_2 + X_3 + \cdots + X_N) \\ - (Y_1 + Y_2 + Y_3 + \cdots + Y_N)$$

and add the X's separately and Y's separately:

$$\Sigma(X - Y) = \Sigma X - \Sigma Y$$

CONCLUDING REMARKS

It would be unrealistic to expect a first course in statistical methods to transform a beginner into a polished researcher or research analyst. If you find that one of your primary interests is conducting research, you will undoubtedly choose one or more additional courses in this area. Since different textbooks and different instructors may use other systems of notation and methods of approach in the advanced courses, it is difficult to write an introductory textbook that will prepare everyone equally well for future courses that they may take. The approach used in this book is to present the material in an intuitive fashion, stressing the understanding of basic concepts, so that there will be maximum transfer to the next course you take. Symbols may differ and formulas may be slightly altered, but if you understand the elementary principles presented, you should be able to make the transition to an advanced course with a minimum of discomfort.

STUDY QUESTIONS

1. Why is a pictogram often misleading in representing the number in each of several categories?
2. In general, what is the "task" of statistics?
3. In what ways are descriptive and inferential statistics the same? In what ways are they different?
4. Give an example of each of the four types of scales.
5. What does the symbol X_i indicate?

EXERCISES

1. Indicate which scale (nominal, ordinal, interval, or ratio) would be used for the following tasks.
   a. Neighbors compare numbers on Powerball lottery tickets.
   b. Five judges choose the best lasagna recipe in the Annual Lasagna Bake-off.
   c. Fifth-graders learn the difference between the Fahrenheit and Celsius temperature scales.
   d. Beagles are ranked 72nd out of 80 breeds on canine intelligence.
   e. A college professor posts the scores for her multiple-choice test on Asian history.
   f. A realtor reports that the model home for showing this Sunday has 2,500 square feet.
   g. A total of 3,580 registrants for the Midwest Marathon are issued pin-on numbers from 1 to 3580.
   h. Football fans measure the hang time (how long the kicked football is in the air) for a punter in the National Football League.
2. Classify the following statements as reflecting nominal, ordinal, interval, or ratio data.
   a. Mary left sometime after lunch.
   b. Did you vote Republican, Democratic, or Independent?
   c. Are you left-handed?
   d. This is the brightest tie of all.
   e. How cold is it out today?
   f. Just how much time should I spend brushing my teeth?
   g. "Mirror, mirror, on the wall. Who's the fairest one of all?"
   h. I got five wrong on the geometry quiz.
3. Simplify the following expressions using summation notation.
   a. $X_3 + X_4 + X_5$
   b. $Y_1^2 + Y_2^2 + Y_3^2 + Y_4^2$
   c. $X_1 + X_2 + X_3 + X_4$
   d. $X_1 + X_2 + X_3 + \cdots + X_N$

4. Write the summation symbol you would use to express the following operations.
   a. For a column of test scores (X) you want to add all the scores from the fifth one to the 21st.
   b. Each student's score (X) is squared, and you would like to add all the squared scores.
   c. You would like to add the first six scores in a column.
5. Describe what operations are indicated by the following symbols.

   a. $\displaystyle\sum_{i=3}^{6} X_i$ c. $\displaystyle\sum_{i=1}^{N} X_i$

   b. $\displaystyle\sum_{i=1}^{7} X_i$ d. ΣX

6. Use the summation rules to expand the following expressions (remember that C is a constant).
   a. $\Sigma(X - Y - C)$
   b. $\Sigma(CY)^2$
   c. $\Sigma(X + C)$
   d. $\Sigma(X - Y)^2$

CHAPTER 2

Frequency Distributions and Graphical Methods

Lisa has always had difficulty in reading her school assignments. She doesn't "hate" to read books that her teacher recommends, but reading seems to take too much time when she would rather be doing something else. But now her reading class has changed, with the teacher showing videos highlighting excerpts from certain books and interviews with their authors. Other times, the teacher conducts "booktalks" to increase interest in and motivation toward more reading. Lately, Lisa seems to be spending more time reading, especially when studying at home. Her mother thinks that Lisa is actually enjoying reading some of the stories, especially those about animals, Lisa's favorite topic.

Lisa's situation is similar to one that was studied recently in a research project on how to get middle-level students to read more.* The researcher chose five sixth-grade reading classes at random from a school of 1,100 students. Two classes were designated as the control group ($N = 55$) and three as the experimental group ($N = 75$). The instrument to measure the degree of like or dislike of reading was the Estes Reading Attitude Scale (Estes, 1971). The Estes contains items on which students indicate their agreement

*Adapted from K. M. Brandt, *The effect of booktalks on students' attitudes towards reading* (unpublished master's thesis, Moorhead State University, MN, 1996).

or disagreement on a five-point scale with statements like "Most books are too long and dull" and "Reading turns me on." High scores indicate a positive attitude toward reading; lower scores indicate a more negative attitude.

In order to assess the students' attitudes toward reading *before* the booktalks and videos were used, the Estes was given during the first week of classes (the pretest phase of the study).

In the last chapter we noted that one of the tasks of statistics was to describe a mass of numbers in a meaningful way. The mass of numbers may represent such diverse measurements as test scores, survey results, medical records, or family income—but they are similar in that the final computer printouts, scoring sheets, or file folders result in a batch of numbers that defy any reasonable attempt to make sense out of them. Consider Table 2.1, which shows the Estes Reading Attitude Pretest scores for the 55 students in the control group.

Notice how difficult it is to get any meaning out of this collection of scores. With some effort we can find the highest score, 99, or the lowest score, 54. But we would be hard pressed indeed to find out where the concentrations of scores were, or how many students scored above 85, or how many people had a score of 82. In short, this collection of data gives us very little information about the group's reading attitudes. So, to bring a semblance of order to a group of observations, we resort to a technique that is often used to display this kind of information in a meaningful way—the *frequency distribution*.

Table 2.1
Reading attitude pretest scores

76	76	75	69	69
71	73	67	74	89
68	73	78	88	81
76	83	74	75	85
58	76	91	73	74
91	64	79	72	78
54	80	94	76	59
66	84	77	84	62
62	77	82	75	79
67	74	65	70	99
70	89	82	80	76

Source: Adapted from K. M. Brandt, *The effect of booktalks on students' attitudes towards reading.* (Unpublished master's thesis, Moorhead State University, MN, 1996.)

FREQUENCY DISTRIBUTIONS

Basically, the frequency distribution is simply a table constructed to show *how many times* a given score or group of scores occurred.[†] For example, we could set up a table where the highest score is at the top and the lowest at the bottom, with all possible scores in between, and indicate how often each score occurred. Such a table is called a *simple frequency distribution;* this technique is shown for the reading attitude scores in Table 2.2.

Although the simple frequency distribution may be convenient for a teacher assigning grades on a class achievement test, the *pattern* of the distribution does not emerge as it should. It is still difficult to readily see the concentrations of scores in such a distribution.

Table 2.2
Simple frequency distribution
of reading attitude scale
scores

Score	f	Score	f
99	1	76	6
98	0	75	3
97	0	74	4
96	0	73	3
95	0	72	1
94	1	71	1
93	0	70	2
92	0	69	2
91	2	68	1
90	0	67	2
89	2	66	1
88	1	65	1
87	0	64	1
86	0	63	0
85	1	62	2
84	2	61	0
83	1	60	0
82	2	59	1
81	1	58	1
80	2	57	0
79	2	56	0
78	2	55	0
77	2	54	1

[†]We will often use the term *scores* even though the numbers may represent heights, weights, reaction times, heart rates, or numbers of eyelashes, for instance.

Table 2.3
Poor illustration of a
grouped frequency
distribution of reading
attitude scores

Scores	f
90–99	4
80–89	12
70–79	26
60–69	10
50–59	3
	$N = 55$

Table 2.4
Better illustration of a
grouped frequency dis-
tribution of reading attitude scores

Scores	f
95–99	1
90–94	3
85–89	4
80–84	8
75–79	15
70–74	11
65–69	7
60–64	3
55–59	2
50–54	1
	$N = 55$

The most common form of the frequency distribution is the *grouped frequency distribution*, which is shown for the reading attitude scores in Table 2.3. Note that instead of displaying how often *each* score occurred, the scores have been grouped into intervals (thus the name *grouped* frequency distribution) and the number in the frequency column *f* tells how many scores are in the given interval. For example, in Table 2.3, 4 students had scores from 90 through 99.

Unfortunately, Table 2.3 has only five intervals, resulting in a frequency distribution that does not tell us very much about the pattern of distribution of our reading attitude scores. It would be better to have a frequency distribution with more and smaller intervals. Such an example is shown in Table 2.4, where there are now ten intervals. Notice that this frequency distribution gives us a better idea of the spread and concentration of our scores. We can easily see the clustering of scores about the center of the distribution, with fewer and fewer scores at the extreme ends of the distribution.

DEFINING SOME TERMS

Before we can get at the business of constructing frequency distributions, we must define some concepts that are essential to understanding the nature of the data to be displayed in a frequency distribution. The concepts described will all refer to the frequency distribution of the reading attitude scores of Table 2.4.

Real Limits and Apparent Limits

The top interval in Table 2.4 is 95–99, with a frequency of 1. In other words, one student scored somewhere from 95 through 99, the *apparent limits* of this interval. The next interval shows three scores from 90 through 94. However, to preserve the continuity of our measuring system for calculations to be discussed later on, we cannot leave a gap between 94 (the top score in the 90–94 interval) and 95 (the lowest score in the 95–99 interval). For this reason, it is understood that the *real limits* of any interval extend from 1/2 *unit below the apparent lower limit to* 1/2 *unit above the apparent upper limit*. Thus the real limits of the 95–99 interval are 94.5 and 99.5, while the real limits of the 90–94 interval are 89.5 and 94.5. The real lower limit is designated L and the real upper limit is U. So for the 60–64 interval, $L = 59.5$ and $U = 64.5$. There will be more said about real limits in a later section on continuous and discrete data.

Midpoints

The exact center of any interval is called its *midpoint,* abbreviated MP. The MP of any interval is found by adding the apparent upper limit to the apparent lower limit and dividing by 2. In Table 2.4, the MP of the 75–79 interval is 77 (75 + 79 divided by 2), and the MP for the 80–84 interval is 82.

Interval Size

The *size* of the interval, denoted by the symbol i, is the distance between the real lower limit and the real upper limit. In other words you can determine the size of the interval simply by subtracting L from U. For example, in Table 2.4, using the 70–74 interval, you would calculate $i = U - L = 74.5 - 69.5 = 5$. Note that i is the same for all the intervals in Table 2.4. And, in Table 2.3, you will note that the interval size is 10 (99.5 − 89.5 = 10).

Frequency

It should be obvious by now that frequency (the symbol is f) simply indicates how many scores are located in each interval. In Table 2.4, $f = 4$ for the 85–89 interval, indicating that four students scored between 85 and 89.

Number

As was mentioned in the last chapter, in connection with summation notation, the number of scores in a distribution is denoted by the symbol N. In Table 2.4, $N = 55$. Note that N is the total of all the frequencies for the different intervals; that is, $\Sigma f = N$.

CONSTRUCTING THE FREQUENCY DISTRIBUTION

The first step in constructing a frequency distribution from any group of data is to locate the highest and lowest scores. For the data of Table 2.1, the two extremes are 99 and 54. These give us a range of 99 − 54 = 45. A convenient rule of thumb is to have from 8 to 15 intervals, depending on the size of the group. With only 50 scores, 8 to 10 intervals would serve very nicely, while for a group of 200 you might get more information from your frequency distribution if you used from 12 to 15 intervals.

After you have calculated the range between the highest and lowest scores, the next step is to determine i, the size of the interval. You do so by dividing the range by the number of intervals you wish to employ.

For the reading attitude scores, the range of 45 divided by 8 would give 5.6 or 6. However, 6 is rarely used for i, and most commonly you will see i values of 3, 5, 10, 25, 50, and other multiples of 10. But our calculation of 5.6 is also close to 5, a very often-used interval size, so that is the interval size employed in Table 2.4. *The choice of the number of intervals and the size of the interval is quite arbitrary.*

Whatever your choice of the number of intervals and the size of i, your main concern is to have the frequency distribution display as much information as possible concerning concentrations and patterns of the scores. Obviously, the top interval should contain the highest score, and the bottom interval the lowest score. The bottom interval begins with a multiple of the interval size. The lowest score among those of Table 2.4 might be 50, 51, 52, 53, or 54, but the interval would still begin at 50.

Table 2.5
Worksheet for frequency distribution of reading attitude scores

Scores	Tally	f
95–99	I	1
90–94	III	3
85–89	IIII	4
80–84	ℕℕ III	8
75–79	ℕℕ ℕℕ ℕℕ	15
70–74	ℕℕ ℕℕ I	11
65–69	ℕℕ II	7
60–64	III	3
55–59	II	2
50–54	I	1
		$N = 55$

After you have determined the size of i and the number of intervals you will use, you simply place the intervals in a column labeled "Scores" at the left side of a worksheet and then begin going through the data, placing a tally mark by the interval in which each score lies. Each entry in the frequency column is simply the addition of these tally marks for each interval. Your original worksheet for the reading attitude scores would look like Table 2.5, and the finished product would, of course, look like Table 2.4.

STEM-AND-LEAF DISPLAYS

A lot of attention has been given to frequency distributions in the last few pages because this method is the traditional way to find some meaning in a mass of data. Another technique called the *stem-and-leaf display* has come into more frequent use recently and is worthwhile exploring.

Let us use the reading attitude data from the simple frequency distribution of Table 2.2 to construct a stem-and-leaf display. For two-digit numbers such as the reading attention scores, the first digit (the "tens" digit) goes in the *stem* column. The trailing digit (the "ones" digit) is placed to the right in the *leaf* columns opposite the first digit. For example, a score of 68 would be indicated by an 8 in the leaf columns to the right of the 6. Within each row, the numbers go from smallest to largest.

Table 2.6 shows the 55 scores in a stem-and-leaf display. Notice that it is conventional in these displays to have the smaller values at the top of the table and the larger ones at the bottom—just the opposite of our grouped frequency distributions. Also notice that the interval size is 5, so that the intervals would be 50–54, 55–59, . . . , and 95–99. The main advantage of the stem-and-leaf display is that the identities of the individual scores are preserved. It is easy to see at a glance the

Table 2.6
Stem-and-leaf display for reading attitude scores

Stem	Leaf
5	4
5	8 9
6	2 2 4
6	5 6 7 7 8 9 9
7	0 0 1 2 3 3 3 4 4 4 4
7	5 5 5 6 6 6 6 6 6 7 7 8 8 9 9
8	0 0 1 2 2 3 4 4
8	5 8 9 9
9	1 1 4
9	9

highest and lowest scores, frequently occurring scores, or nonexistent scores. For example, in Table 2.6 we can easily see that six students had scores of 76, while the highest score was 99, but the next highest was 94. Another advantage is that rotating the table 90° produces a bar graph that shows the distribution of scores.

We have considered only two-digit numbers, but it should be obvious that other numbers could also be handled in the stem-and-leaf display. For example, if your data consisted of two- and three-digit numbers, say scores from 97 to 132, your stems would be 9 through 13, with the leaves being the single digits 0–9 as before.

CONTINUOUS VERSUS DISCRETE DATA

The data that constitute the raw material for studies in education and the behavioral sciences are numbers representing quantities such as reaction time, IQ, age, test scores, and the like. It is convenient at this time to point out that some of the measurements that describe an individual's characteristics are *continuous* and some are *discrete*.

If the precision of a measurement or observation depends upon the accuracy of the measuring instrument, we say we have continuous data. For example, in measuring an individual's reaction time in pushing the brake pedal on a driving simulator in response to a red light, we may get a reaction time of 0.32 seconds. However, if we had a more accurate clock we might measure the same reaction as 0.324 seconds, or even as 0.3241 seconds. Or, in a similar vein, a person's height might be 5 feet 10 inches, but with a better measuring instrument we might find it to be 5 feet 10.3 inches or even 5 feet 10.317 inches.

In any case we usually report just how accurate our measures are. If our reported reaction time is 0.32 seconds, we note that the measure is accurate to the nearest hundredth of a second. If our height is 5 feet 10 inches, we note that it is accurate to the nearest inch. Whenever we work with continuous data, we must be conscious of the *real limits* of the reported values, which extend from one-half unit below the reported value to one-half unit above. In the present examples, any reaction time between 0.315 and 0.325 seconds would be reported as 0.32 seconds, and any height from 5 feet 9.5 inches to 5 feet 10.5 inches is reported as 5 feet 10 inches. If the measurement answers the question "How much?" we are talking about continuous data.

However, if data are of the *frequency* or *counting* type (and answer the question "How many?"), we are speaking of *discrete* data. If there are 51 divorces for 100 marriages, or 17 auto fatalities in December, or 183 cases of Asian flu, then we have discrete data. There are no "in-between" values, since you cannot have 0.35 of a divorce or 1/2 a case of the flu. This fact does not stop the statistician from reporting fractional values, and you may have read that the average family size is 3.5 persons (see Figure 2.1) or that the average worker may change jobs 3.8 times before retiring. Statements of this kind, of course, can be meaningful, provided you

THE FAR SIDE   By GARY LARSON

"Bob and Ruth! Come on in .... Have you
met Russell and Bill, our 1.5 children?"

Figure 2.1
Care is needed in interpreting statistics based on discrete data. (*Source*: THE FAR
SIDE © 1988 FARWORKS, INC. Used by permission of Universal Press Syndicate.
All rights reserved.)

remember that the basic data consisted of discrete numbers. Later on in this book
you will find that for purposes of calculation it will be necessary to assume that,
for example, 3 children means between 2.5 and 3.5 children—but deep in our
hearts we know that these are discrete data, and the fractions are for computational purposes only.

One very common type of measure deserves special consideration—that of
test scores, especially those reported in number of items correct. If a student gets
43 items correct out of a possible 60 items, it sounds as if we are dealing with discrete data, since you cannot get part of an item correct. However, test scores in
terms of items correct are considered continuous data, *since the underlying variable that is being measured is assumed to be continuous*. A 60-item test may be
measuring mathematics achievement, and it is assumed that the amount of
achievement is continuous, with a score of 43 extending from 42.5 to 43.5. We are
simply assuming that some students scoring 43 may have slightly less achievement

than what is represented by the 43 but still greater than what is represented by a score of 42. Those with slightly more achievement than a score of 43, but not quite enough to obtain a score of 44, would still get a score of 43. So, when the underlying variable is assumed to be continuous, it is meaningful to consider a score of 43 extending from 42.5 to 43.5.

GRAPHING THE FREQUENCY DISTRIBUTION

Our noble ancestor who first uttered the now well-worn cliché about a picture being worth a thousand words was undoubtedly looking at the first graph. One can hardly read an assignment in a textbook or scan a newspaper or magazine without running into a graphical presentation of one form or another. Because graphical methods are such an important part of the statistical tools of the educator or behavioral scientist, it is essential that we spend considerable time and energy on this topic. There are many different kinds of graphs, but we will focus our attention on two main types: graphs that display the frequency distribution and graphs that represent a functional relationship between two variables.

By inspecting the frequency distribution of the reading attitude scores in Table 2.4, we can see that a few people made low scores and a few made high scores, but the majority of the scores are concentrated toward the middle of the distribution. It is difficult, however, to picture the entire distribution as a whole. For example, certain irregularities in the distribution may easily escape a casual glance. Since a pictorial representation of the data enables us to see the pattern of the distribution almost instantaneously, it is desirable to graph the frequency distribution. The most common graphical methods for the frequency distribution are the *histogram* and the *frequency polygon*.

Histogram

The histogram is similar to the familiar bar graph that you have seen quite frequently, and it can be interpreted in much the same way. Figure 2.2 shows a histogram based on the frequency distribution of the reading attitude scores of Table 2.4. Note that the height of each column represents the *frequency* in each interval.

When we examine the histogram of the reading attitude scores in Figure 2.2, we see that it is not symmetrical and that the shape is irregular. However, there is a tendency for many scores to fall toward the center of the distribution, with progressively fewer scores as you move in either direction from the "hump." We also see that there is a wide variation in the scores.

Certainly, if we worked at it long enough we could get this information from the frequency distribution itself, but the graphical method gives us the information at a glance. Also, in a later section, when we get into the topic of the different kinds of shapes that distributions may take, it will be much easier to compare several graphs instead of frequency distributions.

The steps in the construction of a histogram are as follows:

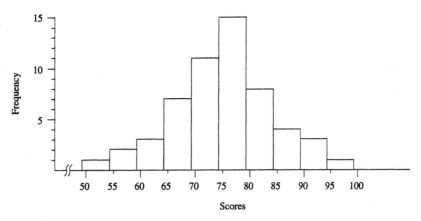

Figure 2.2
Histogram of reading attitude scores.

1. Lay out an area on a sheet of graph paper that corresponds roughly to the proportions of Figure 2.2. It is a good practice to have the height of the graph about three-fourths of the width. The horizontal line, called the x-axis or the abscissa, is drawn long enough to include all of the scores plus a little unused space at each end. Label this axis ("Scores" in this example) and put a number of scores at appropriate intervals (50, 55, 60, etc., are logical choices here).

2. At the left end of the x-axis draw a vertical line (the ordinate, or y-axis). Divide the y-axis into units so that the largest frequency will not quite reach the top of the graph. Number these units and label this axis "Frequency."

3. Now you can complete the histogram simply by drawing lines parallel to the x-axis at the height of the frequency for each interval and connecting the lines to the x-axis by vertical lines to the *real* limits of the intervals. For example, as shown in Figure 2.2, three people scored in the 60–64 interval, so the horizontal line above this interval is drawn 3 units up from the x-axis, and vertical lines extend down to the real limits of 59.5 and 64.5.

4. Give the histogram a title, either above or below the figure. The title should be a clear statement of what the histogram represents.

Frequency Polygon

Probably, most pictorial representations of the frequency distribution take the form of the *frequency polygon,* which is a line graph instead of the bar-type graph of the histogram. The frequency polygon for the distribution of statistics exam scores is shown in Figure 2.3.

Note that we get the same information from the frequency polygon as we did from the histogram, that is, the concentrations and spread of the scores. Since most graphs of the frequency distribution are frequency polygons, it might be a good

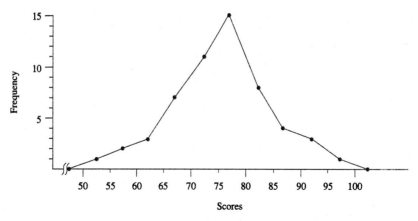

Figure 2.3
Frequency polygon of reading attitude scores.

idea to become thoroughly acquainted with the construction of a frequency polygon. Especially note that the points plotted in Figure 2.3 are directly above the *midpoint* of each interval and that the polygon drops down to the baseline (zero frequency) at both ends of the graph.

The steps in the construction of the frequency polygon are these:

1. Lay out the area for the graph with the proper proportions and label the *x*- and *y*-axes just as you did for the histogram.

2. Instead of drawing a bar corresponding to the frequency for each interval as you did for the histogram, place a *dot* above the *midpoint* of each interval. For example, three persons scored in the 60–64 interval. *MP* = 62 for this interval, so you would place a dot opposite a frequency of 3 and above the score of 62. After you place the points for all intervals, simply connect the points with straight lines.

3. It is mathematically incorrect and artistically unsatisfying to leave the polygon suspended in midair, so the curve connecting the points drops down to the baseline at the extreme ends of the distribution. The curve touches the baseline at the *midpoint* of the adjacent interval, whose frequency, of course, is 0. For example, on the right side of Figure 2.3 the curve connects the point at 97 (the midpoint of the 95–99 interval) with the *x*-axis at 102 (the midpoint of the nonexistent 100–104 interval). The same method is used to connect the point at 52 with the *x*-axis at 47.

Cautions on Graphing.   A certain amount of care has to be exercised in transforming the ordinary frequency distribution into a frequency polygon. The greatest single error committed by the novice is in using incorrect proportions in draw-

Note 2.1
Where Do the Scores Lie?

We have to remember that in gaining a bit of efficiency we have lost a little accuracy. Note that when scores are placed in a frequency distribution (and graphed as a polygon or histogram) the *identity* of an individual score is lost. In the reading attitude data we see that seven individuals scored between 65 and 69. Once the data are in the form of a frequency distribution we cannot determine the exact values of the individual scores. We only know that the seven scores lie somewhere in the 65–69 interval. Several statistical techniques to be presented later on will make different assumptions regarding the precise location of the scores in an interval. But we will leave that topic for a later section and for now will note that the frequency polygon shown in Figure 2.3 assumes that the *average* of all the scores in any interval falls at the *midpoint* of that interval.

Of course, this caution does not apply to the stem-and-leaf display. The advantage of such a display is that we know the identity of all the scores.

ing the graph. In the last section we noted that the height of the graph should be about three-fourths of the width. It is essential to follow this convention, since most graphs that you will be examining in books and journal articles will have the same general proportion. It is a lot easier to analyze someone else's graph if you have been using a similar layout and format all along.

Figure 2.4 shows the reading attitude scores represented in two incorrectly drawn frequency polygons. The polygon of Figure 2.4a has the scale of the ordinate too great with respect to that of the abscissa, while the one in Figure 2.4b is just the reverse. Although these figures are obvious exaggerations, it must be noted that it does not take much deviation from the three-fourths rule of thumb to produce a distortion that interferes with interpreting the graph.

Comparing Two Distributions.   One very common use of the frequency polygon is in presenting data from two frequency distributions with approximately equal values of N. This procedure permits a comparison of two sets of scores on the same variable, in addition to providing information on each distribution separately. Just such a comparison is shown in Figure 2.5 for coordination test scores for a group of 90 seventh-grade girls and 85 seventh-grade boys. Note the ease with which you can make direct comparisons regarding the relative abilities of the two groups and the spread and concentrations of scores. It is obvious from the graph that the ability of the girls as shown by this particular coordination test is superior to that of the boys.

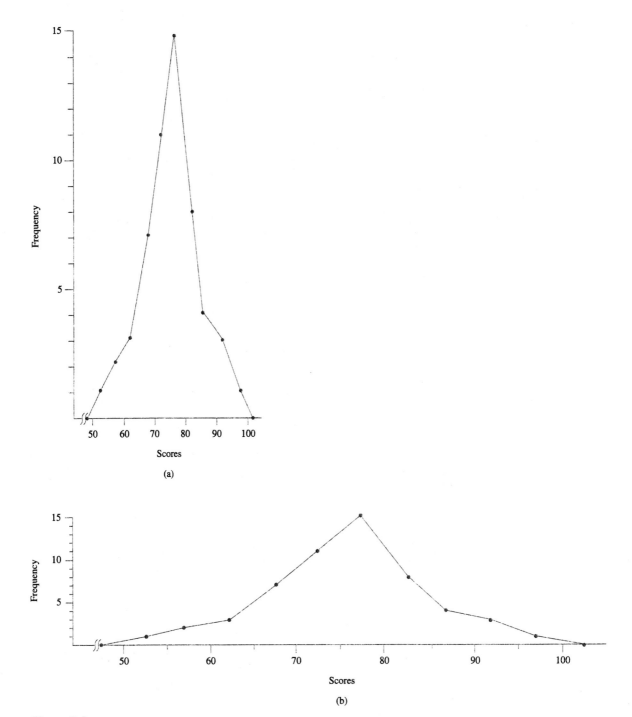

Figure 2.4
Graphical distortion produced by improper proportion in reading attitude scores.

Figure 2.5
Coordination scores for seventh-grade boys and girls.

TYPICAL AND NOT-SO-TYPICAL
FREQUENCY DISTRIBUTIONS

The Normal Curve

You have all heard of, and probably used, the term *normal curve*. Many physiological measurements (e.g., height, weight, length of nose, and number of eyelashes) and behavioral measurements (IQ scores, eye blink response, and aptitude test scores) are normally distributed in the population. By "normally distributed" we mean that the frequency polygon for the distribution of measurements closely approximates the mathematical model shown in Figure 2.6. This bell-shaped, symmetrical curve is called a *normal curve*. If this were a frequency polygon of test scores, it would show the typical concentration of scores in the middle of the distribution, with fewer and fewer scores as you approach the extremes. For example, if this curve represented the distribution of the heights of American adult males, the curve would be the highest (greatest frequency) around 5 feet 9 inches and would get progressively lower (smaller and smaller frequency) as you got out toward 6 feet 5 inches or 5 feet 1 inch. The curve would almost touch the baseline (very small frequency of occurrence) at a height of 7 feet 1 inch or 4 feet 8 inches.

The frequency polygon of the reading attitude scores of Figure 2.3 bears only a slight resemblance to the normal curve. When we have only 50 scores we must expect a lack of symmetry in the distribution. If the reading attitude scale had been given to 500 students, we would expect that some of the irregularities would disappear, resulting in a smoother, more symmetrical curve. If the attitude scores were obtained from several thousand individuals, the resulting frequency polygon would come even closer in appearance to the normal curve model of Figure 2.6.

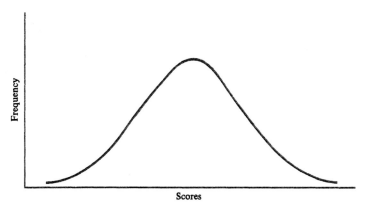

Figure 2.6
A normal curve model.

Even though the data with which we will most often be working will never be exactly normally distributed, we will find that the normal curve model has some very useful properties in relation to our data. In fact, these properties are a foundation for a very important part of statistical techniques, and we will have occasion to devote an entire chapter to these properties later on in this text.

Skewness

There will be times when a graph of the frequency distribution will not have the typical, symmetric bell shape with the majority of scores concentrated at the center of the distribution. Instead you might find that the majority of the scores are clustered at either the high end or the low end of the distribution. This concentration of scores at one end or the other of the distribution is called *skewness*.

If the scores are concentrated at the upper end of the distribution so the tail of the curve skews to the *left,* we say that the curve is *negatively skewed*. Figure 2.7 shows the results of a national achievement exam in mathematics given to all ninth-graders in a school system enrolled in accelerated classes in mathematics. As you can see, there is a large concentration of high scores with progressively fewer low scores as you go to the left. This graph is telling us that the exam was too easy for the majority of the students, which was to be expected, since they are in accelerated classes.

If the scores are clustered at the lower end of the distribution so the tail of the curve skews to the right, we say that the curve is *positively skewed*. Positive skewness is characterized by a preponderance of low scores, such as would occur if a difficult test were administered to an average group or an ordinary test administered to a below-average group. Another set of data that is usually positively skewed is the distribution of earned incomes. Figure 2.8 shows the incomes of 14,000 workers with a high school education or less who took part in a national survey. You can see that there is an obviously positive skew, since the majority of

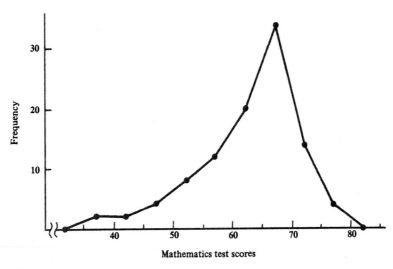

Figure 2.7
Negatively skewed mathematics achievement scores.

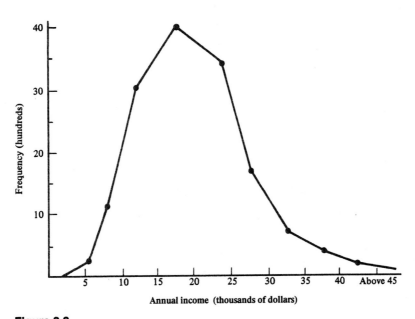

Figure 2.8
Positively skewed distribution of annual incomes of 14,000 workers with high school education or less.

Note 2.2
Remembering Which Skewness Is Which

A handy device for determining whether a curve is negatively or positively skewed is to look at the *tail* of the curve (the tail is on the opposite side from the concentration of scores). If you remember your algebra, you know the direction *left* is negative, so if the tail goes to the left, the skewness is negative. If the tail points to the right, since the direction *right* is positive, you have positive skewness. In checking this with Figures 2.7 and 2.8, note that in Figure 2.7 the tail points to the left (negative skewness) while in Figure 2.8 it points to the right (positive skewness).

incomes fall between $12,500 and $22,500, at the lower end of the distribution, while other incomes extend a considerable distance to the right.

We noted that the mathematics achievement scores in Figure 2.7 were negatively skewed, with more scores near the upper end of the distribution. This type of skewness is quite common in academic situations, especially in college-level classes. Since most college classes represent quite a high level of ability, there usually will be more higher scores than lower scores. To put it another way, there usually are more A and B letter grades than D and F grades.

We have been using the "eyeball" method for examining the skewness of a distribution, and this may be perfectly adequate in most situations. However, if you want a more precise, mathematically defined method for measuring the amount of skewness, see one of the texts listed in the References.

Kurtosis

Another property of a frequency distribution besides the amount of symmetry (symmetry is the opposite of skewness) is its *kurtosis*. When we speak of kurtosis we are referring to the "peakedness" or "flatness" of a frequency polygon. If the curve has a very sharp peak, it indicates an extreme concentration of scores about the center, and we say that it is *leptokurtic*. If the curve is quite flat, it would tell us that while there is some degree of concentration at the center, there are quite a few scores that are dispersed away from the middle of the distribution; we say the curve is *platykurtic*. The curve that represents a happy medium is a *mesokurtic curve*. The normal curve model of Figure 2.6 is mesokurtic. All three degrees of kurtosis are shown in Figure 2.9.

We ordinarily do not worry too much about the type of kurtosis in a set of data from test scores, surveys, and experiments, where we are interested in describing the performance of a group of individuals. However, when we consider theoretical issues in sampling procedures and statistical tests in later chapters, we will come back to the concept of kurtosis.

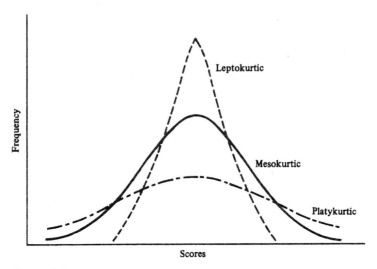

Figure 2.9
Types of kurtosis.

J-Curves

Before leaving our discussion of the shapes of frequency distributions, we should make note of a special type of extreme skewness—the J-curve. The J-curve hypothesis of social conformity was first proposed by Floyd Allport and is related to conforming behavior among groups of people. The large majority of scores fall at the end of the scale representing socially acceptable behavior, while the small minority of scores represents a deviation from this social norm.

Nelson and Nilsen (1984) assessed drivers' behavior at a four-way stop sign under two conditions: when a marked police car was parked near the intersection and when no police car was present. The speed with which each driver entered the intersection was tabulated, and the results are shown in Figure 2.10.

Note 2.3
Remembering Which Kurtosis Is Which

A colleague of mine uses some vivid imagery to illustrate the different types of kurtosis. He notes that the platykurtic curve is flat and rounded like the back of a duckbilled platypus. The other type of kurtosis reminds him of a kangaroo, since the leptokurtic curve looks as if it is "lepping" around. He claims that not a single student has forgotten the difference between platykurtic and leptokurtic curves!

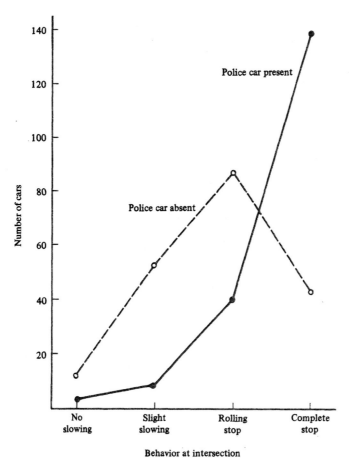

Figure 2.10
Conforming behavior at a four-way stop sign with a marked police car present or absent.

The J-shaped curve for the drivers' behavior with the police car present is the result of extreme skewness, since the great majority of the drivers either made a "complete stop" or a "rolling stop." However, a few only slowed down slightly and two went through the intersection without slowing down at all, resulting in the J-shaped curve. As you can see, the curve has an entirely different shape when the police car was absent.

This type of curve can be found in a number of situations where a group standard can be quantified and deviations from the social norm observed. Some examples might be the length of time drivers will park in a no parking zone, the time of arrival at a concert or religious service, and the number of drinks consumed during the social hour preceding a banquet.

THE CUMULATIVE FREQUENCY AND CUMULATIVE PERCENTAGE DISTRIBUTIONS

Before we leave the topic of frequency distributions and their graphs, we need to consider one more variation—the cumulative frequency distribution and its cousin, the cumulative percentage distribution. We need these distributions to answer questions about a score and its relationship to the rest of the distribution.

For example, if Angela scored 26 on the English subtest of a college entrance exam, what percent of college-bound high school seniors scored below Angela? If Brian had a score of 65 on the Estes Reading Attitude Scale, what percent of the control group scored higher than he? What is the reading attitude score that separates the top half ("positive attitude toward reading") from the lower half ("negative attitude toward reading")?

We are talking about *percentiles,* of course, and no doubt you remember that the percentile is a way of expressing the location of a given score in a distribution. In the example, Angela later learned that her score of 26 on the English exam placed her at the 87th percentile ($P_{87} = 26$). In other words, 87 percent of the college-bound seniors scored below Angela. And it turned out that Brian's score of 65 on the reading attitude scale was located such that 13 percent of the group had scores lower than he ($P_{13} = 65$).

Constructing the Cumulative Percentage Curve

Answers to questions like those we have posed can be determined from a graph of the cumulative percentage distribution. This graph is called a *cumulative percentage curve,* or *ogive* (say "Oh'-jive"), and is constructed from a slightly modified grouped frequency distribution such as is shown in Table 2.7. This table contains the scores on the reading attitude scale shown earlier in Table 2.4.

To the grouped frequency distribution we have added two more columns: a *cumulative frequency (cum f)* column and a *cumulative percentage (cum percentage)* column. The *cum f* column is simply the addition of the frequencies in each interval as you count up from the bottom. For example, there is 1 score in the 50–54 interval and 2 in the 55–59 interval, so the cumulative frequency for the 55–59 interval is 3. There are 3 scores in the 60 to 64 interval, so the cumulative frequency for the 60–64 interval is 6, since in *that interval and below* there are 6 scores. Technically speaking, the entry in the *cum f* column gives the number of scores *below the real upper limit of the interval.* For example, the 6 in the *cum f* column opposite the 60–64 interval indicates that there are 6 scores below a score of 64.5. Similarly, there are 39 scores below a score of 79.5. This is an important point because the accuracy of your graph depends on this fact.

The *cum percentage* column contains the same information as the *cum f* column, except that the entries have been converted to percentages. Instead of saying that 6 scores are below 64.5, we can say that 11% of the group are below 64.5. To obtain the entries in the *cum percentage* column, you divide each entry in the

Table 2.7
Cumulative percentage distribution of reading
attitude scores

Scores	f	Cum f	Cum Percentage
95–99	1	55	100
90–94	3	54	98
85–89	4	51	93
80–84	8	47	85
75–79	15	39	71
70–74	11	24	44
65–69	7	13	24
60–64	3	6	11
55–59	2	3	5
50–54	1	1	2
	$N = 55$		

cum f column by the total number of scores, N, and multiply by 100. So, for the entry opposite the 80–84 interval, you would calculate $(47/55) \times 100 = 85\%$. You know that 85% of the scores fall below 84.5.

After the cumulative percentage distribution has been prepared as shown in Table 2.7, the steps in the construction of the cumulative percentage curve are as follows:

1. Lay out the area on a sheet of paper with the usual proportions, and label the *x*- and *y*-axes as shown in Figure 2.11.

2. Place a dot above the *real upper limit* opposite the cumulative percentage on the *y*-axis for all the intervals. For example, in Figure 2.11, there is a point above 69.5 and opposite a percentage value of 24.

3. Include a point at the real lower limit of the bottom interval opposite a percentage value of 0. In Figure 2.11 the curve drops to 0 at a score of 49.5.

4. Connect the dots by straight lines.

Reading Percentiles and Percentile Ranks from the Cumulative Percentage Curve

Before we make use of the cumulative percentage curve, we need to make a distinction between a *percentile* and a *percentile rank*. If you wish to know what score is the point below which a given percentage of the distribution falls, you are interested in a *percentile*. If you wish to know what percentage of the distribution falls below a given score, you are concerned with *percentile rank*. If you have trouble discriminating, remember the following:

1. *Percentile:* Given the percentage, find the score.

2. *Percentile rank:* Given the score, find the percentage.

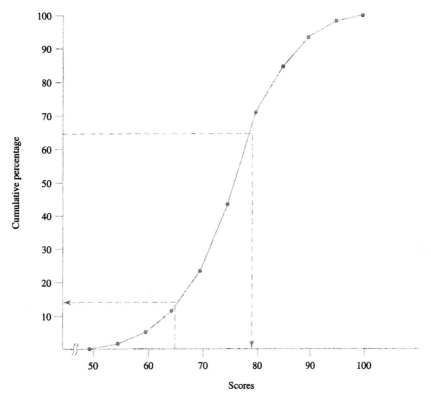

Figure 2.11
Cumulative percentage curve of the reading attitude scores.

If you want to find a particular *percentile*, you simply draw a horizontal line from the cumulative percentage scale on the *y*-axis until it intersects the curve. At the point of intersection you drop a vertical line perpendicular to the *x*-axis and read the score where the perpendicular line touches the *x*-axis. For example, in Figure 2.11, a percentile of 65, P_{65}, is found by the above method to be a score of 78.

The reverse procedure is used to determine the *percentile rank* of a particular score. You draw a vertical line from the score until the line intersects the curve, and a horizontal line from that point of intersection over to the cumulative percentage scale on the *y*-axis. That point is the percentile rank of the score. For example, in Figure 2.11, Brian's score of 65 has a percentile rank of 13. In other words, 13 percent of Brian's group had reading attitude scores lower than he.

Any percentile or percentile rank can be found using these methods, but the accuracy of the procedure depends on how precisely the graph is drawn. Remember that any point on the curve tells us *what percent of the distribution scored that value or below*.

Comparing Cumulative Percentage Curves for Two Different Distributions

A very useful technique that is often employed is a comparison of two frequency distributions. In Figure 2.5 there was a comparison of the frequency polygons of motor coordination test scores for a group of seventh-grade boys and girls. The distributions have been converted to cumulative percentage curves and are shown in Figure 2.12.

It is obvious from Figure 2.12 that the coordination test performance of seventh-grade girls was superior to that of their male counterparts. But by using the techniques we have described for reading percentiles and percentile ranks directly, we can gain a great deal of specific information as well and can do such things as the following:

Comparing Scores. If the test manual states that anyone with a score of 27 or below should be given remedial exercises, how do boys and girls compare? A vertical line from the score of 27 intersects the girls' curve at about 4% and the boys' at about 20%. In other words only 4% of the girls but 20% of the boys would score below 27, or in the "remedial" range.

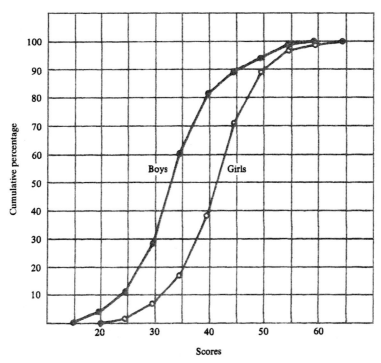

Figure 2.12
Cumulative percentage curves for coordination scores for seventh-grade boys and girls.

Comparing Percentiles.   In Figure 2.12, it is easy to compare various percentiles. For example, what score has to be made to place a boy or girl in the top 25% of his or her group? The value that you want is, of course, the 75th percentile, P_{75}, and a horizontal line from the 75th percentage value intersects the boys' curve at a score of 38 and the girls' curve at a score of about 45.5. Comparatively speaking, the examinee would need a coordination score of at least 46 to be in the top 25% of the girls' group but only 38 to be in the top 25% of the boys' group.

GRAPHING THE FUNCTIONAL RELATIONSHIP

After spending considerable time and energy on frequency distributions and the graphical methods for displaying such data, we will have to shift our frame of reference slightly in order to take up the topic of graphing a *functional relationship*. We will be directing our attention not to a pictorial representation of the frequency distribution but rather to a pictorial image of the *relationship* between two variables.

In the broadest sense we might say that the objective of educators and behavioral scientists is to discover functional relationships between variables. An educator might be interested in knowing if the number of siblings (brothers and sisters) that a child has will have an effect on his or her social relationships in nursery school. If an investigator finds that the only child has more difficulty in getting along with others than the child with two siblings, we say that the researcher has demonstrated a *functional relationship* between the two variables of number of siblings and amount of social adjustment.

An economist might be interested in learning what effect the amount of leisure time has on the individual's expenditures for recreational items such as snowmobiles, speedboats, camper trailers, and the like. If she finds that people working a 48-hour week spend 3% of their take-home pay on recreation while those working a 36-hour week spend 7%, we say that she has found a functional relationship between hours worked and leisure expenditures.

In still another example, an engineering psychologist might be concerned with the brightness of a car's brake lights and the reaction time of the driver in the following car. If he finds that the reaction time of 100 drivers decreases as the brightness of the brake light is increased, we would say that he has established a functional relationship between reaction time and brake light brightness.

Independent and Dependent Variables

In all of the examples given we have noted that there is a relationship between two variables—the *independent* variable and the *dependent* variable.

The independent variable is the one that is manipulated in some way by the researcher, who may choose to compare an only child with a child who has two siblings, or workers working a 48-hour workweek with those working a 36-hour workweek, or three different brightness levels of brake lights. The *independent variables* are, respectively, number of siblings, length of workweek, and brake light brightness.

The dependent variable is dependent (hence the name) upon the value of the independent variable. It is always a measurement of some sort—in the examples we are using it would be the amount of social adjustment, the amount of money spent on recreation, and the speed of reaction. It is sometimes called the *response variable,* since it is always the measure of some type of response. If there is a relationship between the independent and dependent variables, we note that the dependent variable changes in response to changes in the independent variable. As you vary the independent variable, you note that the dependent variable, which you are measuring, also changes.

These changes are best shown in the form of a graph such as Figure 2.13. As we mentioned earlier, a researcher might be investigating how the reaction time of a driver to a brake light depends on the brightness of the brake light. Note that the dependent variable (reaction time) is plotted on the *y*-axis while the independent variable (brake light brightness) is plotted on the *x*-axis. As you can see from the graph, when a dim brake light is used as a stimulus, the response time is about 0.35 seconds. The driver's response is somewhat faster when a moderately bright brake light is used, and the response is the fastest (about 0.30 seconds) when a bright brake light is used. There is no doubt about it—the researcher has demonstrated a functional relationship between the two variables. Reaction time does indeed depend on the brightness of the stimulus, and the graph displays this functional relationship very efficiently.

The rules for graphing functional relationships are much the same as for graphing the frequency distribution as far as proportion, labeling of axes, and so

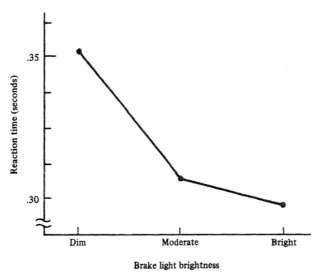

Figure 2.13
Reaction time to three brake light systems.

on. And, as we have mentioned, the dependent variable—what the researcher is measuring—always goes on the *y*-axis. One important difference that should be noted is that the curve does not drop down to 0 at the baseline as was the case with the frequency polygon. If it did this in Figure 2.13, for example, it would imply that we had some measurements at other brightness levels than dim, moderate, and bright. Since reaction times were not measured at "very dim" or "very bright," we cannot extend the curve to those points.

The preceding discussion was not intended to be a thorough and exhaustive presentation of the topic of functional relationships. A complete treatment of functional relationships and different types of variables more properly belongs in a textbook of experimental design or advanced statistics. Our purpose for considering the topic at this point was twofold: A discussion of graphical methods would not be complete without it, and there will be several occasions in future chapters when we will want to consider ways to measure the *amount* of relationship that exists between two variables.

SAMPLE PROBLEM—MANUAL SOLUTION

We will use the techniques described in this chapter to analyze the data on part-time jobs. We will want to produce a frequency distribution and a frequency polygon to help us describe the part-time job hours worked by college students.

The College Life Questionnaire was administered to a random sample of 219 full-time freshmen students at a small midwestern state university. Forty-seven percent, or 104, indicated that they had a part-time job either on or off campus. They were asked to list the number of hours they worked each week. The results follow.

2	11	9	6	10	5	10	6	8	5
5	3	11	9	11	5	10	10	10	7
9	5	3	10	12	8	15	6	5	8
10	5	6	4	13	10	22	9	12	9
7	8	13	6	4	16	10	16	12	6
7	10	9	6	8	4	5	6	10	5
18	10	8	6	5	12	4	10	15	10
8	6	20	15	14	18	6	4	25	9
8	15	6	15	8	12	7	9	4	11
6	7	20	5	14	4	12	9	5	4
9	8	10	10						

To construct a frequency distribution from these data, we first note that the highest "score" is 25 hours worked per week and the lowest is 2. With a

(continued)

SAMPLE PROBLEM—MANUAL SOLUTION *(CONTINUED)*

range of $25 - 2 = 23$, we could use 9 intervals with $i = 3$. We could use 8 intervals if we began the bottom interval at 2, but the frequency distribution might be more descriptive if we begin with zero.

Once we have decided on the bottom interval of 0–2, we list the remaining intervals in a column and go through the table of raw data, placing a tally mark beside the interval where each score falls. In Table 2.8 the worksheet is shown on the left and the finished product is on the right.

The frequency polygon for these data is shown in Figure 2.14. Note that for easy readability the score values on the horizontal axis are in multiples of 5, even though $i = 3$ for this distribution. Also note that the points are plotted above the midpoints for each interval.

In analyzing the frequency polygon, we note that there is a rather marked degree of positive skewness; that is, the tail skews to the right. This would indicate that most freshmen with part-time jobs work a moderate number of hours (3 to 11 hours per week), but there are a few who are working 15 or more while carrying a full load of course work.

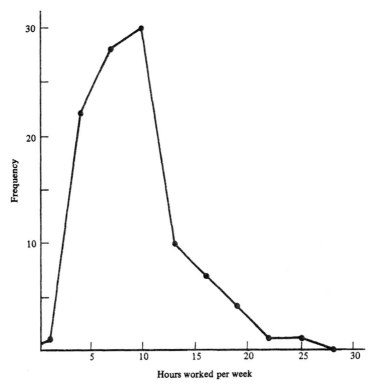

Figure 2.14
Hours worked at a part-time job by college freshmen.

Table 2.8
Number of hours worked per week at a part-time job

Scores	Tally	Scores	f
24–26	I	24–26	1
21–23	I	21–23	1
18–20	IIII	18–20	4
15–17	JHT II	15–17	7
12–14	JHT JHT	12–14	10
9–11	JHT JHT JHT JHT JHT JHT	9–11	30
6–8	JHT JHT JHT JHT JHT III	6–8	28
3–5	JHT JHT JHT JHT II	3–5	22
0–2	I	0–2	1
			N = 104

Sample Problem—Computer Solution

A lab assistant for a physiological psychologist recorded the number of times 40 different rats pressed a lever while in a Skinner box for two minutes. The number of responses for each rat is shown in Table 2.9. This is our first encounter with computer-aided data analysis, and, as you can see, we can have considerably more detail with less effort.

Table 2.10 shows the SPSS output for a simple frequency distribution and cumulative percentage distribution, along with the stem-and-leaf plot and a histogram. The *simple frequency distribution* is contained in the first two columns with the *cumulative percentages* shown in the fifth column. Note that in the *stem-and-leaf plot*, the single digits (3, 4, 6, 7, and 8) have a stem of 0. We can see that the number of responses ranged from 3 to 40, with the majority of the responses being in the middle of the distribution (15 rats had responses of 15 to 19, and 8 had responses from 26 to 29).

Table 2.9
Number of lever presses during a two-minute interval in a Skinner box

30	28	17	3	19	40	22	28
6	10	15	8	19	28	33	20
4	36	18	29	16	34	7	13
12	19	27	26	15	18	15	19
15	17	27	18	29	15	30	40

(continued)

Table 2.10
SPSS output for lever-pressing data

Frequencies

Frequency Distributions for Lever Press Responses

	Frequency	Percent	Valid Percent	Cumulative Percent
Valid 3	1	2.5	2.5	2.5
4	1	2.5	2.5	5.0
6	1	2.5	2.5	7.5
7	1	2.5	2.5	10.0
8	1	2.5	2.5	12.5
10	1	2.5	2.5	15.0
12	1	2.5	2.5	17.5
13	1	2.5	2.5	20.0
15	5	12.5	12.5	32.5
16	1	2.5	2.5	35.0
17	2	5.0	5.0	40.0
18	3	7.5	7.5	47.5
19	4	10.0	10.0	57.5
20	1	2.5	2.5	60.0
22	1	2.5	2.5	62.5
26	1	2.5	2.5	65.0
27	2	5.0	5.0	70.0
28	3	7.5	7.5	77.5
29	2	5.0	5.0	82.5
30	2	5.0	5.0	87.5
33	1	2.5	2.5	90.0
34	1	2.5	2.5	92.5
36	1	2.5	2.5	95.0
40	2	5.0	5.0	100.0
Total	40	100.0	100.0	
Total	40	100.0		

Stem-and-Leaf Plot

Number of Lever Presses: Stem-and-Leaf Plot

Frequency	Stem & Leaf
2.00	0. 34
3.00	0. 678
3.00	1. 023
15.00	1. 555556778889999
2.00	2. 02
8.00	2. 67788899
4.00	3. 0034
1.00	3. 6
2.00	4. 00

Stem width:	10
Each leaf:	1 case

Histogram

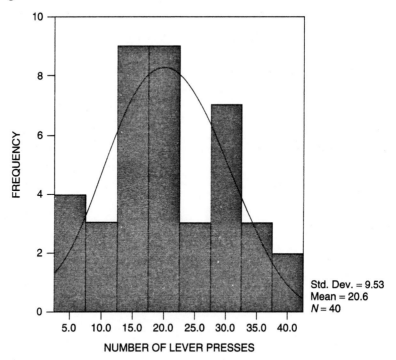

In the *histogram*, notice that a normal curve has been superimposed, which allows us to note similarities to or deviations from a "normal" distribution. For example, we would note that a greater number of responses occurred at the interval with a midpoint of 30 than what we would expect. Such variations in a small sample are, of course, not unexpected.

STUDY QUESTIONS

1. Why might a frequency distribution with 10 intervals be preferred to one with only 4 or 5 intervals?
2. When might you prefer a frequency distribution where $i = 1$?
3. List the steps you would use in constructing a frequency distribution.
4. In what ways are a frequency distribution and a stem-and-leaf display similar? In what ways are they different?
5. What is the difference between discrete and continuous data?
6. What are the steps you would use in constructing a frequency polygon?
7. How do a histogram and a frequency polygon differ?

8. Describe the shape of a distribution that is negatively skewed, and give an example. Do the same for a distribution that is positively skewed.

9. How does a cumulative percentage curve differ from a frequency polygon?

10. What is the difference between the independent variable and the dependent variable? Which goes on the x-axis? Which goes on the y-axis?

EXERCISES

1. For the following intervals, give the real lower and upper limits, the midpoint, and the size of the interval.
   a. 30–39
   b. 4–5
   c. 6.5–6.9
   d. 76–78
   e. 23.0–23.4
   f. 60–89
   g. 100–124
   h. 20–39
   i. 45–49
   j. 0.01–0.03

2. For the following intervals, give the real lower and upper limits, the midpoint, and the size of the interval.
   a. 50–99
   b. 1–4
   c. 7.0–7.9
   d. 30–44
   e. 54.7–54.8
   f. 50–69
   g. 200–249
   h. 10–19
   i. 45.5–45.9
   j. 0.08–0.09

3. Indicate whether the following statistics represent discrete or continuous data.
   a. The United States' infant mortality rate due to pneumonia in 1937.
   b. Free-throw shooting percentage of Michael Jordan.
   c. Number of college students who do not own a car at Duke University.
   d. Average knee-jerk reflex time (in msec.) of college freshmen after a tap on their patellar tendons.
   e. Average weight of the members of the U.S. Senate.
   f. Number of items correct on a mathematics test.
   g. The proportion of college freshmen who study more than 10 hours per week.
   h. Average number of swimsuits each lifeguard owns at Santa Cruz beach.
   i. Amount of milk consumed by ten children at a day-care facility in Idaho.
   j. Percent of cars in a used-car lot that are red.

4. Indicate whether the following statistics represent discrete or continuous data.

   a. Average number of popcorn kernels needed to pop one cup of popcorn.

   b. Amount of time needed to drive from Rochester, Minnesota, to Dallas, Texas, traveling at 60 miles per hour.

   c. The number of people who attended the last Garth Brooks concert.

   d. Average age of patients at Pine View Nursing Home.

   e. Percentage of restaurants that serve free popcorn to their customers.

   f. Proportion of left-handed students in a freshman class at Arizona State University.

   g. Average amount of hot chocolate consumed by residents of Michigan from December 20 to January 20.

   h. Percentage of U.S. men and women over age 65 who work full-time.

   i. Average monthly snowfall in Maine from November 1 to April 1.

   j. Number of turnovers in the first game of the season between the Boston Celtics and the New York Knicks.

5. The shoe sizes of 40 female college students follow. Half sizes were rounded up to the nearest whole number. Construct a simple frequency distribution ($i = 1$) from these data.

5	12	4	6	10	8	7
8	7	6	7	9	9	9
6	8	10	10	12	8	6
8	9	12	8	4	9	8
7	10	6	7	7	8	11
9	10	8	6	7	7	

6. Thirty-six gymnasts were judged on their floor routines. Construct a frequency distribution with $i = 1$.

6	9	2	9	8	6
9	8	7	8	9	5
10	5	6	9	7	8
8	9	5	7	6	9
4	9	8	9	8	7
5	8	9	10	9	6

7. The weights of 42 college students follow.

120	145	230	154	168	138	154
180	186	195	129	179	164	208
200	173	206	178	242	152	156
173	124	129	192	173	128	143
154	133	138	132	106	139	265
212	190	162	141	146	148	189

   a. Construct a frequency distribution with $i = 10$.

   b. Construct a stem-and-leaf display using the same intervals.

8. A random survey of 42 male CEOs of U.S. corporations asked each man how many business suits he owned.

6	3	13	6	11	5	6
9	1	16	14	22	16	14
15	12	21	7	10	15	8
17	22	5	24	15	1	12
23	9	2	18	4	21	15
26	5	4	9	6	12	9

a. Construct a frequency distribution with $i = 3$.
b. Construct a stem-and-leaf display.

9. An owner of a busy restaurant kept track of the number of guests her restaurant served each night from 5 to 6 P.M. over a two-month period.
a. Construct a simple frequency distribution ($i = 1$) for these data.
b. Construct a grouped frequency distribution with $i = 3$. Note that the pattern of scores is more obvious than with $i = 1$.

155	152	162	154	152	171
184	184	162	169	164	171
173	173	180	176	180	163
162	164	173	189	173	154
151	166	154	178	179	166
177	188	158	160	164	179
188	172	153	173	150	180
156	151	179	165	158	150
174	170	164	173	155	164
185	185	173	162	153	173

10. A 50-item unit exam was given to 98 members of an introductory psychology class, and the number of items correct for each student is shown below.
a. Construct a simple frequency distribution ($i = 1$) for this group of scores.
b. Construct a grouped frequency distribution with $i = 3$. Note that the pattern of scores is more obvious than with $i = 1$.

32	29	35	26	32	22	33	30	27	30
36	29	33	38	32	43	29	39	36	30
18	35	37	38	33	30	39	31	38	32
36	30	19	29	37	35	33	34	30	38
30	39	30	39	30	42	36	22	36	33
39	31	26	30	39	31	42	25	35	30
38	38	33	39	32	42	36	34	35	31
41	44	47	31	39	36	34	37	37	30
46	31	31	41	43	37	44	42	40	37
24	28	25	41	33	30	36	28		

11. A dental care survey asked 80 women, ages 20 to 27, to record how many times they brushed their teeth in a one-week period.

a. Construct a grouped frequency distribution ($i = 3$) for these data.
b. Draw a frequency polygon of this frequency distribution.
c. What type of skewness is shown here?

14	17	13	19	11	21	7	16	24	14
14	21	17	16	22	13	15	17	22	17
15	7	11	18	20	21	24	13	12	22
23	21	24	20	17	18	15	13	14	18
17	16	19	17	15	13	12	8	10	20
21	14	16	29	17	25	15	11	14	19
14	17	19	18	23	27	25	26	22	16
14	15	16	19	20	27	28	26	13	14

12. Researchers wanted to know if men and women differed in the frequency with which they brushed their teeth. A study similar to the one in exercise 11 used male subjects and produced the following data.
a. Construct a grouped frequency distribution ($i = 3$) for these data.
b. Draw a frequency polygon of this frequency distribution.
c. What type of skewness is shown here, if any?

14	13	16	15	13	21	18	17	16	13
7	8	11	17	9	10	23	19	18	14
17	16	15	18	14	12	17	19	21	13
7	9	16	18	15	14	14	14	13	20
15	15	13	14	19	22	27	17	19	14
13	20	19	18	15	17	16	20	10	8
16	19	18	15	13	13	16	12	9	24
12	15	18	15	13	19	23	20	14	17

13. A local taco establishment reported the number of hours worked by 30 part-time employees in one week. A grouped frequency distribution of the employees' hours is shown below.

Hours/Week	f
27–29	2
24–26	3
21–23	0
18–20	2
15–17	1
12–14	7
9–11	5
6–8	6
3–5	3
0–2	1

a. Construct a histogram of these data.
b. Construct a frequency polygon for these data.
c. What type of skewness is shown here?

14. An exercise physiologist was wondering if self-employed workers exercised more or less than company-employed workers. To begin her research, she asked 30 self-employed workers chosen at random how many times they exercised in one month.
    a. Construct a histogram of these data.
    b. Construct a frequency polygon for these data.
    c. What type of skewness is shown here?

Hours Spent Exercising	f
24–26	1
21–23	0
18–20	2
15–17	3
12–14	4
9–11	5
6–8	4
3–5	3
0–2	8

15. Indicate the shape of the curve (normal, positively skewed, or negatively skewed) that you would be most likely to find in the following data.
    a. College entrance exam results of members of a high school honors class.
    b. Test scores on a sixth-grade mathematics test taken by fifth-graders.
    c. Number of conversations with strangers initiated by introverted individuals in one month.
    d. Exam scores of a sophomore high school class in biology.
    e. Anxiety measurements of workers taken on the first day of their new job at a toxic waste disposal site.
    f. Test scores on a fifth-grade mathematics test taken by sixth-graders.
16. Give an example of data that would likely be negatively skewed.
    a. Draw a hypothetical frequency polygon that would describe these data, and label the axes.
    b. Do the same for an example of positive skewness.
17. A soap company is in the process of marketing a new soap and is studying whether the color of the soap affects consumer satisfaction with the soap. Two groups of consumers, one group between the ages 21 and 40, and another group between the ages of 41 and 60, were given the unlabeled soap bar in three different colors—red, white, and brown. The consumers were asked to rate how satisfied they were with each of the three colored soaps on a scale of 1 (very dissatisfied) to 7 (very satisfied).
    a. Graph the results given below.
    b. Which is the dependent variable? Which is the independent variable?
    c. What is the relationship between the color of the soap and consumer satisfaction? How is this relationship affected by the age group of the consumer?

Average Rating of Soap

Group	Brown	White	Red
Age 21–40	2	5	4
Age 41–60	1	7	3

18. A professor at a state university wanted to see if a student's GPA in college is related to his or her annual income once out of school. The professor located ten students who had been out of school for ten years and located their cumulative college GPA's. The professor's results are shown below.
    a. Graph these data.
    b. What was the dependent variable? The independent variable?
    c. On the basis of this meager sample, what would you conclude about the relationship between a student's college GPA and annual income ten years later?

GPA	Income Level
3.8	51,000
3.2	31,000
3.5	76,000
4.0	46,000
3.9	23,000
3.0	58,000
3.1	29,000
3.8	30,000
3.6	39,000
3.4	22,000

19. A marketing specialist is analyzing the monthly sales of a popular magazine to determine which months out of the year the magazine company should increase their advertising. Draw a graph of these data for the specialist to present at the company sales meeting.

Month	Number of Issues Sold
Jan.	101,728
Feb.	96,543
Mar.	99,229
Apr.	102,491
May	103,624
June	103,399
July	104,012
Aug.	104,801
Sept.	105,009
Oct.	102,969
Nov.	110,628
Dec.	111,211

20. College students wearing glasses were compared with those wearing contact lenses on their reaction times in pushing a switch when a stimulus light came on. The lights were located at different positions in the visual field. One light was at center (0°), and the others were at 20°, 40°, 60°, and 80° to the left and right of the center light. Use graph paper to plot the functional relationship between reaction time (in milliseconds) and position in the visual field, and note the differences between those wearing glasses and those wearing contacts.

(Left)				Position				(Right)
80°	60°	40°	20°	0°	20°	40°	60°	80°
Contacts 576	570	554	545	540	544	548	560	579
Glasses 597	578	564	550	542	548	558	576	595

21. Use the cumulative percentage curve of the reading attitude scores of Figure 2.11 to answer the following.
    a. Find the 50th percentile for this group of children.
    b. Thirty percent of the children had scores below what?
    c. What percent of the children had scores of 74 or above?

22. Use the cumulative percentage curve of the boys' and girls' coordination scores in Figure 2.12 to determine the following.
    a. The top 10% of the boys are considered to be highly coordinated. What coordination test score would be necessary to be in this group?
    b. What percent of girls are at this score or above?
    c. What percent of the boys scored lower than the girls' 50th percentile of 41?

23. Doctors recommend drinking eight glasses of water a day. To determine how often this recommendation is actually followed, health and nutrition majors at a private college asked 50 of their classmates how many glasses of water they drank on an average day. Calculate the values for a *cumulative f* column and a *cumulative percentage* column, and use a sheet of graph paper to draw a cumulative percentage curve for these data.

Number of Glasses	f
10	3
9	4
8	5
7	6
6	5
5	7
4	8
3	7
2	5

a. What was the 50th percentile for these students?
b. What percentage of the students polled drank at least eight glasses of water a day?

c. The health and nutrition majors decided to send out letters of encouragement to drink more water to those students who scored in the bottom 40% of the group. These students drank less than _____ glasses of water a day.

24. College students who held part-time jobs were polled to determine the number of hours they worked per week. The grouped frequency distribution of hours worked per week follows. Calculate the *cumulative f* and the *cumulative percentage* columns and use graph paper to draw a cumulative percentage curve of the data.

Hours Worked	*f*
27–29	1
24–26	3
21–23	1
18–20	12
15–17	9
12–14	9
9–11	49
6–8	55
3–5	51
0–2	7
	$N = 197$

a. A dormitory counselor believes that students working 15 or more hours per week will have serious academic difficulties. According to this study what percent of the students will be affected?

b. How many hours per week did the top 20% of the students holding part-time jobs work?

c. What number of hours was at the 50th percentile?

COMPUTER EXERCISES FOR APPENDIX 4 DATA BANK

C1. Construct a *simple frequency distribution* for men for the Self-Monitoring data. Do the same for the women. Are there any noticeable differences in the two distributions?

C2. Construct a histogram for the men's Type A scores. Is there any skewness present? If so, what kind?

C3. Construct a stem-and-leaf display of the women's BSRI Masculinity scores. Is there any skewness present? If so, what kind?

C4. Construct a histogram for the women's BSRI Femininity scores. Does the histogram show any skewness?

C5. Construct a cumulative percentage distribution for the JAS Type A scores. How high would you have to score to be in the top one-third of this distribution?

CHAPTER 3

Central Tendency

More than three-fourths of adult Americans report drinking coffee regularly. Most coffee drinkers are aware that the critical ingredient in their brew is the drug caffeine. Health researchers have reported a wide variety of psychological and physiological effects of caffeine, especially effects on the cardiovascular system.

In one study (Green & Suls, 1996) the subjects were given capsules containing either caffeine or cornstarch (placebo condition) and took a capsule with each cup of decaffeinated coffee. Green and Suls reported that both systolic and diastolic blood pressures as well as heart rate were elevated after ingesting caffeine equal to the consumption of the average American coffee drinker.

Hardly a day goes by that we do not hear some reference to the concept of "average" performance. Studies like the one just mentioned have reported that the "average" coffee drinker consumes five or six cups a day. And, of course, we are all familiar with energy-conscious drivers who tell us that their cars will average 40 miles per gallon and with sports fans who are forever discussing some ballplayer's batting average or earned run average or their own bowling averages. Figure 3.1 suggests that measures of average performance even are topics for the comic strips.

The "average" used so frequently by the layperson is part of the concept of *central tendency*. As you saw in the last chapter, frequency distributions and stem-and-leaf displays, along with the histogram and frequency polygon, are valuable devices that enable us to extract meaning from a mass of data. However, we

Figure 3.1
The concept of central tendency is even noted in the comic strips. (*Source:* PEANUTS ©
United Feature Syndicate. Reprinted by permission.)

would like more efficient ways of expressing our results than a mere picture of the
distribution as a whole. Specifically, we would like to have a statistical method that
would yield a *single value* that would tell us something about the entire distribution.

One such single value is called a measure of *central tendency*. It is the single
value that best describes the performance of the group as a whole. Since much of
our research efforts involve comparing the performance of two or more groups, it
will make our job much easier if we can describe a group's performance with a
single value. For example, the average net income in one county might be
$27,500, or the average weight of the defensive linemen of the Minnesota Vikings
might be 280 pounds, or the average test score in an educational psychology
course might be 83.2. All of these single values cited have one thing in common:
They are values that best characterize the group as a whole. No person actually
had a score of 83.2 on the educational psychology exam, but the average of 83.2
is the best single value that represents the performance of that group of students.

There are a number of measures of central tendency, all designed to give representative values of some distribution. In this chapter we will concentrate on
three of the most commonly used: the arithmetic mean, the median, and the mode.
But keep in mind as we discuss the characteristics of these measures of central
tendency that our eventual aim will be to find one that best describes the performance of the group as a whole.

MEAN

The *average,* referred to a bit earlier, is more correctly called the *arithmetic mean,*
or often just the *mean*. I am sure you remember from some previous mathematics
classes that to calculate the mean you simply add up all the numbers and divide
by how many numbers there are. So, if you paid 69 cents, 49 cents, 98 cents, 59
cents, and 95 cents for 5 items in the supermarket, the average, or mean, price
paid per item would be $3.70 divided by 5, or 74 cents.

However, statisticians tend to get a little nervous when terms are not precisely
defined, so let us be more formal with the terminology. Table 3.1 shows the num-

Table 3.1
Calculating the mean: Number of cups of coffee consumed per day by 10 office personnel

X
6
9
10
7
9
2
4
5
6
2
$\Sigma X = 60$

$$\overline{X} = \frac{\Sigma X}{N} = \frac{60}{10} = 6$$

ber of cups of coffee consumed by 10 office personnel and the terms ΣX and N, which we first met in Chapter 1. We remember that ΣX is the symbol for the sum of the X values, and N is the number of values. In Table 3.1, the addition of the X values yields $\Sigma X = 60$, and N is, of course, 10. The formula for the mean, whose symbol is $\overline{X}$ (say "X bar"), would be

$$\overline{X} = \frac{\Sigma X}{N} \tag{3.1*}$$

which simply states that we obtain the mean by summing all the X values and dividing by N, the number of observations. So, for the data of Table 3.1, the mean would be

$$\overline{X} = \frac{\Sigma X}{N} = \frac{60}{10} = 6$$

So what does the mean mean? What does $\overline{X} = 6$ in Table 3.1 tell us about the data? In short, we would say that the value of 6 is the best single value that describes this distribution. Since these values were the number of cups of coffee drunk by 10 office personnel, we would conclude that the mean of 6 is the best single value that represents the number of cups of coffee consumed by the 10 office personnel as a whole.

Another useful feature of the mean is that it makes it possible to compare an individual's performance with the rest of the group. Was Bob's coffee consumption

*Computational formulas in this book will be identified by a number that indicates the chapter number and the location of the formula in the chapter. Thus formula 3.1 is the first formula listed in Chapter 3.

above the mean or below it? Was Erin's consumption above or below average? How far above or below was she? We can answer these questions in terms of deviation or distance from the mean. Using the coffee data again, we list each worker and number of cups consumed in Table 3.2. In addition to the number of cups drunk (X) there is another column ($X - \overline{X}$), which shows how far each value is from the mean. The column headed ($X - \overline{X}$) contains deviations, and these are obtained, obviously, by subtracting the mean from each value. For example, Bob's deviation would be 3 (9 minus 6), indicating that his consumption is located 3 units above the mean. In a similar fashion we calculate that Fay, who drank only 2 cups, would have a deviation of −4 (2 minus 6), locating her 4 units below the mean.

The reason for belaboring the obvious in the previous paragraph is to demonstrate that the algebraic sum of the deviations is always 0. Note that the sum of the ($X - \overline{X}$) column in Table 3.2 is 0. This is the formal definition of the arithmetic mean. It is calculated in such a way that it is directly in the center of these deviations, making the algebraic sum of these deviations 0. In our usual notation, $\Sigma(X - \overline{X}) = 0$.

This point is best shown by the illustration in Figure 3.2. Note that the mean is the fulcrum and that the entire group of observations is in balance.

We need to make one last point about the calculation of the mean. In Chapter 1, if you remember, quite a case was made for the necessity of determining what level of precision we have in a group of data, that is, whether the observations are from a nominal, an ordinal, an interval, or a ratio scale. As was mentioned, we need to know this information before we can calculate any statistic based on the data. As you progress through this book, you will note that for each statistic discussed there will always be an accompanying comment on what type of data is appropriate for a given statistic. So with this fact in mind, we conclude that since the mean takes into account the distances between observations, the

Table 3.2
Cups of coffee shown as deviations from
the mean

Employee	X	$(X - \overline{X})$
Al	6	0
Bob	9	3
Chad	10	4
Darla	7	1
Erin	9	3
Fay	2	−4
Greg	4	−2
Helen	5	−1
Ivan	6	0
Jody	2	−4
	$\Sigma X = 60$	$\Sigma(X - \overline{X}) = 0$

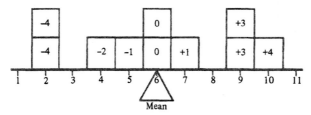

Figure 3.2
Arithmetic mean expressed as a balancing point.

measurements from which the mean is calculated must be at least of the interval type. A mean calculated from ordinal data (e.g., mean rank) may be misleading.

Simple Frequency Distributions

Most likely you will be calculating means for *raw data,* that is, data that have not yet been treated in any organized fashion. Such data will usually wind up as a column of numbers, with one value in each row. For such data, formula 3.1 will work very well. However, if your data are already in the form of a *simple frequency distribution,* such as shown in Table 3.3, the process of calculating the mean can be simplified greatly.

Table 3.3 shows the heights (in inches) of 39 college women, with the data already organized into a simple frequency distribution. The first two columns (*Scores* and *f*) are the usual columns of the simple frequency distribution. The third column, *fX,* is simply the result of multiplying each score by its *f* value. For example,

Table 3.3
Calculating the mean from a
simple frequency distribution:
Heights of college women
(inches)

Scores	f	fX
70	1	70
69	3	207
68	6	408
67	3	201
66	6	396
65	5	325
64	3	192
63	6	378
62	5	310
61	1	61
	39	2,548

the score of 68 is multiplied by its frequency, 6, and the product, 396, is entered in the fX column. The f and fX columns are then summed. The formula for the mean for data in a simple frequency distribution is

$$\overline{X} = \frac{\Sigma fX}{N} \tag{3.2}$$

For the women's height data of Table 3.3,

$$\overline{X} = \frac{2{,}548}{39} = 65.33$$

So we conclude that the mean height for this sample of 39 college women is 65.33, or approximately 5 feet $5\frac{1}{3}$ inches.

MEDIAN

The median is probably most familiar to you as the 50th percentile. *The median is the value that exactly separates the upper half of the distribution from the lower half.* It is obviously a measure of central tendency in that the median is the point located in such a way that 50% of the scores are lower than the median and the other 50% are greater than the median. It is important to note that while the mean was the exact center of the *deviations* or distances of the scores from the mean, the median is the exact center of the scores themselves.

The calculation of the median requires that we first arrange the set of scores in order of magnitude—usually with the highest score on top. The median is then found by counting up from the bottom $(N + 1)/2$ scores. The procedure is slightly different depending on whether we have an odd number of scores or an even number of scores.

Median: N Is Odd.   In the first column of Table 3.4 are an odd number of observations. The column shows the resting heart rate of 11 members of a senior citizens' exercise class before the class began. Counting up from the bottom $(11 + 1)/2 = 6$ scores, we find that the median is 73. Here, the median is simply the central score in the ordered distribution. One-half of the heart rates are higher than 73, and one-half are lower.

Median: N Is Even.   In the second column of Table 3.4 are an even number of observations—the heart rates of eight class members after five minutes of mild exercise. We again count up $(N + 1)/2$ scores from the bottom, but $(8 + 1)/2 = 4.5$, a decimal fraction. This simply means that our median is halfway between the fourth and fifth scores from the bottom. This would be the average of the two values, or $(80 + 88)/2 = 84$. Here, the median is not one of the actual values in the distribution. But, by definition, one-half of the heart rates are above 84 and one-half are below.

Table 3.4
Calculating the median: Comparing resting and exercise heart rates

Resting Heart Rate	Exercise Heart Rate
$N = 11$	$N = 8$
100	110
88	102
82	100
78	88 ← *Med* = 84
77	80
73 ← *Med* = 73	77
72	76
71	75
62	
61	
58	

What If Some Scores Are the Same?   The eight exercise heart rates in the second column of Table 3.4 are all different. What if the fourth and fifth heart rates were both 88? The median for the set of heart rates, 75, 76, 77, 88, 88, 100, 102, 110 would be again the $(8 + 1)/2 = 4.5$th score. But halfway between 88 and 88 is still 88, so the median is 88.[†]

For larger data sets, it is not always easy to eyeball the middle value, so the $(N + 1)/2$ method is essential. All that is necessary is that the scores are in order of magnitude. For any size data set, the stem-and-leaf plot is an easy method to use. Table 3.5 shows the number of home runs hit by American League batters with 400 or more plate appearances. We can see that the number of home runs varied from 1 to 52 and that the distribution is positively skewed. For the 95 hitters, the median would be the $(95 + 1)/2 = 48$th score from the bottom. (In the case of the stem-and-leaf display, remember to start with the *smallest* values, 1, 1, 2, 2, 4, . . . etc.) The 48th score is an 18, so we would say that the median number of home runs by American Leaguers was 18. By definition, 18 is the center of the distribution of home runs.

The median is a valuable measure of central tendency for measurements that are only of the ordinal type. Since no assumptions are made concerning distances between observations, it is meaningful to talk about median ranks, for example. So the median is an appropriate measure of central tendency for data that are ordinal or above.

[†]Some text authors use an interpolation method when some scores are duplicates, especially when the duplicate scores are near the center of the distribution. This method will give a more accurate value for the median, but except in highly skewed distributions, the difference between the two is usually minimal. If you need to use the interpolation method, see Fox, Levin, and Harkins (1993) for an easy-to-follow description.

Table 3.5
Stem-and-leaf display of home runs hit in the American League during the 1996 regular season[a]

Stem	Leaf
0	1 1 2 2 4 4
0	5 5 5 6 6 6 7 7 8 8 9 9
1	0 0 0 0 0 0 1 1 1 2 2 2 3 3 3 3 3 4 4 4 4
1	5 5 6 6 7 7 7 8 8 8 9 9 9 9
2	0 1 2 2 2 2 2 2 3 4 4
2	5 5 5 6 6 6 7 7 8 8 8 9
3	0 1 3 4 4
3	5 6 6 8 8 9
4	0 4 4
4	7 8 9
5	0 2

[a]Players with 400 or more at bats.

MODE

The French expression *à la mode* literally means "in vogue" or "in style." That is exactly what the mode is—*the score that is made most frequently,* or seems to be "in style." It is classed as a measure of central tendency, since a glance at a graph of the frequency distribution (e.g., Figure 2.3, in the last chapter) shows the grouping about a central point, and the mode is the highest point in the hump, or the most frequent score. The mode is easily obtained by inspection, but it is the crudest measure of central tendency and is not used as often as either the mean or the median. Table 3.6 shows the number of sit-ups completed in 60 seconds by 14 members of a noon-hour fitness class before beginning an eight-week exercise program. We note that the mode is 21, since that score appears most often. However, there are three scores of 19, so it is necessary to distinguish between the *principal mode* and the *secondary mode.* Whenever there are two peaks or concentrations in a frequency distribution, we have what is known as a *bimodal distribution.* For example, if we were to measure the heights of a random sample of high school seniors, we would very likely get a bimodal distribution—one peak corresponding to the concentration about an average for women and another peak for men.

The chief value of the mode lies in the fact that it is easily obtained by inspection and is useful in locating points of concentration of like scores in a distribution. The mode may be calculated from measurements that are of the nominal type or above.

Table 3.6
Determining the mode: Number
of sit-ups by a fitness class
before starting an exercise
program

X	
24	
23	
22	
21 ⎫	
21 ⎬ Principal mode = 21	
21 ⎭	
21	
20	
19 ⎫	
19 ⎬ Secondary mode = 19	
19 ⎭	
18	
17	
16	

COMPARISON OF THE MEAN, MEDIAN, AND MODE

If a measure of central tendency is a single value that best represents the performance of the group as a whole, which single value should be used? If you compute the mean, median, and mode for the same set of scores, you very rarely will
find that all three are identical. Which one will give us the "best single value" that
describes the entire distribution?

The answer to this question is by no means a simple one. First of all, we can
ignore the mode, since it is a rather crude measure of central tendency. This leaves
the mean and median to be considered, and, as you probably have guessed, the
mean is most often given as a measure of central tendency. Whenever you see the
term *average* used in books, magazines, and newspapers in describing some distribution, most often the author is referring to the mean.

However, there are many instances where the median is a valuable statistic. It
is not affected by extreme or atypical values as much as is the mean, so it is very
useful in situations where the distribution is either positively or negatively skewed.
For example, suppose we would like to calculate the average income for people
living in a small midwestern town. Let us assume that in this community there is
one millionaire and the rest of the residents are earning what we would judge to
be ordinary incomes. This is a slight exaggeration, but it will serve to illustrate the
usefulness of the median when distributions are markedly skewed. The mean,
since it takes into account the exact value of each score, would be unduly influenced by the millionaire's income, and this measure of central tendency would be

Note 3.1
The Effect on the Mean of Adding a Constant

If some number, such as 3 (in other words, a constant), is added to all the scores in a distribution, the mean is increased by the amount of the constant. For instance, the mean of the scores 5, 2, 9, 6, and 3 is 25/5 = 5. If the constant 3 were added to each score you now would have 8, 5, 12, 9, and 6, with a mean of 40/5 = 8. Stated symbolically, if a constant C is added to each score in a distribution with a mean $\overline{X}$, the mean of the new distribution will be $\overline{X} + C$. This fact probably does not come as a startling revelation to you, but in later chapters we will have occasion to make use of this peculiar property of the mean. For the mathematically inclined, the proof is very simple. Given the mean of a set of scores:

$$\overline{X} = \frac{\Sigma X}{N} = \frac{X_1 + X_2 + \cdots + X_N}{N}$$

a constant is added to each score:

$$\overline{X} = \frac{(X_1 + C) + (X_2 + C) + \cdots + (X_N + C)}{N}$$

Combining terms, and noting that the sum of a constant is equal to N times the constant:

$$\overline{X} = \frac{\Sigma X + \Sigma C}{N} = \frac{\Sigma X + NC}{N} = \frac{\Sigma X}{N} + \frac{NC}{N}$$

So the mean of the new distribution is

$$\overline{X} = \frac{\Sigma X}{N} + C = \overline{X} + C$$

much too high. The median, on the other hand, is the center of the distribution and would not be affected very much by the addition of a single score at the extreme end. Clearly, the median would give the most accurate picture of the income for this situation.

The ability of the median to resist the effect of skewness is demonstrated in Table 3.7 with the personal incomes of 8 members of a drug rehabilitation group shown in the left column. The original group has a mean income of $9,375 and median income of $9,500. Now suppose a new member joins the group, and let us say he or she has an income of $60,000. Look what happens to the mean and median income of this new group. The mean jumps to $15,000, which is higher than 7 of the 9 incomes. The median is not affected nearly as much, increasing only to $11,000. Again, the median gives a much more representative picture of the entire group.

Table 3.7
The effect of skewness on mean and median incomes

Original Drug Rehabilitation Group	Same Group Plus New Member
$17,000	$60,000
14,000	17,000
12,000	14,000
11,000	12,000
8,000	11,000
6,000	8,000
4,000	6,000
3,000	4,000
$\Sigma X = 75,000$	3,000
	$\Sigma X = 135,000$

$$\overline{X} = \frac{75,000}{8} = \$9,375 \qquad \overline{X} = \frac{135,000}{9} = \$15,000$$

Med = $9,500   *Med* = $11,000

The relationship of the mean and median in skewed distributions is demonstrated in Figures 3.3 and 3.4. The negatively skewed distribution of mathematics achievement scores discussed in Chapter 2 is reproduced in Figure 3.3. Note that the mode has the highest value, 67, while the mean is at 62.9, and the median is between the two at 64.9. This result illustrates a general rule: *In negative skewness, the mean is the lowest value of the three measures of central tendency.*

In Figure 3.4 the distribution of incomes of 14,000 workers discussed in Chapter 2 as an example of positive skewness is reproduced. Note that the mode is the lowest value, at $17,590, the median is $19,480, and the mean is the highest, at $21,430. *In positive skewness, the mean is the highest value of the three measures of central tendency.*

As you can see from the last two examples, the mean is affected greatly by the extreme or atypical scores in a skewed distribution, since it is "pulled" in the direction of the atypical values. It is for just this reason that the median is the preferred measure of central tendency when there is a marked degree of skewness in the distribution. It is much more likely to be the best single value that describes the distribution as a whole.

Stability

If the median is the preferred measure of central tendency in skewed distributions, why isn't it used all the time for all distributions? The answer to this question is that the *mean* is the most *stable* of the three measures of central tendency. By stability, we mean that in *repeated sampling* the means of the samples will tend to vary the least among themselves.

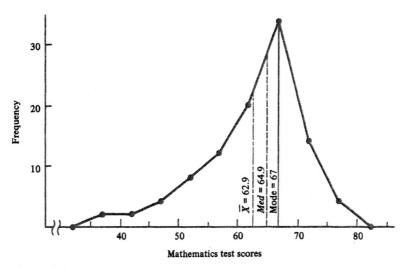

Figure 3.3
Three measures of central tendency in negative skewness.

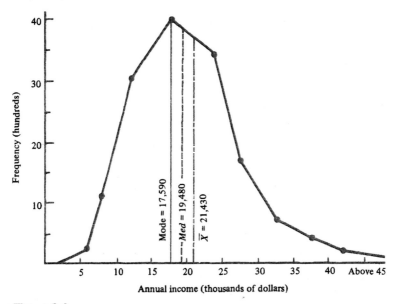

Figure 3.4
Three measures of central tendency in positive skewness.

A complete treatment of *sampling* and *populations* will be coming up in a later chapter, but for the time being we can illustrate this concept by an example. If we took repeated samples of some variable in the population (e.g., IQ scores of 100 10-year-olds, chosen at random) and calculated the three traditional measures of central tendency for various batches of samples, each containing 100 IQ scores, we would find that the means would be most like each other. Since we often want to estimate what the population value is from just one sample, we naturally would want to use the measure of central tendency that is the most reliable or consistent. So the mean is used most often as the measure of central tendency, since it fluctuates the least from sample to sample.

MEAN OF A POPULATION VERSUS THE MEAN OF A SAMPLE

The formula $\overline{X} = \Sigma X/N$ that we have been using is technically the formula for calculating the mean of a *sample*. The distinction between sample and population, as mentioned in the preceding paragraph, will be discussed at length in a later chapter, but at this point we need to distinguish between the mean of a sample and the mean of a population.

By *population,* we mean a group of elements that are alike in one or more characteristics as defined by the researcher. A population could be all the college students in the United States, or all the voters in a state, or all the seventh-graders in a school system, or all the dairy cattle in a county. The important thing to remember is that the population is defined by a researcher *for a particular purpose* and *all* the elements satisfying the criteria are members of that population. Size

Note 3.2
Rounding Off Measures of Central Tendency

How many significant digits should you report when you calculate a measure of central tendency? The mean, since it is obtained by dividing ΣX by N, could have a whole string of digits to the right of the decimal point. For example, if $\Sigma X = 93$ and $N = 7$, you could report the mean as 13.3 or 13.29 or 13.286 or 13.2857. The problem is that the more digits you include, the more precision is implied—and the precision may be totally unwarranted. For that reason it is conventional to report measures of central tendency to *two more decimal places* than you have in your data. Therefore, for test scores that are whole numbers, such as 84, 72, and so on, your mean might be 58.62. Also, if your data consisted of reaction time measured in hundredths of seconds, such as 0.37, 0.29, and so on, your mean might be 0.3261. The median is treated in a similar fashion.

alone does not determine whether or not a group of elements is a population, although in practice most populations turn out to be rather large.

The formula for the mean of a population, μ, is[‡]

$$\mu = \frac{\Sigma X}{N} \tag{3.3}$$

which contains the identical components ΣX and N as did the *sample* mean. The only difference, as should be obvious by now, is that the calculation of μ is based on *all* the elements of a population, whereas $\overline{X}$ is based on a smaller group of observations called a sample.

CALCULATING A MEAN FOR SEVERAL GROUPS

There will be occasions when you will want to calculate a mean from a number of other means. For example, if the mean reading test score for a group of fourth-graders is 31.3, and for a group of fifth-graders it is 42.7, what is the mean for the combined group of fourth- and fifth-graders? With only this information, *you cannot calculate a combined mean.* You cannot simply "average" the two means to get a combined mean for the two groups (except in the unlikely event that the values of N for the two groups are identical). In order to calculate the combined mean for a group of means, you must know the size of each sample, or N. Then the formula is

$$\overline{X} = \frac{N_1\overline{X}_1 + N_2\overline{X}_2 + N_3\overline{X}_3 + \cdots}{N_1 + N_2 + N_3 + \cdots} \tag{3.4}$$

where
N_1 = the size of sample 1
$\overline{X}_1$ = the mean of sample 1
N_2 = the size of sample 2
$\overline{X}_2$ = the mean of sample 2
and so on.

Table 3.8 shows the means for a motor coordination test for three groups of 10-, 11-, and 12-year-olds, and our objective is to find the combined mean, for all 80. Note that in the calculation of the combined mean, the mean of each separate group is multiplied by its own N. The sum of these products is then divided by the combined N, giving a mean of 21.13 for all three groups together. This is obviously different from what you would have obtained if you had incorrectly "averaged" the three means themselves.

[‡]To avoid confusion, we will use Greek letters anytime we are talking about population values. The Greek letter μ, pronounced "myoo," is the symbol for the population mean.

Table 3.8
Calculation of a combined mean for motor coordination

10-Year-Olds	11-Year-Olds	12-Year-Olds
$N = 10$	$N = 30$	$N = 40$
$\bar{X}_1 = 17$	$\bar{X}_2 = 20$	$\bar{X}_3 = 23$

$$\bar{X} = \frac{N_1\bar{X}_1 + N_2\bar{X}_2 + N_3\bar{X}_3}{N_1 + N_2 + N_3}$$

$$= \frac{10(17) + 30(20) + 40(23)}{10 + 30 + 40}$$

$$= \frac{170 + 600 + 920}{80} = \frac{1{,}690}{80}$$

$$= 21.13$$

Note 3.3
What the Combined Mean Formula Really Means

The formula for finding a mean of means is very easy to remember if you stop and note that $N\bar{X} = \Sigma X$. In other words, all that we are doing is converting the data for each group back to the original sum of the scores. After we have done this for all the groups, we add the individual sums together to get one grand sum of the scores, or a combined ΣX. This is then divided by the combined N for all groups, and the result is the ordinary mean

$$\frac{\Sigma X}{N}$$

By the way, the process of multiplying each $\bar{X}$ by its own N is called *weighting* the mean by its N. This makes sense if you refer to Table 3.8 and note that there are only ten 10-year-olds, while there are forty 12-year-olds. Since there are many more 12-year-olds, their mean should have a greater *weight* in the calculation of the combined mean. Or, stated another way, the mean of 23 is weighted by an N of 40, while the mean of 17 is weighted by only 10. We will have occasion to refer to the process of weighting in later chapters.

SOME CONCLUDING REMARKS

There should be no doubt in your mind what the purpose of a measure of central tendency is. Quite clearly, it is an attempt to find the best single value that represents the performance of the group as a whole. A measure of central tendency of 57.5 would be the best single value that describes the performance of a group of high school seniors in terms of number of items answered correctly on a college entrance exam, or a group of white rats in terms of number of seconds taken to run a maze, or a group of job applicants in terms of number of pins correctly placed in a manual dexterity test.

The problem arises when a decision must be made concerning *which* measure of central tendency is the best one to use for a given set of data. The mean, because it is the most stable measure of central tendency, is preferred in most cases. Since, as we indicated in Chapter 1, we are often interested in making inferences concerning the population, the mean is preferred because it is the most reliable. However, as we noted in the case of skewed distributions, the mean may not be the most representative value, and for this reason the median may give a better picture of the distribution as a whole.

SAMPLE PROBLEM—MANUAL SOLUTION

The following table presents the results of a study on sex stereotyping of occupations by children. We will use the methods covered in this chapter to calculate the three measures of central tendency. The sex-typing of occupations by children was studied by means of test of memory. Thirty fourth-graders were presented with flash cards containing pairs of proper names and occupations. Each received 12 cards with traditional sex-typed pairs (e.g., Carpenter-Bob, Nurse-Sue). Each flashcard was shown for 3 seconds with a 2-second interval in between. One minute after all cards had been viewed, the children were asked to recall as many of the pairs as they could. The number of errors made by each child is shown below (perfect recall = 0 errors).[§] Calculate the mean and median for the error scores.

0	2	2	2	0
1	0	0	1	6
4	8	2	0	0
4	2	2	0	0
2	2	0	2	2
2	2	2	4	0

[§]Adapted from D. Blaske, Occupational sex-typing by kindergarten and fourth-grade children, *Psychological Reports, 54* (1984): 795–801.

$$\text{Mean: } \bar{X} = \frac{\Sigma X}{N} = \frac{54}{30} = 1.80 \text{ errors}$$

Median: We first place the 30 error scores in order of magnitude. We calculate $(N + 1)/2 = (30 + 1)/2 = 15.5$, so the median would be halfway between the 15th and 16th scores. Counting in from the zero end we find that the 15th and 16th scores are both 2s, so *Med* = 2.

$$\downarrow$$
0, 0, 0, 0, 0, 0, 0, 0, 0, 0, 1, 1, 2, 2, 2, 2, 2, 2, 2, 2, 2, 2, 2, 2, 2, 4, 4, 4, 6, 8

Mode: The most frequent error score was 2.

SAMPLE PROBLEM—COMPUTER SOLUTION

An English instructor administered a midterm exam to a class of 50 college freshmen. The group of exam scores is shown in Table 3.9.

Table 3.10 shows the SPSS output. The first box shows a group of statistics called *descriptives,* followed by a stem-and-leaf plot of the scores and a histogram. Although some of the descriptives have not yet been covered in this text, you quickly spot the mean of 36.30 and the median of 37.00. Also familiar are the minimum and maximum scores and the range. Several of the measures in the descriptives box will be unfamiliar to you, but most will be covered later on in the text.

Also included are the stem-and-leaf display and a histogram. We can check on the accuracy of the median in the descriptives box by counting in $(N + 1)/2 = (50 + 1)/2 = 25.5$, or halfway between the 25th and 26th scores. Counting in from the zero end of the stem-and-leaf display, we see that both the 25th and 26th scores are 37s, so *Med* = 37, the same value given in the descriptives box.

Table 3.9
English midterm examination scores

40	37	38	22	28	28	46	48	33	37
50	31	20	27	41	35	40	43	34	37
38	26	44	35	26	37	23	31	28	49
39	32	39	39	24	38	25	47	44	28
45	42	35	35	46	53	31	42	41	38

(continued)

SAMPLE PROBLEM—COMPUTER SOLUTION *(CONTINUED)*

Table 3.10
SPSS output for descriptive statistics for English exam scores

Descriptives

			Statistic	Std. error
SCORES	Mean		36.30	1.13
	95% Confidence Interval for Mean	Lower Bound	34.04	
		Upper Bound	38.56	
	5% Trimmed Mean		36.31	
	Median		37.00	
	Variance		63.357	
	Std. Deviation		7.96	
	Minimum		20	
	Maximum		53	
	Range		33	
	Interquartile Range		11.75	
	Skewness		–.093	.337
	Kurtosis		–.654	.662

Scores

Scores: Stem-and-leaf plot

Frequency	Stem & Leaf
4.00	2. 0234
8.00	2. 56678888
6.00	3. 111234
15.00	3. 555577778888999
9.00	4. 001122344
6.00	4. 566789
2.00	5. 03

Stem width: 10
Each leaf: 1 case

The mode is not very informative in this distribution, with 28, 35, 37, and 38 all having the highest frequency of four. However, the histogram shows the typical cluster of scores toward the center of the distribution. We

Graph

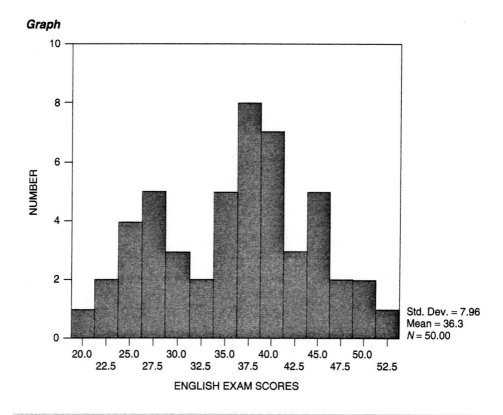

ENGLISH EXAM SCORES

Std. Dev. = 7.96
Mean = 36.3
N = 50.00

might note, though, that the distribution comes close to being bimodal, with a second grouping of scores at the left side (lower scores) of the distribution.

STUDY QUESTIONS

1. What is meant by the concept of central tendency?
2. How does the mean differ from the median?
3. What does $\Sigma(X - \overline{X}) = 0$ mean?
4. When would you use the formula $\overline{X} = \dfrac{\Sigma fX}{N}$ for calculating the mean?
5. When might the median be preferred to the mean?
6. The mean is the most stable measure of central tendency. What does this statement mean?
7. In calculating a mean for several groups, each individual mean is weighted. What does this term mean?

EXERCISES

1. A newspaper published football season averages for area high schools. The following table lists the points Jefferson High scored against their opponents in the 1996 football season. Calculate the mean number of points scored and also demonstrate that $\Sigma(X - \overline{X}) = 0$.

6	0	28	20	21	14
6	0	7	14	13	0

2. A telephone company has decided to reduce its rates for customers who spend an average of 75 dollars for long-distance calls per month. Following is the monthly amount of money the McDeer family has spent in long-distance calls over the past year. Calculate the mean for this distribution and demonstrate that $\Sigma(X - \overline{X}) = 0$. Does the McDeer family qualify for a reduced long-distance billing rate?

68	111	90	77
72	76	67	89
62	88	51	85

3. A college communications instructor listened to 24 three-minute student speeches and counted the number of times "uh," "um," or "ah" was verbalized. Calculate the mean and median for these data.

20	10	16	12	17	0
11	9	5	11	9	6
15	17	7	3	13	12
10	0	8	12	20	2

4. The same instructor as in exercise 3 decided she would let her students leave class 10 minutes early on the next speech day if the students could average less than five "um," "uh," and "ah"'s per speech. Calculate the mean and the median for this distribution. Were the students allowed to leave 10 minutes early that day?

5	3	2	7	1	0
5	6	8	4	9	1
3	7	4	2	9	8
2	4	1	0	0	4

5. A study comparing the typical household incomes for cities in Oklahoma and Texas was initiated to see where differences in household incomes lie across

regions. The mean household incomes for a sample of 75 different families in three Texas cities are shown in the following table. Calculate a combined mean to obtain the average household income for all 75 families in the Texas sample.

Odessa	Houston	Amarillo
$N = 30$	$N = 25$	$N = 20$
$\overline{X} = \$36,093$	$\overline{X} = \$50,411$	$\overline{X} = \$45,768$

6. The study described in exercise 5 showed the following results for a sample of 300 families in three cities in Oklahoma. Calculate a combined mean household income for all 300 families in the Oklahoma sample.

Tulsa	Enid	Lawton
$N = 121$	$N = 87$	$N = 92$
$\overline{X} = \$41,890$	$\overline{X} = \$40,900$	$\overline{X} = \$31,266$

7. An optimism–pessimism scale was administered to several different self-help groups meeting at a local community center, with means and sample sizes as follows. Calculate a combined mean for all groups.

Alateen	Single Parents	Ostomy Group	Parkinson's
$N = 22$	$N = 8$	$N = 12$	$N = 10$
$\overline{X} = 24$	$\overline{X} = 21$	$\overline{X} = 25$	$\overline{X} = 22$

8. An eighth-grade English teacher administered a unit exam to one of her classes and found that the majority of the items were too difficult. Calculate the mean and the median for the 50-point exam. What kind of skewness is illustrated here?

26	31	30	21
32	27	17	18
29	23	22	19
16	33	25	22
29	13	16	29
25	24	21	30

9. A freshman psychology student completed a project for extra credit in his general psychology class. He was told to conduct a survey on 30 people about any topic he chose and calculate the mean and median for his data. He asked 30 college students how many pizzas they ordered in one month.

What is the mean? The median? Is there skewness in this distribution? If so, what kind?

7	4	2	2	2
5	3	4	2	1
3	4	3	2	1
2	2	2	1	1
2	2	0	1	2
2	0	2	1	1

10. Another student in the same statistics course asked 30 classmates how many hours it takes them to travel home from college. Calculate the mean and median for her data.

6.5	3.5	5	4	3.5
2.75	6	3.5	2	2.5
4	3.75	4.5	4	1.75
2.5	1.5	2.5	2.75	0.25
1.5	2	1.5	1	2
1	3.5	0.75	3.5	3

11. Sales gain is the increase in sales for a particular product compared to the sales brought in for that same product in the previous year. A department store sold $360,000 worth of men's jeans in the fall of 1996 and was aiming for a 9% increase in sales for the fall of 1997. Reaching this goal would require selling $675 worth more jeans per week as compared to the previous year. Following is the weekly sales gain dollar amount for jeans in the fall of 1997. Calculate the mean and the median weekly sales gain. Did the department store reach its sales gain goal?

664	680	679	675
660	667	678	674
681	673	662	668
674	671	678	680

12. The mayor in a town of 16,000 would like to see each of her police officers ticket an average of three traffic violations per day. A new recruit is told to keep a daily record of the traffic violations he reports. Below are his data from 30 working days. Calculate the mean and the median number of traffic violations he reports per day. Did he meet his quota?

4	0	3	4	2	1
1	4	2	3	3	0
0	7	5	0	1	2
5	3	3	2	2	2
4	1	0	1	2	6

13. Guest count average (GCA) is computed hourly by restaurants and reports the average amount of money each guest spends at the restaurant. Servers are encouraged to increase their guests' GCA by offering soups, sides, beverages, and the like. The manager on duty is offering the seven servers working a 5 to 8 P.M. shift a free-meal card if their combined GCA averages $6.05. Below are the seven servers' hourly GCA averages. Calculate the mean GCA for the restaurant for the 5 to 8 P.M. shift. Did the servers get free-meal cards?

	5–6 P.M.	6–7 P.M.	7–8 P.M.
Server 1	$5.45	$6.01	$6.23
Server 2	$5.30	$5.83	$5.95
Server 3	$4.89	$6.35	$7.26
Server 4	$5.68	$6.75	$7.27
Server 5	$5.95	$7.04	$6.71
Server 6	$4.50	$5.64	$4.59
Server 7	$7.83	$7.56	$8.24

14. The 1996 Agricultural Statistics Summary reported that farmers in one midwestern state farmed an average of 1,263 acres. The following table lists the number of acres farmed by a sample of 35 farming families throughout the state. Calculate the mean number of acres farmed for this sample. Does the mean from this sample represent the state mean? Explain why or why not.

200	500	1,200	2,000	4,500
6,700	345	5,600	26,000	100
3,400	6,800	7,000	450	340
780	1,500	5,600	3,200	900
3,000	4,500	400	990	1,200
780	1,100	700	2,000	700
7,000	500	990	3,400	780

COMPUTER EXERCISES FOR APPENDIX 4 DATA BANK

C1. Calculate several descriptive statistics for the male college students on the Physical Symptoms Inventory. Include the mean, median, minimum score, maximum score, and range. Also construct a histogram of the symptoms scores.

C2. Calculate the same statistics as you did in C1 for the female college students. How do men and women compare on the various statistics?

C3. Calculate the measures of central tendency for the women on the Self-Monitoring Inventory.

C4. Did the women who were high on self-monitoring (above the median) report more symptoms than those who were low (below the median)?

CHAPTER 4

Variability

A critical issue in the field of learning disabilities is whether students with learning disabilities are any different from students who are low achievers. Various diagnostic tests have been developed to assess a wide range of learning deficits. For example, cognitive abilities and school achievement are assessed by measures such as the Woodcock-Johnson Psycho-Educational Battery and the Peabody Individual Achievement Tests.

Several studies have shown a difference between students with learning disabilities and students who are low achievers in some factors but not others. For example, students with learning disabilities scored lower on the Picture Vocabulary subtest of the Woodcock-Johnson, while there was no difference between learning-disabled and low-achieving students on Spatial Relations (Algozzine, Ysseldyke, & McGue, 1995).

This short introduction to the controversy is not intended to promote one view or the other, but simply to supply some background information before we examine examples of results from several of the test instruments used by school psychologists and special education teachers.

If one thing is obvious from a casual observation of human behavior, it must be the notion of variability. Some people are short, some are tall, others are in between, One five-year-old might be forward, aggressive, and noisy, while her playmate is withdrawn, passive, and quiet. A teacher or school psychologist giving one of the diagnostic tests that we have mentioned will find some students getting low scores, a few getting high scores, and a majority clustering in the center of the group. Or you may notice that your car averages 21 miles per gallon, but you know that on a long trip you can squeeze 26 out of it, while in downtown traffic the mileage drops to a mere 13.

Not only is there variation among different people and among different things, but the same person or thing may vary from time to time in certain characteristics. Although Michael Jordan might score an average of 30 points a game during the National Basketball Association's regular season, he has broken away for a season's high of 69, but has also shot a relatively cold 20. Similarly, a B student will get A's on occasion and also a few C's.

We said earlier that the task of statistics was to reduce large masses of data to some meaningful values. In Chapter 3 you saw how a measure of central tendency yielded the best *single* value that described the performance of the group as a whole. It was a value that best represented the entire group of observations. But as you noted in the first couple of paragraphs of this chapter, there is more to describing a group of observations than noting the *average* performance, since a measure of central tendency tells you nothing concerning the variation about the average. In preparing frequency distributions and calculating measures of central tendency in earlier chapters, you noted that some observations fell below the mean while some were above the mean. This fluctuation of scores about a measure of central tendency is called variability.

In short, to describe a set of observations accurately we need to know not only the central tendency but also the variability of the observations. For example, let us suppose that Jones and Smith, seventh-grade mathematics teachers in two different school districts, give the same national achievement test in mathematics to their classes. They happen to run into each other at a fast-food restaurant one day, and Jones states that her classes had an average of 72. Smith stops short and remarks that it certainly is a coincidence because the average for his classes was also a 72.

A naive observer would tend to say that the abilities of the two groups of students must be quite similar, since they were equal on the achievement test. But note that nothing has been said about the variability of the two groups. It is possible that Jones has the usual classes with a few very bright students, a few slow ones, and the rest just ordinary, plain, average seventh-graders. Smith on the other hand teaches in a district that has resource rooms and some self-contained classrooms for those with learning disabilities and also several accelerated classes for gifted and talented students. Let us further suppose that the results on the mathematics exam for these special classes are not included in Smith's data.

The frequency polygons shown in Figure 4.1 illustrate this somewhat contrived, but not uncommon, example. The scores of Jones' students are spread out over a wide range (approximately 42 to 97), since her group contains a few excellent students and several poor students. The scores from Smith's class, on the other hand, show much less dispersion (scores from 51 to 85), which is what you would expect when those students likely to make the high scores and the low scores are not included. In Figure 4.1 the greater variability of Jones' class is obvious, and there is no doubt that despite the fact that the two classes have equal means, the scores of Jones' students are different from those of Smith.

Clearly, a measure of central tendency is not enough to describe a distribution accurately. Some unkind stories concerning statisticians have arisen from just this

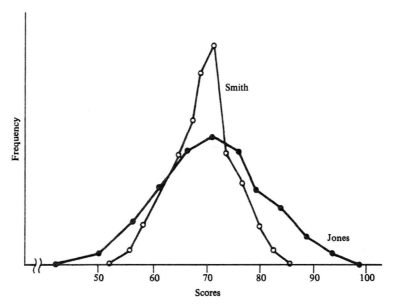

Figure 4.1
Frequency polygons for two distributions of mathematics achievement scores.

last point—you may have heard such things as "A statistician drowned in a river whose average depth was 4 feet" or "A statistician is one who with feet in the oven and head in the refrigerator is, on the average, quite comfortable." And in Figure 4.2, even Garfield takes advantage of reporting only a measure of central tendency.

Since a measure of central tendency does not give information about the variability of a group of observations, it is necessary to have some way to measure precisely the amount of variability (scatter, dispersion, spread, or variation) that is present in a distribution of scores. We would like to have a convenient and con-

Figure 4.2
A measure of central tendency alone can be misleading. (*Source:* © Copyright Universal Press Syndicate.)

cise measure that tells us instantly something about how much the scores are spread out. The frequency polygons in Figure 4.1 tell us this, of course, but a single measure would be much more efficient. This measure would do for the characteristic of variability what the mean or median did for central tendency. Let us examine several ways of measuring variability.

RANGE

One of the simplest and most straightforward measures of variability is the *range*. This statistic can be calculated for measurements that are on an interval scale or above. The range is simply the difference between the *highest* and the *lowest* scores in a distribution. For example, if a distribution of weights of 100 college men showed the heaviest at 225 pounds and the lightest at 132 pounds, the range would be 225 − 132 = 93 pounds. Or in the example described previously in Figure 4.1, Jones' classes had a range of 97 − 42 = 55, while the range for Smith's classes was 85 − 51 = 34. Obviously, this single value tells us something about the scattering or spread of scores, and the range of 55 for Jones' classes indicates considerably more variability in the mathematics achievement scores than the range of 34 for Smith's.

Although the range is a handy preliminary method for determining variability, it has two serious weaknesses. First of all, one extreme value can greatly alter the range. These extreme values are called *outliers,* and we will have more to do with them later. For now, we will note that an outlier could affect the outcome of our data analysis. For example, in Figure 4.1, note that the lowest score in Jones' class is a 42. If the student making that score had been sick that day, the next lowest score might have been a 50. In this case the range would be 97 − 50 = 47, which is considerably less than the original range of 55, and all because an outlier stayed home with a flu bug.

The second, and most serious, drawback is that since the range is based on only two measures, the highest and the lowest, it tells us nothing about the *pattern* of the distribution. A good illustration of this drawback is shown in Table 4.1.

Table 4.1 shows scores for 20 students on the Spatial Relations subtest of the Woodcock-Johnson Battery, measuring the students' ability to match random shapes visually. Scores for the 10 students labeled as low achievers are shown under "Group A" and scores for 10 students identified as learning disabled are shown under "Group B." Groups A and B have identical means, 32.5, and identical ranges, 15, but a glance at the *pattern* of the distributions shows how dissimilar they are. The scores of group A range from 25 to 40, with most of the other values clustered tightly around the mean of 32.5. Group B's scores also range from 25 to 40, but note that most of the scores are grouped at the extreme ends of the distribution. In this case the range is misleading as a measure of variability, since it says that groups A and B have equal variability although it is obvious that there are rather severe differences between the two.

Table 4.1
Two distributions with equal ranges but dissimilar patterns of dispersion

Group A		Group B	
40		40	
33	$\overline{X} = \dfrac{325}{10} = 32.5$	39	$\overline{X} = \dfrac{325}{10} = 32.5$
33		39	
33		38	
33		38	
32	Range = 40 − 25 = 15	27	Range = 40 − 25 = 15
32		27	
32		26	
32		26	
25		25	
$\Sigma X = 325$		$\Sigma X = 325$	

It is this last point that is important for our attempt to measure variability in an accurate way. We need a method that depends on *all* the measures in a distribution, not just the two extremes. If we define variability as the fluctuation of the scores about some central point, we need a method that will tell us *how* much these scores are fluctuating about that point, or how far they are from the mean. In Table 4.1 the majority of the scores of group A do not deviate very far from the mean, while those of group B are scattered quite a distance from the mean. Clearly, we need a method that will be sensitive to how far each individual observation deviates from the mean, so let us take a look at one method that might be of help in measuring the amount of deviation.

AVERAGE DEVIATION

You will recall from Chapter 3 that the mean was defined as the center of the deviations, and to prove it we subtracted the mean from each score. For example, if a distribution consisted of five scores, 14, 12, 9, 17, and 8, the mean would be 60/5 = 12. Subtracting the mean from each score $(X - \overline{X})$, we would get values of 2, 0, −3, 5, and −4.

It should be obvious that if we want a measure of variability that takes into account how far each score deviates from the mean, the deviation score $(X - \overline{X})$ would give us this information. If the values of $(X - \overline{X})$ are relatively small, it would indicate that there is not much variability and that the scores are near the mean, while if the values of $(X - \overline{X})$ are large the scores must be scattered farther from the mean.

To construct a measure of variability, it would be necessary only to add the $(X - \overline{X})$ values to get an overall picture of how much variation there was. However, we noted in Chapter 3 that the sum of the deviations about the mean,

$\Sigma(X - \overline{X})$, is always 0. We could easily overcome this problem by ignoring the sign of the deviation score (in other words, using the *absolute* value) and then dividing this sum by N to get the average deviation. For example, for those five scores listed earlier with a mean of 12, the scores deviate, on the average, 2.8 units from the mean.

From an intuitive point of view the average deviation makes good sense. The value of 2.8 in the example would tell us that on the average each observation deviates 2.8 units from the mean. So the average deviation is a sensible, easily understood, accurate measure of variability.

Unfortunately, it is hardly ever used. One thing that you will become aware of should you go on to more advanced courses in statistics is that all of the statistical techniques are linked together by certain theoretical foundations—and that the average deviation simply doesn't fit into this framework. So it is doubtful that you will ever see any reference to the average deviation again. The only reason that it was brought up at this point was to emphasize the use of the deviations from the mean $(X - \overline{X})$ as a way of indicating the amount of variability. These deviations will be an important part of the measure of variability to be discussed in the next section.

STANDARD DEVIATION

The most widely used measure of variability is the *standard deviation*. This statistic makes use of the deviation of each score from the mean, but the calculation, instead of taking the absolute value of each deviation, squares each deviation to obtain values that are all positive in sign. You will remember from elementary algebra that when two numbers of the same sign are multiplied together the product is always positive. So when we square each of the deviations, we get positive numbers whether our original deviations were positive or negative. We add these squared deviations to obtain $\Sigma(X - \overline{X})^2$ (read "sum of the squared deviations"), divide the sum by $N - 1$ to obtain a sort of average, and then take the square root of that result in order to get back to our original units of measurement. The standard deviation may be calculated from any set of measurements that are at least of interval nature.*

To summarize the steps just described, we can state the formula for the standard deviation as

$$s = \sqrt{\frac{\Sigma(X - \overline{X})^2}{N - 1}} \qquad (4.1)$$

*The meaning of the standard deviation will become clearer when it is interpreted in terms of the normal curve later in this chapter. It is simply the distance on the x-axis between the mean and the steepest part of the normal curve, (e.g., between μ and -1σ or μ and $+1\sigma$ in Figure 4.3).

where

s = standard deviation

$\Sigma(X - \overline{X})^2$ = the sum of all the squared deviations from the mean

N = number of observations

This formula for the standard deviation is called the *deviation formula* because it is calculated from the deviations themselves. In the next section a formula will be used that simplifies the calculation of s by eliminating the time-consuming step of subtracting the mean from each score. But before we get ahead of ourselves, let us use the deviation formula to calculate s for the set of data shown in Table 4.2. These 8 scores are representative of the Numbers Reversed subtest of the Woodcock-Johnson Battery, measuring the ability to say groups of random numbers backward. Substituting into formula (4.1) we obtain

$$s = \sqrt{\frac{\Sigma(X - \overline{X})^2}{N - 1}} = \sqrt{\frac{30}{7}}$$

$$s = \sqrt{4.29}$$

$$s = 2.07$$

Our standard deviation for the data of Table 4.2 is $s = 2.07$.

The example shown in Table 4.2 uses the deviation formula to obtain s. Although this method was used here to show you how s is based on squared deviations from the mean, it is not often used in practice because its calculations are time-consuming and laborious. It is necessary to subtract the mean from each score, square these deviations, divide by $N - 1$, and extract the square root. However, some of the concepts involved in this method, especially the sum of squares, $\Sigma(X - \overline{X})^2$, will be useful to us in a later chapter. As was mentioned earlier, the deviation method illustrates the concept of variability very well in that each score is treated as a deviation from the mean.

Table 4.2
Calculation of the standard deviation (deviation method)

X	$(X - \overline{X})$	$(X - \overline{X})^2$	
6	1	1	$\overline{X} = \dfrac{\Sigma X}{N} = \dfrac{40}{8} = 5$
8	3	9	
2	-3	9	
4	-1	1	$s = \sqrt{\dfrac{\Sigma(X - \overline{X})^2}{N - 1}} = \sqrt{\dfrac{30}{7}}$
4	-1	1	
3	-2	4	$s = \sqrt{4.29}$
7	2	4	
6	1	1	$s = 2.07$
$\Sigma X = 40$	0	$\Sigma(X - \overline{X})^2 = 30$	

COMPUTATIONAL FORMULA FOR THE STANDARD DEVIATION

The preceding method for calculating s employed the deviation of each score from the mean, but it was mentioned that there was a more efficient method. It does not take much thought to realize that the calculation in Table 4.2 would have been much more time-consuming and prone to error if ΣX had been 41 instead of 40. Then the mean would have been $41/8 = 5.125$. Consider for a moment subtracting 5.125 from each score and then squaring the deviation. Instead of pondering this plodding, time-consuming process, let us move on to the computational formula.

Table 4.3 shows the number of cups of coffee consumed by 10 office employees that we first examined in Table 3.1. The computational formula is

$$s = \sqrt{\frac{\Sigma X^2 - \dfrac{(\Sigma X)^2}{N}}{N - 1}} \tag{4.2}$$

where

ΣX^2 = the sum of the squared scores
$(\Sigma X)^2$ = the square of the sum of the scores
N = number of observations

Note the difference between ΣX^2 and $(\Sigma X)^2$. The symbol ΣX^2 indicates that you are to square each individual score and then sum these squared scores. The term $(\Sigma X)^2$ indicates that you are to add all the scores first and then square that sum. To clarify these terms, let us calculate s for the coffee-drinking data of Table 4.3 using the computational formula.

Table 4.3
Calculating ΣX and ΣX^2 for coffee-drinking data

X	X^2
6	36
9	81
10	100
7	49
9	81
2	4
4	16
5	25
6	36
2	4
$\Sigma X = 60$	$\Sigma X^2 = 432$

$$s = \sqrt{\frac{\Sigma X^2 - \dfrac{(\Sigma X)^2}{N}}{N-1}} = \sqrt{\frac{432 - \dfrac{(60)^2}{10}}{9}}$$

$$= \sqrt{\frac{432 - 360}{9}} = \sqrt{\frac{72}{9}} = \sqrt{8.00}$$

$$s = 2.83$$

We will be using the computational formula for s throughout the rest of this text, since rounding errors are minimal.

Note 4.1
Calculating the Standard Deviation with a Pocket Calculator

Calculators, as you very well know, come in all shapes and sizes (and prices). There are basically two kinds, and advertising displays in electronic and discount stores show "scientific" calculators and a simpler arithmetic version (with memory and square root functions). If you have a scientific calculator, it will most likely have a "statistics" mode or function, and you need only to follow the instructions to enter a column of data, and push appropriate keys to obtain $\overline{X}$, s, N, and so on.

However, if you are using the simpler version, there are some excellent shortcuts to speed up your calculation of the standard deviation. After you have calculated ΣX in the usual way, the quantity ΣX^2 can be obtained by squaring each number and entering the square in your M+ storage. For example, in Table 4.3 you would multiply the first score, 6, by itself to obtain 36 and enter this in the memory by pushing the M+ key. The second score, 9, would be squared and entered into M+ and so on until you reached the last score, 2, and entered its square, 4, into M+. You would then recall memory to obtain $\Sigma X^2 = 432$.

You can now perform the operations called for in the computational formula,

$$s = \sqrt{\frac{\Sigma X^2 - \dfrac{(\Sigma X)^2}{N}}{N-1}}$$

You would first enter 432 on the keyboard and store in M+. You would next calculate $(\Sigma X)^2$ by multiplying $60 \times 60 = 3,600$, dividing by 10, and subtracting 360 from memory by pressing the M− key. You would now recall the result, 72, from memory and divide by 9 to get 8. Pressing the square root key now yields 2.83, the standard deviation for the coffee-drinking data of Table 4.3.

Now that we have spent the time and effort on the calculation of s, what does it do? What does it tell us about a distribution of scores? Obviously, it tells us in a relative fashion how much the scores in a distribution deviate from the mean. If s is small, there is little variability, and the majority of the observations are tightly clustered about the mean. If s is large, the scores are more widely scattered above and below the mean. One of the primary uses of s is to compare two or more distributions with respect to their variability. Let us repeat Table 4.1, where we noted that groups A and B had equal ranges on the Spatial Relations subtest, but the scores were distributed differently in the two distributions. The results are shown in Table 4.4.

Table 4.4
Comparing the standard deviations of two different distributions

GROUP A		GROUP B	
X	X^2	X	X^2
40	1,600	40	1,600
33	1,089	39	1,521
33	1,089	39	1,521
33	1,089	38	1,444
33	1,089	38	1,444
32	1,024	27	729
32	1,024	27	729
32	1,024	26	676
32	1,024	26	676
25	625	25	625
$\Sigma X = 325$	$\Sigma X^2 = 10{,}677$	$\Sigma X = 325$	$\Sigma X^2 = 10{,}965$

$$\overline{X}_1 = \frac{\Sigma X}{N} = \frac{325}{10} = 32.5 \qquad \overline{X}_2 = \frac{\Sigma X}{N} = \frac{325}{10} = 32.5$$

$$s_1 = \sqrt{\frac{\Sigma X^2 - \frac{(\Sigma X)^2}{N}}{N-1}} \qquad s_2 = \sqrt{\frac{\Sigma X^2 - \frac{(\Sigma X)^2}{N}}{N-1}}$$

$$= \sqrt{\frac{10{,}677 - \frac{(325)^2}{10}}{9}} \qquad = \sqrt{\frac{10{,}965 - \frac{(325)^2}{10}}{9}}$$

$$= \sqrt{\frac{114.5}{9}} \qquad = \sqrt{\frac{402.5}{9}}$$

$$= \sqrt{12.7222} \qquad = \sqrt{44.7222}$$

$$s_1 = 3.57 \qquad s_2 = 6.69$$

There can be no doubt that s is sensitive to the pattern of scores in a distribution. The scores of group A are tightly clustered about the mean, and s is 3.57. Compare this result with 6.69 for group B, where the scores are more widely dispersed from the mean. We have accomplished what we said we would do, that is, develop a measure of variability that reflects the distance each score deviates from the mean. The variable s is just this measure. The importance of s cannot be overemphasized, and, if there are some concepts that are still not clear, it would be a good idea to review the preceding sections before going on to the next topic.

VARIANCE

Before completing the chapter on measures of variability, we should take a quick look at a measure of variability that will be of considerable importance in later chapters. This measure is called the *variance;* it is simply the square of the standard deviation. In Table 4.2, you will note that the deviation formula for the standard deviation is

$$s = \sqrt{\frac{\Sigma(X - \overline{X})^2}{N - 1}}$$

and so the formula for the variance is simply

$$s^2 = \frac{\Sigma(X - \overline{X})^2}{N - 1}$$

For the data of Table 4.2, s is 2.07, and the variance (s^2) is 4.28.

We will have occasion to discuss the concept of variance in several future chapters, but, for the time being, consider variance (s^2) as just another method for describing the amount of variation in a set of scores. For example, in Table 4.4, s^2 for group A is $(3.57)^2 = 12.74$, while for group B it is $(6.69)^2 = 44.76$. Obviously, there is greater variability in the scores of group B than in those of group A.

Note 4.2
Rounding Off the Standard Deviation

We noted in Chapter 3 that the mean is conventionally rounded off to two more decimal places than we have in our set of raw data. The same convention applies to the standard deviation, so for whole numbers such as the test scores for group A shown in Table 4.4, we report a mean of 32.50 and a standard deviation of 3.57. Also, if you had a set of reaction time scores measured in hundredths of seconds, your mean might be 0.3261 with a standard deviation of 0.0942.

Note 4.3
Dividing by N or $N - 1$?

In our calculations of s and s^2, we have been using $N - 1$ as the denominator. You may have a calculator that computes two different standard deviations: one divides by N and the other divides by $N - 1$ (see Note 4.1). The instruction manual may use the symbol σ_N and divide by N and σ_{N-1} and divide by $N - 1$. For calculating the standard deviation of our sample, we will always divide by $N - 1$.

CALCULATING THE VARIABILITY OF A POPULATION USING σ AND σ^2

Just as we distinguished between the mean of a sample, $\overline{X}$, and the mean of a population, μ, back in Chapter 3, we must do the same for measures of variability. The symbols σ (lowercase Greek letter sigma) and σ^2 (say "sigma squared") represent the population standard deviation and population variance, respectively. The formulas for σ and σ^2 are

$$\sigma = \sqrt{\frac{\Sigma(X - \mu)^2}{N}}$$

$$\sigma^2 = \frac{\Sigma(X - \mu)^2}{N}$$

It is obvious that these two formulas are very much like the formulas for s and s^2. All we have to remember is that σ and σ^2 are calculated using *all* the elements of a population, while s and s^2 are calculated using $N - 1$ observations.

THE STANDARD DEVIATION AND THE NORMAL CURVE

It was noted earlier that frequency distributions of much of the data in education and the behavioral sciences approximate the normal curve. The normal curve will be discussed in detail in the next chapter, but at this point it will be helpful to see the relationship of the standard deviation and the normal curve. If we can assume that a variable (height, weight, IQ score, coordination score, etc.) approximates the shape of the normal curve, we can even better understand the concept of variability. Figure 4.3 shows a normal curve, with its mean, μ, and standard deviation, σ, units on the baseline.

In the normal curve of Figure 4.3, the mean is erected from the baseline, and this vertical line divides the distribution into two equal parts. In other words 50%

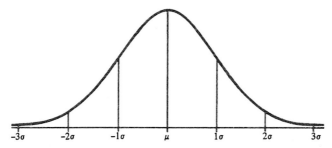

Figure 4.3
Normal curve with mean (μ) and standard deviation (σ) units.

of the scores lie below the mean (to the left) and 50% above the mean (to the right). Vertical lines are also erected from the baseline corresponding to the different σ units so that the area under the curve (e.g., number of scores) between 1σ unit below the mean and 1σ unit above the mean is approximately 68% of the total area. Similarly, approximately 95% of the distribution lies between −2 and +2σ units from the mean, and about 99% of the distribution lies between −3 and +3σ units from the mean. These statements are represented graphically in Figure 4.4.

Let us apply this approach to a real-life setting in Figure 4.5. The mean of a well-known intelligence test is 100 with a standard deviation of 16. If this variable is normally distributed in the population, we can make some inferences using the normal curve model shown in Figures 4.3 and 4.4. With what we know about the normal curve, we are able to make statements to the effect that approximately 68% of the population would have tested IQ scores between μ ± 1σ, or 100 ± 16, or between 84 and 116. As you can see from Figure 4.5, intervals could be constructed to describe IQ scores between μ ± 2σ or μ ± 3σ that would include 95% and 99% of the population, respectively. In the next chapter we will spend considerable time on the normal curve; it was introduced at this point to show the interpretation of the standard deviation when variability is being studied in a variable that approximates the normal curve.

z SCORES

It is a little awkward in discussing a score or observation to have to say that it was "2 standard deviations above the mean" or "1.5 standard deviations below the mean." To make it a little easier to pinpoint the location of a score in any distribution, the *z* score was developed. The *z* score is simply a way of telling how far a score is from the mean in standard deviation units. In Table 4.3, we noted the number of cups of coffee consumed and calculated a standard deviation of $s = 2.83$, based on a mean $\overline{X} = 6$. Let us use these coffee-drinking data to demonstrate the calculation of the *z* score as shown in Table 4.5.

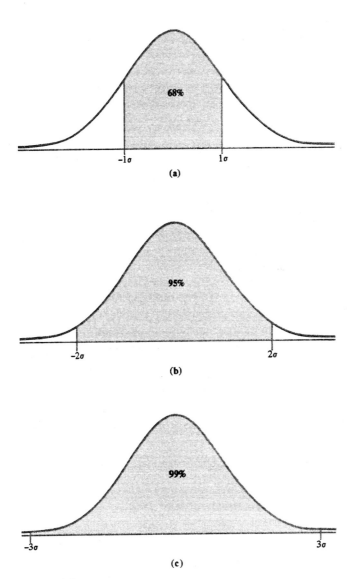

Figure 4.4
Percentage of area under the normal curve.

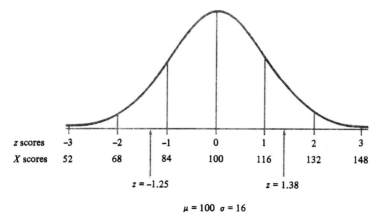

Figure 4.5
Population distribution of IQ scores.

The formula for converting any score (*X*) into its corresponding *z* score is

$$z = \frac{X - \overline{X}}{s} \qquad (4.3)$$

where

z = the z score
X = the observed score
$\overline{X}$ = the mean of the distribution of scores
s = the standard deviation of the distribution

Table 4.5
Calculation of selected *z* scores for coffee-consumption data

X	
6	
9	
10	$X = 9, z = ?$
7	
9	$z = \dfrac{X - \overline{X}}{s} = \dfrac{9 - 6}{2.83} = 1.06$
2	
4	$X = 2, z = ?$
5	
6	$z = \dfrac{X - \overline{X}}{s} = \dfrac{2 - 6}{2.83} = -1.41$
2	
$\overline{X} = 6.0$	
$s = 2.83$	

From Table 4.5, what would be the z score for an observed value of 9 cups of coffee? Using Formula 4.3, we obtain

$$z = \frac{X - \overline{X}}{s} = \frac{9 - 6}{2.83} = \frac{3}{2.83} = 1.06$$

Again, in Table 4.5, what would be the z score for an observed value of 2 cups of coffee?

$$z = \frac{X - \overline{X}}{s} = \frac{2 - 6}{2.83} = \frac{-4}{2.83} = -1.41$$

Note that when a z score is positive, it is located *above* the mean, and when negative it is *below* the mean. Observe the location of these last two z scores in Table 4.5. If you have difficulty understanding just what a z score is, remember that it is a way of telling how much a score deviates from the mean in standard deviation units. The value of 2 just calculated is 1.41 standard deviations below the mean.

A z score may also be used to find the location of a score that is a normally distributed variable. Using the example again of a population of IQ test scores shown in Figure 4.5, we may want to determine the location of an IQ score of, say, 80 or 122. Since the mean is now μ and the standard deviation is σ, the formula for the z score is changed accordingly to

$$z = \frac{X - \mu}{\sigma} \qquad (4.4)$$

where
  z = the z score
  X = the observed score
  μ = the population mean
  σ = the population standard deviation

Let us calculate z scores for IQs of 122 and 80 and locate them on the normal curve of Figure 4.5.

$$z = \frac{X - \mu}{\sigma} = \frac{122 - 100}{16} = \frac{22}{16} = 1.38$$

$$z = \frac{X - \mu}{\sigma} = \frac{80 - 100}{16} = \frac{-20}{16} = -1.25$$

We can observe, both graphically and algebraically, that a score above the mean results in a positive z score and a score below the mean results in a negative z score.

Another compelling reason for using a z score is to make comparisons between different distributions. Knowing that Stacy got a score of 78 on a mathematics achievement test, 115 on a natural science aptitude test, and 57 on an En-

Table 4.6
Means, standard deviations, and Stacy's scores (X) on
three tests

Mathematics	Natural Science	English
$\mu = 75$	$\mu = 103$	$\mu = 52$
$\sigma = 6$	$\sigma = 14$	$\sigma = 4$
$X = 78$	$X = 115$	$X = 57$

glish usage exam tells us nothing about her performance in relation to the rest of the group. But if these three variables are normally distributed in the population (a reasonably safe assumption), we can make direct comparisons by using the z score approach. For example, Table 4.6 shows the means and standard deviations for the three tests just mentioned.

In comparing z scores for the three tests, you would first calculate the z scores for the three tests as follows:

$$\text{Mathematics:} \quad z = \frac{X - \mu}{\sigma} = \frac{78 - 75}{6} = \frac{3}{6} = 0.5$$

$$\text{Natural science:} \quad z = \frac{115 - 103}{14} = \frac{12}{14} = 0.86$$

$$\text{English:} \quad z = \frac{57 - 52}{4} = \frac{5}{4} = 1.25$$

So we find that Stacy, in terms of the rest of the group, did best on the English test and poorest (though still above average) on the mathematics exam.

Because a z score can be interpreted in relation to the rest of the distribution without knowledge of the observed scores themselves, z scores will be used frequently throughout the rest of this book. Their relation to the normal curve, which you were introduced to in Figure 4.5, will be explained further in the next chapter.

OTHER STANDARD SCORES

The z score is sometimes called a *standard score,* since it is based on standard deviation units. However, there are several minor disadvantages in the use of the z score. There are negative values for any scores below the mean, the mean of the z score distribution is 0, and the z scores are decimal fractions—all of which results in a certain amount of computational complexity.

A number of other standard score systems have been devised that do not have these disadvantages. These are listed (along with the familiar z scores for comparison) in Table 4.7.

Note 4.4

Finding the Observed Score When z Is Given

There will be times when you will have to calculate the observed score when the z score is known. If you are not particularly proficient in algebra, the z score formulas (4.3 and 4.4) can be reworked so that you solve for X. By appropriate algebraic manipulation,

$$z = \frac{X - \overline{X}}{s} \qquad \text{becomes} \qquad X = z(s) + \overline{X}$$

and

$$z = \frac{X - \mu}{\sigma} \qquad \text{becomes} \qquad X = z(\sigma) + \mu$$

For example, in Figure 4.5 what IQ score corresponds to a z of -1.75? Solving for X, we get

$$X = z(\sigma) + \mu = -1.75(16) + 100 = -28 + 100 = 72$$

Thus 72 is the IQ score that corresponds to a z of -1.75. Notice that your choice of $X = z(s) + \overline{X}$ or $X = z(\sigma) + \mu$ depends on whether you are working with a *sample* of scores or making a statement about a normally distributed variable in the *population*.

The standard scores of Table 4.7 are only a small sample of possible standard score systems in current use. However, they are all related to the z score, since they still tell us the basic fact: how far any score deviates from the mean in standard deviation units.

The z score formula is used to determine how many standard deviation units a given score in one of these distributions deviates from the mean. Where in the CEEB distribution, for example, does a score of 437 lie?

$$z = \frac{X - \mu}{\sigma} = \frac{437 - 500}{100} = \frac{-63}{100} = -0.63$$

Table 4.7
Typical standard score systems

z scores:	$\mu = 0$	$\sigma = 1$
T scores:	$\mu = 50$	$\sigma = 10$
General Aptitude Test Battery (GATB):	$\mu = 100$	$\sigma = 20$
College Entrance Examination Board (CEEB):	$\mu = 500$	$\sigma = 100$

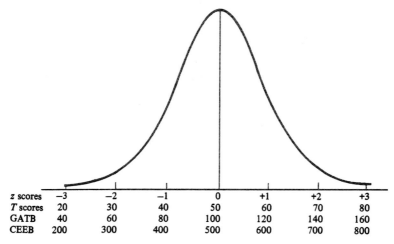

z scores	−3	−2	−1	0	+1	+2	+3
T scores	20	30	40	50	60	70	80
GATB	40	60	80	100	120	140	160
CEEB	200	300	400	500	600	700	800

Figure 4.6
The normal curve and standard scores.

Thus a CEEB score of 437 lies 0.63 of a standard deviation below the mean of 500. Similarly, a T score of 62 yields a z of 1.2, which indicates it is 1.2 σ units above the mean. Figure 4.6 shows the relationship of various derived scores to the normal curve.

STANDARD DEVIATION: MISCELLANEOUS TOPICS

Negative Numbers under the Radical Sign

In computing s using the computational formula, you may get a negative number under the radical sign. If you get this result, *you have made a mistake.* You must recheck your work, perhaps the addition of the X^2 column, to find the error. A negative number under the radical sign indicates an error in your calculations.

Effect of Adding a Constant to Each Score

It can be shown that when a constant is added to each score in a distribution, s remains unchanged. The addition of a constant to each score does not change each score's relative position with respect to the new mean, and, since s is based on deviations from the mean, the deviations themselves would remain unchanged. Table 4.8 shows distribution A with its mean and s and distribution B, where the constant 3 has been added to each score of distribution A. The deviation method for calculating s is used so you can see that the deviations remain unchanged.

As you remember from Chapter 3, the addition of a constant to every score *did* alter the mean in that the mean increased by an amount equal to the constant.

Table 4.8
Adding a constant does not affect the standard deviation

Distribution A

X	$(X - \bar{X})$	$(X - \bar{X})^2$
9	3	9
7	1	1
6	0	0
5	−1	1
3	−3	9
$\Sigma X = 30$	0	$\Sigma(X - \bar{X})^2 = 20$

$$\bar{X} = \frac{\Sigma X}{N} = \frac{30}{5} = 6$$

$$s = \sqrt{\frac{\Sigma(X - \bar{X})^2}{N - 1}}$$

$$= \sqrt{\frac{20}{4}} = \sqrt{5}$$

$$s = 2.24$$

Distribution B (A + 3)

X	$(X - \bar{X})$	$(X - \bar{X})^2$
12	3	9
10	1	1
9	0	0
8	−1	1
6	−3	9
$\Sigma X = 45$	0	$\Sigma(X - \bar{X})^2 = 20$

$$\bar{X} = \frac{45}{5} = 9$$

$$s = \sqrt{\frac{20}{4}} = \sqrt{5}$$

$$s = 2.24$$

However, this addition of a constant, as shown in Table 4.8, does not change the standard deviation.

SEMI-INTERQUARTILE RANGE

There are times when it is convenient to be able to examine the variability of a group of observations about the *median* rather than the mean. Such a measure of variability is the *semi-interquartile range* (sometimes called the quartile deviation, or Q), which can be used with any data that are appropriate for the median, that is, with data that are of an ordinal nature or above.

The semi-interquartile range is one-half the distance between P_{25} and P_{75}. The formula for Q is

$$Q = \frac{P_{75} - P_{25}}{2} \tag{4.5}$$

In a normal distribution we would expect that about 50% of the observations would be covered in the range $Med \pm Q$. For example, in the Sample Problem at the end of this chapter, the median is 7.0. If P_{75} were 9.5 and P_{25} were 4.5, Q would be calculated as

$$Q = \frac{P_{75} - P_{25}}{2} = \frac{9.5 - 4.5}{2} = \frac{5}{2} = 2.5$$

We would then assume that approximately 50% of the distribution would be between 7.0 ± 2.5, or between 4.5 and 9.5.

The semi-interquartile range has not been a popular statistic in recent years, but you still may run across it in older books and journal articles. Because of its limited use, we will not have any more to do with it.

SAMPLE PROBLEM

A clinical psychologist was studying the prevalence of Type A behavior in college students and used the Jenkins Activity Survey (JAS). The JAS assesses the extent of Type A behaviors, such as aggression, competitive achievement striving, sense of time urgency, and potential for hostility, that have been shown to be linked to coronary heart disease. The JAS items survey such everyday behaviors as eating rapidly, hurrying to get places even when there is plenty of time, and the ability to control one's temper. Scores on the student version of the JAS can range from 0 to 21 where a score of 21 would indicate extreme Type A behavior. The psychologist administered the JAS to a sample of 52 college women chosen at random from courses in introductory psychology. Calculate the mean, range, and s for this distribution.

X	X^2	X	X^2	X	X^2
12	144	3	9	4	16
7	49	8	64	6	36
7	49	3	9	12	144
12	144	4	16	5	25
8	64	8	64	12	144
7	49	11	121	7	49
3	9	3	9	9	81
8	64	8	64	11	121
6	36	5	25	1	1
7	49	2	4	1	1
8	64	10	100	8	64
6	36	8	64	13	169
8	64	11	121	1	1

(continued)

SAMPLE PROBLEM (CONTINUED)

14	196	5	25	6	36
10	100	14	196	6	36
3	9	9	81	9	81
3	9	6	36	1	1
11	121				

Summary: $\Sigma X = 370$ $\Sigma X^2 = 3270$ $N = 52$

Calculator Solution

Mean:

$$\bar{X} = \frac{\Sigma X}{N} = \frac{370}{52} = 7.12$$

Range:

$$\text{Range} = 14 - 1 = 13$$

Standard Deviation:

$$s = \sqrt{\frac{\Sigma X^2 - \frac{(\Sigma X)^2}{N}}{N - 1}} = \sqrt{\frac{3,270 - \frac{(370)^2}{52}}{51}}$$

$$= \sqrt{\frac{3,270 - 2,632.6923}{51}} = \sqrt{12.4962}$$

$$s = 3.54$$

If Ann scored 5 on this test, what would be her z score? And if Sally was told that her z score was 1.39, what was her score on the test?

Ann: $X = 5, z = ?$

$$z = \frac{X - \bar{X}}{s} = \frac{5 - 7.12}{3.54} = \frac{-2.12}{3.54} = -0.60$$

Sally: $z = 1.39, X = ?$

$$X = z(s) + \bar{X} = 1.39(3.54) + 7.12 = 12.04$$

Computer Solution

Table 4.9 shows the SPSS output for the standard deviation, as well as other descriptive statistics. Other statistics besides the mean and standard deviation are part of the SPSS program for descriptive statistics, and these statistics as well are shown in Table 4.9. Also shown is a simple frequency distribution and a histogram of the Type A scores. The frequency distribution and the histogram, of course, add to our interpretation of the data.

Table 4.9
SPSS output for the standard deviation and other descriptive statistics

Frequencies

Statistics

	N		Mean	Median	Mode	Standard Deviation	Variance	Range
	Valid	Missing						
Type A	52	0	7.12	7.00	8	3.54	12.50	13

Type A

	Frequency	Percent	Valid Percent	Cumulative Percent
Valid 1	4	7.7	7.7	7.7
2	1	1.9	1.9	9.6
3	6	11.5	11.5	21.2
4	2	3.8	3.8	25.0
5	3	5.8	5.8	30.8
6	6	11.5	11.5	42.3
7	5	9.6	9.6	51.9
8	9	17.3	17.3	69.2
9	3	5.8	5.8	75.0
10	2	3.8	3.8	78.8
11	4	7.7	7.7	86.5
12	4	7.7	7.7	94.2
13	1	1.9	1.9	96.2
14	2	3.8	3.8	100.0
Total	52	100.0	100.0	
Total	52	100.0		

Graph

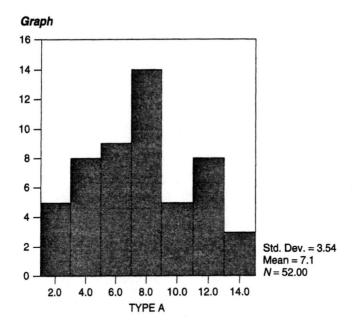

Std. Dev. = 3.54
Mean = 7.1
N = 52.00

TYPE A

STUDY QUESTIONS

1. Give a definition of the term *variability*.
2. What would be an example of the definition of variability?
3. Why is the range inadequate as a measure of variability?
4. What is meant by the operation $\Sigma(X - \overline{X})^2$?
5. How is the quantity $\Sigma(X - \overline{X})^2$ related to the concept of variability?
6. What is the difference between ΣX^2 and $(\Sigma X)^2$? Demonstrate the difference in these two operations by choosing 5 numbers and calculating both values for each.
7. What is the difference between s and σ?
8. What does $z = 1.32$ indicate? What about $z = -2.43$?

EXERCISES

1. Calculate the standard deviation for the 10 quiz scores that follow, using the two formulas described in this chapter.

9	3
11	7
16	8

8	6
2	1

2. Fifteen subjects in a problem-solving experiment are measured on how long it takes to form a word from a scrambled set of letters. Calculate the standard deviation using the two formulas described in this chapter.

15	13
12	11
11	10
11	10
14	13
11	11
12	13
13	

3. A sample of the number of acres farmed in a midwestern state first listed in exercise 14 of Chapter 3 is repeated here. Calculate the range for these data. Why would the range be an inferior measure of variability in this instance?

200	500	1,200	2,000	4,500
6,700	345	5,600	26,000	100
3,400	6,800	7,000	450	340
780	1,500	5,600	3,200	900
3,000	4,500	400	990	1,200
780	1,100	700	2,000	700
7,000	500	990	3,400	780

4. The heights in inches of 15 physical education majors at a university are shown. Calculate the range and the standard deviation. Why could the range be a misleading measure of variability in this case?

77	68	70	68	60
68	67	71	70	68
69	70	69	71	70

5. Twenty university students applying for the position of teaching assistant in chemistry laboratory classes were given a 30-point quiz. Calculate the mean and the standard deviation for these data.

28	24	22	23	30
30	29	27	28	28

25	30	28	29	27
26	26	24	30	26

6. The monthly long-distance bill for the McDeer family first listed in exercise 2 of Chapter 3 is repeated here. Calculate the mean and the standard deviation for these data.

68	111	90	77
72	76	67	89
62	88	51	85

7. The dietary guidelines of the U.S. Department of Agriculture recommend consuming no more than 30% of calories from fat. This would amount to less than 65 grams of fat per day based on a 2,000-calorie diet. The following list gives the number of fat grams found in a one-ounce serving of various kinds of snack chips. Calculate the mean and the standard deviation for these data.

6	4	9	1
8	2	6	1
12	0	3	5
14	7	7	

8. The USDA dietary guidelines recommend consuming no more than 2,400 milligrams of sodium per day. The amount of sodium found in 11 ounces of various kinds and brands of canned soups are as follows. Calculate the mean and the standard deviation for these data.

2,250	1,850	2,300	1,750
2,000	1,600	1,900	1,675
1,020	1,950	1,700	2,025
2,125	2,000	1,625	2,400

9. In 1993 the average life expectancy for newborns in the United States was estimated at 75.4 years with a standard deviation of 7.4 years. Redraw Figure 4.5 marking off the life expectancies for 1993 newborns corresponding to $\mu \pm 3\sigma$.

10. The Word Fluency Inventory (WFI) for assessing word skills in bilingual children has a mean of 32 with a standard deviation of 4.9. Assume that this distribution is normally distributed in the population of bilingual children, and redraw Figure 4.5, marking off WFI scores corresponding to $\mu \pm 3\sigma$.

11. Means and standard deviations for the English, Mathematics, Reading, and Science Reasoning subtests of the 1995 ACT (American College Testing Program) are shown in the following table. Carrie scored 22, 20, 24, and 23, respec-

tively, on the four subtests. Assume that these test scores are normally distributed in the population, and calculate Carrie's corresponding z scores. On which test did she do the best? The worst?

	English	**Mathematics**	**Reading**	**Science Reasoning**
μ	20.2	20.2	21.3	20.8
σ	5.3	4.9	6.0	4.6

12. Matthew scored a 25 on all four subtests of the ACT described in exercise 11 and claims he has equal ability in the four areas. Use the z score method to show why you would dispute his claim.
13. Amy, Cheri, and Jen scored 17, 25, and 21, respectively, on the English subtest of the ACT described in exercise 11. Sketch a normal curve similar to Figure 4.5 and locate their z scores on the normal curve.
14. Patrick, Ryan, and Phil scored 23, 17, and 29, respectively, on the Science Reasoning subtest of the ACT described in exercise 11. Sketch a normal curve similar to Figure 4.5 and locate their z scores on the normal curve.

COMPUTER EXERCISES FOR APPENDIX 4 DATA BANK

C1. Calculate descriptive statistics for the JAS S&I distribution for those women who were high in self-monitoring (see C4 in Chapter 3). Include the mean, median, minimum score, maximum score, range, and standard deviation.
C2. Do the same as in C1 for those women who scored low in self-monitoring.
C3. In comparing the values found in C1 with those found in C2, did you find any marked differences in any of the statistics?
C4. Some social scientists believe that men exhibit greater variability in many behaviors than women. Calculate the standard deviations for physical symptoms, self-monitoring, and the JAS A, S&I, and HDC scales. Do men and women differ in variability on these particular measures?

CHAPTER 5

The Normal Curve

We have had several occasions in previous chapters to refer to the normal curve in a cursory fashion, but it is necessary at this point to devote an entire chapter to this much maligned and misunderstood statistical concept. Technically, this chapter is not consistent with the rest of the text as far as presenting techniques for either describing a set of data or making inferences about the nature of the population. Rather, it is a necessary interruption in order to introduce a mathematical concept that is a foundation for many statistical concepts, and it is essential to insert the material at this point. This chapter is somewhat similar to the interruption of an auto mechanic's on-the-job training with a study unit on the theory of automotive electronics. Comparatively speaking, we will temporarily put aside our statistical wrenches and screwdrivers for a short dissertation on the properties of the normal curve.

In previous chapters we noted that many physiological and psychological measurements were "normally" distributed; that is, a graph of the measurements took on the familiar symmetrical, bell-shaped form. The graph of IQ test scores shown in Figure 5.1 is but one of many examples of such a distribution.

THE NORMAL CURVE AS A MODEL

One of the reasons for the tremendous progress of the sciences over the last few decades has been their utilization of *mathematical models*. Without getting bogged down in technical jargon, we can say that scientists are overjoyed when the data of whatever they happen to be observing "fit" a particular mathematical model that they have chosen. Astronomers noted very early that the orbital path of planets seemed to be elliptical in form (an oval is one type of an ellipse), and by using

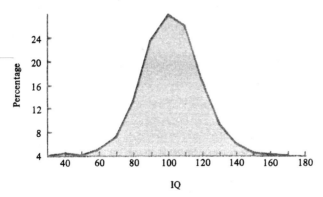

Figure 5.1
Stanford-Binet IQ scores of 1937 standardization group. (From L. M. Terman and
N. Merrill, *Stanford-Binet Intelligence Scale* [Boston, 1960], p. 18. Copyright 1960 by The
Riverside Publishing Company. Used by permission of the publisher.)

this model they were able to predict such things as eclipses and the existence of, at that time, still undiscovered planets. In a similar way, physicists and other scientists have used such mathematical models as exponential or logarithmic functions, wave motion, and ballistic mechanics to study the behavior of electrons, light, body motion, and other natural phenomena. And—here is the point of the whole discussion—mathematical models were used to help scientists *picture* or *visualize* the nature of the data and to enable them to *predict* the outcome of data to be gathered in the future.

Applications of the normal curve were developed in much the same way. Borrowing from the work of several earlier mathematicians (see Note 5.1), Adolphe Quetelet (1796–1874), a Belgian mathematician and astronomer, was the first to note that the distribution of certain body measurements appeared to approximate the normal curve. He found that the heights of French soldiers and chest circumferences of Scottish soldiers yielded frequency distributions that fit the characteristic bell-shaped curve. Sir Francis Galton (1822–1911) continued with Quetelet's approach and studied the distributions of a wide variety of physical and mental characteristics. Quetelet, Galton, and countless researchers in innumerable investigations since those early days have made good use of the normal curve model to describe a set of data and to predict the results of future investigations.

So, why are we so excited (or, at least, mildly enthusiastic) over the possibility of using the normal curve as a model for data in education and the behavioral sciences? Simply because, if we can assume that the *population* of measurements from which we draw our sample is normally distributed, we can make use of the known properties of the normal curve both to visualize our data and to make predictions based on our sample. Since prediction is such an important part of statistics, we shall examine in detail the properties of this mathematical concept, the normal curve, in the remainder of this chapter.

Note 5.1
Origin of the Normal Curve

The noble art of mathematics was very early applied to problems in probability posed by gamblers. One very knotty problem concerned such questions as "What is the probability that in 10 flips of a coin heads will result 6 times?" or "What is the probability that in 20 throws of a die a '2' will show 7 times?" Although solutions to these simple problems occurred quite early, it remained for a general application to cover the impossible calculations involved in answering a question such as "What is the probability that in 12,000 tosses of a coin heads will occur 1,876 times?" In 1733, Abraham de Moivre (1667–1754) developed a mathematical curve that would predict the probabilities of events associated with such things as flipping coins and rolling dice. The curve that de Moivre developed was, of course, what we now call the normal curve.

You may also have seen this curve referred to as the "Gaussian curve," after C. F. Gauss (1777–1855), who developed the normal curve independently of de Moivre in 1809. His interest was primarily in errors of measurement or observation in astronomy, and he noted that the curve described a distribution of errors. But, as was mentioned earlier, it was probably Quetelet who first applied the curve to a variety of physical data.

Some Characteristics of the Normal Curve

Since the normal curve is a mathematical function, it has a formula, which is

$$y = \frac{1}{\sigma\sqrt{2\pi}} \, e^{-\frac{(X-\mu)^2}{2\sigma^2}}$$

where

   y = height of the curve
   σ = standard deviation of the population
   π = pi, or 3.14
   e = natural logarithm, approximately 2.718
   X = any score value
   μ = the population mean

Admittedly, the formula is an imposing one, and fortunately we will have very little to do with it as such. It is mentioned here so that we are aware of the fact that the normal curve is indeed a mathematical function, and because we must call attention to some of the terms in the formula.

There is a whole family of normal curves, depending on the values for the population mean (μ) and the population standard deviation (σ). That is, we can change the position of the curve on a scale of measurement by altering the mean, or we can change the spread of the curve by altering the standard deviation. We

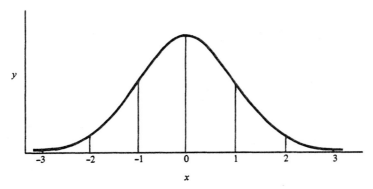

Figure 5.2
The unit normal curve.

could have a normal curve by substituting into the formula a mean of 10, 50, or 100 and a standard deviation of 2, 17, or 29, or any value that suited our fancy.

In Figure 5.2 a normal curve with a mean of 0 and a standard deviation of 1 is shown. This is called the *unit normal curve,* and it is the one we will be working with throughout this chapter. It is called the unit curve because the *area* under the curve is exactly equal to 1 square unit. As we shall see later, using this area of exactly 1 will simplify our computations greatly.

Note that the units on the *x*-axis of Figure 5.2 are the familiar *z* scores that we dealt with in the last chapter. As you discovered then, a *z* score is a way of specifying a location on the scale that holds for whatever mean or standard deviation you have. The *z* score simply tells where a particular value lies in terms of standard deviation units from the mean. For example, in Figure 5.2 a *z* of 2.5 is obviously 2.5 standard deviations to the right of a mean of 0. (If having a mean of 0 bothers you, consider the mean as a point that is 0 standard deviations from the mean!)

AREA UNDER THE CURVE

The last characteristic of the normal curve that we will be concerned with is an important one indeed—that of determining the amount of *area* under the curve. We will find ourselves using this technique throughout the remaining chapters in the book, and it might be an understatement to say that any student of statistics *must* show at least a minimum level of competency in working with normal curve areas.

Some of the areas under the curve are obvious, and a quick glance at Figure 5.2 should reveal that, if the total area under the curve is 1.00, then 0.50 must be the area to the left of the mean and 0.50 the area to the right of the mean. Also, as you may remember from the last chapter, we found that about 68% of the total area (0.68

in decimal terms) is under the curve between a *z* of –1 and a *z* of +1, 95% between *z* scores of –2 and +2, and about 99% between *z* scores of –3 and +3.

However, we are usually interested in the "in-between" values, and we must resort either to some high-level mathematics or a table of normal curve areas to determine the answers to such questions as "How much of the area under the curve lies between the mean and a *z* of 1.53?" or "How much of the area under the curve lies between a *z* of –2.38 and a *z* of 1.92?" Fortunately, we have Table A in Appendix 3, which makes it very simple to answer a variety of questions relating to normal curve areas. Note that the left side of the pairs of columns in Table A lists the *z* score, and the entry opposite gives the area under the normal curve *between that* z *score and the mean.* So to answer the question "How much of the area lies between the mean and a *z* of 1.53?" you simply look up the *z* value of 1.53 in Table A and note that 0.4370, or 43.7%, of the total area is included under the curve between those points. The shaded area in Figure 5.3a illustrates this graphically.

The *z* scores of Table A are all positive, but since the curve is perfectly symmetrical we use the same tabled values for negative *z* scores. For example, if we wanted to know the area under the curve between the mean and a *z* of –1.53, we would get the same answer as before: 43.7%. The only thing that would be different would be the location of the shaded area in Figure 5.3a, and we would see that the area under consideration would be to the *left* of the mean, between –1.53 and the mean.

Two techniques will be demonstrated in the following sections, with variations of each illustrated in Figures 5.3 through 5.5. Basically, we have two approaches: we either know the *z* score and use Table A to find an area, *or* we know the area and use Table A to determine the appropriate *z* score.

Given a *z* Score, Find the Area

In the preceding section Table A was described as giving a direct answer to finding the area under the curve between a *z* score and the mean, and the answer was illustrated in Figure 5.3a. The following examples show how to determine the area *above* or below a *z* score or *between* z scores.

Figure 5.3b. *How do you find the area under the curve above a positive* z *value* (*or* below *a negative* z)? You cannot read the value directly from Table A, since the areas in Table A are *between* z *and the mean.* In this case you must *subtract* the tabled value from 0.5000. For example, if you want to find what percentage of the area under the curve lies above a *z* of 1.65, the tabled value from Table A is 0.4505. But this value is the area between *z* and the mean, so you must subtract 0.4505 from 0.5000 to obtain 4.95%, which is the area above a *z* of 1.65. Figure 5.3b demonstrates this point graphically. A similar approach would be used to find the area below a negative *z* value.

Figure 5.3c. *How do you find the area below a positive* z *score?* In this case it is necessary to add the tabled value to 0.5000, since the value in Table A gives only

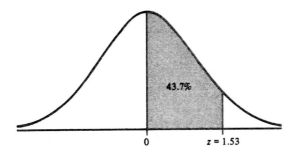

(a) 43.7% between the mean and a z of 1.53.

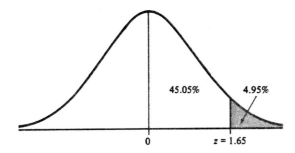

(b) 4.95% above a z of 1.65.

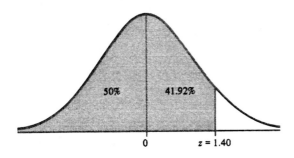

(c) 91.92% below a z of 1.40.

Figure 5.3
Determining areas under the normal curve.

the area from the z value down to the mean. Figure 5.3c shows what is done to answer a question such as "What percentage of the area under the curve lies below a z of 1.40?" Table A shows the area from a z of 1.40 down to the mean to be 0.4192, which, when added to 0.5000, would give 91.92% of the area below a z of 1.40.

To determine the percentage of the area *between* two z scores, it is necessary to use one of two techniques, depending on whether the z scores are on the same side of the mean or on opposite sides.

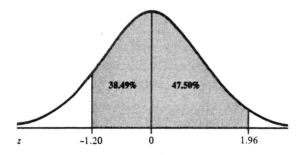

(a) 85.99% between z scores of –1.20 and 1.96.

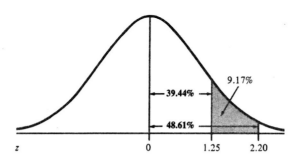

(b) 9.17% between z scores of 1.25 and 2.20.

Figure 5.4
More areas under the normal curve.

Figure 5.4a.   How do you determine the area under the curve between two z scores on different sides of the mean? Figure 5.4a shows how you would find the area between a negative z and a positive z, for example, –1.20 and 1.96. Since Table A gives the area from the z score to the mean, it is only necessary to add the two areas to arrive at the answer. As you can see, the area between the mean and a z of –1.20 is 0.3849, and the area between the mean and a z of 1.96 is 0.4750, for a total area between the two of 0.8599 or 85.99%.

Figure 5.4b.   How do you determine the area under the curve between two z scores on the same side of the mean? You simply subtract the smaller area from the larger area. For example, if we wish to determine the area between a z score of 1.25 and 2.20, we look up the tabled value for 2.20 and find that 0.4861 of the total area lies between the mean and a z of 2.20. We then look in Table A for the area between the mean and a z of 1.25 and find the value to be 0.3944. We then subtract 0.3944 from 0.4861 to show that 0.0917 or 9.17% of the area lies between a z of 1.25 and 2.20. This calculation is illustrated graphically in Figure 5.4b.

Given an Area, Find the z Score

The preceding section just about exhausts all the possible ways in which Table A can be used when the z score is known and we wish to find the area. However, there are many occasions when we will have a known percentage of area under the curve and will use Table A to find the appropriate z score. Such occasions are obviously the reverse of the problems described in the preceding section, but the same general logic is used. Only the procedure is changed, in that you go to Table A with a percentage of area and look for a z. Figure 5.5 shows several examples of how Table A can be used in this way.

Figure 5.5a.   How do you find what z scores form the boundaries of a centrally located area? All you have to do is divide the area by 2 (since Table A gives values only for one-half of the curve) and look up the z score that corresponds to that value. For example, the middle 95% of the area is between what two z scores? Figure 5.5a shows that one-half of the area, or 47.5%, would be on either side of the mean. We then go to Table A and look in the *area* column to locate 0.4750 and find that the z score that marks off 47.5% of the area from the mean is 1.96. Since the curve is symmetrical, we know that a z score of −1.96 would mark off 47.5% of the area below the mean. So we conclude that z scores of −1.96 and 1.96 are the boundaries enclosing the middle 95% of the distribution.

Figure 5.5b.   How do you find the z score corresponding to a given percentile? In an earlier chapter we noted that a percentile is a point below which lies a given percentage of the distribution. So to answer the question "What is the z score that corresponds to the 65th percentile, or P_{65}?" we note that in Figure 5.5b, since 50% of the distribution is below the mean, 15% would be above. We then look up 15% in the *area* column of Table A, because the areas shown in Table A are between the mean and the z value. We find that the exact value of 0.1500 is not listed in Table A, so we take the value *closest* to 0.1500, which is 0.1517, and see that the corresponding z score is 0.39. So the z score at P_{65} is 0.39.

Figure 5.5c.   What if the percentile is below the mean? As you can see, the situation is a little different if the percentile falls below the mean, at P_{15}, for instance. Since the areas of Table A are between the mean and the z score, it is necessary to subtract 0.1500 from 0.5000 to get 0.3500 with which to enter Table A. The nearest value in Table A is 0.3508, and the corresponding z score is 1.04. Since the percentile in question is below the mean, the z value for P_{15} is −1.04.

It should be evident by now that in any problems involving normal curve areas, it is a good idea to draw a rough sketch of the curve, both so you can follow the procedure (i.e., use Table A correctly) and so you get a pictorial representation that helps you visualize the reasoning behind the procedure. In some of the practical applications to follow, we will find such a pictorial approach very helpful in visualizing variables that otherwise would be difficult to understand.

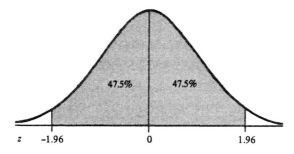

(a) z scores of –1.96 and 1.96 enclose the middle 95%.

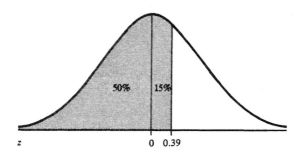

(b) P_{65} falls at a z score of 0.39.

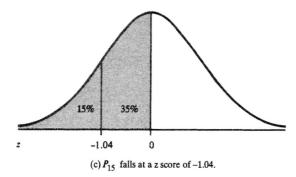

(c) P_{15} falls at a z score of –1.04.

Figure 5.5
Still more areas under the normal curve.

Some Practical Applications

The preceding section was basically a set of instructions on the use of a normal curve table, at best a mechanical and mathematical procedure. We have already seen that the scientist is looking for mathematical models for understanding and predicting, so we now turn to a very important activity of behavioral scientists— applying the normal curve to real-life situations.

In Chapter 2 we saw that many of the data of a psychological and physiological nature are normally distributed in the population. Variables, such as height, weight, and test scores, approximate this normal curve model. But in the remaining sections of this chapter we must keep in mind the distinction between the mathematical model and the distribution of observed data. The mathematical characteristics of the normal curve printed in Table A (z scores and corresponding areas under the curve) apply to the model only, and the accuracy of our predictions regarding the real world depends on how close the population "fits" the normal curve model.

With these reservations in mind, let us use the normal curve model in a practical setting to make predictions about the variable of tested IQ scores. We noted in the last chapter that according to one popular IQ test the mean IQ is 100 with a standard deviation of 16. With only this information (and the assumption that IQ is normally distributed in the population) we can make a number of predictions based on the normal curve model.

Figure 5.6a. In the early years of intelligence testing, some researchers considered a child with an IQ score of 70 or below to be "mentally retarded." What percentage of the population would be expected to score 70 or below? The first step in answering this question is to convert the score of 70 to a z score. The formula given in Chapter 4 for a z score in a population was $z = (X - \mu)/\sigma$. So a score of 70 in the distribution of IQ scores would have a z of

$$z = \frac{X - \mu}{\sigma} = \frac{70 - 100}{16} = \frac{-30}{16} = -1.88$$

Referring to Figure 5.6a and Table A of Appendix 3, you can see that a z of -1.88 is below the mean, and the area between z and the mean is 0.4699. But the question asked concerned the population *below* 70, so we must subtract 0.4699 from 0.5000 to get 0.0301. Thus we would conclude that 3.01% of the population has a tested IQ of 70 or below.

Figure 5.6b. Some researchers on "gifted" children have used a tested IQ score of 140 as a criterion. What percentage of the population would be expected to score 140 or above? Since we need a z score to enter Table A, we find that the z score corresponding to an IQ of 140 is

$$z = \frac{X - \mu}{\sigma} = \frac{140 - 100}{16} = \frac{40}{16} = 2.50$$

Using Table A and Figure 5.6b, we note that 0.4938 of the area is between the mean and the z of 2.50, leaving 0.0062 or 0.62% of the area above the z score. So we conclude that 0.62% of the population would have tested IQ scores above 140.

Figure 5.6c. If the range of "average" IQ scores is 90 to 110, what percentage of the population is considered average in intelligence? Converting IQ scores to z scores, we get

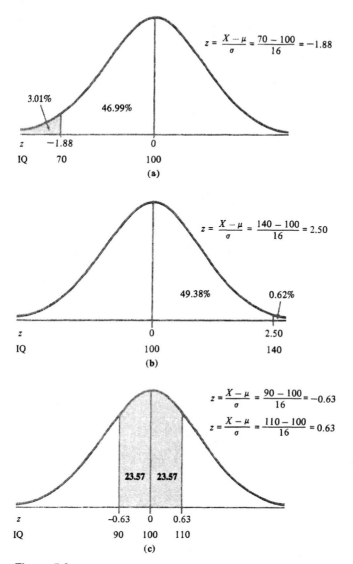

Figure 5.6
Normal-curve applications with IQ test scores.

$$z = \frac{X - \mu}{\sigma} = \frac{90 - 100}{16} = \frac{-10}{16} = -0.63$$

$$z = \frac{X - \mu}{\sigma} = \frac{110 - 100}{16} = \frac{10}{16} = 0.63$$

We see that the area of the curve in question is that between z scores of -0.63 and 0.63. Referring to Table A, we find that 0.2357 of the area lies between the mean and a z of 0.63. Since the curve is symmetrical, we know that the same area lies between the mean and a z of −0.63, for a total area of 0.2357 + 0.2357, or 0.4714. So we conclude that 47.14% of the population would have IQ scores between 90 and 110.

The careful reader will note that the three preceding examples were similar in that a decision had to be made about the location of a score in the distribution, the score was converted to a z score, and Table A was used to find the percentage of area above, below, or between the z scores. In terms of the earlier section on the use of Table A, we are again saying, "Given a z, find the percentage." The reverse procedure—"Given a percentage, find the z"—can also be used in practical applications, and Figure 5.7 illustrates this fact.

Figure 5.7a.   The middle 95% of the population have IQ scores between what two values? Dividing the distribution into two equal parts on each side of the mean gives 47.5% on each side. Table A shows us that the z scores corresponding to these areas are −1.96 and 1.96, so we know that the middle 95% have IQ scores between z values of −1.96 and 1.96. However, the question is stated in terms of IQ scores, not z scores, so we must convert our z values to IQ scores, and we find

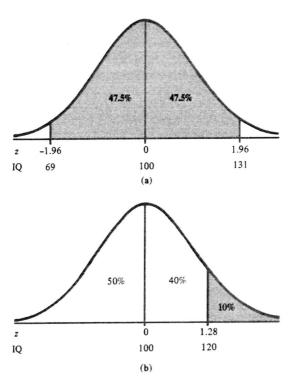

Figure 5.7
More normal-curve applications with IQ test scores.

$$X = z\sigma + \mu = -1.96(16) + 100 = -31.36 + 100 = 68.64$$
$$X = z\sigma + \mu = 1.96(16) + 100 = 31.36 + 100 = 131.36$$

So, as Figure 5.7a indicates, the middle 95% of the population have scores between 69 and 131.

Figure 5.7b.   How high does an individual's IQ have to be to place among the top 10% of IQ scores? By drawing a quick sketch, you can see at a glance that we want the score that corresponds to the 90th percentile, since that would divide the bottom 90% from the top 10%. As Figure 5.7b shows, we use Table A to find the z score that marks off 40% of the area, and we note that the closest value to 40% is 0.3997 and its corresponding z score is 1.28. Converting the z score to an IQ score, we find

$$X = z\sigma + \mu = 1.28(16) + 100 = 20.48 + 100 = 120.48$$

Thus we conclude that an individual must have an IQ score of at least 120 to be considered in the top 10% of the population.

PROBABILITY AND THE NORMAL CURVE

As we noted earlier in the chapter, especially in Note 5.1, the development of the normal curve was directly linked to some practical applications involving probability—mostly questions that gamblers might ask on the probability of the flip of a coin or the roll of a die. Although a complete treatise on probability is beyond the intended scope of this book, it will be helpful to become acquainted with some of the terms used in probability, since we must be aware of just how the normal curve can assist us in making probability statements.

Coins, Cards, Dice, and People

The topic of probability might not be uppermost in our minds at any given point in time. But whether we are aware of it or not, we are constantly surrounded by probability statements. In a single evening the news, weather, and sports on television might all contribute statements directly related to probability. The news anchor might comment on the increase in car insurance rates, the weather reporter will report a 30% chance of rain for the next 24 hours, and the sports editor will note that the boxer being interviewed is a 5-to-1 favorite for tomorrow's middleweight match. Also if, during a TV commercial, the announcer spins a wheel to determine the lucky winner of a prize holstein, we will have seen demonstrated all the different types of probability in a single evening! With these examples in mind, let us sort out two different types of probability.

Classical.   The classical type of probability is undoubtedly the most familiar to us, since we all have flipped coins, rolled dice, drawn a playing card from a deck, and maybe even had a chance to spin a roulette wheel. We define probability, p, in this case by the following formula:

$$p = \frac{\text{Number of ways the event in question can occur}}{\text{Number of events possible}}$$

So the probability of getting heads in the flip of a coin is 1/2, since the 1 event is getting heads on a normal coin, and the total number of events possible (represented by the 2) is a head and a tail. Similarly, the probability of rolling a "4" on one toss of a die is 1/6, since only one side of a die has four spots while there is a total of six possible sides on the die. The probability of drawing an ace of spades from a well-shuffled deck would, of course, be 1/52, while the probability of drawing *any* ace from the deck would be 4/52. The typical roulette wheel has 38 numbered spaces and 1 blank space, so the probability that your number will come up on a fair spin of the wheel is 1/39.

Although we have been using *fractions* to illustrate these probability situations, it is conventional to state probabilities in terms of *proportions*. So, instead of $p = 1/2$, $p = 1/6$, or $p = 1/52$, it is more common to see $p = .50$, $p = .17$, or $p = .02$. A quick glance at the general probability formula should demonstrate that the probability of a "certainty" or "sure thing" is 1.0. Thus the probability of flipping *either* a head *or* tail is 2/2 or 1.0.

One lucky by-product of stating probabilities in terms of proportions is that they are so easily converted to percentages when we talk about the frequency of occurrence in the "long run." For example, if the probability of rolling a "4" in one throw of a die is $p = .17$, we can expect a "4" to appear approximately 17% of the time. Or, in the long run, we could expect to pull an ace of spades from a well-shuffled deck approximately 2% of the time. There are advantages to thinking of probabilities in terms of percentages, as we shall see when we apply probabilities to areas under the normal curve.

Empirical.   The characteristic that differentiates empirical probability from classical is that empirical probabilities can be calculated only from previous observations. How would one calculate the probability that the next baby born at a given hospital will be a boy? If records for the past five years show 7,223 babies born at this hospital, 3,720 of them boys, our empirical probability that the next birth will be a boy would be $p = 3,720/7,223 = .515$. Or, again using the "long-run" concept, we would say that 51.5% of the births would be boys.

In a similar fashion, the weather reporter's prediction of a 30% chance of rain is based on a number of past situations when meteorological conditions were identical to present conditions. Some precipitation occurred in the surrounding area on 30% of the occasions when these conditions were present, so she is predicting that $p = .30$ for some rain during the next 24 hours. (Not everyone comprehends this system, as illustrated by Figure 5.8.) The same interpretation can be applied to the car insurance rates and the betting results for the boxer. Past results (amount of insurance claims or amount bet on the boxer to win versus amount bet on him to lose) in each case determine the probability associated with each event.

Figure 5.8
Probability statements in weather forecasts are not universally understood. (*Source:* © Tribune Media Services, Inc. All Rights Reserved. Reprinted with permission.)

It should be clear by now that the way to compute an empirical probability is simply to calculate the percentage of times that the event in which you are interested has occurred in past situations and convert that percentage to a proportion. So, if you find that there are 800 freshmen, 680 sophomores, 578 juniors, and 492 seniors at a college with a total enrollment of 2,550, you would simply convert these to percentages to find that there are 31% freshmen, 27% sophomores, 23% juniors, and 19% seniors. Thus the probability that a name drawn at random from the student directory will be that of a senior would be $p = .19$, since 19% of the student body are seniors.

The "Addition" and "Multiplication" Rules

The preceding examples illustrated the probability of occurrence of a single item, such as rolling a "4" or drawing an ace. But what about questions such as the probability of rolling *either* a "4" *or* a "5"? Or, in two draws from a deck of cards, what is the probability of drawing two aces?

Addition Rule. Now we are talking about the probability of occurrence of several events, and the probability of occurrence of *either one event or the other* is simply the *sum* of the individual probabilities. For example, the probability of drawing an ace is $\frac{4}{52}$ and of drawing a king is also $\frac{4}{52}$. So the probability of drawing *either* an ace *or* a king is $\frac{4}{52} + \frac{4}{52} = \frac{8}{52} = .1538$. In the "long run" we would expect to draw either an ace or a king approximately 15 percent of the time. The addition rule is stated more formally as follows:

> *The probability of occurrence of two or more mutually exclusive events is the sum of their individual probabilities.*

"Mutually exclusive" simply means that if one event occurs, another event cannot. If you flip a head, a tail cannot occur; if you draw an ace, a queen cannot occur.

Multiplication Rule. To answer probability questions such as "What is the probability of rolling a 2 on two successive throws of a die?" or "In two draws from a deck of cards, what is the probability that one would be a queen and the other an ace?", we resort to the multiplication rule. In using the addition rule, we could see that the key word was "or" (drawing an ace *or* a king). Now, however, the key word is "and," since we are talking about the occurrence of two or more events. The probability of this multiple occurrence is the *product* of the individual probabilities. For example, the probability of drawing a queen is 4/52, and that of drawing an ace is 4/52 (assuming we replace our first card and shuffle the deck before we make our second draw).[*] The probability of the first card being a queen and the second an ace would then be $4/52 \times 4/52 = 16/2{,}704 = .0059$. Using the "long-run" concept, such an occurrence would happen less than one percent of the time. The multiplication rule would be formally stated as follows:

> *The probability of both A and B occurring is equal to the probability of occurrence of A times the probability of occurrence of B, if A and B are independent events.*

"Independent events" means that the occurrence of one has no effect on the occurrence of the other. If in the preceding example we got a queen on our first draw but did not put the card back into the deck, the probability of drawing an ace on the second draw would now be 4/51, instead of the usual 4/52. Since sampling in this case is with replacement, A and B can be considered independent.

Reading Probabilities from the Normal Curve Table

We can go directly from the normal curve areas of Table A to statements of probability. This convenient arrangement is possible because probability in this case can be defined as

$$p = \frac{\text{Area under a portion of the curve}}{\text{Total area under the curve}}$$

For example, what is the probability of a z score being equal to or greater than 1.0? From Table A we note that 0.1587 of the area of the normal curve lies above a z of 1.0 $(0.5000 - 0.3413)$, so

$$p = \frac{.1587}{1.0} = .1587$$

In other words, the proportions given in Table A *are* probabilities, since dividing by the total area of 1.0 always yields the numerator. So, in this example we would conclude that the probability of a z score being 1.0 or greater is $p = .1587$ or .16.

---

[*]Calculated probabilities will differ slightly if we do not replace the first card before drawing the second. We will examine this topic again in the section "Sampling with Replacement" in the next chapter.

What is the probability of a z score being between −1.96 and 1.96? Since 95% of the area under the curve is between these two values, $p = .95$ that any z score would be between those values.

It should be obvious by now that in any of the previous examples where we calculated a percentage of the area under the curve we could easily make a probability statement. In Figure 5.6a, for example, we found that 3.01% of the population would have an IQ score of less than 70. Thus the probability that a person selected at random would have an IQ score below 70 is $p = .03$. Similarly, in Figure 5.6b and 5.6c, $p = .006$ that a person would have an IQ score above 140, and $p = .47$ that an individual would have a score between 90 and 110.

Odds and Ends

Any observer of the American sporting scene is aware of a unique way of stating the probability of success in a sporting event—in terms of the "odds for" or "odds against" a particular outcome. A football power might be a 2-to-1 favorite, a horse might be a 40-to-1 long shot, or the chances of being a winner in a three number lottery would be 1 in 999. Of course, such statements are not limited to sporting events or games of chance but are often made about political elections, weather forecasts, and any other event where the outcome is something less than a certainty.

Undoubtedly, most of these statements are rather subjective, as shown by Figure 5.9, and are based upon hunches, past experiences, and the like. For example, in horse racing, the "morning line" of a newspaper contains the day's picks by one or more sportswriters, and statements like "Whirligig is a 100-to-1 long shot" simply imply that this creature may not even make it from the stable area to the starting gate. However, in some cases, actual data may be involved; thus the fact that a sample of voters has given two-thirds of their votes to one candidate may lead to a statement that "Senator Blank is a 2-to-1 favorite."

It would be interesting to continue discussing horseflesh and gambling, but we will have to confine our treatment of the topic to classical probability and areas under the normal curve. We will then be able to use "odds for" or "odds against"

Figure 5.9
An example of a subjective odds statement. (*Source:* PEANUTS © United Feature Syndicate. Reprinted by permission.)

as just another way of stating probability. A homely way of stating the *odds for* an event to occur would be

Frequency of occurrence to frequency of nonoccurrence.

Thus the *odds for* obtaining a "3" in the roll of a die would be 1 to 5, since out of six possible ways the die can land 1 is the frequency of the specified event and 5 is the frequency of the remaining events. In a similar fashion, the *odds for* drawing an ace of spades from a deck of cards would be 1 to 51, and the *odds for* drawing any ace would be 4 to 48. You might note that the *odds for* flipping a head, with an unbiased coin, would be 1 to 1; that is, the odds are even. In all cases note that the total frequency in the odds statement adds up to the total number of ways *any* event can occur. That is, 1 to 5 = 6 sides, 1 to 51 = 52 cards, and so on.

The *odds against* an event occurring are given simply by reversing the *odds for* statement. The *odds against* rolling the "3" are 5 to 1, and the *odds against* drawing the ace of spades are 51 to 1.

When odds statements are made concerning areas under the normal curve, we are able to go directly from probability to odds by using 100 as the base figure. For example, we noted that about 68% of the area under the curve lies between z's of −1.0 and 1.0. We then stated that the probability of a z score chosen at random being between −1.0 and 1.0 was $p = .68$. Thus the *odds for* a z score being between −1.0 and 1.0 are 68 to 32. Similarly, in Figure 5.6, the *odds for* an individual having an IQ of less than 70 would be 3 to 97, the *odds for* an individual having an IQ greater than 140 would be less than 1 to 99 (actually 6 to 994), and the *odds for* an individual having an IQ between 90 and 110 would be 47 to 53.

SOME CONCLUDING REMARKS

As was mentioned earlier, the discussion of probability in this chapter is a very superficial treatment of the topic. We did, however, spend quite a bit of time with the normal curve, both examining its mathematical properties and applying these characteristics to some practical situations. But you still must be aware of the fact that we have just barely scratched the surface as far as the normal curve goes. By using this normal curve model, mathematical statisticians have been able to solve a number of theoretical issues that would otherwise be extremely tedious if not impossible. Many of the techniques to be discussed in later chapters are based on such a theoretical foundation. It should be noted that several recent studies have questioned blind adherence to the normal curve, and nonnormal population shapes may not be all that rare. This is a relatively recent controversy in mathematical statistics, and if this topic has whetted your appetite for a mathematical approach to statistics, by all means pursue the matter with your favorite mathematics department.

SAMPLE PROBLEM

A manufacturer of hockey equipment is designing a new set of protective gear for male college hockey players, and the design engineers are basing their model on an average college male chest measurement of 39 inches with a standard deviation of 2.5 inches. We will assume that chest circumferences are normally distributed in the college male population.

What percentage of the population has a chest measurement of 44 inches or over?

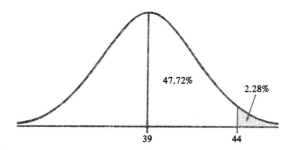

After drawing the curve, we calculate the z score for 44, which is $z = (44 - 39)/2.5 = 2.0$. In Table A we note that 47.72% of the area is between a z of 2.0 and the mean, leaving a total of 2.28% with a chest measurement of 44 inches or more.

If the engineers want their design to fit the middle 99% of all males, what range of chest measurements will be covered?

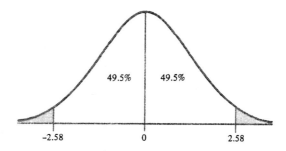

The middle 99% would be divided so that 49.5% of the distribution is on either side of the mean. In Table A we see that z scores of -2.58 and 2.58 are the boundaries for this 99%. Converting the z scores to chest measurements, we have

$$X = z\sigma + \mu = -2.58(2.5) + 39 = 32.6$$
$$X = 2.58(2.5) + 39 = 45.5$$

(continued)

SAMPLE PROBLEM (*CONTINUED*)

So we conclude that the design would have to be adjustable from 32.6 inches to 45.5 inches in order to fit the middle 99% of all males.

A husky defenseman claims that he is in the top 1% in chest expansion. What would his measurement have to be in order for him to make this claim?

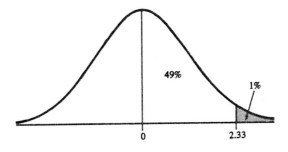

From the drawing and Table A we note that 49% of the area would be between the mean and the point needed, which would give a z score of 2.33. Converting the z score to inches, we would have

$$X = z\sigma + \mu = 2.33(2.5) + 39 = 44.8$$

His chest measurement would have to be 44.8 inches.

What is the probability that a male student, chosen at random, would have a chest measurement of less than 37 inches?

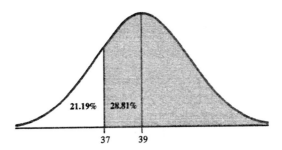

After drawing the curve, we calculate the z score for 37, which is $z = (37 - 39)/2.5 = -0.8$. In Table A we note that 28.81% of the area is between the mean and a z of -0.8. This would leave 21.19% below this point, so the probability that any male student chosen at random would have a chest measurement of less than 37 inches would be $p = .21$.

STUDY QUESTIONS

1. Mathematical models are used for what two purposes?
2. How is the unit normal curve different from other normal curves?
3. A score equivalent to a z of -2.3 is located where in the normal curve?
4. How would you find the area under the normal curve between two negative z scores?
5. What is the difference between classical and empirical probability?
6. What is the relationship between a probability p and the "long run"?
7. How is the addition rule used in determining probabilities? The multiplication rule?
8. How are odds statements used in classical probability? In empirical probability?
9. What is the difference between the statement "The odds are a thousand to 1 against my getting that job" and the statement "The odds are 3 to 1 for the mayor to win reelection?"

EXERCISES

1. What percentage of the area under the normal curve lies within the following boundaries?
   a. Between the mean and a z of 1.27.
   b. Between the mean and a z of -0.91.
   c. Between z scores of -1.84 and 1.39.
   d. Between z scores of -2.58 and 2.58.
   e. Above a z of 1.96.
   f. Below a z of -2.58.
   g. Above a z of -1.72.
   h. Below a z of 1.96.
2. What percentage of the area under the normal curve lies
   a. Between the mean and a z of 1.47?
   b. Between the mean and a z of -2.13?
   c. Between z scores of -1.50 and .89?
   d. Between z scores of -1.96 and 1.96?
   e. Below a z of 1.66?
   f. Below a z of -1.45?
   g. Above a z of 2.01?
   h. Above a z of -1.01?
3. According to the National Center for Health Statistics, the average male college student weighs 154 pounds, and the distribution of weights has a standard deviation of 21.4 pounds. Assume that this distribution is normally distributed in the population to answer the following.
   a. What percent of college men weigh 200 pounds or more?
   b. Tami tells her friends that she will not date any man that weighs less than she does. Tami weighs 125. What percent of the college men need not bother to call?

    c. Bill states that he is heavier than 99 percent of the college male population. How much would Bill have to weigh to make this statement?

    d. A hot air balloonist wants to hire a male assistant who weighs 140 pounds or less. What percent of the college male population would be eligible for this job?

    e. The middle 95% of the college male population would be included between what two weights?

    f. What weight corresponds to the 90th percentile?

4. The National Center for Health Statistics also states that the population of college women has a mean height of 5 feet 4 inches with a standard deviation of 2.48 inches. Assume that this variable is normally distributed in the population to make the following predictions.

    a. What percent of college women are 5 feet or shorter?

    b. An eccentric restaurant owner wants his waitresses to be 5 feet 10 inches or taller. What percent of college women would be eligible for these jobs?

    c. Kim states that she is so short that she is in the bottom 10% of women's heights. What height would she have to be to make that statement?

    d. Pete says that he will not date any woman who is taller than he. Pete's height is 5 feet 6 inches. What percent of college women are missing this opportunity?

    e. The middle 99% of college women are between what two heights?

    f. What height corresponds to the 98th percentile?

5. A popular college entrance examination has a mean of 60 and a standard deviation of 7. Assume that this variable is normally distributed in the college-bound population.

    a. What percent of the population would score 53 or below?

    b. The office of admissions at one college decided to admit anyone who scored 56 or above. What percent of the population is *not* eligible for admission?

    c. Peter learns that his test score is in the top 5% of the distribution. If this information is true, how high must his test score be?

    d. A guidance counselor claims that no one scoring in the bottom 20% should consider going to college. This group would have scores below what value?

6. The National Heart, Lung, and Blood Institute completed a large-scale study of cholesterol and heart disease. They estimated that the average serum cholesterol reading in the United States was 210 milligrams per deciliter of blood (mg/dl) with a standard deviation of 33 mg/dl. Assume that this variable is normally distributed in the population to answer the following.

    a. One of the requirements for participation in the study was to have a cholesterol reading of 265 mg/dl or greater. What percent of the population would fulfill this requirement?

    b. Some physicians have recommended that anyone with a reading of 240 mg/dl or more should go on a low-cholesterol diet and take cholesterol-lowering drugs. What percent of the population would be in this category?

c. Some authorities believe that even though the "average" cholesterol reading in the population is 210 mg/dl, it is too high and should be lowered to where the present 38th percentile now is. What average cholesterol level are they recommending?

d. Sue is proud of her nutrition and exercise program and claims that her cholesterol reading is in the bottom 20% of the population. How low would her reading have to be to enable her to make that statement?

7. A convention center is holding a conference for health professionals interested in arterial blood flow in the brain. Eighty-seven people convene. Of these 87, 57 are neurosurgeons, 12 are clinical psychologists, 15 are general physicians, and 3 are dentists.

a. One of the health professionals walks out of the conference room for a drink of water. What is the probability that he or she is a neurosurgeon?

b. What is the probability that he or she is a dentist?

c. Use the term "in the long run" to explain your answer in part a.

d. What are the odds for him or her being a neurosurgeon? Odds against?

8. A bag of fruit-flavored round candies contains 50 candies: 13 strawberry, 12 grape, 11 cherry, 7 orange, 5 lemon, and 2 piña colada. You close your eyes and reach into the bag to grab one piece of candy.

a. What is the probability that the candy is cherry flavored?

b. What is the probability that the candy is lemon flavored?

c. Use the term "in the long run" to explain your answer in part a.

d. What are the odds for the candy being cherry flavored? Odds against?

9. In the distribution of college men's weights discussed in exercise 3:

a. What is the probability that a man chosen at random would weigh 200 pounds or more? What are the odds for this occurrence? Odds against?

b. What is the probability that a man chosen at random would not meet Tami's requirements? Odds for? Odds against?

10. In the distribution of college women's heights discussed in exercise 4

a. What is the probability that a college woman chosen at random would be 5 feet or shorter? What are the odds for this occurrence? Odds against?

b. What is the probability that a woman chosen at random would be eligible for the restaurant job? Odds for? Odds against?

11. The distribution of scores for a popular college entrance exam was discussed in exercise 5.

a. What is the probability that a college-bound examinee chosen at random would score 53 or below?

b. What is the probability that a college-bound examinee chosen at random would score 56 or above?

12. The distribution of cholesterol readings was discussed in exercise 6.

a. What is the probability that someone chosen at random would have a cholesterol reading of 265 mg/dl or greater?

b. What is the probability that someone chosen at random would have a cholesterol reading of 240 mg/dl or greater?

13. A card is drawn from a well-shuffled deck. What is the probability that this card is an ace of diamonds? What is the probability that this card is either an ace of diamonds or a black queen?

14. In another card-drawing exercise, a card is drawn and returned to the deck, and a second card is drawn. What is the probability that both of these cards are aces? What is the probability that both are hearts?

15. In a computer science class of 48, there are 16 freshmen, 20 sophomores, 8 juniors, and 4 seniors. The name of each student is written on a slip of paper, and the slips are placed in a shoe box. A name is drawn at random. What is the probability that this person is a junior? What is the probability that this person is either a junior or a senior?

16. In the class of 48 students described in exercise 15, a name is drawn at random; it is returned to the box; and another name is drawn. What is the probability that one of the names is a freshman and the other a senior? What is the probability that both are seniors?

CHAPTER 6

Sampling Theory for Hypothesis Testing

Your friend Teri is a fan of extrasensory perception and claims to have the ability to tell what is written on a piece of paper that is face down. You devise a simple test to check out her claim. You take two slips of paper, write an *A* on one and a *B* on the other, and place them face down on the table while Teri's back is to you. You quickly and thoroughly mix them around so even you don't know which one is which. You then ask her to turn over the two in order—first the *A* and then the *B*. She studies the two slips of paper, then reaches down and—turns over the *A* and then the *B*!

Would this prove to you that she possesses ESP? No? Just luck? Would you believe her if, instead of two, you had tried three slips with *A*, *B*, and *C* written on them, and she had turned them over in the correct order? No? Just chance? Would you be a believer if you had asked her to turn over four slips with an *A*, *B*, *C*, and *D* in the correct order? No? Yes? At what point can you rule out chance, and say she *definitely* has ESP?

In Chapter 4 we noted the controversy over the interpretation of test scores for students with learning disabilities and non-learning-disabled students. One study (Ysseldyke, Algozzine, Shinn, & McGue, 1982) administered a battery of achievement tests and cognitive tests, including the Wechsler Intelligence Scale for Children–Revised (WISC–R). They found a WISC–R full-scale score mean of 99.92 for a sample of students with learning disabilities. Researchers would agree that there is really no difference between this mean and the traditional mean IQ of 100. They would agree that this small observed difference (after all, 99.92 and 100 *are* different!) is simply due to chance.

But how low would the mean have to be before we could say there *is* a difference between the scores of students with learning disabilities and the expected value of 100? 99.5? 97? 95? At what point could we say that the difference between an obtained mean and 100 is *definitely* not due to chance?

It should be obvious that the two situations described in the preceding paragraphs are in some way different from the concepts that we have discussed in previous chapters. In earlier chapters on central tendency and variability we calculated means and standard deviations to *describe* a collection of data. But in the present situations we are not content to merely describe the data at hand. We want to use the data to draw conclusions about some events in general.

In Chapter 1, we first noted the distinction between descriptive statistics and inferential statistics, and it is with this chapter that we begin to be concerned about making *inferences* about the *population* instead of being content merely to describe a particular distribution of data. To be sure, descriptive statistics are useful—even indispensable—for a teacher measuring the performance of a class of algebra students or a college administration calculating grade-point averages, but as Chapter 1 pointed out, educators and behavioral scientists often gather evidence from samples for the express purpose of generalizing their results to the population.

DESCRIPTIONS VERSUS INFERENCES

If a social psychologist wants to know the relationship between TV violence and aggression in children, or if a guidance counselor wants to know if participation in extracurricular activities is an indicator of a healthy self-image, or if a human resources specialist wants to see if performance on a keyboard dexterity test will predict job success as a data-entry operator, all three will undoubtedly select a group of individuals, gather data, and generalize the results from the small sample to a much larger population. And in the case of Teri's ESP claims, we can use a small sample of her results to draw conclusions about a puzzling phenomenon.

Note that the difference between descriptive statistics and inferential statistics is not in the *kind* of statistical measures employed but in the *purpose* for doing the measuring. If your intent is merely to describe a collection of data, you will construct a frequency distribution and frequency polygon in order to picture the distribution, and you will calculate a mean, median, or mode to discover its central tendency and a standard deviation to find its variability. All of these procedures, of course, *describe* the distribution.

Now, if your purpose is to make *inferences* about a population, you will still calculate means and standard deviations, but your interest will focus on how well these statistics estimate a *population* mean and standard deviation. The rest of this chapter will be devoted to procedures for taking samples and for estimating the population values by using the sample statistics.

The terms *sample* and *population* were formally defined in Chapter 3, but a review might be in order. Basically, a *population* is a group of elements that are alike on one or more characteristics as defined by the researcher, such as all fourth-graders in a state or all college students in the United States or all property owners in a county. Or in terms of the social psychologist, the guidance counselor, and the human resources specialist mentioned earlier, the populations could be all the preschool children in Illinois, all the junior high school students in a metropolitan school district, or all the data-entry operators in the claims office of a large insurance company.

The important thing to remember is that the population is defined by a researcher *for a particular purpose* and *all* the elements satisfying the criteria are members of that population. Size alone does not determine whether or not a group of elements is a population, although in practice most populations turn out to be rather large.

A *sample,* on the other hand, is a group of elements that is selected from the population and is *smaller* in number than the size of the population. A sample may be chosen in a number of ways, and you can have random samples, stratified samples, or cluster samples. Each type involves a different procedure for determining how the data are to be gathered. Since the theoretical background for the statistical procedures were developed primarily for random samples, we will spend our time and energy investigating random sampling.

RANDOM SAMPLES

The random sample is chosen in such a way that *each element in the population has an equal chance of being in the sample*. This is an important definition and one that must be strictly followed before the procedures outlined in this chapter can be applied. But how does one draw a random sample in practice?

As an example, let us say that we would like to interview a random sample of college students on a given college campus about their attitudes toward the college administration. It would be simple to stand in the entrance to the student union and pick the first 50 students that come by, but the result would *not* be a random sample. The fact that many polls are conducted in just this fashion does not make it right, and we must look for a more statistically defensible procedure. There are two generally acceptable ways of obtaining a random sample: a table of random numbers and a "counting-off" technique. The random number method is preferred, although the counting method will usually approximate a random sample.

Table of Random Numbers

Table K in Appendix 3 is a collection of random numbers, random in that any digit or any grouping of four digits bears no relationship to any other digit or grouping of digits in the table. In other words, in terms of our definition of a random sample, in any position in the table, each digit from 0 to 9 has an equal chance of appearing.

To obtain a random sample from a college population of 5,000 students, we would first obtain a listing of all students and assign each one a number from 1 to 5,000. We would then enter Table K at a point determined by chance (a colleague of mine closes his eyes and stabs at the page with his fingertip or a pencil). From this starting point, we would take as many numbers from the columns as we needed for our sample. If we ran across a duplicate number, we would ignore it and go on to the next one. If we wanted one-, two-, or three-digit numbers, we would use the same procedure but would take only the first one, two, or three digits of the four-digit numbers. The students with the numbers corresponding to the ones we selected would constitute our sample.

Counting-Off Procedure

The technique described in the preceding section can be quite time-consuming when the population is large; assigning a number to all the names in a metropolitan telephone directory, for instance, would require great dedication. In such a case it may be more convenient to use a counting-off procedure and take every hundredth or every thousandth name in the list. For example, if we wanted a random sample of 200 from a population of 60,000, we would take every 300th name. A counting-off procedure is used frequently in consumer surveys, where a questionnaire may be inserted in every 30th box of the manufacturer's product or mailed along with a monthly billing to every 10th credit card customer.

Sometimes referred to as "systematic sampling," this procedure involves entering a directory or list of names by making the first draw a random one. For example, if we wanted a sample of 50 from a list of 500 names, we would need every 10th name on the list. The starting place for counting would be determined by a table of random numbers, so we would choose a number from 1 to 10 at random. If the number 6 came up, we would begin our drawing at the 6th name on the list and take every 10th name after that.

MORE ON SAMPLING

Before progressing to the mathematics of sampling theory, we need to be aware of other terms and concepts that we are likely to encounter in reference to sampling.

Size of Sample

All other things being equal, a sample is more likely to be accurate (i.e., to faithfully describe the population characteristics) as it increases in size. Size alone does not insure an accurate sample, but it is safe to say that a larger sample is more likely to reflect the characteristics of the population. Later in the chapter we will have occasion to demonstrate mathematically the effect of the size of a random sample on the accuracy of results.

Biased Samples

Any time that our samples contain a systematic error, they are said to be *biased*. A very common example of bias in sampling is the case in which copies of a ques-
mailed out to a number of people and only a fraction of the total are
ssible that those returning the questionnaire, thereby vol-
ta examined, are different in some respect from those
he classical study on sexual behavior in men by Alfred C.
ome on just this point; the critics felt that those men will-
nation in explicit detail were somehow different from the
pulation.

tituting the foundation for theories in education and the be-
inate in studies using college students. It seems that intro-
ourses are a very handy source of subjects for an infinite va-
and it is not unusual to have each student participate in one
s as a course requirement. Critics of this technique are quick
llege sophomores in the introductory psychology course may
ve of even college students in general, to say nothing of the
ze. Whenever such *incidental sampling* is employed (grade
college faculty, county welfare recipients, etc.), it is difficult, to
generalize to a population of all grade schools, college faculties,
ents. The particular sample at hand may be unique, so that the re-
simply cannot be generalized to a larger population without seri-
, if incidental sampling must be used because of cost considera-
ns must be taken to examine the sample for any possible biases.

ith Replacement

n samples are drawn from a comparatively small population, it is usu-
ry to replace the observation before taking the next one. If your pop-
sists of a deck of cards, a bag of colored marbles, numbers in a hat, or
ou should return the card or whatever to the group before making an-
other draw. For example, let us say a bag contains 15 yellow, 3 blue, and 2 red marbles. The probability of drawing a blue marble would be 3/20 or $p = .15$. However, if you didn't get a blue one on your first draw, the probability of getting a blue one on the second draw depends on whether or not you return the first marble to the bag. If you don't, the probability is now 3/19 or $p = .16$. Similarly, the probability of pulling an ace from a well-shuffled deck is 4/52 or $p = .077$. If you don't get an ace on the first draw and do not replace the card, the probability on

the second draw is now 4/51 or $p = .078$. The differences due to nonreplacement in these examples are small, but nonreplacement could affect your calculations in a complex probability problem.

Parameters versus Statistics

In the sections to come we will have occasion to talk about means, medians, standard deviations, and other characteristics of samples, as well as means and standard deviations of a population. We will attempt to avoid confusion by referring to these measures of central tendency and variability as *statistics* when they describe a *sample* and as *parameters* when they describe a *population*. In other words the mean and standard deviation of a sample are *statistics*, and their namesakes in the population are *parameters*. As we noted earlier in Chapters 3 and 4, we use the lowercase Greek letter μ (mu) for the population mean and the lowercase Greek letter σ (sigma) for the population standard deviation. As before, $\overline{X}$ and s are the sample mean and standard deviation, respectively.

ESTIMATING THE POPULATION MEAN

Much of the energy expended in inferential statistics goes toward the *estimation* of population parameters. This estimation process is necessary because in most cases it is virtually impossible to measure an entire population due to its size and ever-changing nature. If one wants to know the average IQ of high school seniors, manual dexterity of aerospace electronics technicians, reading readiness scores of six-year-olds, or what have you, the respective populations are so large and inaccessible that the only reasonable procedure is to take a random sample and estimate the population values from this sample alone.

Although this procedure may seem questionable to you, it is the only practical approach to the problem. Statisticians have worked out the necessary formulas, tested mathematical models, and developed techniques to enable us to take a sample, calculate its mean, and estimate with a given degree of certainty how well this sample $\overline{X}$ estimates the "true" mean or population mean, μ. The following sections will describe the theory behind the techniques and the methods to be followed in estimating population parameters.

The Sampling Distribution

Let us suppose that we would like to know the average number of hours worked per week by college students with part-time jobs. We follow the methods described earlier for obtaining a random sample and, using a sample size of 100, we come up with a mean of 11.7 hours and a standard deviation of 3.9 hours. The sample $\overline{X}$ of 11.7 is called an *unbiased estimate of the population mean,* μ. By *unbiased,* we mean that if we continued to take samples like the one we just did, the *mean of all these sample means* would approach the value of the population mean.

After we have gathered our data and calculated the sample mean, we ask, "How good an estimate of the population mean is our sample mean of 11.7 hours? Is it too high? Too low? Just about right?" Since we rarely know the true mean (population mean), we can never answer these questions exactly, but we can make a *probability statement* about its most likely value.

In order to make such a statement, we must first indulge in a mathematical fantasy. Let us perform a hypothetical exercise in which we continue to take samples of size 100 and calculate the mean of each sample. Keeping track of these means, we might get

$$\overline{X}_1 = 11.7$$
$$\overline{X}_2 = 10.9$$
$$\overline{X}_3 = 12.1$$
$$\overline{X}_4 = 11.2$$

and so on.

If we continued this exercise for an *infinite* number of samples (you see why it is a *hypothetical* exercise), the following would occur:

1. A batch of means, called a *sampling distribution of means,* would result.
2. The mean of this sampling distribution, $\mu_{\overline{X}}$ (say "mean of means"), would be equal to the population mean, μ.
3. The batch of sample means would be normally distributed around the mean of the distribution, $\mu_{\overline{X}}$, with a standard deviation of $\sigma/\sqrt{N}$.

This last point illustrates the *central limit theorem,* and it is an important foundation for much of our work in statistical inference. Stated more precisely, the central limit theorem in this instance says,

If a population has a mean μ and a standard deviation σ, then the distribution of sample means drawn from this population approaches a normal distribution as N increases, with a mean $\mu_{\overline{X}}$ and a standard deviation of $\sigma/\sqrt{N}$.

Regardless of the shape of the population from which we draw our samples, the sampling distribution of means will be normal *if the sample size is sufficiently large.* What is a "sufficiently" large sample? There is no easy answer, because the required sample size depends on the shape of the population distribution. You will find some statistics texts specifying an N of 30, and others an N of 50; certainly an N of 100 would remove all doubt about the resultant shape of the sampling distribution. In any event, the central limit theorem enables us to solve sampling problems without worrying whether or not the population from which we are sampling is normal.

The three characteristics of a sampling distribution listed above are of primary importance, so let us look at each in greater detail.

Note 6.1
Chance, "Dumb Luck," and Sampling Error

There will be a number of occasions in the remaining chapters when we will be talking about *chance* or *sampling error*. Decisions must be made to determine whether some result is due to chance (i.e., sampling error), or whether the result represents a real departure from purely chance fluctuations. If you regularly take a coffee break with a friend and flip a coin to see who pays, you expect in the long run to win about half the time. In other words, who winds up paying on a given day is strictly due to "chance." But, as you well know, there might be times when one of you will win, three, or even four days in a row. Such fluctuations can still be chance effects and would be called, simply "sampling error."

On the other hand, if your friend seems to win the toss 90% of the time, you would probably demand to examine her coin, since such a departure from what you expect to happen "just by chance" leads you to suspect something other than an unbiased coin toss. But where do you draw the line? How much of a deviation from a 50-50 split do you endure before you can say that there is something uncanny about your friend's coin-tossing ability? 60-40? 70-30? 80-20? At what point do you say that the deviation is no longer sampling error but is a *real* nonchance happening? Decisions such as these are typical of inferential statistics, and we will be spending considerable time on just how such decisions are made.

Sampling Distribution of Means. We would note as we calculated mean after mean that most of them tended to cluster about some central point, just as our frequency distributions tended to do back in Chapter 2. We should not be surprised that all the samples do not have the same mean; we expect that because of *chance* fluctuations the means will tend to vary slightly. Just as we would not expect to get 5 heads and 5 tails every time we flipped a coin 10 times, we also do not expect that all sample means would be the same.

Let us assume that the mean of means, $\mu_{\bar{X}}$, in our hypothetical exercise on hours worked per week on part-time jobs turned out to be 12 hours. We would notice that many of the sample means would be quite close to $\mu_{\bar{X}}$, say 11.8, 12.3, or 11.6. However, we would also notice that a few of the sample means would be scattered a little farther away from $\mu_{\bar{X}}$, such as 10.2 or 14.1. And an occasional sample mean would be as far away as 7.9 or 15.2. We expect the sample means to be distributed in this fashion, *and this scattering of $\bar{X}$'s about $\mu_{\bar{X}}$ is due to sampling error.*

The Mean of Means. The mean of the sampling distribution of means, $\mu_{\bar{X}}$, is equal to the population mean, μ. What we are saying is that if we take all possible samples of a given size from a population and calculate the mean of each sample, the mean of all these sample means will be identical to the population mean. The mathematical proof for the relationship between $\mu_{\bar{x}}$ and μ is beyond the scope of this book, but this is a handy relationship, as we shall soon see.

Normal Sampling Distribution.   Since the sampling distribution of means is normal, we can use the characteristics of the normal curve that we noted back in Chapter 5. For example, we could say:

1. 68.26% of all the sample means would fall between −1 and 1 standard deviations from the mean, $\mu_{\bar{x}}$.
2. 95% of all the sample means would fall between −1.96 and 1.96 standard deviations from the mean, $\mu_{\bar{x}}$.
3. 5% of all the sample means would fall outside the same interval, −1.96 and 1.96 standard deviations from the mean, $\mu_{\bar{x}}$.

Similarly, the probability statements we made concerning the normal curve would apply to this sampling distribution as well.

1. The probability that a sample mean falls between $\mu_{\bar{x}} \pm 1$ standard deviation would be .68.
2. The probability that a sample mean falls between $\mu_{\bar{x}} \pm 1.96$ standard deviations would be .95.
3. The probability that a sample mean falls outside the same interval, $\mu_{\bar{x}} \pm 1.96$ standard deviations, would be .05.

With these probability statements in mind, let us get back to our original question, "How well does our sample mean of 11.7 hours estimate the true mean?" In Figure 6.1, the hypothetical sampling distribution of means is shown with its mean, $\mu_{\bar{x}}$, of 12. Basically, we are asking, "Where in this distribution of sample means does our mean of 11.7 fall?"

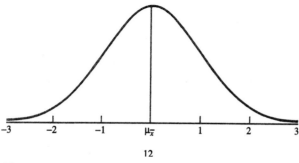

Figure 6.1
Sampling distribution of means with $\mu_{\bar{x}} = 12$.

STANDARD ERROR OF THE MEAN

As you can see from Figure 6.1, we could locate our sample mean of 11.7 and make probability statements about it, *if we knew the standard deviation of this distribution*. If the standard deviation were 1.0 hours, 11.7 would be very close to $\mu_{\bar{X}}$. However, if the standard deviation were 0.1 hours, the sample mean of 11.7 hours would be 3 standard deviations below $\mu_{\bar{X}}$.

The standard deviation of this sampling distribution of means is called the *standard error of the mean* and, as we noted earlier, is given by

$$\sigma_{\bar{X}} = \frac{\sigma}{\sqrt{N}} \tag{6.1}$$

where

$\sigma_{\bar{X}}$ = the standard error of the mean
σ = the standard deviation of the population from which the samples
     were drawn
N = size of the sample

The term *standard error of the mean* may sound awkward, but it is to be interpreted in the same way as any other standard deviation. We could just as well say "standard deviation of the mean," but convention is convention, and we will have to learn to live with the standard *error* of the mean. The important thing is that *standard error of the mean* means the standard deviation of the sampling distribution of means.

Note that this formula requires that we know the value of the population standard deviation, σ. For the situations where σ is *not* known, a different formula and procedure are required; these will be discussed in detail in Chapter 9.

Once we have calculated the standard error of the mean, $\sigma_{\bar{X}}$, we can make probability statements about where our sample mean falls in the sampling distribution and, by inference, just how good an estimate of the population mean our sample mean is. To illustrate the reasoning behind this procedure, let us use the example of our sample of the hours worked per week at part-time jobs by 100 college students with $\bar{X} = 11.7$. We will assume that the standard deviation of the population of hours worked from which our sample came is $\sigma = 4.0$ hours.

To calculate the standard error of the mean, we substitute into the formula

$$\sigma_{\bar{X}} = \frac{\sigma}{\sqrt{N}} = \frac{4}{\sqrt{100}}$$

$$\sigma_{\bar{X}} = 0.4$$

Some Trial Estimates of μ

Now with our sample mean, $\bar{X}$, of 11.7 and our standard error, $\sigma_{\bar{X}}$, of 0.4, is it possible for the population mean, μ, to be 12? Figure 6.2a shows the sampling distri-

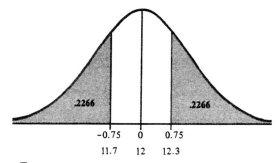

(a) $\overline{X}$ deviates 0.3 hours or more from $\mu_{\overline{X}}$; $p = .2266 + .2266 = .4532$

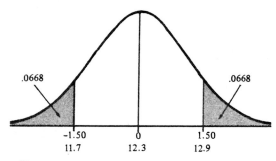

(b) $\overline{X}$ deviates 0.6 hours or more from $\mu_{\overline{X}}$; $p = .0668 + .0668 = .1336$

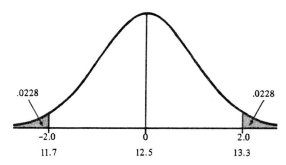

(c) $\overline{X}$ deviates 0.8 hours or more from $\mu_{\overline{X}}$; $p = .0228 + .0228 = .0456$

Figure 6.2
Sample mean with different hypothesized true means.

bution with $\mu_{\bar{X}}$ of 12 and its standard deviation ($\sigma_{\bar{X}}$) of 0.4. If the true mean (remember that $\mu_{\bar{X}} = \mu$) is actually 12, where does our sample mean of 11.7 lie?

The z score is used to determine where in the distribution our mean of 11.7 is located. However, the usual z score formula, $z = (X - \bar{X})/s$, must be modified slightly in order for us to use it in a sampling distribution. Since the mean is $\mu_{\bar{X}}$, the standard deviation is the standard error of the mean, $\sigma_{\bar{X}}$, and the "score" is our sample mean, $\bar{X}$, the z formula would now read

$$z = \frac{\bar{X} - \mu_{\bar{X}}}{\sigma_{\bar{X}}} \tag{6.2}$$

It is still the same old z score, but the terms in the formula are changed to apply to a sampling distribution.

Could μ Be 12?   The z score for our sample mean of 11.7 would be $z = (11.7 - 12)/0.4 = -0.75$. In other words our sample mean is three-fourths of a standard deviation from the hypothesized true mean of 12. Since by sampling error it is just as easy to wind up with a sample mean 0.3 hours *above* $\mu_{\bar{X}}$, we can rephrase our original question as follows: "What is the probability that any sample mean would deviate from the population mean by 0.3 hours or more?" Using Figure 6.2a and Table A of Appendix 3 we see that the sample means in the sampling distribution that deviate by 0.3 hours or more are shown *below* a z score of −0.75 and *above* a z of 0.75, and that 45.32% of the normal curve area lies outside these two points. In other words, 45.32% of all sample means would fall outside these two z values, *so the probability that a sample mean, picked at random, would deviate 0.3 hours or more from this hypothesized true mean of 12 hours is .4532.*

From these results does it seem likely that the true mean is actually 12 hours? Remember that we do not know the exact value of the true mean but are simply hypothesizing a value and, on the basis of our sample, trying to make a decision about the most likely value of the true mean.

Could μ Be 12.3?   Suppose that we had hypothesized that the true mean was 12.3 hours. We then would have the situation shown in Figure 6.2b. With our sample mean again of 11.7, our question would now be "What is the probability that any sample mean would deviate from this hypothesized population mean by 0.6 hours or more?" If the true mean were in fact 12.3, the sampling distribution would look like Figure 6.2b, and we could calculate a z score for our sample mean of 11.7 as $z = (11.7 - 12.3)/0.4 = -1.50$. Since the deviation could be either plus or minus (again, remember that from a sampling point of view we are just as likely to get a sample mean that is 0.6 hours *above* the mean as one that is 0.6 hours below the mean), we can see from Figure 6.2b that this area is represented under the curve below a z of −1.50 and above a z of 1.50. We then conclude that if the true mean were 12.3, 13.36% of all the means in this sampling distribution would fall outside the two z scores of −1.50 and 1.50, or outside 11.7 and 12.9, so $p = .1336$ that any sample mean would fall outside these values.

With these results is it possible that the true mean could actually be 12.3? Is it possible with a sample mean of 11.7 to have a population mean that is 12.3? Let us postpone an answer to these questions until we look at one more example.

Could μ Be 12.5?   Suppose that we had hypothesized that the population mean was 12.5 hours with the hypothetical frequency distribution shown in Figure 6.2c. With our sample mean again of 11.7, what is the probability that a sample mean, drawn at random, would deviate 0.8 hours or more from the true mean? The z score for our sample mean of 11.7 would now be $z = (11.7 - 12.5)/0.4 = -2.0$. Again, since this much of a deviation from the mean could be above the mean, we see in Figure 6.2c that this area is represented under the curve below a z of -2.0 and above a z of 2.0. We then conclude that if the true mean were actually 12.5, only 4.56% of all sample means in this sampling distribution would fall outside the two z scores of -2.0 and 2.0, or outside 11.7 and 13.3. The probability, then of any sample mean chosen at random being outside these two values is $p = .0456$.

Sampling Error Versus a Real Difference

At last we have come to the point where we can make a decision about how good our sample mean is as an estimate of the population mean. (Again, keep in mind that we do not know the actual value of the population mean.) In Table 6.1 are the results of our three hypothetical estimates of the population mean, along with the probability of a sample mean deviating by as much as or more than our sample mean of 11.7 does. Examine this table carefully and, at the same time, inspect the three sampling distributions of Figure 6.2.

Note in Table 6.1 and Figure 6.2 that the farther away the hypothesized population mean is from our sample mean, *the smaller the probability that a given sample mean, drawn at random, would deviate by that amount or more.* On the basis of these three examples we note the following:

1. When we hypothesized a population mean of 12 hours, we saw that more than 45% of all sample means would miss μ by as much as (or more than) our mean of 11.7 did. Since the probability of any sample mean, chosen at random (as ours was), deviating by as much as or more than that was .4532, we

Table 6.1

Hypothesized population means and associated probabilities of a greater deviation than our sample mean of 11.7 hours

Hypothesized Population Mean	Amount of Deviation from μ	Probability of Deviation
12 hours	0.3 hours or more	$p = .4532$
12.3 hours	0.6 hours or more	$p = .1336$
12.5 hours	0.8 hours or more	$p = .0456$

Note 6.2
How Large a Difference Is Still Due to Chance?

The example of Teri's ESP claim may be helpful in illustrating the dilemma posed in statements 3a and 3b (p. 149), where we were faced with the problem of determining if the discrepancy between our sample mean of 11.7 and a hypothesized population mean of 12.5 was due to sampling error. We noted at the beginning of the chapter that with two slips of paper, Teri turned up first the *A*, then the *B*, as she said she would. Does this feat demonstrate ESP ability?

Before you decide, let us take a careful look at her task. We know that there are only two possible ways that she can respond—she can turn up the *A*, then the *B*; or she can turn up the *B* first, then the *A*. Whether she has ESP or not, one of the two orders is correct, and we say that she would be right 50% of the time *just by chance*. The probability that she would be correct just by chance would, of course, be $p = .50$. If she were correct on this simple task, we would be unimpressed, since anyone, ESP or no, would be right 50% of the time.

But what about three slips of paper, lettered *A*, *B*, and *C*, and requiring her to put them in order in the same manner? There are now six possible ways in which she could turn them over: *ABC*, *ACB*, *BAC*, *BCA*, *CAB*, and *CBA*. Since only one of these orders is correct, we know that the probability of her being correct, *just by chance*, is 1/6, or $p = .17$. If she were correct, we would probably still be unimpressed, since anyone would be right 17% of the time just by chance.

How about making the task still more difficult by requiring her to order correctly four, five, six, or more slips of paper? The probabilities are as follows.

The point of this whole discussion is this: There is *no time* that you can say that your friend's performance is not due to chance and is definitely due to ESP. If she picks up four slips of paper and places them in the correct order, we begin to suspect her of possessing some kind of strange power, but we definitely cannot say that it is not chance, since it is still possible (4 chances out of 100) that the result is simply due to chance. If the test is set up with five slips, the probability due to chance of her ordering them correctly is pretty

Number of Slips	Possible Orders	Probability of Correct Order
2 *AB*	2	$p = 1/2 = .50$
3 *ABC*	6	$p = 1/6 = .17$
4 *ABCD*	24	$p = 1/24 = .042$
5 *ABCDE*	120	$p = 1/120 = .008$
6 *ABCDEF*	720	$p = 1/720 = .001$

slim (8 chances out of 1,000), but it is still possibly a chance effect. The same reasoning applies to the test with six slips, but note that the correct order would happen just by chance only 1 time out of 1,000 ($p = .001$).

So, you ask, when is the result definitely, positively, irrevocably due to ESP (or whatever is responsible for your friend's strange ability) and *not* due to chance? You *never* know for certain; you just have varying degrees of certainty that the result could have happened by chance alone. If the probability of a result happening by chance is .042, we are more certain that this result could have happened by chance than a result whose probability due to chance was .008. Clearly, what we need are some guidelines to help us make our decision as to whether chance is responsible for our results.

could conclude that it is entirely possible that the population mean is in fact 12, and our sample mean of 11.7 represents *sampling error* due to chance effects present in any sampling situation.

2. When we hypothesized that $\mu = 12.3$ hours, we saw that about 13% of all sample means would miss μ by as much as or more than 0.6 hours. The probability, then, of any sample mean deviating by that much or more than that was $p = .1336$, and we would probably conclude that it would be entirely possible for μ to be 12.3 and that our sample mean of 11.7 is due to sampling error. But, noting that fewer sample means (13% versus 45%) deviate by this larger amount, we begin to feel a little uneasy about one of two possibilities. Either we doubt our hypothesis about the value of μ, or we wonder about the accuracy of our sample mean.

3. When we hypothesized that $\mu = 12.5$ hours, we noted that less than 5% of all the sample means would miss μ by as much as 0.8 hours or more. The probability of any sample mean, chosen at random, deviating by this much or more is $p = .0456$, and now we really begin to feel uneasy. Our sample mean deviates so much that less than 5% of the sample means deviate by this much or more by *sampling error.* There are two possibilities, as indicated in statement 2.

   a. The population mean could really be 12.5 and our sample mean of 11.7 is a rare occurrence, one of the few that we expect would deviate this much by sampling error.

   b. Our hypothesis is dead wrong. We have made a big mistake in hypothesizing the value of the population mean.

It turns out that we must rely on our *sample* mean, so, if the discrepancy between our sample mean and some hypothesized population mean is too large, *we must reject the hypothesized population mean as being untenable.* When there is a conflict between the value of the sample mean and the hypothesized population mean, we will go along with the sample mean.

Significance Levels

It should be obvious by now that the crux of the whole problem is where to draw the line. At what point do you say that your result is such a rare occurrence that it is highly unlikely to be sampling error? When do you start rejecting the notion that the discrepancy is due to sampling error? Fortunately, statisticans have rallied to our cause and have proposed the concept of *significance levels*. Simply stated, a significance level is the probability that a result is due to sampling error, *and, if this probability is small enough, we reject the notion that sampling error is the cause.* We then conclude that there is a real difference between our result and what would logically be expected by chance. Traditionally, these significance levels have been set at .05 and .01. Significance levels are sometimes called *alpha* levels (Greek letter α).

The .05 Significance Level ($\alpha = .05$).   If the probability that our result happened by chance is .05 or less, we say that our results are significant at the .05 level. If the discrepancy between our result and what would be expected by chance alone would happen 5% of the time or less, we reject the notion that it is sampling error.

The .01 Significance Level ($\alpha = .01$).   If the probability that our result happened by chance is .01 or less, we say that our results are significant at the .01 level. If the discrepancy between our result and what would be expected by chance alone would happen 1% of the time or less, we reject the notion that it is sampling error.

Statisticians will be the first to admit that these levels are set in an arbitrary manner, but at least they represent some guidelines to use in making a decision. Let us apply these guidelines to our earlier problem—that of determining how good our sample mean is as an estimate of the population mean, μ.[*]

The Confidence Interval Approach to Estimating μ

In an earlier example we tested various hypothesized values of the population mean and observed the hypothetical sampling distributions for possible population means of 12, 12.3, and 12.5 hours. We noted that as the hypothesized values deviated more and more from our sample mean of 11.7, the probability that we would obtain a sample mean that deviated by as much as or more than ours grew smaller and smaller.

So why not hypothesize a population mean that is the *same* value as our sample mean? With our sample mean of 11.7 and a population mean of 11.7, we would not have to worry at all about sampling error. Whenever we wished to estimate μ from a sample $\overline{X}$, all we would have to do is say that the most likely value of the population mean is the value of our sample mean.

---

[*]There is considerable ongoing controversy on the use of significance levels to evaluate the results of an experiment. Your instructor may have one or more alternate approaches to replace the one presented here. The methods presented in the following chapters are those currently in use in the majority of scientific journals. However, these practices will probably change over the next few years.

However practical this approach may sound, there is an error in this type of reasoning. The population mean is a *fixed* value, *and it is the sample means that deviate about this fixed value.* As you saw in Figure 6.2, for any given value of μ, the sample means were normally distributed about this point. So instead of talking about possible values that μ may take, given our sample $\overline{X}$, we are better off in setting up a *confidence interval* in which the true mean probably lies.

As an example let us use the information presented in Figure 6.2c, where we hypothesized a population mean of 12.5 and noted that 95.44% of all sample means fell between this mean ±2$\sigma_{\overline{X}}$, or between 11.7 and 13.3. You will remember from the last chapter that in a normal curve the interval containing the mean ±1.96 standard deviations contained 95% of the cases and the mean ±2.58 standard deviations contained 99% of the cases. So, in a similar manner, we could calculate the interval about the hypothetical sampling distribution with its mean of 12.5. This interval would be $\mu_{\overline{X}} \pm 1.96\sigma_{\overline{X}}$, or 12.5 ± 1.96(0.4) = 12.5 ± 0.78, or 11.72 to 13.28. So we would say that 95% of the sample means would fall between 11.72 and 13.28 if the population mean were 12.5. Similarly, with the interval of $\mu_{\overline{X}} \pm 2.58\sigma_{\overline{X}}$, we would have 12.5 ± 2.58(0.4), or 11.47 to 13.53. In this case we can say that 99% of the sample means would fall between 11.47 and 13.53.

However, when we use the confidence interval approach, we set up an interval with the *sample mean as the center.* We now have a technique that allows us to feel reasonably certain that the population mean is included in an interval, without having to start out by hypothesizing a specific value for μ.

The 95% Confidence Interval.   To determine the 95% confidence interval, we simply calculate the interval

$$\overline{X} \pm 1.96\sigma_{\overline{X}} \qquad (6.3)$$

where $\overline{X}$ is the *sample mean* and $\sigma_{\overline{X}}$ is the standard error of the mean. So, for our sample mean of 11.7 and standard error of 0.4, we would have

$$\overline{X} \pm 1.96\sigma_{\overline{X}} = 11.7 \pm 1.96(.04)$$
$$= 11.7 \pm 0.78$$
$$= 10.92 \text{ to } 12.48$$

Since the probability is .95 that the population mean is included in all intervals similarly constructed from all possible sample means, we are reasonably certain that the population mean is between 10.92 and 12.48.[*]

The 99% Confidence Interval.   To determine the 99% confidence interval, we calculate the interval given by

$$\overline{X} \pm 2.58\sigma_{\overline{X}} \qquad (6.4)$$

---

[*]We might be tempted to say that the probability is .95 that μ is between 10.92 and 12.48. However, mathematicians remind us that meaningful probability statements are made only about variables (such as $\overline{X}$) and not fixed values (such as μ).

which gives

$$\overline{X} \pm 2.58\sigma_{\overline{X}} = 11.7 \pm 2.58(0.4)$$
$$= 11.7 \pm 1.03$$
$$= 10.67 \text{ to } 12.73$$

Since the probability is .99 that the population mean is included in all intervals similarly constructed from all possible sample means, we are even more certain (than with the 95% interval) that the population mean is between 10.67 and 12.73. Or, stated in still another way, if we continued to take more and more samples of the same size, we would find that 99 out of 100 times the population mean would be included in the interval.

Comparison of the Two Confidence Intervals.   In practice, which of the two intervals do you use? Note that the 99% confidence interval is *wider* (10.67 to 12.73) than the 95% confidence interval (10.92 to 12.48). This result is to be expected, since in order to be more certain, you must have a slightly wider interval. We have sacrificed some precision in order to be more certain, and as the saying goes, "We are more and more certain of less and less."

Let us use the confidence interval approach in an example and see how it can help us in estimating the population mean, μ. Suppose that we administer a college entrance exam to a random sample of 200 high school seniors and calculate a mean of 102. From the examiner's manual accompanying the test, we learn that the standard deviation of all high school students tested is 12.0. So, in summary, we have $N = 200$, $\overline{X} = 102$, and $\sigma = 12$.

The 95% confidence interval, $\overline{X} \pm 1.96\sigma_{\overline{X}}$, requires us to calculate first the standard error of the mean, $\sigma_{\overline{X}}$, as follows:

$$\sigma_{\overline{X}} = \frac{\sigma}{\sqrt{N}} = \frac{12}{\sqrt{200}} = \frac{12}{14.14} = 0.85$$

Substituting into the interval formula yields

$$\overline{X} \pm 1.96\sigma_{\overline{X}} = 102 \pm 1.96(0.85)$$
$$= 102 \pm 1.67$$
$$= 100.33 \text{ to } 103.67$$

and we can be reasonably certain that the population mean is in that interval.

To calculate the 99% confidence interval, we substitute to obtain

$$\overline{X} \pm 2.58(0.85) = 102 \pm 2.19$$
$$= 99.81 \text{ to } 104.19$$

and we are even more certain that this wider interval contains the population mean.

Testing Hypotheses: The One-Sample Case

It is a simple step to go from calculating a confidence interval to testing a specific hypothesis. This is usually called the "one-sample case," since we are working with only one sample and using it to draw a conclusion about possible population values. Let us say that a friend of yours feels that college women are much taller today than when he was in school 10 years ago. He claims the average height of college women today is 5 feet 6 inches. To check out his claim, you take a random sample of 49 college women and find a mean of 65 inches. Then from an insurance company's table of ideal heights and weights, you find that the standard deviation of women in this age group is 2.5 inches. To summarize, $N = 49$, $\overline{X} = 65$ inches, and $\sigma = 2.5$ inches. Could your friend's claim of 66 inches be correct? With what degree of confidence?

The Null Hypothesis.   Stated another way, your friend has a hypothesis that we want to test. His hypothesis that the average college woman's height is 66 inches is called a *null hypothesis,* abbreviated H_0. It is often stated more formally, so we would write H_0: $\mu = 66$ inches. The symbol H_0 is saying that in the population of college women, the population mean, μ, is 66 inches.

Hypothesis testing always involves a second hypothesis, the *alternate hypothesis, H_A.* The alternate hypothesis complements the null hypothesis, in that if we reject H_0, we assume that H_A is true. In the women's heights example, H_0: $\mu = 66$ inches. If we can show that this hypothesis is unlikely, we reject H_0 in favor of the alternate hypothesis, H_A: $\mu \neq 66$ inches. Both H_0 and H_A are statements about the population mean, μ. Let us test H_0: $\mu = 66$ inches.

Calculating the standard error of the mean and both the 95% and 99% confidence intervals would give

$$\sigma_{\overline{X}} = \frac{\sigma}{\sqrt{N}} = \frac{2.5}{\sqrt{49}} = \frac{2.5}{7} = 0.36$$

95% CI: $\overline{X} \pm 1.96\sigma_{\overline{X}} = 65 \pm 1.96(.36)$
                              $= 64.29$ to 65.71

99% CI: $\overline{X} \pm 2.58\sigma_{\overline{X}} = 65 \pm 2.58(.36)$
                              $= 64.07$ to 65.93

In this example we can be very confident that μ is included in the interval 64.07 to 65.93. We would have to deny your friend's claim that the average college woman is 66 inches tall, since we are reasonably certain that the population mean is in the 64.07 to 65.93 range and 66 is outside that interval. Or stated in terms of our null hypothesis, H_0: $\mu = 66$ inches and alternate hypothesis, H_A:$\mu \neq 66$ inches, we would say we reject H_0 in favor of H_A.[†]

Confidence Intervals and Significance Levels

A few paragraphs ago we had occasion to consider the concept of levels of significance, and we noted that this concept referred to the probability of a result

---

[†]The "null" in the null hypothesis does *not* mean zero. Cohen (1994) noted that for R. A. Fisher, an eminent British statistician, the null hypothesis was the hypothesis to be nullified.

being caused by sampling error. Let us consider this last example of women's heights to show how confidence intervals, significance levels, and sampling error are related.

We note that your friend's claim that the average college woman's height is 66 inches is really a hypothesized value for the mean of the population of college women. However, our random sample of 49 women yields a mean of 65. Our question is "If the population mean is in fact 66, could we through sampling error come up with a sample mean of 65?" Using the 99% confidence interval, we found that we are reasonably certain that the population mean is included in the 64.07 to 65.93 interval, *which does not include 66.*

So we are again faced with the dilemma of determining whether the discrepancy between the hypothesized population mean of 66 and our sample mean of 65 is one of sampling error or whether the hypothesized population mean is incorrect. If we use the 95% confidence interval, the probability that all possible intervals include the population mean is .95. But this also means that the probability is .05 that they do *not* include the population mean. Similarly, with the 99% confidence interval, the probability is .01 that these intervals do not include the population mean.

Since the discrepancy between a possible $\mu = 66$ and our sample $\overline{X} = 65$ is such a rare occurrence (happening less than 1% of the time just by sampling error), we conclude that the discrepancy is *not* sampling error but that the hypothesized μ is incorrect. But there is a slight chance (probability less than .01) that we are wrong and that the discrepancy *is* due to sampling error.

We can summarize by making two general statements. With the 95% confidence interval, in the long run we stand to be in error 5% of the time; that is, 5% of the time our intervals will *not* contain the population mean. If we use the 99% confidence interval, we could be wrong 1% of the time; that is, 1% of the time our intervals would *not* contain the population mean.

These points can best be illustrated in the graph of Figure 6.3, which shows a number of 95% confidence intervals calculated from different samples. The population from which the samples were drawn consisted of the heights of college women, and the population mean is shown as $\mu = 65.3$ inches. The confidence intervals have been constructed around the mean of each sample, with the dot in the center of each interval representing the mean, and the horizontal bars representing lower and upper limits of the interval. For example, the first confidence interval shown (sample 1) was constructed from our sample with a mean height of $\overline{X} = 65$ inches and the 95% CI limits of 64.29 inches to 65.71 inches.

Notice that most of the intervals include the population mean of 65.3 inches. However, sample 4 has a confidence interval that does *not* include a μ of 65.3 inches. If we use the 95% confidence interval, we expect that 5% (or 5 out of every 100) of the samples will yield a confidence interval that will not include μ and, like sample 4, will miss μ on either the high end or low end. If we use the 99% confidence interval, we expect that 1% of the confidence intervals will not include μ.

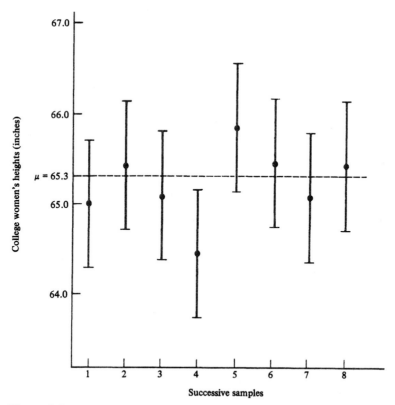

Figure 6.3
Interval estimates of the population mean of college women's heights in successive samples.

Standard Error and Size of Sample

In previous sections we have looked at how we go about the business of estimating an unknown population mean on the basis of the data from a single sample. You have seen that we do not attempt to specify a *single* value for μ but
rather an *interval* in which μ is most likely included. It should be obvious that
we would like to have the confidence interval as *narrow* as possible, since we
then have a better idea of what the population mean "really" is. Knowing that
the IQ of the average college sophomore is between 110 and 130 is not very
helpful; an interval of 118 to 123 would give us a much clearer picture of what
is going on.

What factors are responsible for reducing the width of the interval (without
causing a less stringent probability level, such as .90 or .80) so we can more ac-

curately pinpoint the population mean? In examining the formula for the standard error of the mean:

$$\sigma_{\bar{X}} = \frac{\sigma}{\sqrt{N}}$$

you note that σ and N are the two variables affecting $\sigma_{\bar{X}}$ and consequently the confidence interval itself. We could reduce the size of $\sigma_{\bar{X}}$ either by *decreasing* the standard deviation of the population or by *increasing* the size of the sample. Since we obviously do not have any control over the amount of variability in the population, we must concentrate our efforts on increasing the sample N. Table 6.2 shows how the confidence interval is reduced as you go from a sample size of 10 to 20 to 50. It follows that we would like to have our sample size as large as possible.

But What If We Do Not Know the Population Standard Deviation, σ?

We noted earlier that the formula for the standard error of the mean, $\sigma_{\bar{X}} = \sigma/\sqrt{N}$, requires that we know the value of the population standard deviation, σ. If you will remember, in all of the preceding examples we knew the value of σ and were able to calculate the standard error of the mean ($\sigma_{\bar{X}}$), use it in a confidence interval (e.g., $\bar{X} \pm 1.96\sigma_{\bar{X}}$), and make a statement regarding the possible value of the population mean.

But what do we do if we do not know the exact value of σ? Since *most* of the

Table 6.2
Decreasing the 95% confidence interval by increasing the sample size

	Sample $\bar{X} = 60$	**Population $\sigma = 5$**
If $N = 10$,	$\sigma_{\bar{X}} = \dfrac{\sigma}{\sqrt{N}} = \dfrac{5}{\sqrt{10}} = \dfrac{5}{3.1623} = 1.58$	
	$\bar{X} \pm 1.96\sigma_{\bar{X}} = 60 \pm 3.10 = 56.90$ to 63.10	
If $N = 20$,	$\sigma_{\bar{X}} = \dfrac{\sigma}{\sqrt{N}} = \dfrac{5}{\sqrt{20}} = \dfrac{5}{4.4721} = 1.12$	
	$\bar{X} \pm 1.96\sigma_{\bar{X}} = 60 \pm 2.20 = 57.80$ to 62.20	
If $N = 50$,	$\sigma_{\bar{X}} = \dfrac{\sigma}{\sqrt{N}} = \dfrac{5}{\sqrt{50}} = \dfrac{5}{7.0711} = 0.71$	
	$\bar{X} \pm 1.96\sigma_{\bar{X}} = 60 \pm 1.39 = 58.61$ to 61.39	

time we will *not* know what σ is, we will have to use a different formula than $\sigma_{\bar{x}} = \sigma/\sqrt{N}$ and use it in a slightly different procedure. But we will leave these new concepts until Chapter 9, and remember that the techniques described in this chapter require that we know the population standard deviation when we are trying to estimate the population mean.

Other Sampling Distributions

The bulk of this chapter has been spent on the sampling distribution of means, the standard error of the mean, and estimated confidence intervals for the population mean. We could go into depth for other statistics, such as the median, standard deviation, and proportion. However, in an introductory textbook it is just not possible to cover all these topics, and you are referred to any advanced statistics textbook for a treatment of these sampling distributions. But the method of approach is similar for each statistic. Each has its own sampling distribution with its standard deviation being, for example, the standard error of the median or standard error of the proportion.

In light of an earlier discussion we might briefly examine the formula for the standard error of the median, which is

$$\sigma_{Med} = \frac{1.253\sigma}{\sqrt{N}}$$

Note that the standard error of the median is approximately 1.25 times as large as the standard error of the mean. In an earlier discussion we noted that the mean was a more *stable* measure of central tendency than was the median. This fact should now be obvious, since the confidence interval using the standard error of the mean about the population *mean* is narrower than the confidence interval using the larger standard error of the median about the population *median*. This is just another way of saying that *means* of repeated samples will vary less than will the *medians* of repeated samples.

RANDOM VERSUS REPRESENTATIVE SAMPLES

Let us close out this chapter by recalling an earlier discussion of the topic of a representative sample. We noted that a representative sample was a "miniature" population that contained all the relevant characteristics of the population. Now that we have covered a number of topics on random sampling, we should remember that a random sample may or may not be a representative one; that is, a random sample may not necessarily be an accurate representation of the population. Using again the example of a "population" of colored marbles, let us say that a bag contained 50 blue, 30 red, and 20 yellow marbles. A sample of 10 that contained 5 blue, 3 red, and 2 yellow marbles would certainly be a representative sample. On the other hand, in that sample of 10, it would be entirely possible for a *random* sample to contain 10 blue marbles (remember sampling error?) and obviously not be representative of the population at all.

So why don't we use other methods of sampling, where we are likely to obtain representative samples, and dispense with random sampling altogether? The reason is that we know the shape of the sampling distribution for random samples and can estimate its standard deviation in order to set up confidence intervals, but we do not always know the nature of the distribution for other kinds of samples. As a result we may freely use representative samples for opinion polls, consumer surveys, and the like, but when we need to set up confidence intervals for estimating population means, we resort to the old reliable random sample.

SAMPLE PROBLEM 1

A group of researchers was investigating the effect of early childhood intervention on the IQ tested later on in the upper elementary grades. A well-known IQ test with a mean of 100 and a standard deviation of 16 was used to assess intelligence (i.e., $\mu = 100$ and $\sigma = 16$). A group of 40 ten-year-olds from an economically disadvantaged area of a midwestern city was given this IQ test, and a mean of 82 was calculated.

1. Calculate the 95% CI for the true mean.
2. The project director felt that children that had received early intervention should have an average score of 90 when tested at age 10. Does this study support her belief?

Our first step is to calculate the standard error of the mean.

$$\sigma_{\bar{X}} = \frac{\sigma}{\sqrt{N}} = \frac{16}{\sqrt{40}} = \frac{16}{6.3246} = 2.53$$

1. The 95% CI, $\bar{X} \pm 1.96\sigma_{\bar{X}}$, would give

$$82 \pm 1.96(2.53)$$
$$82 \pm 4.96$$
$$77.04 \text{ to } 86.96$$

2. We would be reasonably certain that the true mean for the population from which this sample came would be between approximately 77 and 87. Since an IQ of 90 is not included in the interval, we would have to conclude that the project director's statement that this age population would have an average IQ of 90 is not supported.

SAMPLE PROBLEM 2

The National Heart, Lung, and Blood Institute completed a large-scale study of cholesterol and heart disease, and reported that the national average for blood cholesterol level for 50-year-old males was 210 mg/dl with a standard deviation of 33. A total of 89 men with cholesterol readings in the average range (200 to 220) volunteered for a low cholesterol diet for 12 weeks. At the end of the dieting period their average cholesterol reading was 204 mg/dl.

1. Calculate the 95% CI for the true mean.
2. Is it possible that after 12 weeks of dieting the true mean could still be 210?

Calculating the standard error of the mean, we find

$$\sigma_{\bar{X}} = \frac{\sigma}{\sqrt{N}} = \frac{33}{\sqrt{89}} = \frac{33}{9.4340} = 3.50$$

1. The 95% CI, $\bar{X} \pm 1.96\sigma_{\bar{X}}$, would yield

$$204 \pm 1.96(3.50)$$
$$204 \pm 6.86$$
$$197.14 \text{ to } 210.86$$

2. We would be reasonably certain that the true mean for the population from which this sample came would be between approximately 197 and 211. Since the population mean of 210 is still within this interval, we would have no reason to believe that the low-cholesterol diet was effective in lowering blood cholesterol readings. Or stated in statistical terms, with a population mean of $\mu = 210$, it is possible that we could have gotten a sample with a mean of $\bar{X} = 204$ just by sampling error.

STUDY QUESTIONS

1. How are the terms *descriptive* and *inferential* used with the terms *sample* and *population*?
2. Twenty thousand students are enrolled at an eastern university. Describe the procedure you would use to obtain a random sample of 500.
3. Give some examples of *biased* samples. What might be done to protect against bias in these examples?
4. What is a sampling distribution of means? What do the symbols $\mu_{\bar{X}}$ and $\sigma_{\bar{X}}$ represent in this distribution?

5. How does the central limit theorem apply to a sampling distribution of means?
6. Define the *standard error of the mean*.
7. What do the terms *sampling error* and *chance* mean?
8. What is the purpose of the *one-sample case*?
9. How is the sampling-error-versus-real-difference dilemma "solved" by using arbitrary significance levels (e.g., .05 or .01)?
10. What effect does sample size have on the size of $\sigma_{\bar{X}}$? On the size of the confidence interval?

EXERCISES

1. Differentiate among the terms *sample, sampling distribution,* and *population*.
2. Sketch a sample distribution, a sampling distribution of means, and a population distribution. Indicate $\bar{X}$ and s, $\mu_{\bar{X}}$ and $\sigma_{\bar{X}}$, and μ and σ on these distributions, and note what they tell us about each distribution.
3. Draw a sampling distribution of means and mark off $-1.96\sigma_{\bar{X}}$ and $1.96\sigma_{\bar{X}}$. What percentage of the sample means will fall in the region outside $\pm1.96\sigma_{\bar{X}}$?
4. Using the same sketch you drew in exercise 3, darken the region outside $\pm1.96\sigma_{\bar{X}}$. What is the probability that a sample mean will deviate by this much or more just by sampling error?
5. You are in charge of testing a random sample of 121 college-bound seniors. You administer the American College Testing (ACT) program college entrance exam and calculate the means of the following four subtests.

English	*Mathematics*	*Reading*	*Science Reasoning*
$\bar{X} = 20.2$	$\bar{X} = 20.2$	$\bar{X} = 21.3$	$\bar{X} = 21.0$

   a. According to the test publisher, the standard deviation of the population of scores on the Science Reasoning subtest is $\sigma = 4.6$. Calculate the 95% CI for this subtest.
   b. A friend of yours says that the national average on the Science Reasoning subtest is around 20. In light of the confidence interval you calculated in part a, is it likely that $\mu = 20$? Why or why not?
6. Again, let us use the ACT data from exercise 5.
   a. According to the test publisher, the standard deviation of the population of scores on the mathematics subtest is $\sigma = 4.9$. Calculate the 95% CI for this subtest.
   b. Is it likely that the population mean would be 20? Explain your answer.
7. A random sample of 90 vegetarians has a mean cholesterol level of 202 mg/dl. The NHLBI study described in Sample Problem 2 reported a population stan156dard deviation of 33 mg/dl.
   a. Calculate the 95% CI for this data.
   b. Is it likely that the true mean is 210?
8. What conclusions would you have reached in exercise 7 if you had obtained the same results but had a sample size of 32? What would you conclude concerning the relationship between sample size and estimating μ?

9. A sample of 36 fourth-graders is given a popular intelligence test, and a mean of 105 is calculated. Sample Problem 1 noted that according to this test the standard deviation of IQ scores in the population was $\sigma = 16$.

   a. Calculate the 95% CI.

   b. A friend of yours is looking over your shoulder and remarks that the average IQ should be 100. Given the confidence interval that you calculated in part a, is your friend's comment likely to be true?

10. What conclusions would you have reached in exercise 9 if you had gotten the same results but had a sample size of 85? What does this result say about the relationship between sample size and estimating μ?

CHAPTER 7

Correlation

The primary duty of science is to establish
relationships between variables.

—*Anonymous*

No one would doubt for a minute that most of the great advances we have seen in medicine and technology started with an investigation of some rather simple relationship. For example, the link between cigarette smoking and lung cancer and heart disease was first reported during the 1940s by researchers who noted that the incidence of disease was directly related to the number of cigarettes smoked per day and the number of years one had smoked. Another example would be the relationship between the number of high-risk sexual behaviors and incidence of HIV infection.

Less spectacular maybe, but certainly of equal importance is the study of relationships between variables in education and the behavioral sciences. Haven't we all, at some time or another, heard questions such as "What is the relationship between high school grades and college success?" or "What is the relationship between your IQ and your ability to remember?" or "What is the relationship between college entrance exam scores and college performance?"

Questions such as these about relationships can be answered by a statistical technique called *correlation*. If there is a relationship between two variables, such as high school grades and college success, we say that they are *correlated*. The statistical techniques to be developed in Chapters 7 and 8 will demonstrate two major functions of correlation. First, we would like to develop techniques that indicate the *strength* or *amount* of the relationship so that a single value will tell us at a glance how two variables are related. Second, we would like to be able to *predict* scores on one variable from knowledge of another variable. For example, if there is a relationship between high school grades and college success, we would like to be able to actually predict your college grades on the basis of your high school grades.

Before beginning such an ambitious undertaking, let us first consider the meaning of correlation by looking at two approaches to this new concept. The first is an intuitive approach, and the second is a graphical method, called a *scatter diagram* or *scatter plot*.

AN INTUITIVE APPROACH

Let us use a rather homely example of correlation and assume that we would like to see if there is a relationship between athletic ability and scholastic ability. Are good athletes also good students? Or are the best athletes poor students, while the poorer athletes are good students? To test our hypotheses, we choose five college women soccer players and have the coach rank them on their soccer ability. (Obviously, we would want more than five subjects in an actual study, but such a small number will make our illustration easier.) After the coach has ranked the five on soccer ability, we consult the registrar's office and obtain the players' grade-point averages (GPAs), which are a measure of their academic success. We then rank the five on their scholastic ability and get the results shown in Table 7.1.

Note that Ann was the best soccer player and also the best student of this small sample. Bobbi was second best at both, and so on down to poor Erin, who is ranked last as the poorest soccer player and the poorest student. This is an illustration of *perfect positive correlation*. It is *perfect* because there are no reversals or changes from the 1-1, 2-2, 3-3, 4-4, 5-5 pairs of ranks, and it is *positive* because both variables *increase together*. If you are high on one variable, you are high on the other, and, if you are low on one, you are low on the other. *Perfect positive correlation is denoted by a coefficient of +1.00.* (We will come back to the meaning of a coefficient later, but for now regard it as a descriptive number.)

Table 7.1
Ranks on soccer ability and GPA: Positive correlation

Player	Soccer Ability	GPA
Ann	1	1
Bobbi	2	2
Cindy	3	3
Darla	4	4
Erin	5	5

Table 7.2
Ranks on soccer ability and GPA: Negative
correlation

Player	Soccer Ability	GPA
Ann	1	5
Bobbi	2	4
Cindy	3	3
Darla	4	2
Erin	5	1

But let us suppose that our little experiment had turned out just the opposite way and the rankings on soccer ability and GPA resulted in the data shown in Table 7.2.

As you can see, there is a definite relationship here, but in just the opposite direction. Ann, who is the *best* in soccer, has the *worst* GPA, the second-*best* soccer player has the second-*worst* GPA, and so on down to Erin, who is the worst soccer player but has the highest GPA. This is an illustration of *perfect negative correlation*. It is *perfect* because there are no changes or reversals from the best–worst, second-best–second-worst, third-best–third-worst, and so on, pairs of ranks, and it is *negative* because as one variable *increases* the other *decreases*. The better one is at soccer, the poorer one is at getting grades. *Perfect negative correlation is denoted by a coefficient of −1.00.*

Of course, there is the possibility that we would find no relationship at all between soccer ability and GPA. Ann might be the best at soccer and the third-best student, while Cindy might be the third best at soccer and the second-best student. In other words, there might be no pattern of relationship shown in the data. Thus there would be no correlation, and the coefficient would be simply 0, indicating no relationship.

The first two examples illustrate the extreme cases, where the correlation was either perfect positive or perfect negative, that is, 1.00 or −1.00. In practice we find that correlation coefficients may take any value between −1.00 and 1.00, such as −.80, .43, or .60. These three hypothetical examples are shown on a continuum in Figure 7.1 and might illustrate the correlation between juvenile street crime and socioeconomic level (−.80), manual dexterity and assembly line production (.43), and height and weight (.60).

Let us ponder further the correlation between height and weight. What does a correlation coefficient of .60 tell us about the data? Any coefficient less than perfect means that there have been some reversals or changes in the relative ranking. In Table 7.1, for example, suppose that Cindy had a GPA ranking of 4 while Darla's GPA ranking was 3. This reversal would result in a coefficient that was less than 1.00, but it would still be quite high and would still be positive, maybe

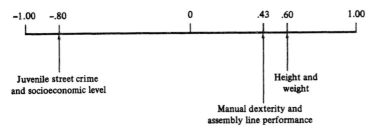

Figure 7.1
Examples of correlation coefficients on a continuum from –1.00 to 1.00.

around .90. We would still say that the relationship between soccer ability and GPA was "high" and "positive." We would say that the better players "tended to be" the better students while the poorer players "in general" were poorer students.

As there get to be more and more reversals in the relative ranks, we find that the correlation gets lower and lower. In our height-weight example with a coefficient of .60, we would note that, in general, taller people are heavier and shorter people are lighter—but there are an ample number of reversals, with some tall, skinny, light people and some short, stocky, heavy people.

There are two important characteristics of a correlation coefficient to keep in mind when evaluating a relationship: first its *sign* and then its *size*. If the sign is positive, we know that as one variable increases so does the other. So, if the relationship between height and weight or between manual dexterity and assembly line performance is positive, we know that tall people tend to be heavier than short people, or that factory workers with high dexterity scores will produce more units than their lower-scoring fellow workers. If, on the other hand, the sign is negative, we know that as one variable increases, the other decreases. Thus, if the correlation between coordination and age is negative for people over age 40, we know that as age increases, coordination decreases. Also, in the example shown in Figure 7.1, the negative relationship between juvenile street crime and socioeconomic level indicates that as socioeconomic level increases, the incidence of juvenile street crime decreases.

The *size* of the coefficient, as we noted earlier, indicates the *amount* of relationship. In Tables 7.1 and 7.2, there were no reversals in relative ranking, and the resultant coefficients were a perfect 1.00. As there get to be more and more changes in the relative rankings, the coefficient becomes lower and lower until it finally reaches 0, indicating no relationship between the variables. The correlation of .60 between height and weight, as we saw earlier, indicated that "in general" tall people tended to be heavier and short people lighter, but there would be a number of exceptions. The correlation of .43 between manual dexterity and assembly line performance shows a considerably poorer relationship than that between height and weight. We would still say that there is a tendency for good manual dexterity to be matched with good assembly line production, but there are a lot of exceptions.

THE GRAPHICAL APPROACH

There is always something appealing about an intuitive approach to an unfamiliar topic, but, unfortunately, we cannot stop with the preceding section. We must push on to a graphical and a mathematical interpretation of correlation. The intuitive approach was presented to provide a frame of reference for discussing correlation in general terms, and many of the concepts to be discussed in future sections will be a little more familiar because of that earlier treatment.

The graphical approach to correlation uses a *scatter diagram*. A scatter diagram is simply a graph showing the plotted pairs of values of the two variables being measured. In keeping with mathematical convention, we designate the vertical axis (the ordinate) as Y and the horizontal axis (the abscissa) as X, and plot each X, Y pair for all the pairs in our data. As an illustration let us say we would like to see if there is a relationship between height and weight among college males. We select a random sample of 20 college men, measure their height and weight, and enter the paired scores (X = height, Y = weight) on a data sheet, as in Table 7.3.

These X, Y pairs are plotted according to the method described in Chapter 2 for graphing a functional relationship. The resulting scatter diagram is shown in Figure 7.2. Examining this scatter diagram you would expect the correlation to be positive (since those with greater heights tend to weigh more) and quite high. However, the correlation certainly is not perfect, since you can find a number of reversals. Student P, for example, is 3 inches taller than student I but weighs 6 pounds less. If you will find those two points on the scatter diagram (student I is at [66, 159], and student P is at [69, 153]), you will see that they contribute to the "scattering" of the points away from a straight line. Anyway, there are not many of these reversals in the height-weight data, and the actual correlation coefficient is .81, which is quite high.

Table 7.3
Heights and weights of 20 college men

Student	X Height (inches)	Y Weight (pounds)	Student	X Height (inches)	Y Weight (pounds)
A	70	177	K	64	147
B	69	174	L	70	162
C	72	190	M	70	177
D	70	174	N	65	147
E	72	177	O	72	180
F	67	162	P	69	153
G	71	186	Q	68	168
H	67	165	R	68	150
I	66	159	S	71	168
J	70	171	T	69	159

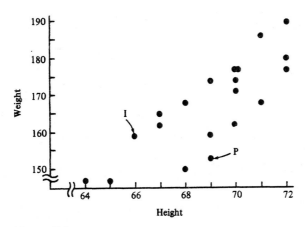

Figure 7.2
Scatter diagram of heights and weights.

Scatter Diagrams and Size of Correlation

The height-weight data of Figure 7.2, with a correlation coefficient of .81, illustrated a certain degree of "scattering" of the plotted points. Let us now take a look at a number of scatter diagrams with different patterns of plotted points and see how they are related to the size of the correlation coefficient. Four sets of data and their associated scatter diagrams are shown in Figure 7.3.

Figure 7.3a. Note that with perfect positive correlation the plotted points lie on a *straight line* going from the lower left-hand corner to the upper right-hand corner. There are no reversals in X and Y; each increase in X is accompanied by a corresponding increase in Y.

Figure 7.3b. As the correlation coefficient decreases to .83, note that there is a scattering away from the straight line of Figure 7.3a. The pattern of points is elliptical, but its major axis is still from lower left to upper right, indicating positive correlation. In general, low scores in X are paired with low scores in Y, and high values of X are paired with high values of Y. You can see that exceptions to this general statement contribute to the scattering away from the major axis of the ellipse.

Figure 7.3c. By the time the coefficient drops to near 0 (.09 in this example), the pattern of points is almost circular, and it is difficult to tell whether the relationship is positive or negative. Note that some high values of X are accompanied by *high* values of Y while other high values of X are paired with *low* values of Y. The same can be said of lower values of X. There apparently is little or no relationship between X and Y, and this fact is reflected in the coefficient of nearly 0.

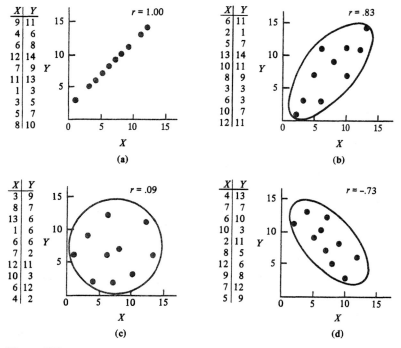

Figure 7.3
Scatter diagrams and size of correlation coefficients.

Figure 7.3d. When the relationship between *X* and *Y* is *negative*, you can see that the points lie in an ellipse whose major axis goes from the upper left-hand corner to the lower right-hand corner. This pattern, of course, occurs because *low* values of *X* are paired with *high* values of *Y* and *high* values of *X* with *low* values of *Y*. And since a correlation of −.73 is quite high, we do not expect much scattering away from a straight diagonal line but a rather tight ellipse, as shown.

CALCULATING THE PEARSON *r* (*z* SCORE METHOD)

We have finally reached the point where we are ready to actually calculate a correlation coefficient. There are a number of techniques used to calculate a measure of correlation, but one stands alone as far as popularity and universality go. This coefficient is called the Pearson *r* (after Karl Pearson [1857–1936], an English statistician), and it is derived from the *z* scores of the two distributions to be correlated. The Pearson *r* may be computed for interval or ratio data.

As an example, let us say that we would like to see if there is any relationship between proficiency in algebra and proficiency in geometry. An algebra and a

Table 7.4
The z score method for calculating the Pearson r

Individual	Algebra			Geometry			
	X	$X - \overline{X}$	z_X	Y	$Y - \overline{Y}$	z_Y	$z_X z_Y$
A	14	1	0.38	24	3	0.96	0.3648
B	16	3	1.15	23	2	0.64	0.7360
C	17	4	1.53	25	4	1.28	1.9584
D	13	—	—	21	—	—	—
E	13	—	—	20	−1	−0.32	—
F	14	1	0.38	23	2	0.64	0.2432
G	14	1	0.38	23	2	0.64	0.2432
H	10	−3	−1.15	18	−3	−0.96	1.1040
I	9	−4	−1.53	17	−4	−1.28	1.9584
J	10	−3	−1.15	16	−5	−1.60	1.8400
							$\Sigma z_X z_Y = 8.4480$

$$\overline{X} = 13 \qquad\qquad \overline{Y} = 21$$
$$s_X = 2.62 \qquad\qquad s_Y = 3.13$$

$$r = \frac{\Sigma z_X z_Y}{N - 1} = \frac{8.4480}{9} = .94$$

geometry test are given to 10 high school sophomores, with the result shown in Table 7.4.

In Table 7.4 are 10 pairs of scores, each individual having a score on X (the algebra test) and a score on Y (the geometry test). In addition to these raw scores, a z score has been calculated for both X and Y for each individual, by the simple division of each score's deviation from its mean by the standard deviation for that distribution. For example, individual A has an X score of 14, which is 1 unit above the mean of 13. That $(X - \overline{X})$ is then divided by the standard deviation of the X distribution, 2.62, for a resultant z score of 0.38. Similarly, A's z score on Y would be $z = (Y - \overline{Y})/s_Y = (24 - 21)/3.13 = 0.96$.

The next step in calculating the Pearson r is to obtain the *products of the pairs of z scores for each individual*. Each individual's z score on X is multiplied by his or her z score on Y. For individual A, $z_X = 0.38$ and $z_Y = 0.96$, so A's $z_X z_Y$ product would be 0.38×0.96, or 0.3648. Similarly, individual B would have a $z_X z_Y = 1.15 \times 0.64 = 0.7360$. After $z_X z_Y$ products are obtained for all individuals, the $z_X z_Y$ column is summed, and $\Sigma z_X z_Y$ is obtained.

The final step in the calculation of the Pearson r is the division by $N - 1$, where N is the number of pairs.

$$r = \frac{\Sigma z_X z_Y}{N - 1} \qquad\qquad (7.1)$$

For the data of Table 7.4,

$$r = \frac{8.4480}{9} = .94$$

With $r = .94$ we would conclude that there is a high positive correlation between X and Y in the data of Table 7.4. If a person has a high level of ability in algebra, he or she also excels at geometry.

Let us stop a moment and consider just what these $z_X z_Y$ products are telling us about the data and how they indicate the amount of relationship between two distributions. Consider three examples: high positive, low positive, and high negative correlations.

High Positive Values of r.   If the correlation between two variables is high positive, we expect high scores in one variable to be matched with high scores in the other variable. In terms of z scores, if a person's z_X is high, his or her z_Y should also be high. For example, in Table 7.4, individual C has a z_X of 1.53 and a z_Y of 1.28. These results, of course, indicate that C is well above the mean in both the X and Y distributions. We also expect in a situation where r is high and positive that an individual who is low in X will also score low in Y. This point is illustrated in Table 7.4 by individual J, who had a z_X of -1.15 and a z_Y of -1.60, well below the mean in both distributions.

Note that in either example the $z_X z_Y$ products are both large and *positive*. If both of a pair of z scores are positive, the resultant $z_X z_Y$ product is, of course, positive. And, if both of a pair of z scores are negative, the resultant $z_X z_Y$ product is *still positive*. Thus the sum of the products $\Sigma z_X z_Y$, will be large and positive, yielding a high value of r.

Low Positive Values of r.   In light of the preceding discussion, can you see what factors are responsible for decreasing the value of r? Just what happens as the scores become more and more scattered, as shown earlier, in Figure 7.3? Instead of finding each positive z_X paired with a positive z_Y or a negative z_X paired with a negative z_Y, we now begin to see instances where some individuals scoring high on X score lower on Y. As a result, some large positive z scores on X are paired with small positive z scores on Y, which, of course, eventually produce a smaller $\Sigma z_X z_Y$ and a smaller r. As the strength of the relationship decreases still further, some individuals with a positive z_X may score *below* the mean on Y, resulting in a negative z_Y. The resultant $z_X z_Y$ product for such individuals would be negative, and this would reduce the size of $\Sigma z_X z_Y$, and of r.

In the case where r is near 0, we would note that there would be about as many positive $z_X z_Y$ products as there were negative $z_X z_Y$ products, making $\Sigma z_X z_Y$ and r about 0.

High Negative Values of r.   We noted in the introductory material to the topic of correlation that if there were a high negative correlation between two variables, high scores on X would be paired with low values on Y, and low values on X

would be matched with high values on Y. In terms of z scores, note that this means that a large *positive* z score on X is paired with a large *negative* z score on Y, and a large *negative* z_X is paired with a large *positive* z_Y. As a result the $z_X z_Y$ product for most individuals will be negative. This, of course, means that the sum of the cross products, $\Sigma z_X z_Y$, will also be negative and will yield a negative r.

Computational Formula for the Pearson r

The z score method, just described, for calculating r is extremely tedious and time-consuming, since computing a $z_X z_Y$ for each individual involves a number of different steps. A much more convenient technique requires only the sums of the various columns on a correlation worksheet. The computational formula is

$$r = \frac{N\Sigma XY - \Sigma X \Sigma Y}{\sqrt{N\Sigma X^2 - (\Sigma X)^2} \; \sqrt{N\Sigma Y^2 - (\Sigma Y)^2}} \tag{7.2}$$

where N is the number of pairs and the rest of the terms are simply the sums of the X, X^2, Y, Y^2, and XY columns. All the terms are familiar except ΣXY, which is the sum of the products of each person's pair of scores. For example, in Table 7.5, the XY product for individual A is $14 \times 24 = 336$; for individual B it is $16 \times 23 = 368$, and so on. The sum of this column is $\Sigma XY = 2,799$.

Table 7.5 shows the calculated r between the algebra and geometry scores to be .93, almost the same as the r calculated by the z score method shown in Table 7.4. The z score and computational formulas are algebraically identical, and the difference between .93 and .94 is due simply to rounding error.

Although the computational formula may look somewhat imposing, this formula will simplify computations considerably. It should be emphasized that, compared to the z score method, the computational formula will result in the most accurate calculation of r, since it is less subject to rounding error.

The computational formula is obviously preferred, since the z score method, as was mentioned earlier, requires a number of tedious steps with each score value. However, the z score formula was included to show just what the Pearson r is measuring, since with the raw score methods it is not possible to see what the individual pairs of scores are doing.

Testing r for Significance

Up to this point we have been treating r simply as a descriptive statistic, meaning that it describes the mathematical relationship between pairs of scores. A descriptive statistic is useful, to be sure, and there are many times when we may wish to know the amount of relationship in a set of data without needing to make inferences concerning a population. However, if we wish to use correlational techniques to *predict* one variable from another, or to make inferences regarding the amount of relationship between two variables in the *population*, we find that correlation is indeed a very powerful tool in statistical analysis.

Table 7.5
Calculating the Pearson r: Computational formula

Individual	Algebra X	Geometry Y	X^2	Y^2	XY
A	14	24	196	576	336
B	16	23	256	529	368
C	17	25	289	625	425
D	13	21	169	441	273
E	13	20	169	400	260
F	14	23	196	529	322
G	14	23	196	529	322
H	10	18	100	324	180
I	9	17	81	289	153
J	10	16	100	256	160
	$\Sigma X = 130$	$\Sigma Y = 210$	$\Sigma X^2 = 1{,}752$	$\Sigma Y^2 = 4{,}498$	$\Sigma XY = 2{,}799$

$$r = \frac{N\Sigma XY - \Sigma X \Sigma Y}{\sqrt{N\Sigma X^2 - (\Sigma X)^2}\ \sqrt{N\Sigma Y^2 - (\Sigma Y)^2}}$$

$$= \frac{10(2{,}799) - (130)(210)}{\sqrt{10(1{,}752) - (130)^2}\ \sqrt{10(4{,}498) - (210)^2}}$$

$$= \frac{27{,}990 - 27{,}300}{\sqrt{17{,}520 - 16{,}900}\ \sqrt{44{,}980 - 44{,}100}}$$

$$= \frac{690}{\sqrt{620}\ \sqrt{880}} = \frac{690}{(24.90)(29.66)}$$

$$r = \frac{690}{738.53} = .93$$

In order to be able to use correlation in this way, we must observe some rules of sampling, just as we did for the mean in the last chapter. These rules, or assumptions, are stated explicitly in Chapter 8, but for now we are concerned primarily with just one—that of a random sample from the population.

If we wanted to know, for example, the relationship between intelligence and school grades for children in the sixth grade, we would want to conduct our study with a *random* sample from a population of sixth-graders. We would then be able to generalize the results from our sample of 100 or 500 or 1,000 to the population of sixth-graders everywhere.

But we face a problem similar to that mentioned in the last chapter: Does our calculated correlation coefficient represent the actual situation out there in the real world, or *is it due to sampling error?* Is it possible that in the population from which we drew our sample the true correlation is 0 and the r calculated from our sample is due simply to sampling error? We can answer this question, at least on a probability basis, by taking the next step in a correlational analysis—testing our obtained *r* for significance. Stated more formally, after we have calculated the *r* for the sample, we must determine if our *r* could have arisen by chance alone from a sampling distribution of *r*'s whose mean is 0.

Chance Correlation.   The preceding statement might be confusing at first, so let us use an example to help clarify some of the important concepts implicit in that statement. Imagine yourself in a room with 39 other people, taking part in a little demonstration. Forty slips of paper are numbered from 1 to 40, dropped in a hat, and mixed thoroughly. The hat is then passed around, and each of you draws a number without looking into the hat. After this is done, another 40 slips of paper, numbered from 1 to 40, are placed in the hat, and the procedure is repeated. Each of you now has two slips of paper, and we ask, "What is the relationship between the first number you drew and the second number?" Since both were random draws, you would undoubtedly say that there is no relationship at all. However, if we calculated *r* for the 40 pairs of numbers we would very likely not get an *r* that is exactly 0. It would probably be very close to 0, such as .07 or −.02, but it certainly does not surprise us that we do not calculate an *r* that is exactly equal to 0. This discrepancy, similar to that noted between a sample mean $(\overline{X})$ and the population mean (μ) in the last chapter, is due to sampling error.

So, we certainly would not be very concerned in this hypothetical demonstration if we actually obtained an *r* that is .07 or −.02 or .11 instead of exactly 0. What *does* concern us is the reverse situation, where we run a correlational study, compute an *r*, and then wonder whether the "true" correlation in the population is really 0 and our *r* is due to sampling error.

The Null Hypothesis Again

We found in Chapter 6 that the null hypothesis was a very efficient way of evaluating the difference between a sample mean and a hypothesized population mean. We can apply the same logic to our sample correlation coefficient. We would begin by assuming that there is no relationship between the two variables in the population. This assumption, of course, means that the population correlation coefficient is assumed to be zero. The symbol for the population correlation coefficient is ρ (Greek letter rho), so our null hypothesis would be $H_0: \rho = 0$. And if we were to believe that H_0 is unlikely, we would reject H_0 in favor of the alternate hypothesis, $H_A: \rho \neq 0$.

We will again use the confidence interval approach that was introduced in Chapter 6 to help us out of our dilemma. But, instead of taking an infinite number of sample *means* from some population and constructing a hypothetical sampling distribution of sample means, let us construct a sampling distribution of sample *r*'s.

Sampling Distribution of r.   We first assume that the true correlation in the population from which we draw our samples is 0. If we then draw an infinite number of random samples from this population and calculate an *r* between the two variables we are interested in, we will have a *sampling distribution* of r. This sampling distribution of r's would be normal (if the size of each of our samples was greater than 30), its mean would be 0, and its standard deviation would be called the standard error of r, s_r.

As with the sampling distribution of means, we could then make such statements as

1. 95% of all sample r's would fall between $0 \pm 1.96s_r$.
2. 99% of all sample r's would fall between $0 \pm 2.58s_r$.

The formula for the standard error of r, which is an estimate of the standard deviation of this sampling distribution of r's, is

$$s_r = \frac{1}{\sqrt{N-1}} \qquad (7.3)$$

where N is the size of the sample.

For an example, let us say that we have tested a random sample of 50 high school juniors to find the correlation between their college entrance exam scores and their scores on a current events test and found $r = .45$.

Testing the Null Hypothesis.　In order to evaluate our sample $r = .45$, we begin by assuming the null hypothesis, H_0: $\rho = 0$. And, as usual, our alternate hypothesis would be H_A: $\rho \neq 0$. We first calculate s_r to begin construction of our confidence interval.

$$s_r = \frac{1}{\sqrt{N-1}} = \frac{1}{\sqrt{50-1}} = \frac{1}{\sqrt{49}} = \frac{1}{7} = 0.143$$

We can now set up a confidence interval and say that if ρ is 0, we would expect 95% of the sample r's to fall between $0 \pm 1.96s_r$. The equation would be as follows:

$$0 \pm 1.96(0.143) = 0 \pm .28 = -.28 \text{ to } .28$$

Similarly, 99% of the sample r's would fall between $0 \pm 2.58s_r$:

$$0 \pm 2.58(0.143) = 0 \pm .37 = -.37 \text{ to } .37$$

Figure 7.4 shows this hypothetical sampling distribution with the 99% confidence interval about the hypothesized mean of 0.

But where does our sample $r = .45$ enter the picture? Note from Figure 7.4 that our $r = .45$ is *outside* this interval and, given the preceding assumptions, would be branded as a very rare occurrence. Specifically, if the true correlation in the population were indeed 0, we would obtain an r as large as or larger than .45 due to sampling error less than 1% of the time. Again, following the logic of the last chapter, we must now make a decision. Is the true correlation really 0

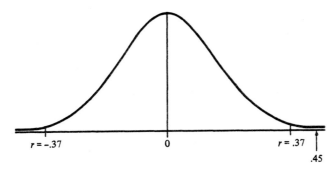

Figure 7.4
Sampling distribution of *r* when hypothesized population correlation is 0.

and our sample *r* one of those rare occurrences caused by sampling error? Or is
it not sampling error at all, and is the true correlation some other value than 0?
Since by sampling error alone, *r*'s as large as or larger than .37 happen less than
1% of the time, we would reject H_0: $\rho = 0$ in favor of H_A: $\rho \neq 0$. We conclude
that our *r* of .45 is not sampling error and that the population ρ is something
larger than 0. In terms of our example, we would conclude that the correlation
between college entrance exam scores and knowledge of current events in the
population is not 0. In effect, we have shown that a relationship could exist on
the basis of our sample. We would state that our sample *r* is significantly different from zero at the .01 level.

Using Table B to Test r *for Significance.*   The confidence interval approach that we
have outlined not only is rather time-consuming but also should be avoided if the
size of your sample is less than 30. The shape of the sampling distribution of *r*
when *N* is less than 30 is *nonnormal,* and the normal curve values of 1.96 and
2.58 for the 95% and 99% confidence intervals would be in error. For this reason
a table of *r*'s necessary for *r* to be significant at the .05 and .01 levels is printed in
Table B in Appendix 3. The tabled values are to be interpreted in the same manner as in the confidence interval approach.

   Before using Table B in an example, you must note that the left-hand column
contains the term *degrees of freedom (df)*. For purposes of using Table B, we must
remember that the degrees of freedom in calculating *r* is equal to *N* − 2, where *N*
is the number of pairs of scores. We will have more to say later about the degrees
of freedom concept, but for now just remember when you use Table B that the
degrees of freedom is equal to *N* − 2.

   As an example of the use of Table B, let us say that we found *r* = .42 for 25
students given a manual dexterity test (*X*) and a hand steadiness test (*Y*). Is this
r significantly different from 0? We turn to Table B and note that for 23 degrees of
freedom (*df* = 25 − 2 = 23), *r* at the .05 level is .396 and at the .01 level is .505.
These values are to be interpreted in the same way as when we constructed a confidence interval; that is, 95% of the sample *r*'s would fall between −.396 and .396

if the true population correlation were 0. Similarly, 99% of the sample r's would fall between $-.505$ and $.505$ if the true correlation in the population were 0.

With our sample value of $r = .42$, we note that this is a rather rare occurrence (since r's outside the $-.396$ to $.396$ interval occur less than 5% of the time by random sampling from a distribution of sample r's whose mean is 0), so we would reject the null hypothesis, H_0: $\rho = 0$ in favor of the alternate hypothesis, H_A: $\rho \neq 0$. We conclude that the true correlation is not 0, and we would say that the obtained r of .42 is significantly different from 0 at the .05 level.

Note that with a sample of this size you would have to obtain an r of at least .505 to be able to say it was significantly different from 0 *at the .01 level*. We would conclude that the probability that our r of .42 arose through sampling error is between .01 and .05.

If we would examine Table B carefully, we would note that with very large sample sizes (an N of 500 or even 1,000) our correlation coefficient can be quite small and still be significantly different from zero. With such large samples a coefficient of .10 or .20 can be declared "very significant." So, it is always necessary to examine the actual size of correlation coefficients, instead of relying on a statement that "the correlation between such and such was highly significant." We will treat this topic again in the "How High Is High?" section at the end of the chapter.

Establishing Confidence Intervals for the True ρ

After one has concluded that the obtained r is significantly different from 0, the logical next step would be to set up a confidence interval for the true correlation, in much the same way that we set up confidence intervals for the true mean in Chapter 6. It would then be possible to make a statement that, for example, $p = .95$ that the population ρ is included in the interval .47 to .61. However, determining confidence intervals for the true correlation is a rather complicated affair, and you are referred to any advanced statistics textbook for this involved operation. The reason that it is not a simple, straightforward technique is that the sampling distribution is nonnormal for population coefficients that are not 0. The sampling distribution of r becomes more and more skewed as the population correlation gets larger. An excellent treatment of establishing confidence intervals for the true correlation can be found in Minium, King, and Bear (1993).

Restrictions on Using the Pearson r

There are two restrictions on the Pearson r (other than the fact that it requires interval or ratio data) that must be kept in mind. First, the relationship between X and Y must be linear. Second, the technique requires pairs of values; that is, for every observation, you must have a value for X and a value for Y. This second restriction is self-explanatory, since you need X, Y pairs to plot a scatter diagram, but the linearity restriction deserves further clarification.

A linear relationship between X and Y means that the plotted points in a scatter diagram ascend (or descend, if r is negative) in a regular fashion such as shown in the scatter diagrams of Figure 7.3a, 7.3b, and 7.3d.

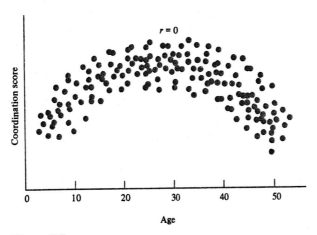

Figure 7.5
A curvilinear relationship: coordination as a function of age.

A nonlinear relationship between X and Y is shown in Figure 7.5, which plots coordination scores as a function of age. There is no doubt that there is a high degree of relationship between age and coordination. As you can see in Figure 7.5, coordination scores increase as the child gets older, up to about age 15. From 15 years of age until about 40, coordination scores stay the same, and they decline after age 40. The scatter diagram indicates a high degree of relationship, since the points are tightly clustered, but $r = 0$ for these data, since the relationship of X and Y is curvilinear (the points are clustered about a curved line). Mathematically speaking, the Pearson r measures the amount of *linear* relationship present in two distributions, and the interpretation of r will be in error if the relationship between X and Y is nonlinear. It is a good practice to plot a scatter diagram to check for nonlinearity when using the correlational method, as well as to check for "outliers," which will be explained shortly.

THE SPEARMAN RANK-DIFFERENCE METHOD

There is a convenient shortcut for calculating the correlation between two variables if N is relatively small, that is, less than 30 or so. The procedure is called the Spearman rank-difference method, and it uses the ranks of the scores instead of the scores themselves. The formula for the Spearman coefficient, r_s, is

$$r_s = 1 - \frac{6\Sigma D^2}{N(N^2 - 1)} \qquad (7.4)$$

where

r_s = the coefficient (some older textbooks use the Greek symbol ρ)
ΣD^2 = the sum of the squared differences between ranks
N = the number of pairs of ranks

Calculating the Spearman r_s

The Spearman r_s can be calculated for data that are already in the form of ranks or that can be converted to ranks. Let us first consider the example of Table 7.6, where a teacher has ranked 10 children on "social responsiveness" and "conversational skills." Is there any relationship between these two variables?

Note that you obtain the quantity ΣD^2 by first listing the pairs of ranks for each individual. Then you subtract the rank on one variable from the rank on the other variable to obtain the difference (D) for each pair. You square these differences to get D^2 and sum the D^2 column to obtain ΣD^2. Note that after you substitute $\Sigma D^2 = 18$ and $N = 10$ into the formula, you subtract the resulting fraction, 0.11, from 1 to obtain $r_s = .89$. A coefficient of .89 would indicate a strong relationship between social responsiveness and conversational skills as judged by this teacher.

Converting Existing Data to Ranks

When one or both of the variables to be correlated are measurements of one sort or another, the scores must be ranked; the highest score receives a rank of 1, the next highest a rank of 2, and so on. As an illustration of this method, let us con-

Table 7.6
The relationship between teacher rankings on social responsiveness and conversational skills

Child	Social Rank	Skills Rank	D	D^2
A	2	1	1	1
B	4	3	1	1
C	1	2	1	1
D	8	8	0	—
E	3	6	3	9
F	6	4	2	4
G	9	10	1	1
H	5	5	0	—
I	10	9	1	1
J	7	7	0	—
				$\Sigma D^2 = 18$

$$r_s = 1 - \frac{6\Sigma D^2}{N(N^2 - 1)} = 1 - \frac{6(18)}{10(100 - 1)}$$

$$= 1 - \frac{108}{990} = 1 - 0.11$$

$$r_s = .89$$

sider an attempt by an avid baseball fan to answer the age-old question of whether there is a relationship between players' salaries and how well the team does. He had recently found an article in the sports pages that listed total salaries for the different teams, and then looked up the final season standings for that year in the American League. The results for the 14 teams are shown in Table 7.7. Let us use the Spearman rank-difference method to determine the correlation between the teams' payrolls (shown in millions of dollars) and their final won-lost percentage.

Note that when there are tied values, *each observation is assigned the average rank for the tied positions*. For example, Baltimore and Detroit both had records of .525. Since these values occupy the rank positions of 5 and 6, both are assigned a rank of 5.5 in the first rank (R_1) column. Similarly, both Minnesota and California had records of .438, which put them in the 11th and 12th positions, so they are both ranked at 11.5.

Table 7.7
Correlation between won-lost records and team payroll for American League baseball teams

Team	Won-Lost Percent	Payroll (Millions)	R_1	R_2	D	D^2
Toronto	.586	52	1	1	0	—
New York	.543	46	3	2	1	1
Baltimore	.525	29	5.5	10	4.5	20.25
Detroit	.525	37	5.5	6	.5	.25
Boston	.494	45	9	3	6	36
Chicago	.580	42	2	4	2	4
Kansas City	.519	40	7	5	2	4
Cleveland	.469	16	10	14	4	16
Minnesota	.438	27	11.5	11.5	0	—
Milwaukee	.426	25	13	13	0	—
Texas	.531	35	4	8	4	16
Seattle	.506	33	8	9	1	1
California	.438	27	11.5	11.5	0	—
Oakland	.420	36	14	7	7	49
						$\Sigma D^2 = 147.50$

$$r_s = 1 - \frac{6 \Sigma D^2}{N(N^2 - 1)} = 1 - \frac{6(147.5)}{14(196 - 1)}$$

$$r_s = 1 - \frac{885}{2,730} = 1 - .32$$

$$r_s = .68$$

Is r_s Significantly Different from 0?

We have already seen that it is possible to obtain a correlation coefficient that is due to chance or sampling error, so we must test our obtained r_s to see if it is significantly different from 0. Table C in Appendix 3 lists the values of r_s that are necessary for r_s to be significantly different from 0 at the .05 and .01 levels of significance. For example, with an N of 20, the tabled value of r_s at the .05 level is .450. As before, this means that an obtained r_s of .450 or greater would happen by sampling error alone less than 5% of the time.

In our example in Table 7.7, we found r_s = .68. Is this significantly different from 0? Entering Table C with an N of 14, we find the tabled values of r_s at the .05 and .01 levels to be .545 and .716, respectively. Since our r_s of .68 is *greater than* .545, we would reject the null hypothesis, H_0: ρ = 0 in favor of the alternate hypothesis, H_A: $\rho \neq 0$. We would conclude that a correlation coefficient of this size did not happen just through sampling error, and we would state that it is significantly different from 0 at the .05 level. In terms of the study, we would conclude that a relationship exists between the players' salaries on a team and the team won-lost record—those teams with the highest paid players had the better won-lost records. However, as we shall soon see, this outcome does not necessarily imply a cause-and-effect relationship.

The Meaning of r_s

The rationale for interpreting the rank-difference method is a simple one. Note that when there is perfect positive correlation between two variables, the pairs of ranks for each individual would be identical. This means that all the differences (D) would be 0, the differences squared would all be 0, and the fraction $6(\Sigma D^2)/N(N^2 - 1)$ would be 0, leaving $r_s = 1 - 0 = 1$.

As the relationship drops, the differences and ΣD^2 increase and r_s, of course, gets smaller. Finally, when there is a negative correlation, the differences and ΣD^2 are very large indeed so that the fraction to be subtracted from 1 is greater than 1, resulting in a negative r_s.

The Spearman r_s can be computed on pairs of measurements where one or both of the variables are expressed in an ordinal scale. The Spearman coefficient is nothing more than the Pearson r applied to *untied* ranks, and it would be interpreted in the same manner as the Pearson r. However, when some of the ranks are *tied*, the formula for r_s does not yield the same result as the formula for r and is only an approximation of r. The difference is negligible if there are not too many tied ranks. Also, since r_s is computed on ordinal data (remember that ranking yields an ordinal scale), it cannot take the place of the Pearson r in the regression equation or the standard error of estimate—two concepts to be discussed in Chapter 8. Given these shortcomings of r_s, we are still likely to see the Spearman method used occasionally because of its computational simplicity.

SOME CONCLUDING REMARKS ON CORRELATION

Correlation is an informative and descriptive tool—one of the few statistics that can be understood by nonstatisticians. However, there are some aspects of the technique that can easily be overlooked and possibly lead to errors of interpretation. Some of these finer points follow.

Correlation versus Cause and Effect

If it should turn out that your calculated r indicates that two variables are correlated, this finding does not necessarily indicate a *cause-and-effect* relationship. After all, the Pearson r merely tells the strength of a *mathematical* relationship between X and Y: It is left to the researcher to determine the reason for the correlation. One may find that there is a correlation between socioeconomic level and school performance, or between family income and a child's IQ, but we cannot say that one causes the other unless we have additional information about the variables involved. The calculation of r is only the first step in a correlational study, and it indicates the *degree* to which two variables are related. The *why* of the relationship is a nonmathematical matter left up to the ingenuity of the researcher.

Is the Relationship of X and Y Due to Z?

A very common result noted in correlational studies is that the relationship between two variables is caused by a third variable. For example, a study of the mental ages of elementary school pupils and their height in inches would indicate a substantial correlation. Such a spurious correlation, obviously, does not mean that there is any meaningful relationship between mental age and height, because the relationship is due to a third variable: the chronological age of the children. Both mental age and height increase with chronological age, and thus the relationship between mental age and height is a statistical artifact. When you read the results of correlational studies, it is a good idea to consider the possibility of other variables contributing to an obtained correlation. There are statistical techniques designed to handle this problem, and you are referred to one of the advanced textbooks listed in the References for information on these techniques. (See also Table 7.10.)

The Effect of Outliers

An *outlier*, as we noted in Chapter 4, is an extreme score, compared to the rest of the distribution. If you are measuring heights in several college men in order to determine how high up on the wall a shelf should go, you would not want to base your range on the 7-foot-2-inch basketball star who happened to show up in your sample. As we saw earlier in the chapters on frequency distributions and central tendency, skewness is often the result of the presence of one or more outliers.

Identifying outliers is especially important in correlational studies, since outliers exert a marked effect on the correlation coefficient. As an example let us re-

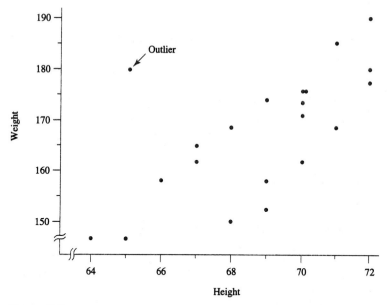

Figure 7.6
Scatter diagram of heights and weights and one outlier.

peat the scatter diagram of the height-weight data of Figure 7.2 where we noted that the correlation between height and weight for 20 college men was $r = .81$. Let us add an outlier—a college male who is short in stature but heavy for his height, 5 feet 5 inches and 180 pounds. This man's height and weight have been plotted on Figure 7.6, and, as can be seen, the point is somewhat above and to the left of the majority of the points on the scatter diagram.

But especially important to note is that the addition of this *single* outlier changes the height-weight correlation from .81 to .65, a considerable drop in the amount of relationship between height and weight shown by the other 20 in the sample. It is important that we be aware of outliers in our data, and plotting a scatter diagram for data in correlational studies is essential to identifying extreme cases.

Restriction of Range

The correlation coefficient is highly sensitive to the range of scores on which it is calculated. As the range becomes more and more restricted, the size of the coefficient decreases. For example, a college entrance exam, given to incoming freshmen during the first week on campus, might correlate .50 with college GPA at the end of the freshman year. However, if we continue to calculate the correlation coefficient at the end of the sophomore, junior, and senior years, we would find a marked reduction in the size of r. One of the reasons for a declining r is that many of those with lower entrance exam scores would drop out of school after an unsuccessful freshman year, a few more after the sophomore year, and so on, and the range of the scores would decrease as these lower scores drop out of the picture.

Similarly, the Graduate Record Exam (GRE), used for screening applicants for admission to graduate school, correlates quite highly with success in postgraduate study. However, if we select a given graduate program (e.g., a psychology department at a large university) and attempt to correlate GRE with course grades, we would be lucky indeed to find an r as large as .35 or .40. (See Table 7.8.) These low coefficients are due to the fact that the range of GRE scores has been severely restricted, since only those with very high GRE scores were initially admitted to this graduate program. There are several techniques for dealing with the problem of a restricted range, but they are beyond the scope of this book; you are referred to one of the advanced textbooks listed in the References.

How High Is High?

It is a very common practice to describe the strength of a correlation by such descriptive adjectives as high, low, moderate, strong, weak, and the like. And some writers encourage this practice by stating that correlation coefficients can be described according to the following scheme:

Very high r = .80 or above
Strong r = .60 to .80
Moderate r = .40 to .60
Low r = .20 to .40
Very low r = .20 or less

Although such descriptors may be convenient for summarizing a series of research studies ("The correlation between manual aptitude tests and job performance on a production line is low"), it makes much more sense to use the actual value of the correlation coefficient itself. When asked how tall a friend of yours is, you don't answer "very tall" if you know he is exactly 6 feet 4 inches. You simply say that he is 6 feet 4 inches tall. So, in the interest of precision, you are encouraged to use the exact value of r (or range of values, if more than one study is being cited) rather than the vague and somewhat ambiguous descriptors that we just listed.

Aside from scientific precision, there is another reason for avoiding descriptive terms for the strength of a correlation. Whether a correlation coefficient is high, moderate, or low depends, to a certain extent, on what variables are being correlated. For example, the correlation between two forms of an intelligence test would be considered low if r = .80, while the correlation between college entrance exam scores and college success would be exceedingly high with the same value of r. Again, the scientist can avoid confusion by stating the exact value of r and letting the readers make their own value judgment.

In fact, there is one area of psychology where the correlation coefficients between variables are consistently small—that of health psychology (Rosenthal,

Table 7.8
Some examples of correlation studies

Variables	*r*
Consummate confidence (bet the mortgage)	
IQ test reliability	.90s
Standardized School Achievement Test reliability	.90s
IQ and school achievement—grade 1	.85–.90
IQ and school achievement—college from high school	.50–.55
GRE and graduate school grade-point average	.00–.40
IQ of identical twins reared apart	.75
IQ of identical twins reared together	.85
IQ of fraternal twins and/or siblings	.50
IQ and memory (higher with age into adulthood)	.50–.70
Height and weight	.55–.60
The ubiquitous .35 correlation	
School achievement (cognitive) and affective	.35
School achievement and socioeconomic status (SES)	.35
School achievement and self-concept	.35
School achievement and motivation	.35
School achievement and student ratings of teacher effectiveness	.35
IQ and self-concept	.35
IQ and creativity	.35
Considerable confidence (bet the rent)	
Traffic fatalities and indices of progress in third world countries	–.70
IQ and age of extremely deprived children	–.70
IQ of parents and children	.50
IQ between spouses	.50
Physical similarity between spouses (believe it or not)	~.40
Different creativity tests	.35
Aversive maternal behavior and aversive child behavior	.55
Reading achievement and television viewing	–.05
Some confidence (don't bet, but say that you did)	
IQ (school achievement) and sibsize	–.30

From John Follman, "Cornucopia of Correlations," *American Psychologist, 39* (1984), 701–702, by permission of the author.

1990). It is not unusual to find a coefficient of .09 between cigarette smoking and lung cancer, or a coefficient of .14 between serum cholesterol and coronary heart disease. The reason these small coefficients are so important is that huge numbers of people are involved. For example, in one study, the correlation between taking an aspirin and incidence of heart attack was only .034. Only 0.94 percent of aspirin users had a heart attack, while 1.71 percent of placebo users had a heart attack.* These small percentages reflect the low correlation, but when one remembers that there are between 1.0 and 1.2 million heart attacks annually in the United States, the small difference in percentages results in a very large number of additional heart attack victims.

As we noted earlier, we need to be aware of the actual size of the correlation coefficient, as well as whether or not it is significantly different from zero, before we can draw conclusions from a correlational study. A third component could well be added to these two—that of repeatability. In other words, if a correlational study is repeated, would we get similar results? In fact, the more often a study is repeated with similar results, the more confidence we have in any single study.

Follman (1984) called attention to the importance of repeatability by classifying a number of correlational studies into three types as shown in Table 7.8. He notes that the correlations reported in the "Consummate Confidence" category have been reported many times, but those in the other two categories have been found less frequently, and he suggests that they be treated accordingly.

But What Does Correlation Really Mean?

We have used a number of techniques to help us interpret different values of r.

1. At first we used an intuitive approach to show how the size of r depended on the number of reversals of ranks in the two variables.

2. Then we proceeded to a graphical approach and examined scatter diagrams. Here we found that a larger value of r would have the points tightly clustered in a skinny ellipse, while a lower value of r would have an almost circular pattern of points.

3. We then looked at the calculation of the Pearson r using the z score method. Here we noted that if scores on X that were well above the mean (yielding large positive z's) were paired with large values of Y, large positive r's would occur. On the other hand, if the relationship of X and Y were *reversed* (i.e., if small x's were paired with large Y's, etc.), large negative r's would occur. And, as more exceptions in either of the preceding cases occurred (some small X's with large Y's, some small X's with small Y's, etc.), the values of r approached zero, indicating, of course, no relationship between X and Y.

Using these three methods, we have learned to understand correlation in *relative* terms. For example, we may find that one r is *larger* than another, or that one r indicates a relationship between X and Y while another r is near zero, or that one r is positive and another is negative. But what does an $r = .50$ mean? It is not 50 percent of something. It does not indicate twice as much of a relation-

---

*From Robert Rosenthal, "How Are We Doing in Soft Psychology?" *American Psychologist, 45* (1990), 775–777, by permission of the author.

Table 7.9
Given all cases above the median on variable 1, percentage of
cases above and below the median on variable 2

True Correlation	Percent Expected on Second Variable[a]	
	Above Median	Below Median
.00	50.0	50.0
.10	53.1	46.9
.20	56.2	43.8
.30	59.5	40.5
.40	63.0	37.0
.50	66.5	33.5
.60	70.3	29.7
.70	74.5	25.5
.80	79.3	20.7
.90	85.3	14.7
1.00	100.0	0.0

From John Duke, "Tables to Help Students Grasp Size Differences in
Simple Correlations," *Teaching of Psychology, 5* (1978), 219–221, by
permission of Lawrence Erlbaum Associates, Inc.
[a]For negative correlations, reverse column entries.

ship as an *r* of .25. It does not indicate a relationship that is one-half of a perfect correlation of *r* = 1.00. If these are what *r* is not, then what information does *r* give us?

One easy procedure to help us understand what an individual correlation coefficient means is possible with the use of Table 7.9. For example, for any positive correlation, we would expect that for those scoring above the median on the first variable, a large percentage of those folks would also score above the median on the second variable.

As an example let us use the *r* = .40 that we noted earlier for the correlation between GRE scores and graduate school GPA. From Table 7.9 we see that of those scoring above the median on the first variable, we would expect that 63 percent would also score above the median on the second variable. However, 37 percent would score *below* the median on the second variable. This figure, of course, is much better than chance (50 percent score above, 50 percent below on the second variable). Nevertheless, this example serves as a reminder that even for relatively high *r*'s, a substantial percentage drop below the median on the second variable. As a further example, at *r* = .90, for those above the median on the first variable, almost 15 percent fall below the median on the second.

Table 7.10
Some other correlational methods

Point-biserial *r:*   One dichotomous variable (yes/no; male/female) and one interval or ratio variable

Biserial *r:*   One variable forced into a dichotomy (grade distribution dichotomized to "pass" and "fail") and one interval or ratio variable

Phi coefficient: Both variables are dichotomous on a nominal scale (male/female versus high school graduate/dropout)

Tetrachoric *r:*   Both variables are dichotomous with underlying normal distributions (pass/fail on a test versus low/high class attendance)

Correlation ratio: There is a curvilinear rather than linear relationship between the variables (also called the eta coefficient)

Partial correlation: The relationship between two variables is influenced by a third variable (e.g., a correlation between mental age and height, which is strongly influenced by chronological age)

Multiple *R:*   The maximum correlation between a dependent variable and a combination of independent variables (a college freshman's GPA as predicted by her high school grades in English, biology, government, and algebra)

It should be noted that the correlation coefficients shown in Table 7.9 are "true correlations," that is, population values. Since the Pearson *r*'s we calculate are based on a limited number of cases, the percentages shown are subject to error. However, we can still get a rough idea of the amount of fluctuation that occurs when the correlation is less than perfect.

Other Correlational Techniques

In our introduction to the concept of correlation, we have just barely scratched the surface of correlational topics, and the inclusion of the Pearson *r* and Spearman r_s in this chapter was dictated mainly by the popularity of these methods. There are a wide variety of other techniques, however, developed for rather specific applications. Some are modifications of the Pearson *r,* while others are based on probability functions. Some of the more popular techniques and possible applications are shown in Table 7.10.

Table 7.10 is not intended to be an exhaustive list of possible correlational methods but a sampling of the possible ways in which correlational research can be used. The serious student is referred to one of the advanced textbooks listed in the References.

SAMPLE PROBLEM

The Drug Enforcement Administration (DEA) provides federal funds to the states for marijuana eradication. The following table presents a random sample of 30 states showing the amount spent (in thousands of dollars) by each state last year and the number (in thousands) of marijuana plants destroyed.

Calculator Solution

Calculate the Pearson r to see if there was a relationship between the amount of money spent and the number of plants reported destroyed. For example, the first state mentioned reported spending $60,000 to destroy 110,000 plants.

From Table B in Appendix 3 we note that with 28 degrees of freedom ($N - 2 = 28$), r at the .01 level is .463. Since our value of .66 exceeds this tabled value, we conclude that $r = .66$ is significantly different from 0 at the .01 level. There are a number of exceptions in the data shown, but *in general* greater numbers of plants eradicated are associated with larger expenditures of funds.

State	Spent (X)	Plants (Y)	X^2	Y^2	XY
1	60	110	3,600	12,100	6,600
2	40	6	1,600	36	240
3	80	88	6,400	7,744	7,040
4	40	23	1,600	529	920
5	75	107	5,625	11,449	8,025
6	30	5	900	25	150
7	55	69	3,025	4,761	3,795
8	15	13	225	169	195
9	20	5	400	25	100
10	15	1	225	1	15
11	22	89	484	7,921	1,958
12	20	4	400	16	80
13	60	107	3,600	11,449	6,420
14	50	62	2,500	3,844	3,100
15	40	2	1,600	4	80
16	15	4	225	16	60
17	10	3	100	9	30
18	23	4	529	16	92
19	15	3	225	9	45
20	70	101	4,900	10,201	7,070
21	21	22	441	484	462
22	30	24	900	576	720
23	20	25	400	625	500
24	30	11	900	121	330
25	25	4	625	16	100
26	10	7	100	49	70
27	60	26	3,600	676	1,560
28	87	32	7,569	1,024	2,784
29	50	16	2,500	256	800
30	25	65	625	4,225	1,625
Sums	1,113	1,038	55,823	78,376	54,966

(continued)

SAMPLE PROBLEM *(CONTINUED)*

Pearson r:

$$r = \frac{N\Sigma XY - \Sigma X\Sigma Y}{\sqrt{N\Sigma X^2 - (\Sigma X)^2}\ \sqrt{N\Sigma Y^2 - (\Sigma Y)^2}}$$

$$= \frac{30(54{,}966) - (1{,}113)(1{,}038)}{\sqrt{30(55{,}823) - (1{,}113)^2}\ \sqrt{30(78{,}376) - (1{,}038)^2}}$$

$$= \frac{1{,}648{,}980 - 1{,}155{,}294}{\sqrt{1{,}674{,}690 - 1{,}238{,}769}\ \sqrt{2{,}351{,}280 - 1{,}077{,}444}}$$

$$= \frac{493{,}686}{\sqrt{435{,}921}\ \sqrt{1{,}273{,}836}} = \frac{493{,}686}{(660.24)(1{,}128.64)}$$

$$= \frac{493{,}686}{745{,}173.27} = .66$$

Computer Solution

Table 7.11 shows the SPSS output for the marijuana plant eradication just described. We note the correlation coefficient between plants eradicated and amount of money spent, the scatter diagram, and, finally, the descriptive statistics.

Let us pay particular attention to the lower half of the correlation matrix. Note that the intersection of "PLANTS" and "SPENT" (in boldface type) shows a correlation coefficient of $r = .663$ or $.66$. Note also that all possible combinations of the variables are printed out—obviously, the correlation of "PLANTS" and "SPENT" would be the same as the correlation of "SPENT" and "PLANTS" so $.663$ is repeated.

The diagonal of all SPSS correlation matrices will show a coefficient of 1.000, since each variable will correlate perfectly with itself. Also included in the matrix is the number of cases (30 here) and the probability that the coefficient was simply due to chance. (The $p = .000$ here indicates that the probability is less than $.001$.) We drew the same conclusion using Table B in the calculator solution example, that is, that the $r = .66$ was significantly different from zero.

The SPSS correlation matrix is especially useful when more than two variables are displayed in a correlational study. Table 7.12 shows a correlation matrix that resulted when several personality and lifestyle measures were administered to 42 college students. The measurement of grade-point average (GPA), daily hassles, optimism, pessimism, study hours (per week),

Table 7.11
SPSS printout for the marijuana eradication expenditures

Correlations

Correlations

		PLANTS	SPENT
Pearson Correlation	PLANTS	1.000	.663**
	SPENT	**.663****	1.000
Sig. (2-tailed)	PLANTS	.	.000
	SPENT	.000	.
N	PLANTS	30	30
	SPENT	30	30

**. Correlation is significant at the 0.01 level (2-tailed).

Graph

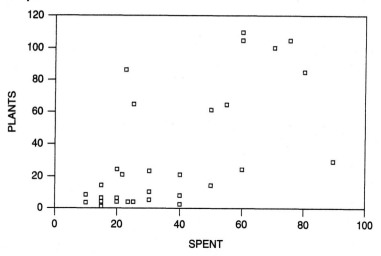

Descriptives

Descriptive Statistics

	N	Minimum	Maximum	Mean	Std. Deviation
PLANTS	30	1	110	34.60	38.26
SPENT	30	10	87	37.10	22.38
Valid N (listwise)	30				

(continued)

SAMPLE PROBLEM (CONTINUED)

Table 7.12
SPSS printout for personality variable correlation matrix

Correlations

Correlations

		GPA	HASSLES	OPT	PESS	STUDYHRS	SYMPT
Pearson	GPA	1.000	−.021	.102	.025	.050	−.106
Correlation	HASSLES	−.021	1.000	.289	.290	.013	.349*
	OPT	.102	.289	1.000	−.142	−.046	−.147
	PESS	.025	.290	−.142	1.000	.200	.353*
	STUDYHRS	.050	.013	−.046	.200	1.000	.020
	SYMPT	−.106	.349*	−.147	.353*	.020	1.000
Sig.	GPA	.	.896	.520	.874	.751	.505
(2-tailed)	HASSLES	.896	.	.063	.063	.936	.023
	OPT	.520	.063	.	.369	.774	.352
	PESS	.874	.063	.369	.	.205	.022
	STUDYHRS	.751	.936	.774	.205	.	.901
	SYMPT	.505	.023	.352	.022	.901	.
N	GPA	42	42	42	42	42	42
	HASSLES	42	42	42	42	42	42
	OPT	42	42	42	42	42	42
	PESS	42	42	42	42	42	42
	STUDYHRS	42	42	42	42	42	42
	SYMPT	42	42	42	42	42	42

*. Correlation is significant at the 0.05 level (2-tailed).

and physical symptoms resulted in the 15 intercorrelations shown. Again we will ignore the 1.000 coefficients on the diagonal, and concentrate on the lower half of the matrix and the highlighted correlation coefficients.

As in Table 7.11, the number of cases (42) and the probability statements for each coefficient are shown. The exact probabilities are shown, and we usually would be interested in those that are .05 or less. A researcher would typically look for the larger coefficients and whether or not they are significantly different from zero. For example, a health psychologist might be very interested in the $r = .349$ ($p = .023$) between physical symptoms and daily hassles, and $r = .353$ ($p = .022$) between symptoms and pessimism.

STUDY QUESTIONS

1. Show how you would use the intuitive approach to explain to a friend the difference between a positive and a negative correlation.
2. Also use the intuitive approach to explain the difference between correlation coefficients of .85 and .62.
3. Use the graphical approach to explain the situations found in questions 1 and 2.
4. How would the scatter diagram plotted for data with $r = .08$ differ from another scatter diagram where $r = -.86$?
5. During the calculation of a Pearson r using the z score formula, how can you tell from glancing at the $z_X z_Y$ column whether r will be positive or negative? Large or small?
6. In the sampling distribution used for testing r for significance, what does s_r represent?
7. What is the mean of the sampling distribution described in study question 6?
8. Under what condition would the Pearson r and the Spearman r_s for a set of data be identical?
9. Why are *outliers* so important in the study of correlation? What is the best way to locate them?
10. Under what conditions might low correlation coefficients be important?
11. How would knowing the percent of a group that scored above or below the median help you in understanding the meaning of the amount of correlation?

EXERCISES

1. For the variables listed, indicate whether you would expect a positive, negative, or zero correlation.
   a. Cholesterol level and incidence of coronary heart disease.
   b. Outside temperature and layers of clothing needed.
   c. Amount of time spent studying and test score.
   d. Grade in school and GPA.
   e. Singing ability and writing ability.
   f. Mileage a car has been driven and selling price.
   g. Age and incidence of Alzheimer's disease.
2. For the variables listed, indicate whether you would expect a positive, negative, or zero correlation.
   a. Furnace fuel consumption and outdoor temperature.
   b. Basketball skills and typing skills.
   c. Number of cigarettes smoked and lung cancer incidence.
   d. High school GPA and college GPA.
   e. Body weight and intelligence.
   f. Time elapsed since you last ate and how full your stomach feels.
   g. Driving ability and number of car accidents you have caused.
3. Mary, a food server at a local restaurant, wanted to know the relationship between the amount of money her guests spend on food and the amount of

money they leave her for a tip. A summary of the food amount and tip amount for a sample of 30 of Mary's tables is shown. Calculate the Pearson r using the computational formula.

X Food Amount (\$)	Y Tip Amount (\$)
$\Sigma X = 597.60$	$\Sigma Y = 71.70$
$\Sigma X^2 = 16{,}376.7150$	$\Sigma Y^2 = 247.2060$
$\bar{X} = 19.92$	$\bar{Y} = 2.39$
$s_X = 12.42$	$s_Y = 1.62$

$$N = 30$$
$$\Sigma XY = 1{,}935.3$$

4. In a study first mentioned in Chapter 2, the number of hours worked at part-time jobs was shown. The researchers wondered what relationship they would find between number of hours the students worked per week and their GPA. In a random sample of 30 students, the number of hours worked and GPA for each student are shown in the following table. Calculate the Pearson r using the computational formula.

Hours Worked	GPA	Hours Worked	GPA
25	2.0	23	3.1
20	3.0	21	2.8
10	3.8	13	3.4
12	2.9	3	3.7
5	4.0	2	3.3
0	3.5	10	3.0
20	2.5	21	2.7
25	2.2	16	2.0
18	2.3	7	2.2
12	3.7	30	2.1
15	3.1	11	2.9
10	2.9	15	2.7
7	3.0	11	3.1
8	3.5	12	3.0
14	2.8	13	2.7

5. Eating disorders are present in men and women of all ages, but are especially problematic among women aged 14–25. Research was conducted to determine whether there was a correlation between scores on the Eating Disorders Inventory (EDI) and GPA of 50 female college students. A score of 20 or above on the EDI was indicative of an eating disorder. A summary of the EDI scores and college GPA is shown. Use the computational formula to calculate the Pearson r for these data.

EDI Scores (X)   GPA (Y)
$$\Sigma X = 509 \qquad\qquad \Sigma Y = 150.2$$
$$\Sigma X^2 = 5,200 \qquad\qquad \Sigma Y^2 = 458.7$$
$$N = 50$$
$$\Sigma XY = 1,534$$

6. A sixth-grade teacher was interested in seeing if there was a relationship between her students' mathematics and spelling skills. She gave each of her 24 students a 30-point spelling test and a 50-point arithmetic test, and the data are summarized as follows. Calculate the Pearson r using the computational formula to see if there was a relationship between the students' spelling ability and mathematics ability.

Spelling (X)   Mathematics (Y)
$$\Sigma X = 481.3 \qquad\qquad \Sigma Y = 840.7$$
$$\Sigma X^2 = 9,889 \qquad\qquad \Sigma Y^2 = 32,607$$
$$N = 24$$
$$\Sigma XY = 17,567$$

7. A criminal justice publication reports the number of robberies and aggravated assaults for cities and towns 10,000 and over in population. The following table lists the number of robberies and aggravated assaults for 20 cities and towns in one state. Calculate the Pearson r to see if there is a relationship between these data.

Robberies	Assaults	Robberies	Assaults
32	76	26	64
50	86	15	80
37	184	73	334
1	7	18	42
92	125	35	169
98	216	10	31
5	10	11	46
16	73	6	8
10	26	10	42
14	163	2	6

8. An exercise enthusiast wondered if there was a relationship between the number of hours people exercise and the hours of sleep that they need. He surveyed 25 people and asked them to estimate the number of hours they exercise per week and the number of hours they sleep per week. The results are shown in the following table. Calculate the Pearson r for these data to determine the relationship.

Hours Sleep per Week	Hours Exercise per Week	Hours Sleep per Week	Hours Exercise per Week
47	8	49	14
56	5	48	8

(continued)

49	10	57	5
42	12	50	4
51	6	39	9
40	8	44	15
35	12	50	4
44	7.5	47	14
59	5.5	49	12
39	7	40	10
53	4	42	10
43	8	51	7
47	9		

9. An aerobics instructor teaches a step aerobics class on Mondays and a water aerobics class on Tuesdays. She asked 18 students to try each class and record their heart rate immediately following a 30-minute routine. Use the Pearson r to determine if there was a relationship between the two measurements of heart rate.

Step Aerobics Heart Rate	Water A.erobics Heart Rate
108	116
124	144
112	124
132	156
108	112
124	136
140	156
166	174
116	134
108	132
140	156
180	196
172	196
164	208
150	168
146	156
132	144
144	162

10. A nutrition instructor believed that in order to lose weight, one should not eat within three hours before going to bed but should eat a healthy breakfast in the morning. She asked 25 junior university students how many times per week they eat later than 10 P.M. and how many times per week they eat break-

fast in the morning. Calculate the Pearson r to see if there was a relationship between the two sets of data.

Eat after 10 P.M. (per Week)	Eat Breakfast (per Week)
4	7
5	4
3	7
0	5
4	6
3	0
4	3
7	1
6	2
5	0
2	2
0	6
3	3
0	7
2	4
4	5
3	6
2	0
4	0
0	6
0	5
1	4
2	6
1	4
3	3

11. An entertainment company surveyed 100 families and found a correlation of .32 between the number of family members living at home and the number of television sets in the home. Was this correlation significantly different from zero?

12. The same company as in exercise 11 conducted another survey to determine the relationship between the number of family members living at home and the number of computers in the home. They surveyed 33 families with home computers and found a correlation of .31. Was this correlation significantly different from zero?

13. Shown in the following table are data from 21 countries on life expectancy (age in years) and the annual infant death rate (number of deaths per 1,000 live births). Was there any relationship between these two variables for the countries chosen for this study? Use the Spearman r_s and Table C to determine this relationship.

	Life Expectancy	Annual Infant Deaths per 1,000 Births*
Japan	78.7	5
Iceland	78.2	5
Switzerland	78.0	7
Canada	77.4	7
Australia	76.9	7
Israel	76.5	9
Britain	76.2	7
United States	75.9	8
Argentina	71.3	29
China	70.6	27
Mexico	70.3	35
Russia	70.0	19
Brazil	66.2	57
Philippines	65.0	40
Egypt	61.6	57
India	60.4	88
Kenya	58.9	66
Turkey	57.9	56
Zaire	51.6	93
Cambodia	51.1	116
Angola	46.5	124

*Source: Jon D. Hull, *The State of the Union*. Copyright 1995 Time, Inc. All rights reserved. Reprinted by permission from TIME.

14. The number of full-time law enforcement employees (includes officers and civilians), the number of male officers, and the number of female officers in 10 different U.S. states are presented in the following table. Use the Spearman r_s to see if there was a relationship between the total number of law enforcement employees and the number of female officers in each state. Is this correlation significantly different from zero? Do the same for the number of male officers.

Total Number of Employees	Male Officers	Female Officers
12,682	8,046	692
1,587	953	72
13,689	7,420	739
6,328	3,874	250
86,935	53,230	6,096
11,089	6,966	815
8,971	6,727	480
2,009	1,452	140
4,780	3,190	935
25,179	16,285	2,192

COMPUTER EXERCISES FOR APPENDIX 4 DATA BANK

C1. Plot a scatter diagram with X = JAS S&I and Y = JAS Type A.

C2. Calculate a correlation matrix for the male college students. Include all the variables except sex.

C3. Note whether each coefficient is significantly different from zero. Now carefully examine the matrix. Are you surprised by any of the relationships? Which ones would you expect to be high? Which would you expect to be low?

C4. Repeat C1 and C2 for the women college students. After you have noted which coefficients are significantly different from zero, compare the coefficients for men and women. Do you find any major differences?

CHAPTER 8

Prediction and Regression

As college and university enrollments began to swell in the late 1950s and early 1960s, admissions officers and test publishers alike sought to develop new entrance exams or improve existing ones that would allow colleges to select high school graduates who were most likely to succeed. For example, as the American College Testing (ACT) program expanded, numerous institutions conducted research to see which of the various entrance exams would do the best job of predicting college success.

One small midwestern college began using the ACT exam scores from 484 incoming freshmen at the beginning of the 1961–62 school year. The correlation between grade-point averages (GPAs) at the end of the freshman year and the ACT composite scores (English, mathematics, social science, and natural science) was $r = .53$. Since this was a significantly higher correlation than the $r = .42$ obtained with the current entrance exam on the same 484 freshmen, the college discontinued the older exam and began using the ACT.

In this chapter we will see how predictions for one variable (e.g., GPA at the end of the freshman year) are made from knowledge of a second variable (e.g., college entrance exam scores). We will also need to be aware of the amount of error in any prediction, and how increasing the value of r (e.g., going from $r = .42$ to $r = .53$) can reduce the amount of prediction error.

The use of correlation research in psychology in order to make predictions about future behavior is one of the more interesting topics in statistical applications to the field of psychology. We are all familiar with the use of diagnostic tests to predict depression, bipolar disorders, and other pathological behavior. And countless other studies have shown us the effects that nutrition, socioeconomic status, education, parental marital status, and a host of other variables have on children's behavior.

However, our interest in research in academic and clinical settings is not the only reason for an interest in prediction. Basically, prediction is a fascinating topic in and of itself. Look at the amount of attention we give psychics, medical doctors, and Super Bowl oddsmakers. And few of us can resist a quick peek at the 10-item "Are You a Good Mate?" or "Are You a Dangerous Driver?" tests in the Sunday supplement. From childhood to old age, we listen to predictions of our school success, athletic prowess, job satisfaction, and life expectancy from teachers, parents, coaches, and physicians. Some of these predictions, fortunately, do not come true.

Most of the examples we have mentioned are predictions based on a multitude of factors; for example, your doctor's diagnosis may be based on 10 or 20 physiological indicators. For the purposes of our discussion in this chapter, however, we will restrict our topic to predictions made from a single variable. In the last chapter we noted that the two purposes of correlation were (1) to indicate the amount of relationship between two variables, and (2) to enable us to predict one variable from the knowledge of another variable. It is this kind of prediction that we will be concerned with here—the prediction of an individual's score on one variable on the basis of that person's score on another variable.

THE USE OF r IN PREDICTION

As we have noted, after a significant correlation has been obtained between two variables, X and Y, we would like to be able to take a score on X and *predict* the associated score on Y. If a correlation has been established between a college entrance exam and college GPA, we would like to develop a method that would allow us to use the exam score of a high school senior and actually predict what the college GPA will be (within limits) after the freshman year. This procedure, which at first glance may appear very complex, is really rather simple if one progresses step by step to the different concepts involved. Let us begin with some very basic algebra.

Equation for a Straight Line

Somewhere back in ninth-grade algebra or earlier, you probably learned that the equation of a straight line was of the general form $Y = bX + a$, and you plotted various values of X and Y to get a graph similar to that of Figure 8.1. The equation of the line in Figure 8.1 is $Y = 0.5X + 2$, and five pairs of X, Y values are plotted. In the general equation $Y = bX + a$, the quantity a is called the *Y intercept* and b is the *slope* of the line. For $Y = 0.5X + 2$, in Figure 8.1, the Y intercept is 2 since the line crosses the Y axis at $Y = 2$. The slope of the line is 0.5, indicating that for an increase of one unit in X, there is an increase of 0.5 units in Y.*

---

*There is an easy way to remember these two concepts. Go one unit to the right of your line and the *slope* is the distance you need to go up (or down) to get back on the line. The *Y intercept* is the value of Y when X is 0.

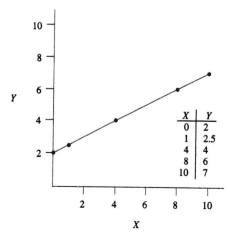

X	Y
0	2
1	2.5
4	4
8	6
10	7

Figure 8.1
Graph of the straight line $Y = 0.5X + 2$.

This graph of $Y = 0.5X + 2$ shows a *functional relationship* between X and Y, with X as the independent variable and Y as the dependent variable. (It might be helpful to review the section "Graphing the Functional Relationship" in Chapter 2.) That is, we can insert any value of X and *predict* the value of Y that is paired with that value of X. For example, in Figure 8.1, we can specify an X of 6 and "predict" that a Y of 5 will satisfy the equation and fall on the same straight line. Note that a similar straight line occurred in Figure 7.3a, where *perfect correlation* is shown between X and Y. When the correlation between X and Y is *perfect* (either positive or negative), we are able to predict Y from X without error. Or in terms of the example of several paragraphs ago, if $r = 1.00$ between a college entrance exam and college GPA, we would be able to predict accurately your college GPA from your exam score alone!

The Prediction Equation

But back to the world of reality. How can you predict Y from X when r is not 1.00 and the points do not all fall on the straight line? The answer is simple: We calculate a straight line that "best fits" the points and from X predict the most likely value of Y. In other words, we can take a group of paired scores, regardless of the value of r (as long as it is significantly different from 0), calculate the best-fitting straight line, and for any given value of X predict the most likely value of Y.

Three sets of data are shown in the scatter diagrams of Figure 8.2, with the best-fitting straight lines for each set. Note that when r is high (.83) most of the points are fairly close to the line and when r is low (.09) the points are scattered well away from this line. Consequently, the higher r is, the better will be

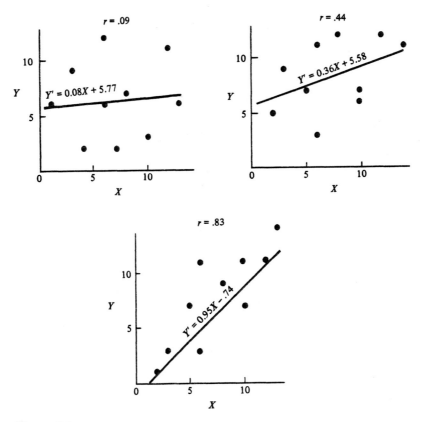

Figure 8.2
Scatter diagrams and best-fitting straight lines.

our predictions of Y from a given X. We will have more to say about this topic later on.

The equation that predicts Y from X is called the *regression equation*, and the best-fitting straight line is called a *regression line*. The formula for the regression equation is

$$Y' = bX + a \qquad (8.1)$$

where

Y' = the predicted value of Y
b = the slope of the regression line
a = the Y intercept
X = the given value of the variable X

Notice that formula 8.1 uses Y' instead of Y. The reason for the difference is that Y represents all the observed Y values that we used to calculate r. Y', on the other hand, is the *predicted* value that we obtain when we substitute a given value of X in the formula. Any Y' falls on the regression line and satisfies the equation. Let us complete the formula by calculating the slope b, and then the Y intercept, a.

Calculating the Slope.   The formula for calculating the slope, b, is

$$b = \frac{N(\Sigma XY) - (\Sigma X)(\Sigma Y)}{N(\Sigma X^2) - (\Sigma X)^2} \qquad (8.2)$$

where N is the number of pairs of scores and the rest of the terms are, as usual, the sums of the X, Y, X^2, Y^2, and XY columns.

Calculating the Y *Intercept.*   The formula for calculating the Y intercept, a, is

$$a = \overline{Y} - (b)\overline{X} \qquad (8.3)$$

where
$\overline{Y}$ = the mean of Y
b = the slope calculated in formula 8.2
$\overline{X}$ = the mean of X

After a and b have been calculated, the values are substituted in the regression formula, $Y' = bX + a$. Let us use the data of the algebra and geometry scores from the last chapter and summarized in Table 8.1. We will use the regression equation to calculate the best-fitting straight line that would predict an individual's geometry score (Y) from his or her algebra score (X).

Calculating the slope, b,

$$b = \frac{N(\Sigma XY) - (\Sigma X)(\Sigma Y)}{N(\Sigma X^2) - (\Sigma X)^2} = \frac{10(2,799) - (130)(210)}{10(1,752) - (130)^2}$$

$$= \frac{690}{620}$$

$$= 1.11$$

And calculating the Y intercept, a,

$$a = \overline{Y} - b\overline{X}$$

$$= 21 - 1.11(13)$$

$$= 21 - 14.43$$

$$= 6.57$$

And, finally, substituting for a and b in the regression equation, $Y' = bX + a$,

$$Y' = 1.11X + 6.57$$

This *regression equation* yields the best-fitting straight line for the algebra–geometry data. We can now plot a scatter diagram as shown in Figure 8.3 from the algebra–geometry data, and locate the line on this scatter diagram.

Table 8.1
Algebra–geometry scores and summary
statistics

Individual	Algebra X	Geometry Y
A	14	24
B	16	23
C	17	25
D	13	21
E	13	20
F	14	23
G	14	23
H	10	18
I	9	17
J	10	16

Algebra (X)	Geometry (Y)
$\Sigma X = 130$	$\Sigma Y = 210$
$\Sigma X^2 = 1,752$	$\Sigma Y^2 = 4,498$
$\overline{X} = 13$	$\overline{Y} = 21$
$\Sigma XY = 2,799$	$r = .93$

To draw the regression line on a scatter diagram, choose a *low* value of X and a *high* value of X and calculate their corresponding Y' values using the regression equation. Looking at the scatter diagram of Figure 8.3, we see that X values of 10 and 16 would do nicely, so calculating Y' by substituting for X in the regression equation would give

$$Y' = 1.11X + 6.57 = 1.11(10) + 6.57 = 11.1 + 6.57 = 17.67$$
$$Y' = 1.11X + 6.57 = 1.11(16) + 6.57 = 17.76 + 6.57 = 24.33$$

These two values of Y' are located on the scatter diagram above X values of 10 and 16, respectively, and a straight line connects these two points. This regression line is the best-fitting straight line for this set of data, and the equation for this line is $Y' = 1.11X + 6.57$.*

The regression equation can now be used to predict the most likely value of Y for any given value of X. For the algebra–geometry data, we can predict the most likely geometry score (Y) from an individual's algebra score alone. For example, let us suppose that some other individual takes the algebra test and scores 15. What would be her predicted geometry score (Y')? Substituting for X in the prediction equation, we would get

---

*"Best-fitting straight line" means that the regression line is so located that the sum of the squared discrepancies between each actual Y and its corresponding predicted Y' is as small as possible [i.e., $\Sigma(Y - Y')^2$ is a minimum]. This approach is called the "least squares criterion."

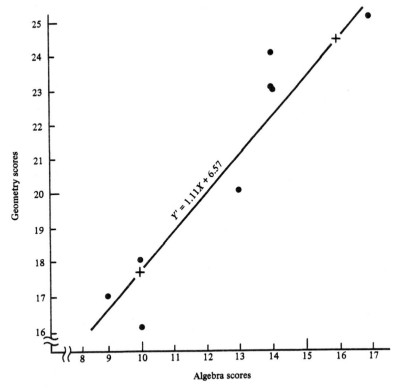

Figure 8.3
Scatter diagram of algebra scores and geometry scores with regression line.

Note 8.1
Origin of the Regression Concept

Sir Francis Galton (1822–1911) undertook a series of studies of inheritance that tested some of the hypotheses of his cousin Charles Darwin. In studying the relation between the heights of parents and the heights of their offspring, Galton noted that the heights of offspring tended to *regress* toward the mean of the general population. In general, tall parents had children who were above average in height but who were not as tall as the parents. Short parents had children who were below average in height but who generally were taller than their parents. This "dropping back" toward the general mean was often referred to as the *law of filial regression*. The term *regression* came to be used whenever the relationship between two variables was studied.

$$Y' = 1.11X + 6.57$$
$$= 1.11(15) + 6.57$$
$$= 16.65 + 6.57$$
$$= 23.2$$

and we conclude that for the individual scoring 15 on the algebra test our best prediction of her geometry score would be 23.2. This score, of course, falls on the regression line of Figure 8.3.

ERRORS IN PREDICTING Y FROM X

In the previous sections we have been discussing the prediction of the "most likely value of Y" without ever really defining what is meant by "most likely." You have probably gathered by now that the accuracy of a predicted value of Y is somehow related to the scattering of the points about the regression line. In Figure 8.3, for example, most of the points lie *near,* but not *on,* the regression line. If you will look back at Figure 8.2, you will note that, as r gets larger, the points are closer to the regression line.

Errors of Estimate

In fact, we can define the *error of estimate, e,* as the distance between the predicted value of Y and the observed score of Y at a given value of X. Stated algebraically, we would have

$$e = Y - Y'$$

where

    e = error of estimate
    Y = the observed value for a given value of X
    Y' = the predicted value of Y for that value of X

The algebra–geometry data are shown again in Table 8.2 with the predicted geometry score (Y') and the error of estimate ($Y - Y'$) shown for each individual.

Let us repeat part of the scatter diagram of the algebra–geometry data in Figure 8.4 and demonstrate this error of estimate for 2 students, A and J. As you can see, student A has an algebra score (X) of 14 and a geometry score (Y) of 24. However, the predicted score Y' for an X of 14 would be

$$Y' = 1.11X + 6.57 = 1.11(14) + 6.57 = 22.11$$

so the error of estimate for student A would be

$$e_A = Y - Y' = 24 - 22.11 = 1.89$$

which indicates that the actual score of 24 is 1.89 score units *above* the predicted Y' of 22.11 on the regression line. For student J, who has an algebra score of 10

Table 8.2
Predicted geometry scores and errors of estimate for algebra–geometry data

Individual	Algebra X	Geometry Y	Predicted Y'	Y – Y'	(Y – Y')²
A	14	24	22.11	1.89	3.5721
B	16	23	24.33	–1.33	1.7689
C	17	25	25.44	–.44	.1936
D	13	21	21.00	0.0	0.0
E	13	20	21.00	–1.00	1.0000
F	14	23	22.11	.89	.7921
G	14	23	22.11	.89	.7921
H	10	18	17.67	.33	.1089
I	9	17	16.56	.44	.1936
J	10	16	17.67	–1.67	2.7889
					11.2102

Summary statistics (from Table 7.5):

$$\overline{X} = 13,\ s_X = 2.62,\ \overline{Y} = 21,\ s_Y = 3.13,\ r = .93$$

Standard error of estimate (deviation formula):

$$s_E = \sqrt{\frac{\Sigma(Y - Y')^2}{N - 2}} = \sqrt{\frac{11.2102}{8}} = \sqrt{1.4013} = 1.18$$

Standard error of estimate (computational formula):

$$s_E = s_Y \sqrt{1 - r^2} = 3.13 \sqrt{1 - (.93)^2} = 3.13 \sqrt{.1351} = 1.15$$

and a geometry score of 16, the predicted value of Y is 17.67, which yields an error of estimate of

$$e_J = Y - Y' = 16 - 17.67 = -1.67$$

which indicates that the actual score of 16 is 1.67 units *below* the predicted Y' of 17.67 on the regression line. These values, 1.89 and –1.67, clearly indicate the amount of error in predicting Y from X in terms of deviations from the regression line.

Table 8.2 shows the errors of estimate for the other 8 individuals. It should be obvious that if, *on the average,* the errors of estimate are quite small, our predictions of Y from a knowledge of X will be relatively accurate. Also, as these errors get larger, our prediction of Y would become less accurate.

Standard Error of Estimate, s_E

These errors of estimate, $Y - Y'$, can be used to develop a statistic that will help us tell how accurate our predictions are. We first take each error, $Y - Y'$, square it

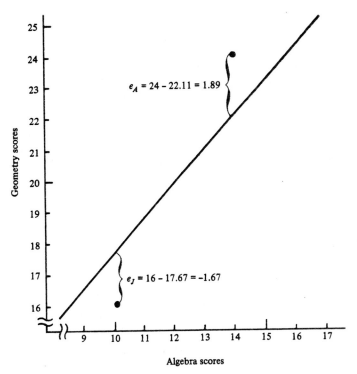

Figure 8.4
Errors of estimate for students A and J.

to obtain $(Y - Y')^2$, and form an additional column shown in Table 8.2. The sum of these squared deviations, $\Sigma(Y - Y')^2$, is then divided by $N - 2$ and the square root is calculated. This statistic is called the *standard error of estimate,* and is given by

$$s_E = \sqrt{\frac{\Sigma(Y - Y')^2}{N - 2}}$$

where

s_E = the standard error of estimate in predicting Y from X
Y = an observed value of the Y variable
Y' = the predicted value associated with each observed value
N = the number of pairs of observations

As you can see in Table 8.2, using this formula we calculate s_E to be 1.18. Before we discuss the meaning of s_E, we should note that this formula for s_E is the *deviation* formula and is a nuisance to calculate. So, as usual, we prefer to use the computational formula:

$$s_E = s_Y \sqrt{1 - r^2} \qquad (8.4)$$

where

     s_E = the standard error of estimate in predicting Y from X
     s_Y = the standard deviation of the Y distribution
     r = the Pearson correlation coefficient between X and Y

Let us use this formula for s_E to calculate the standard error of estimate for the algebra–geometry data. Substituting in the formula for s_Y and r, we have

$$s_E = s_Y \sqrt{1 - r^2}$$
$$= 3.13 \sqrt{1 - (.93)^2}$$
$$= 3.13 \sqrt{1 - .86}$$
$$= 3.13 \sqrt{.1351}$$
$$= 3.13 \,(.3676)$$
$$= 1.15$$

We notice that $s_E = 1.15$ is slightly different from the 1.18 calculated with the deviation formula, but this is merely rounding error.

So, what does this standard error of estimate, s_E, represent? We noted both in Chapters 6 and 7 that a standard error has the properties of a standard deviation. In this case, s_E is a type of standard deviation about the regression line. The smaller the size of the standard error, the tighter the points will be clustered around the regression line.

The Confidence Interval about Y'

In fact, we can use the properties of the standard error of estimate, s_E, to construct a confidence interval about a predicted score, Y', if we can assume that X and Y are normally distributed in the population. In our example, this would mean that ability in algebra and proficiency in geometry are normally distributed in the population, which is a rather reasonable assumption. The formula for constructing the 68% confidence interval is

68% CI: $$Y' \pm s_E \sqrt{1 + \frac{1}{N} + \frac{(X - \bar{X})^2}{(N - 1)s_X^2}} \qquad (8.5)$$

where

     Y' = the individual's predicted score from the regression equation
     s_E = the standard error of estimate
     X = the individual's score on X
     $\bar{X}$ = the mean of the X distribution
     s_X = the standard deviation of the X distribution
     N = the number of pairs of observations

Let us again use the algebra–geometry scores and the summary statistics from Table 8.1 and our calculated standard error of estimate, $s_E = 1.15$. In the example of the woman who scored 15 on the algebra test, we used the regression equation to predict that her geometry score would be $Y' = 23.2$. Calculating the 68% CI using formula 8.5, we have

68% CI:

$$Y' \pm s_E \sqrt{1 + \frac{1}{N} + \frac{(X - \bar{X})^2}{(N - 1)s_X^2}}$$

$$23.2 \pm 1.15 \sqrt{1 + \frac{1}{10} + \frac{(15 - 13)^2}{9(2.62)^2}}$$

$$23.2 \pm 1.15 \sqrt{1.1647} = 23.2 \pm 1.15(1.0792)$$

$$23.2 \pm 1.24 \quad \text{or} \quad 21.96 \text{ to } 24.44$$

In other words, we are 68% certain ($p = .68$) that an individual who scores 15 on X will have a Y score between 21.96 and 24.44. We have accomplished what we set out to do: We can now make a probability statement about the interval in which a given Y score is likely to fall.

Prediction and the Size of r

For prediction purposes we would like to have the confidence interval as narrow as possible. It would not be very helpful, for example, in the algebra–geometry data if our algebra score of 15 resulted in a predicted geometry score of, say, 10 to 33 instead of our 21.96 to 24.44. Since we want the confidence interval as small as possible, we must have s_E as small as possible. A glance at the formula for s_E shows that this is a function of the size of r. When $r = 1.00$, the quantity $s_Y \sqrt{1 - r^2}$ reduces to 0, and s_E is 0. In other words, if r is 1.00, there is no error in predicting Y from X. This conclusion is obvious, because all the points on a scatter diagram would fall on the regression line. As r gets smaller, the quantity $s_Y \sqrt{1 - r^2}$ gets larger, of course; when there is no correlation ($r = 0$), s_E is the same size as s_Y, the standard deviation of the Y distribution. So we would have to conclude that the larger the value of r, the more informative will be our predictions.

What about Predicting X from Y?

All of the preceding sections have been devoted to topics concerning the prediction of Y from X. What about the reverse situation—predicting X from Y? It must be emphasized that we *cannot* take the formulas for the regression equation and the standard error of estimate, and predict X from Y by simply substituting X where Y should be, and vice versa. Because the formulas, as well as their interpretation, are different, you are advised to consult a more advanced statistics textbook given in the References.

As a practical matter, of course, there is no problem. We simply call whatever variable we wish to predict the Y variable, plot our scatter diagram accordingly, and calculate the usual regression equation.

THE COEFFICIENT OF DETERMINATION, r^2

By squaring the Pearson r, we obtain r^2, a statistic named the *coefficient of determination*. It tells us how much of the variation in Y is associated with changes in X. An example may help to clarify this definition.

Again, let us use the example of the relationship between height and weight, with height the X variable and weight the Y variable. Let us say that the correlation was $r = .60$. If we examined the variation of the Y values (the weights), we would see considerable variation of weights about the mean, $\overline{Y}$. What is the source of this variation? We notice that some of the variation in weight must be associated with the heights of the individuals involved, since we did find a relationship between height and weight. After all, taller people should weigh more than shorter people.

But since the relationship is not perfect ($r = .60$, not 1.00), we might find two 6 foot 2 inch males—one weighing 160 pounds and the other 190 pounds. Clearly, factors other than height, such as bone density and muscle mass, cause variations in the weights about the mean, $\overline{Y}$.

Let us use the *variance* as a measure of this variation about the mean of the weights, $\overline{Y}$. We can then write an expression that shows the variation about the mean of weights, $\overline{Y}$, is made up of the variation about $\overline{Y}$ associated with heights, and the variation about $\overline{Y}$ that is due to other factors. In the form of an equation, we would have

$$s_Y^2 = s_{Y \cdot X}^2 + s_{Y \cdot \text{other}}^2$$

where

s_Y^2 = the total variance in weight

$s_{Y \cdot X}^2$ = the variance in weight associated with differences in height

$s_{Y \cdot \text{other}}^2$ = the variance in weight associated with other factors

It can be shown that the coefficient of determination is related to the variances described in the preceding equation by the equation

$$r^2 = \frac{s_{Y \cdot X}^2}{s_Y^2}$$

where

$s_{Y \cdot X}^2$ = the variance in Y associated with differences in X

s_Y^2 = the total variance in Y

In other words, the coefficient of determination, r^2, tells us the proportion of the variation in Y that is associated with changes in X. If the correlation between height and weight is .60, $r^2 = (.60)^2 = 0.36$, or 36% of the variation in the weights is associated with changes in heights. That means that 64% is due to other factors, such as bone mass and muscle mass.

Example of Correlational Research

The preceding sections have covered a number of topics, and it may be helpful at this point to examine an actual research study to see how the various concepts fit together. At the beginning of the chapter, we saw a small midwestern college comparing two different college entrance exams. In one part of the study, researchers found a correlation of $r = .53$ between the ACT composite score and GPA at the end of the freshman year for 484 students. The summary statistics are as follows. The data are plotted in the scatter diagram of Figure 8.5.

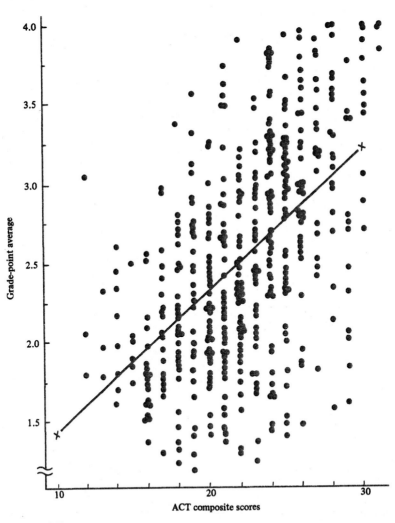

Figure 8.5
Scatter diagram and regression line for predicting GPA from entrance exam scores.

Exam Scores (X)	GPA (Y)
$\overline{X} = 22.21$	$\overline{Y} = 2.53$
$s_X = 4.00$	$s_Y = 0.67$
$\Sigma X = 10{,}750$	$\Sigma Y = 1{,}224.52$
$\Sigma X^2 = 246{,}509$	$\Sigma Y^2 = 3{,}315.3032$

$$N = 484$$
$$\Sigma XY = 27{,}884.06$$

The main interest, of course, is in the possible relationship between the exam scores and the GPAs, so the very first step is the calculation of r.

$$r = \frac{N\Sigma XY - \Sigma X \Sigma Y}{\sqrt{N\Sigma X^2 - (\Sigma X)^2}\ \sqrt{N\Sigma Y^2 - (\Sigma Y)^2}}$$

$$= \frac{484(27{,}884.06) - (10{,}750)(1{,}224.52)}{\sqrt{484(246{,}509) - (10{,}750)^2}\sqrt{484(3{,}315.3032) - (1{,}224.52)^2}}$$

$$= \frac{332{,}295}{(1{,}935.938)(324.28)}$$

$$= \frac{332{,}295}{627{,}785.97}$$

$$= .53$$

After r has been calculated, the next step is to see if it is significantly different from 0. From Table B in Appendix 3 we note that for 400 degrees of freedom (we actually have $484 - 2 = 482$ degrees of freedom, but since Table B does not list that value, we take the next *lowest* value listed). An r must be at least .128 to be significantly different from 0 at the .01 level. Since an r of .53 is outside the $-.128$ to .128 interval, we reject the notion that the true r is 0. We now believe that there is a relationship between entrance exam scores and GPA.

We next determine the regression line by first calculating the slope, b.

$$b = \frac{N(\Sigma XY) - (\Sigma X)(\Sigma Y)}{N(\Sigma X^2) - (\Sigma X)^2}$$

$$= \frac{484(27{,}884.06) - (10{,}750)(1{,}224.52)}{484(246{,}509) - (10{,}750)^2}$$

$$= \frac{332{,}295}{3{,}747{,}586} = .089$$

We then calculate the Y intercept, a.

$$a = \overline{Y} - b(\overline{X})$$

$$= 2.53 - .089(22.21)$$

$$= .55$$

And substituting for b and a in the regression equation, $Y' = bX + a$:

$$Y' = .089X + .55$$

We now position the regression line on the scatter diagram of Figure 8.5 by substituting any two values of X and solving the equation for Y'. Let us use X values of 10 and 30 and solve for the corresponding Y' values as follows:

$$Y' = 0.089X + 0.55 = 0.089(10) + 0.55 = 0.89 + 0.55 = 1.44$$

$$Y' = 0.089X + 0.55 = 0.089(30) + 0.55 = 2.67 + 0.55 = 3.22$$

These Y' values are plotted above their respective X values on the scatter diagram, a straight line is drawn between the two points, and this regression line, $Y' = 0.089X + 0.55$, is the best-fitting straight line for these data.

The last step before we can make predictions about an individual's GPA is to calculate the standard error of estimate, s_E. This is calculated by

$$s_E = s_Y \sqrt{1 - r^2} = 0.67 \sqrt{1 - (.53)^2}$$
$$= 0.67 \sqrt{1 - .28} = 0.67 \sqrt{.72}$$
$$= 0.67(0.85) = 0.57$$

On the basis of this research, the college administration was ready to use the entrance examination for predicting college GPA for the next year's students. If Tara Jones scored 24 on the entrance examination the following year, what would be the best prediction for her college GPA at the end of her freshman year? Using the regression equation, we find

$$Y' = 0.089X + 0.55 = 0.089(24) + 0.55 = 2.14 + 0.55 = 2.69$$

and setting up the 68% confidence interval about Y':

68% CI:

$$Y' \pm s_E \sqrt{1 + \frac{1}{N} + \frac{(X - \bar{X})^2}{(N - 1)s_X^2}}$$

$$2.69 \pm 0.57 \sqrt{1 + \frac{1}{484} + \frac{(24 - 22.21)^2}{483(4)^2}}$$

$$2.69 \pm 0.57(1.0025) = 2.69 \pm 0.57$$

$$2.12 \text{ to } 3.26$$

We would conclude that $p = .68$ that Tara Jones' actual GPA at the end of her freshman year would be between 2.12 and 3.26.

ASSUMPTIONS FOR THE PEARSON *r* IN PREDICTION

We noted in Chapter 7 that we had to make two assumptions before we could meaningfully apply the Pearson method: linearity of X and Y and paired X, Y data. In a similar way, assumptions must be made before the Pearson *r* can be used for purposes of prediction. They are the following:

1. The regression of Y on X is linear (linearity).
2. X and Y are normally distributed in the population (normality).
3. The standard deviation of the Y values about Y' for a given value of X is about the same for all values of Y' (homoscedasticity).

Linearity

We emphasized the importance of linearity in Chapter 7, since *r* measures the degree of *linear* relationship between X and Y. Figure 8.6 shows the scatter diagram of the coordination scores as a function of age that we examined in Chapter 7. But note that the "best-fitting" straight line is a horizontal line at the mean of the Y scores. It is obvious that there is a high correlation between coordination scores and age, but the Pearson *r* is 0, because of the lack of linearity in the data. With a regression line that is horizontal at the mean of the Y scores, our prediction of Y' for any value of X would be the same, $Y' = \overline{Y}$! As we noted in Chapter 7, we certainly would want to draw a scatter diagram, in order to examine the data for possible nonlinearity.

Normality

In order to use the standard error of estimate to establish the accuracy of a predicted Y', it is necessary that X and Y be normally distributed in the population.

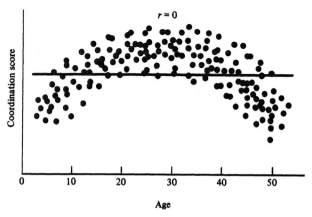

Figure 8.6
A curvilinear relationship: coordination as a function of age.

Homoscedasticity

In order for us to use s_E for any predicted Y' on the regression line, it is necessary that there be homoscedasticity in the values of Y about Y'. Homoscedasticity (this tongue-twisting term can be roughly translated as "equal spread") means that the variance of the Y values around their mean of Y' for a given value of X should be about the same for all distributions of Y values about their respective Y' values. In other words, if we were to calculate the variance (or standard deviation) of all of the Y values for a given value of X, we would expect this variance to be approximately equal to the variance of another group of Y values for some other value of X.

To better understand this concept, let us refer back to Figure 8.5, where the scatter diagram of the entrance exam scores and college GPA is plotted. Let us arbitrarily choose an X value of 20. The Y values for this value of X are distributed about the mean, $Y' = 2.34$, which is on the regression line. If there is homoscedasticity, the variance of this distribution should be about the same as the variance of any of the other columns of Y values.

Strictly speaking, homoscedasticity is a property possessed by samples that are very large, but we can get a rough idea from the shape of the scatter diagram. The scatter diagram of Figure 8.5 is roughly elliptical, but the scatter diagram of Figure 8.7 is not.

In response to a questionnaire, a sample of college sophomores indicated their GPA and the number of extracurricular activities in which they were currently involved. Figure 8.7 shows the shape of the relationship between GPA and participation in extracurricular activities.

Note that students involved in only one or two activities have GPAs ranging anywhere from an average 2.0 almost to a perfect 4.0. However, as the level of ex-

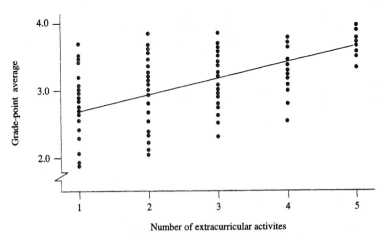

Figure 8.7
Scatter diagram not meeting the homoscedasticity assumption.

tracurricular participation increases, notice that the GPAs of the students increase also, and those most heavily involved (4 or 5 activities) have GPAs almost exclusively in the 3.0 to 4.0 range. This peculiar (i.e., nonelliptical) state of affairs results in an unequal spread of Y values about the regression line, and these data would not meet the assumption of homoscedasticity.

THE IMPORTANCE OF CORRELATION AND REGRESSION

In two chapters we have barely scratched the surface of this extremely important tool in education and the behavioral sciences. Because of the introductory nature of this book and space limitations on what is included, only a brief initiation to some selected topics in correlation and regression is possible. If you are interested in a further treatment of these topics, any of the more advanced textbooks in the References is recommended.

SAMPLE PROBLEM

A human resources director at an assembly plant wants to predict the performance of work inspectors on an assembly line. She develops a visual search test that requires the examinee to identify target letters in a mass of letters and numbers on a computer screen. The score is the number of errors made on 20 screens. The assembly line performance requires the inspector to reject an assembly if it has a broken connection. An error is counted if the assembly gets by the inspector before he or she can see the faulty part and push a reject switch. Each inspector's score is the number of errors made in a two-hour work period.

Calculator Solution

The search test (X) is given to 15 inspectors; later, their assembly line errors (Y) are noted during a two-hour work period. How well does the search test predict assembly line performance?

Worker	Search Test (X)	Assembly Errors (Y)	X^2	Y^2	XY
A	16	9	256	81	144
B	17	12	289	144	204
C	17	10	289	100	170
D	15	8	225	64	120
E	14	8	196	64	112

(continued)

SAMPLE PROBLEM *(CONTINUED)*

F	11	6	121	36	66
G	11	5	121	25	55
H	12	5	144	25	60
I	13	6	169	36	78
J	14	5	196	25	70
K	4	1	16	1	4
L	7	4	49	16	28
M	12	7	144	49	84
N	7	1	49	1	7
O	10	3	100	9	30
	$\Sigma X = 180$	$\Sigma Y = 90$	$\Sigma X^2 = 2{,}364$	$\Sigma Y^2 = 676$	$\Sigma XY = 1{,}232$

Means:

$$\overline{X} = \frac{\Sigma X}{N} = \frac{180}{15} = 12 \qquad \overline{Y} = \frac{\Sigma Y}{N} = \frac{90}{15} = 6$$

Standard deviations:

$$s_X = \sqrt{\frac{\Sigma X^2 - \frac{(\Sigma X)^2}{N}}{N-1}} = \sqrt{\frac{2{,}364 - \frac{(180)^2}{15}}{14}}$$

$$= \sqrt{\frac{2{,}364 - 2{,}160}{14}} = \sqrt{\frac{204}{14}} = \sqrt{14.5714}$$

$$= 3.82$$

$$s_Y = \sqrt{\frac{\Sigma Y^2 - \frac{(\Sigma Y)^2}{N}}{N-1}} = \sqrt{\frac{676 - \frac{(90)^2}{15}}{14}}$$

$$= \sqrt{\frac{676 - 540}{14}} = \sqrt{\frac{136}{14}} = \sqrt{9.7143}$$

$$= 3.12$$

Pearson *r*:

$$r = \frac{N\Sigma XY - \Sigma X \Sigma Y}{\sqrt{N\Sigma X^2 - (\Sigma X)^2}\ \sqrt{N\Sigma Y^2 - (\Sigma Y)^2}}$$

$$= \frac{15(1{,}232) - (180)(90)}{\sqrt{15(2{,}364) - (180)^2}\ \sqrt{15(676) - (90)^2}}$$

$$= \frac{2{,}280}{(55.32)(45.17)} = \frac{2{,}280}{2{,}498.8044}$$

$$= .91$$

Is r significantly different from 0?

From Table B in Appendix 3, we note that with 13 degrees of freedom ($N - 2 = 13$), r at the .01 level is .641. Since our value of .91 exceeds this tabled value, we conclude that $r = .91$ is significantly different from 0 at the .01 level.

Plot the scatter diagram and calculate the regression equation.

Figure 8.8 shows the scatter diagram for the data. Calculating b and a for the regression equation, we get

$$b = \frac{N(\Sigma XY) - (\Sigma X)(\Sigma Y)}{N(\Sigma X^2) - (\Sigma X)^2} = \frac{15(1{,}232) - (180)(90)}{15(2{,}364) - (180)^2}$$

$$= \frac{18{,}480 - 16{,}200}{35{,}460 - 32{,}400} = \frac{2{,}280}{3{,}060}$$

$$= .75$$

$$a = \overline{Y} - b(\overline{X})$$

$$= 6 - .75(12) = 6 - 9$$

$$= -3.0$$

Substituting in the regression equation, we have

$$Y' = .75X - 3.0$$

To plot the regression equation on the scatter diagram of Figure 8.8, we need to choose a small and a large value of X and solve for Y'. Using X values of 5 and 15, we get

$$Y' = 0.75(5) - 3.0 = 3.75 - 3.0 = 0.75$$
$$Y' = 0.75(15) - 3.0 = 11.25 - 3.0 = 8.25$$

We then locate the points (5, 0.75) and (15, 8.25) on the graph and draw a straight line between them to obtain the regression line.

John Jones applies for a job as inspector and makes 9 errors on the search test. What would be our prediction of his performance on the assembly line?

$$Y' = 0.75(9) - 3.0 = 6.75 - 3.0 = 3.75$$

(continued)

SAMPLE PROBLEM *(CONTINUED)*

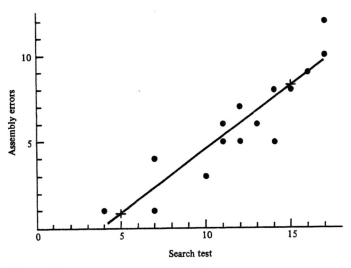

Figure 8.8
Scatter diagram and regression line for assembly line performance.

How accurate is our predicted score? To set up a confidence interval around a predicted Y' score of 3.75, we calculate the standard error of estimate:

$$s_E = s_Y \sqrt{1 - r^2} = 3.12 \sqrt{1 - (.91)^2}$$
$$= 3.12 \sqrt{1 - .83} = 3.12 \sqrt{.17}$$
$$= 3.12(0.41) = 1.28$$

The confidence interval would be calculated as follows:

68% CI:

$$Y' \pm s_E \sqrt{1 + \frac{1}{N} + \frac{(X - \overline{X})^2}{(N - 1)s_x^2}}$$

$$3.75 \pm 1.28 \sqrt{1 + \frac{1}{15} + \frac{(9 - 12)^2}{14 \, (3.82)^2}}$$

$$3.75 \pm 1.28(1.054) = 3.75 \pm 1.35$$

2.40 to 5.10

and we would conclude that $p = .68$ that his actual error performance would be between 2.40 and 5.10.

Computer Solution

The SPSS output for predicting assembly errors from the search test is shown in Table 8.3. The correlation matrix box is shown first with $r = .913$, significantly different from zero at the .01 level. Directly below the correlation box is the scatter diagram with the regression line.

The box marked "Model Summary" repeats the correlation coefficient, but also contains the coefficient of determination, $r^2 = .833$. Also shown is the standard error of estimate, $s_E = 1.3227$.

The second box, "Coefficients," contains the values of b (indicated by B opposite SEARCH, $b = .745$) and a [given as B under (Constant), $a = -2.941$]. Substituting for b and a in the regression equation, $Y' = bX + a$, we get

$$Y' = .745X - 2.941$$

We note that the values of b and a, as well as the standard error of estimate, s_E, are slightly different from those obtained with the calculator solution because of rounding error.

Table 8.3
SPSS printout for predicting assembly errors

Correlations

Correlations

		ASSEMBLY	**SEARCH**
Pearson Correlation	ASSEMBLY	1.000	.913**
	SEARCH	.913**	1.000
Sig. (2-tailed)	ASSEMBLY		.000
	SEARCH	.000	.
N	ASSEMBLY	15	15
	SEARCH	15	15

**. Correlation is significant at the 0.01 level (2-tailed).

(continued)

Graph

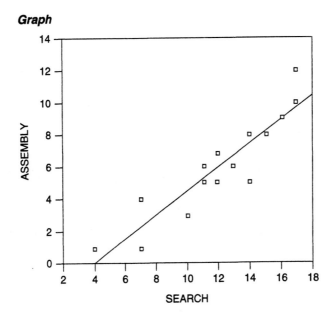

Regression

Model Summary[a,b]

Model	Variables		R	R Square	Adjusted R Square	Std. Error of the Estimate
	Entered	Removed				
1	SEARCH[c]	.	.913	.833	.820	1.3227

a. Dependent Variable: ASSEMBLY
b. Method: Enter
c. Independent Variables: (Constant), SEARCH
d. All requested variables entered.

Coefficients[a]

Model	Unstandardized Coefficients		Standardized Coefficients	t	Sig.
	B	Std. Error	Beta		
1 (Constant)	−2.941	1.163		−2.530	.025
SEARCH	.745	.093	.913	8.046	.000

a. Dependent Variable: ASSEMBLY

STUDY QUESTIONS

1. What is meant by the *slope* of a line? The *Y intercept?*
2. How do you predict *Y* from *X* when all the points on the scatter diagram are not on a straight line?
3. What is the difference between *Y* and *Y'*?
4. In the regression equation, what is *b*? What is *a*?
5. What is meant by the term *best-fitting straight line?*
6. Explain the expression $e = Y - Y'$.
7. In looking at scatter diagrams and their regression lines, such as those of Figure 8.2, how can you tell which would have the larger standard errors of estimate and which would have the smaller?
8. The Pearson *r* tells us the strength of the linear relationship between two variables. What does r^2, the coefficient of determination, tell us about the two variables?
9. List the assumptions for the Pearson *r* when used for prediction, and tell what each means.

EXERCISES

1. On a sheet of graph paper, plot the equation for the line $Y = 2X + 3$. What is the slope of this line? What is its *Y* intercept?
2. Plot the equation for the line $Y = -3X + 5$, and determine its slope and *Y* intercept.
3. In the Sample Problem of Chapter 7 we saw a list of 30 states showing how much money each had spent on marijuana eradication and the number of plants that were destroyed. The relevant statistics (in thousands) are as follows.

Money Spent **X**	Plants Destroyed **Y**
$\overline{X} = 37.1$	$\overline{Y} = 34.6$
$\Sigma X = 1{,}113$	$\Sigma Y = 1{,}038$
$\Sigma X^2 = 55{,}823$	$\Sigma Y^2 = 78{,}376$
$\Sigma XY = 54{,}966$	$r = .66$

   a. Calculate the regression equation for these data.
   b. Another state is planning to spend \$50,000 on marijuana eradication. On the basis of this study what would be our prediction for the number of plants destroyed?
4. A health psychologist investigated the relationship between a college student's optimistic/pessimistic view of life and the frequency of physical symptoms (e.g., headaches, joint pain, nausea). The researcher found a correlation of $r = .59$ between scores of a pessimism scale and physical symptoms for 33 college students. The summary statistics are as follows.

Pessimism	Physical Symptoms
X	Y
$\overline{X} = 6.97$	$\overline{Y} = 37.73$
$\Sigma X = 230$	$\Sigma Y = 1{,}245$
$\Sigma X^2 = 2{,}044$	$\Sigma Y^2 = 64{,}877$
$\Sigma XY = 10{,}332$	$r = .59$

a. Calculate the regression equation to predict symptom frequency from the pessimism scale.

b. Erin scored 10 on the pessimism scale. What would be our prediction for her symptoms score?

5. Calculate the coefficient of determination, r^2, for exercise 3. What does this mean in terms of the relationship between funds expended and number of marijuana plants destroyed?

6. In exercise 4 the correlation between a pessimistic outlook and frequency of physical symptoms is given. Calculate r^2, the coefficient of determination, and tell what this means in terms of predicting physical symptoms from scores on a pessimism scale.

7. In Chapter 7 we met Mary, who wanted to know if there was a relationship between the amount of money her restaurant customers spent on food and the amount they left her for a tip. The statistics for 30 tables are summarized as follows.

Food Amount ($)	Tip Amount ($)
$\overline{X} = 19.92$	$\overline{Y} = 2.39$
$\Sigma X = 597.60$	$\Sigma Y = 71.70$
$\Sigma X^2 = 16{,}376.7150$	$\Sigma Y^2 = 247.2060$
$\Sigma XY = 1{,}935.3$	$r = .87$

a. Calculate the regression equation that would predict the amount of tip from the amount spent on food.

b. A customer's total bill amounts to $30.00. What would be our prediction for the amount of tip that would be left?

8. In Chapter 7 a study on the relationship between eating disorders and GPA found a correlation of $r = .42$ between the Eating Disorders Inventory (EDI) and GPA of 50 female college students. The relevant statistics are as follows.

Eating Disorders Inventory	GPA
$\Sigma X = 509$	$\Sigma Y = 150.2$
$\Sigma X^2 = 5{,}200$	$\Sigma Y^2 = 458.7$
$\Sigma XY = 1{,}534$	$r = .42$

a. Calculate the regression equation that would predict GPA from the score on the EDI.

b. Jodi scored 8 on the EDI. What would be our prediction for her GPA?

9. A professor was interested in the study habits of college students. He was specifically interested in the relationship between how many hours a week

students spent studying and the final grade they received in his course in anthropology. The study hours per week and the final course grades (A = 12, A− = 11, etc.) for 30 students are shown in the following table.

a. Calculate $\bar{X}, \bar{Y}, s_X, s_Y$ for these data.
b. Calculate the Pearson r for these data.
c. Plot a scatter diagram on a sheet of graph paper.
d. Calculate the regression equation, and draw the regression line on the scatter diagram.
e. Dana reports that she studies 22 hours a week. What would be our best prediction for her final course grade?
f. Calculate the 68% CI for Dana's predicted score. What is the meaning of this interval?

Study Hours (X)	Course Grade (Y)	Study Hours (X)	Course Grade (Y)
14	4	16	4
23	12	17	10
10	3	17	3
10	5	22	9
24	10	9	3
15	7	7	2
17	5	22	11
17	7	23	10
16	10	23	8
25	11	13	6
20	5	19	7
15	4	16	5
20	9	17	9
26	12	12	4
16	8	21	7

10. In the development of Skylab, NASA scientists were interested in the relationship between hand steadiness and body balance. Performance on the hand steadiness test was the length of time in seconds that the subject could hold a stylus in an aperture before touching the side of the box (X). Body balance was measured by timing how many seconds subjects could stand on a one-inch wide board before losing their balance (Y). Twenty subjects gave the results shown here:

Steadiness X	Balance Y	Steadiness X	Balance Y
13	8	3	3
12	7	9	9
18	10	14	9
12	8	3	4
13	11	15	11
9	6	6	8

Steadiness X	Balance Y		Steadiness X	Balance Y
16	10		11	7
10	6		5	7
8	5		11	10
12	9		14	8

a. Calculate $\bar{X}$, $\bar{Y}$, s_X, s_Y for these data.
b. Calculate the Pearson r for these data.
c. Plot a scatter diagram on a sheet of graph paper.
d. Calculate the regression equation, and draw the regression line on the scatter diagram.
e. Bob scores 15 on the hand steadiness test. What result would we predict for his body balance test?
f. Calculate the 68% CI for Bob's predicted score.

COMPUTER EXERCISES FOR APPENDIX 4 DATA BANK

C1. Go through the steps necessary to predict the JAS Type A score (Y) from the JAS Hard Driving and Competitive score (X) for all students. Find the following:
   a. Pearson r.
   b. Coefficient of determination, r^2.
   c. Standard error of estimate.
   d. Scatter diagram.
   e. Regression equation.
C2. Conduct a similar analysis predicting the women's JAS Type A score (Y) from the JAS Speed and Impatience score (X).
C3. Conduct a similar analysis predicting the men's JAS Hard-Driving and Competitive score (Y) from their BSRI Masculinity score (X).

CHAPTER 9

The Significance of the Difference between Means

Most of us drivers have experienced the phenomenon of "funneling" or "tunnel vision." When we are driving in light traffic out in the wide-open spaces, we can easily direct our attention to the changing scenery while we manage to stay on the road and avoid other drivers. However, should we approach an unfamiliar metropolitan freeway as traffic density increases and look for a particular exit ramp, we would notice a change in our behavior. Our visual field would be reduced to tracking the car ahead of us, with occasional glances at overhead traffic signs and the stream of vehicles on our right. There is no doubt that funneling has occurred—our increased attention to the central field of view interferes with our ability to respond to what is going on around us.

Traffic safety engineers have conducted numerous studies on the funneling effect to assist them in designing safer roadways. One such laboratory study had two groups of college students monitoring a computer display in the center of the visual field. The display required the "driver" to keep a spot of light aimed at a target moving on the screen. One group of students had a *simple* task with only a few targets moving at a relatively slow speed. The other group had a *complex* task, with more frequent targets moving at a faster speed.

In addition to this central tracking task, four small lights were located to the right and left side of the central task in the peripheral field of vision. Each student pressed a handheld switch whenever he or she detected a light coming on. The reaction time to these peripheral lights was measured in hundredths of a second.

The average reaction time to the peripheral lights was 56 hundredths for the simple task group and 59 hundredths for the complex task group. It would appear that the funneling effect is occurring, with the reaction times to the peripheral lights slower under the complex task ($\overline{X} = 59$) than under the simple task ($\overline{X} = 56$).

Much of the activity of the researcher in education and the behavioral sciences is directed toward comparing the performance of two groups. Such a comparison was just illustrated in the funneling effect—students with the simple central task had shorter reaction times than those with the complex central task. A sampling of other studies might show researchers investigating differences between men and women on mathematical ability, differences between only children and children from large families on introversion, and differences between college GPAs of marijuana users and those of marijuana nonusers. Whenever such differences are established, that is, verified by a number of independent investigators, they become part of our body of scientific knowledge and finally find their place in books on individual differences, child psychology, or drug abuse.

SAMPLING ERROR OR REAL DIFFERENCE?

Verification by the independent work of other researchers is an important part of the scientific method, but how does a single investigator determine whether or not he or she has found a difference in the performance of two groups? For example, suppose that our traffic safety researcher is investigating the relationship between personality factors and traffic violations. As part of a survey, a random sample of university students completed an anxiety scale, and also reported the number of moving traffic violations that they had been ticketed for since they had learned to drive. From this data a group of *safe drivers* (no violations) and a group of *at-risk drivers* (five or more violations) were formed. The mean anxiety scores for both groups are as follows:

Safe Drivers	At-Risk Drivers
$\overline{X} = 49.21$	$\overline{X} = 49.23$

We would certainly agree that there appears to be no difference in anxiety between the safe-driving group and the at-risk group. The slight difference we do observe (obviously 49.21 and 49.23 *are* different) is attributed to *chance* or *sampling error.*

But what if the researcher had obtained the following?

Safe Drivers	At-Risk Drivers
$\overline{X} = 49.21$	$\overline{X} = 49.27$

We would probably still conclude that the .06 difference between the two means was due to sampling error and there basically was no difference between the safe-driving group and the at-risk group.

But just how far apart must the two means be before we can say that our observed difference between the means is *not* due to chance? 49.21 and 49.50? 49.21 and 52.00? 49.21 and 55.00? We are faced with the same dilemma that we noted in the ESP example of Note 6.2. How will we ever be able to know for certain that the difference between two means is *not* due to chance or sampling error?

To help us answer this question, we will have to resort to the sampling distribution, a concept first introduced in Chapter 6. Our ultimate goal is to derive a technique that will enable us to make a probability statement regarding sampling error, just as we did in Chapter 6.

The Sampling Distribution of Differences between Pairs of Means

As an example, let us say that we are interested in seeing if there is any difference between the mathematical ability of college chemistry majors and that of college biology majors. Using appropriate sampling techniques, we select a sample of 100 chemistry majors and 100 biology majors, administer a mathematical aptitude test, and obtain the following results:

Chemistry	Biology
$\overline{X}_1 = 72.9$	$\overline{X}_2 = 68.4$

The obtained difference in the means of the two groups is $72.9 - 68.4 = 4.5$, and we would like to know if this indicates a real difference in mathematical ability on the part of chemistry majors, or if it is simply the result of sampling error.

Hypothesis Testing Again—A Quick Review.   We will solve this "chance" versus a "real" difference by using a sampling distribution and a null hypothesis as we did on two previous occasions. If you remember from Chapter 6, page 152, in the *one-sample case* we used a null hypothesis to test if the average height of college women could be 66 inches, given our sample mean of 65 inches. We set up our null hypothesis, H_0: $\mu = 66$ and found that we would reject H_0. We decided not to attribute the difference between $\mu = 66$ and $\overline{X} = 65$ to chance or sampling error.

We also used the null hypothesis approach in Chapter 7, page 177, to see if our Pearson r was significantly different from zero. Our null hypothesis, H_0: $\rho = 0$, stated that the true correlation in the population was 0. We found the correlation between two motor coordination tests for 25 students to be $r = .42$, and on the basis of the sampling distribution of r (from Table B), we rejected H_0. We decided that it was *not* likely that the true correlation in the population was really 0 and our sample $r = .42$ occurred just by chance or sampling error.

The Null Hypothesis in the Difference between Sample Means.   In order to evaluate the difference between means, we begin by assuming that there is *no differ-*

ence in the means of the populations from which our two samples were drawn. In other words, we assume that the mean mathematical ability of the population of chemistry majors is the same as the mean mathematical ability of the population of biology majors. If μ_1 is the mean ability of all chemistry majors and μ_2 is the mean ability of all biology majors, we are assuming that $\mu_1 = \mu_2$, or $\mu_1 - \mu_2 = 0$. This *null hypothesis, H_0: $\mu_1 - \mu_2 = 0$*, simply states that there is no difference between the means of the two populations from which we drew our two samples.

If this null hypothesis is true and $\mu_1 - \mu_2 = 0$, then our obtained difference of 4.5 is just sampling error. But to see if our assumption that $\mu_1 - \mu_2 = 0$ is true, let us indulge in another bit of fancy, just as we did in Chapter 6. We will conduct a hypothetical exercise by continuing to take pairs of samples and finding the differences in their means. Keeping track of these pairs, we might get the results shown in Table 9.1 (note that we always subtract the biology mean from the chemistry mean to obtain the difference).

As we ran this hypothetical exercise (all the while assuming H_0: $\mu_1 - \mu_2 = 0$), we would note that some of the differences were negative, some were positive, and most would be fairly close to zero.

If we continued this process for an *infinite* number of pairs of samples, the following would occur:

1. A batch of differences, called a *sampling distribution of differences between means,* would result.
2. The mean of this sampling distribution μ_{diff} (say "mean of the differences"), would be 0.
3. The batch of differences would be normally distributed around the mean of the distribution μ_{diff}, with a standard deviation of $\sqrt{\sigma_{\bar{x}_1}^2 + \sigma_{\bar{x}_2}^2}$.

Let us take a closer look at these three results.

Table 9.1
Hypothetical samples of means of mathematical ability of chemistry and biology majors

	Chemistry	Biology	Difference
Sample 1	73.5	73.9	−0.4
Sample 2	74.6	72.1	2.5
Sample 3	72.8	71.3	1.5
Sample 4	73.4	74.6	−1.2
Sample 5	72.9	72.9	0
	.	.	.
	.	.	.
	.	.	.
Means	μ_1	μ_2	μ_{diff}

Sampling Distribution of Differences between Means.   Even though we are assuming that the two populations have equal means, we do not expect that a sample drawn from one population will have a mean exactly identical to the mean of a sample drawn from the second population. We have grown accustomed to sampling error as a fact of life, and we would take for granted that in pairs of means, $\overline{X}_1$ will sometimes be greater than $\overline{X}_2$, and $\overline{X}_2$ will sometimes be greater than $\overline{X}_1$. This, of course, results in a distribution of differences, of which some will be negative and some positive.

The Mean of the Differences.   The mean of this distribution of differences, μ_{diff}, will be 0 under our assumption that $\mu_1 - \mu_2 = 0$. As indicated in the last paragraph, we expect that some differences will be negative and others positive, with the net effect being a mean that is zero.

Normal Sampling Distribution.   Since the distribution of differences is normal, we can use the characteristics of the normal curve to show, for example, that

1. 68.26% of all the differences would fall between −1 and 1 standard deviation from the mean, μ_{diff}.
2. 95% of all the differences would fall between −1.96 and 1.96 standard deviations from the mean, μ_{diff}.
3. 99% of all the differences would fall between −2.58 and 2.58 standard deviations from the mean, μ_{diff}.

Similarly, the probability statements we made concerning the normal curve would apply to this sampling distribution as well; for example:

1. $p = .68$ that any difference would fall between $\mu_{diff} \pm 1$ standard deviation.
2. $p = .95$ that any difference would fall between $\mu_{diff} \pm 1.96$ standard deviations.
3. $p = .05$ that any difference would fall *outside* the same interval, $\mu_{diff} \pm 1.96$ standard deviations.

With these probability statements in mind, let us get back to our original problem—that of deciding whether our obtained difference of 4.5 between the mean mathematical ability of chemistry and biology majors is simply due to sampling error. The first step in the decision process is to establish *where* in the sampling distribution of differences our obtained difference is located. Figure 9.1 shows this hypothetical sampling distribution, which, under the null hypothesis of $\mu_1 - \mu_2 = 0$, has a mean, μ_{diff} of 0.

Using the same logic that was introduced in Chapter 6, we need only find *where* in the sampling distribution of differences our obtained difference falls. If it is located toward the center of the distribution (i.e., between −1.96 and 1.96 standard deviations from the mean), we say that our obtained difference was caused by sampling error. On the other hand, if our difference is so large that it falls way

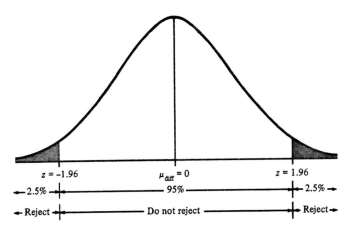

Figure 9.1
Sampling distribution of differences between means assuming the null hypothesis ($\mu_1 - \mu_2 = 0$).

out in either tail of the distribution (labeled "Reject" in Figure 9.1), we know that it would be an extremely rare occurrence, and we would wonder whether our difference is really due to sampling error after all.

The procedure is simple indeed. We need only calculate the z score for our difference and find its location in the sampling distribution of differences, as in Figure 9.1. Under the null hypothesis, H_0: $\mu_1 - \mu_2 = 0$, this sampling distribution of differences has $\mu_{diff} = 0$. Now if the z score of our difference were, for example, 1.23 or −0.67, we would say that our difference of 4.5 points between the mean mathematical ability of chemistry and biology majors could possibly be due to sampling error. However, if the z score of our difference were, for example, 1.98 or −2.37, we would say that it is a rare occurrence in a distribution that has $\mu_{diff} = 0$ and would conclude that μ_1 is not equal to μ_2 (or $\mu_1 - \mu_2 \neq 0$), μ_{diff} is not 0, and our obtained difference is a real difference and not sampling error.

Since that last sentence is crucial to understanding this chapter, let us briefly examine the concepts involved by referring to Figure 9.1.

1. If there is no difference in the populations from which the samples came, the probability that any obtained difference would deviate by ±1.96 standard deviations or more is .05. (Remember that only 5% of the differences are in the two tails of the distribution beyond ±1.96 standard deviations.) These differences are in the shaded portions of Figure 9.1.

2. If, in fact, our obtained difference falls in the *unshaded* portion of the distribution, that is, between −1.96 and 1.96 in Figure 9.1, we say that our difference could be due to sampling error. Since differences with z scores between −1.96 and 1.96 standard deviations happen 95% of the time just by sampling error, we have no reason to believe that our difference is anything but sampling error. We say that the difference is not significant.

3. However, if our obtained difference falls in the region of ±1.96 standard deviations or more (the shaded portions of Figure 9.1 labeled "Reject"), we are faced with two possibilities.

   a. μ_{diff} really *is* 0, and our difference is one of those rare occurrences that happen 5% of the time or less due to sampling error.

   b. μ_{diff} is *not* 0, but some other value, and our difference tells us that there is a real difference between the two populations from which we drew our samples. In this example, we would say that the chemistry majors are higher in mathematical ability than biology majors.

4. In light of the statistical conventions mentioned in Chapter 6, we will conclude that any difference that happens 5% of the time or less by sampling error, that is, $p \leq .05$ (read "probability is equal to or less than .05"), is not due to chance at all but represents a real difference. We say that the difference is significant at the .05 level, and we reject the null hypothesis, H_0: $\mu_1 - \mu_2 = 0$, in favor of an *alternate* hypothesis, H_A: $\mu_1 - \mu_2 \neq 0$.

Standard Error of the Difference between Means

In order to know where our obtained difference is located in the hypothetical sampling distribution of differences, we need to know the standard deviation of this distribution. We can then convert our difference to a z score and locate it precisely in the sampling distribution.

The standard deviation of this sampling distribution is called *the standard error of the difference between means,* and it is denoted by the symbol σ_{diff}. This statistic is to be interpreted as our ordinary, garden-variety standard deviation. For example, we know that 95% of the differences fall between –1.96 and 1.96 standard errors of the difference, or between $\mu_{diff} \pm 1.96\sigma_{diff}$.

When we calculate a z score for the sampling distribution of differences, we must modify the usual z score formula, $z = (X - \overline{X})/s$. The "score" of X is now the difference, or $\overline{X}_1 - \overline{X}_2$. The mean of the sampling distribution is now μ_{diff}, but, as you have seen, $\mu_{diff} = 0$ under our assumption of the null hypothesis, H_0: $\mu_1 - \mu_2 = 0$. The standard deviation of the sampling distribution is now the standard error of the difference, σ_{diff}. So our new formula for calculating a z score in a sampling distribution of differences is

$$z = \frac{(\overline{X}_1 - \overline{X}_2) - 0}{\sigma_{diff}} \tag{9.1}$$

Let us leave the computation of σ_{diff} for a later section and examine now the use of σ_{diff} in determining the significance of an obtained difference in the following hypothetical example. Suppose that in our study of the mathematical ability of chemistry and biology majors, we had obtained the following results.

Chemistry	**Biology**
$\overline{X}_1 = 72.6$	$\overline{X}_2 = 67.6$

$$\sigma_{diff} = 5.0$$

Is this difference between the means due to sampling error, or is it such a rare occurrence that we would suspect a real difference in the mathematical ability of the two groups? Our first step is to calculate a z score for the difference, which would be

$$z = \frac{(\bar{X}_1 - \bar{X}_2) - 0}{\sigma_{\text{diff}}} = \frac{72.6 - 67.6}{5} = \frac{5}{5} = 1.0$$

Since by sampling error it is just as easy to get $\bar{X}_2$ greater than $\bar{X}_1$, we will consider both tails of the curve and ask the question "What is the probability of obtaining a difference of 5 points just by sampling error from a sampling distribution whose mean is 0?" As we just noted, a difference of 5 points results in a z score of 1 (or -1 if $\bar{X}_2$ is greater than $\bar{X}_1$), and we can locate a difference of 5 points in the sampling distribution of differences as shown in Figure 9.2a. By using Table A we would see that 68.26% of the differences would fall between $-1z$ and $1z$, and 31.74% of the differences would result in z scores larger than 1 *if the null hypothesis is true* ($\mu_1 - \mu_2 = 0$, and $\mu_{\text{diff}} = 0$). Converting the percentages to probabilities, we see that $p = .3174$ that *any* obtained difference would deviate by 5 points or more just by sampling error. Since anything that happens 32% of the time is hardly a "rare occurrence," we conclude that the difference of 5 points in mathematical ability between chemistry and biology majors is possibly just due to sampling error.

But suppose, instead, that we had obtained the following results, shown graphically in Figure 9.2b.

Chemistry	Biology
$\bar{X}_1 = 72.6$	$\bar{X}_2 = 65.1$

$$\sigma_{\text{diff}} = 5.0$$

$$z = \frac{(\bar{X}_1 - \bar{X}_2) - 0}{\sigma_{\text{diff}}} = \frac{72.6 - 65.1}{5} = \frac{7.5}{5} = 1.5$$

Our calculations show that our obtained difference of 7.5 between the two means results in a z score of 1.5. What is the probability of obtaining a difference this large or larger just by sampling error from a sampling distribution whose mean is 0? By referring to Figure 9.2b and using Table A, we see that differences as large as 7.5 and larger will happen only 13.36% of the time just by sampling error, or $p = .1336$ that *any* obtained difference will be that large or larger. Since something that happens 13% of the time just by chance is not really a "rare occurrence," we would state that a difference of 7.5 points between the means of the two groups may simply be due to sampling error. But note that if the null hypothesis is *really* true ($\mu_1 - \mu_2 = 0$, and $\mu_{\text{diff}} = 0$) a difference as large as 7.5 is less likely to occur just by chance than is a difference of 5.0 (13% versus 32%).

As a final example, let us suppose that we had obtained the following results on the mathematical ability of chemistry and biology majors.

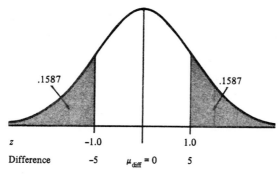

(a) Probability of difference larger than 5 is $p = .3174$.

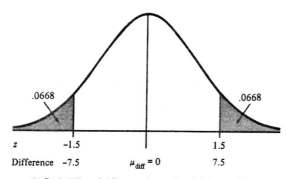

(b) Probability of difference larger than 7.5 is $p = .1336$.

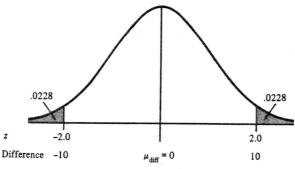

(c) Probability of difference larger than 10 is $p = .0456$.

Figure 9.2
Probabilities of obtaining differences as large as or larger than a result by sampling error.

$$\begin{array}{cc} \textbf{Chemistry} & \textbf{Biology} \\ \overline{X}_1 = 72.6 & \overline{X}_2 = 62.6 \end{array}$$

$$\sigma_{\text{diff}} = 5.0$$

$$z = \frac{(\overline{X}_1 - \overline{X}_2) - 0}{\sigma_{\text{diff}}} = \frac{72.6 - 62.6}{5} = \frac{10}{5} = 2$$

What is the probability of obtaining a difference of 10 points or more just by sampling error? Figure 9.2c and Table A show that we expect only 4.56% of the differences to be 10 points or more, if the null hypothesis that $\mu_1 - \mu_2 = 0$ is true. In other words, less than 5% of the differences would be this large or larger, so $p < .05$ that *any* obtained difference would be this large or larger. Since this is a relatively rare occurrence, we reject the null hypothesis that μ_{diff} is really 0 and state that there is a significant difference between the average mathematical ability of the population of chemistry majors and that of the population of biology majors.

In summary, the steps involved in determining the significance of a difference are as follows:

1. Assume a null hypothesis—usually that the means of the two populations from which the samples are drawn are equal (H_0: $\mu_1 - \mu_2 = 0$).

2. Calculate the z score for your obtained difference between the means of the two samples and locate it in the sampling distribution of differences whose mean, μ_{diff}, is 0.

3. If the resulting z score falls between $\mu_{\text{diff}} \pm 1.96\sigma_{\text{diff}}$, assume that the difference in sample means is due to sampling error.

4. If the resulting z score falls *outside* the interval $\mu_{\text{diff}} \pm 1.96\sigma_{\text{diff}}$, reject the null hypothesis, H_0: $\mu_1 - \mu_2 = 0$, in favor of the alternate hypothesis, H_A: $\mu_1 - \mu_2 \neq 0$. In other words, we will state that our obtained difference is significant at the .05 level.

Calculating the Standard Error of the Difference between Means

The standard error of the difference between means, as we noted earlier, is the standard deviation of the hypothetical sampling distribution of differences, and it is given by the following formula:

$$\sigma_{\text{diff}} = \sqrt{\sigma_{\overline{X}_1}^2 + \sigma_{\overline{X}_2}^2} \qquad (9.2)$$

where

σ_{diff} = the standard error of the difference between means
$\sigma_{\overline{X}_1}$ = the standard error of the mean of one distribution
$\sigma_{\overline{X}_2}$ = the standard error of the mean of the other distribution

However, we noted in Chapter 6 that the standard error of the mean, $\sigma_{\overline{X}}$, is calculated from the *population* standard deviation, so formula 9.2 is of little value to us, since we rarely know the value of σ. As a result, we must have a formula for the standard error of the difference that permits us to use the standard deviations of our samples.* The formula that we shall use extensively is

$$s_{\text{diff}} = \sqrt{\frac{(N_1 - 1)s_1^2 + (N_2 - 1)s_2^2}{N_1 + N_2 - 2} \left[\frac{1}{N_1} + \frac{1}{N_2}\right]} \qquad (9.3)$$

where

s_1 = the standard deviation of the first sample
s_2 = the standard deviation of the second sample
N_1 and N_2 = the sizes of the respective samples

TESTING FOR SIGNIFICANT DIFFERENCES: THE *t* TEST FOR TWO INDEPENDENT SAMPLES

We must note that s_{diff} is an *estimate* of σ_{diff}, and because s_{diff} is based on the standard deviations of the samples, it is subject to sampling error. When the standard deviations of the populations are not known (so σ_{diff} cannot be calculated), the normal distribution can no longer be used, which, of course, means that the z score values of 1.96 and 2.58 cannot automatically be used to describe the region of rejection in the tails of the distribution.

So, instead of the normal distribution with the usual z values, we use what is called the *t* distribution, and the statistical procedure is known as the *t* test. We calculate a *t* value and locate its position in the *t* distribution, just as we did earlier for the z score. The procedure is the same as before, but we no longer use 1.96 and 2.58 as dividing lines for acceptance or rejection of the null hypothesis. The *t* statistic, in fact, has the same formula as the z score used earlier, except the denominator is now s_{diff}.

$$t = \frac{(\overline{X}_1 - \overline{X}_2) - 0}{s_{\text{diff}}} \qquad (9.4)$$

The *t* Distribution

The *t* distribution (sometimes called "Student's *t*," after W. S. Gossett, who published under the pseudonym "Student") looks very much like the normal curve, except that the tails for the *t* distribution are higher and we must go farther out to find the *t* values that mark off the 5% and 1% regions in the distribution. This difference is illustrated graphically in Figure 9.3.

Note that the normal curve has 95% of its area between the usual z scores of −1.96 and 1.96 while the *t* distribution shown in Figure 9.3 for a combined sam-

---

*Note that the symbol for the standard error of the difference is σ_{diff} when the standard error of the mean, $\sigma_{\overline{X}}$, is calculated from the population σ. When it is calculated from the sample standard deviation, s, we will use the symbol s_{diff}.

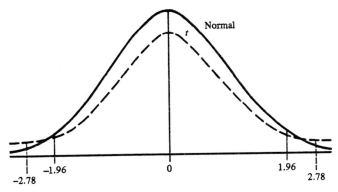

Figure 9.3
Comparison of a normal distribution and a *t* distribution (*N* = 6) showing the 95% limits for each distribution.

ple size of 6 has 95% of its area between −2.78 and 2.78. As the sample size gets larger, the *t* distribution looks more and more like the normal curve, and, when the *N* of the combined samples is about 30, the curves are approximately identical. As a result, of course, as the size of your samples gets smaller, you need a larger *t* value to reject the null hypothesis.

Since the normal curve and the *t* distribution are exactly identical only with an *infinitely large* sample size, it has become conventional always to use the *t* distribution, *regardless of sample size*. This means that we can ignore the *z* values of 1.96 and 2.58 in favor of a specific *t* value that is determined by the size of our samples or, more properly, the *degrees of freedom* in our samples.

The Degrees of Freedom (*df*) Concept

Before we can look at the different *t* distributions, we must become acquainted, at least superficially, with a concept known as *degrees of freedom*. Although a knowledge of advanced statistical theory is necessary to completely understand this concept, we can say that the degrees of freedom in a sample is *the number of observations that are free to vary*.

For example, if we put a restriction on a set of five numbers, such that $\Sigma X = 12$, we may pick any *four* numbers we like, but the *fifth* one is not free to vary, since it, added to the others, must meet the requirement of $\Sigma X = 12$. If we choose 3, 2, 4, and 7, we *must* use −4 as the fifth number in order to meet this requirement, since 3 + 2 + 4 + 7 = 16 and only a −4 would yield $\Sigma X = 12$. In this case we have $N - 1$ degrees of freedom, since only one observation is restricted in meeting the requirement. Stated more formally, $df = N - 1$.

In the calculation of a *t* test, each of the two samples has $N - 1$ degrees of freedom. This means that the total *df* for *both* samples would be $(N_1 - 1) + (N_2 - 1)$, which would sum to $N_1 + N_2 - 2$. Thus the total *df* for our samples is 2 less than the combined sample size. For example, if we had 20 students in one group and 10 students in the second group, our total *df* would be $(20 - 1) + (10 - 1) = 19 + 9 = 28$.

Using the *t* Table

As we noticed earlier, there is a different *t* distribution for every sample size. Therefore, we could have a table of *t* values similar to a normal curve table for every sample size from 2 to infinity! In the interest of brevity, we do not usually consider all areas of the curve, but only those points that indicate the usual significance levels, such as .05, .01, and .001. Table D in Appendix 3 lists the *t* values that must be equaled or exceeded for these usual significance levels for various sample sizes (in terms of degrees of freedom). Note that the table gives both one-tailed and two-tailed values. Let us consider for now only the two-tailed values. We will interpret the one-tailed values later on in the chapter.

For the example of the preceding subsection, with 28 degrees of freedom, how large must our *t* value be in order to be significant at the .05 level? From Table D, we see that for a *df* of 28, the tabled value of *t* is 2.048. We know that our calculated *t* must be at least 2.048 before we can reject the null hypothesis at the .05 level.

As another example, suppose that you had 7 students in one group and 12 in a second group. How large would your *t* value have to be in order for it to be significant at the .01 level? Again, from Table D we see that for 17 degrees of freedom $(df = 6 + 11)$, we would need a *t* of at least 2.898 in order to reject the null hypothesis at the .01 level.

Calculating the *t* Test for Independent Samples[†]

Although the formula for s_{diff} looks somewhat complicated, it is relatively easy to use in practice, since it requires only the standard deviations of the samples and the *N* of each sample. Table 9.2 shows the calculation of s_{diff} and its use in determining the significance of a difference between the number of study hours reported by low-anxious and high-anxious college students.

Following the four steps listed earlier, we note in the example of Table 9.2 that a null hypothesis would state that the mean number of study hours for a population of low-anxious students is the same as the population mean for high-anxious students, or $\mu_1 - \mu_2 = 0$. A sample of 14 low- and 13 high-anxious students from these two populations shows a mean difference of $15.79 - 18.77 = -2.98$.

After calculating *t* to be -1.40, we consult Table D for 25 degrees of freedom. We note that a *t* value of ±2.060 marks off the 5% region of rejection. Since our calculated value of -1.40 is well within the central region (as shown in Figure 9.4), it is hardly a "rare occurrence" and we have no reason to believe that the null hypothesis should be rejected. We pronounce the obtained difference not significant,

---

[†]By *independent samples* we mean that the selection of a member of one group does not influence the selection of any member of the second group.

Table 9.2
Testing for significant differences in self-reported study hours for low-anxious and high-anxious students

	Low Anxious	High Anxious
	$\bar{X}_1 = 15.79$	$\bar{X}_2 = 18.77$
	$s_1 = 5.38$	$s_2 = 5.70$
	$N_1 = 14$	$N_2 = 13$

$$s_{diff} = \sqrt{\frac{(N_1-1)s_1^2+(N_2-1)s_2^2}{N_1+N_2-2}\left[\frac{1}{N_1}+\frac{1}{N_2}\right]}$$

$$= \sqrt{\frac{(14-1)(5.38)^2+(13-1)(5.70)^2}{14+13-2}\left(\frac{1}{14}+\frac{1}{13}\right)}$$

$$= \sqrt{\frac{376.2772+389.88}{25}}(.0714+.0769)$$

$$= \sqrt{30.6463(0.1483)}$$

$$= \sqrt{4.5448}$$

$$= 2.13$$

$$t = \frac{\bar{X}_1-\bar{X}_2-0}{s_{diff}} = \frac{15.79-18.77}{2.13} = \frac{-2.98}{2.13} = -1.40$$

Not a significant difference at the .05 level, so we write $t(25) = -1.40$, $p > .05$.

since the probability is greater than .05 ($p > .05$) that this result could be produced by sampling error alone.

Table 9.2 illustrated a typical research study, with the statistical logic behind the decision to conclude that an observed difference was not significant. Let us consider a recent study that led the investigators to conclude that the differences were significant. The mean GPA was calculated for a sample of 30 marijuana users and 30 nonusers on a college campus. The calculations are shown in Table 9.3.

In analyzing the data of Table 9.3, we would first state a null hypothesis, that the mean college GPA for the population of marijuana users would be the same as the population mean for nonusers, $\mu_1 - \mu_2 = 0$. A sample of 30 marijuana users and 30 nonusers from these two populations shows a mean difference in college GPA of $3.05 - 2.75 = 0.30$.

After calculating a t of 2.31, we note from Table D that ±2.009 marks off the 5% region of rejection (we are conservative and use the tabled value for $df = 50$, since the value for $df = 58$ is not listed). Note that our calculated t of 2.31 is outside the interval, as shown in Figure 9.5. Since this is a rare occurrence, happen-

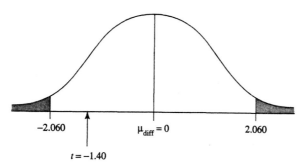

Figure 9.4
Nonsignificant difference in study hours of low-anxious and high-anxious students, with a *t* of −1.40.

ing less than 5% of the time by sampling error ($p < .05$), we conclude that it is not likely that $\mu_1 - \mu_2 = 0$. We reject this null hypothesis in favor of $\mu_1 - \mu_2 \neq 0$ and say that there is a significant difference in the grade-point averages of marijuana users and nonusers.

Significance Levels

In the preceding discussion and in the examples of Tables 9.2 and 9.3, we have seen that any difference occurring 5% of the time or less through sampling error is labeled a "significant" difference. Our concluding statement is that the difference is "significant at the .05 level," or "the null hypothesis is rejected at the .05 level." As you saw in Chapter 6, a significance level (or alpha) is the *p* that a result is due to chance. There is nothing magic about the 5% point; it is simply an arbitrary designation that has become a convention or rule of thumb. Presumably, the 6% or 4% levels could be similarly justified.

However, many statisticians feel that there should be some way to indicate just how rare a rare occurrence is under the null hypothesis, so the .01 level and .001 level have been added to the familiar .05 level.[‡] If a difference is significant at the .01 level, we are saying that the obtained difference would happen by sampling error 1% of the time or less. Similarly, if a difference is stated as significant at the .001 level, the obtained difference would happen by sampling error 0.1% of the time or less. To summarize:

1. If a difference would happen 5% of the time or less by sampling error but is not large enough so that it reaches the 1% level, we state that the difference is significant at the .05 level, or $p \leq .05$ that the obtained difference would

---

[‡]As noted in Chapter 6, there is some controversy over the use of significance levels to inform us where a difference is located in the sampling distribution. Your instructor may prefer an alternate approach to the one described here.

Table 9.3
Testing for significant differences in college GPA among
marijuana users and nonusers.

	Nonusers	Users
	$\bar{X}_1 = 3.05$	$\bar{X}_2 = 2.75$
	$s_1 = 0.60$	$s_2 = 0.40$
	$N_1 = 30$	$N_2 = 30$

$$s_{diff} = \sqrt{\frac{(N_1 - 1)s_1^2 + (N_2 - 1) s_2^2}{N_1 + N_2 - 2} \left[\frac{1}{N_1} + \frac{1}{N_2}\right]}$$

$$= \sqrt{\frac{(30 - 1)(.60)^2 + (30 - 1)(.40)^2}{30 + 30 - 2} \left(\frac{1}{30} + \frac{1}{30}\right)}$$

$$= \sqrt{\frac{10.44 + 4.64}{58} (.0667)}$$

$$= \sqrt{\frac{15.08}{58} (.0667)}$$

$$= \sqrt{.0173}$$

$$= 0.13$$

$$t = \frac{\bar{X}_1 - \bar{X}_2 - 0}{s_{diff}} = \frac{3.05 - 2.75}{.13} = \frac{.30}{.13} = 2.31$$

There is a significant difference at the .05 level, $t(58) = 2.31$, $p < .05$.

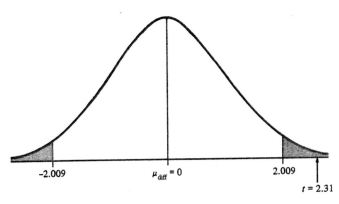

Figure 9.5
Significant difference in college GPA of marijuana users and nonusers with a t of 2.31.

happen by sampling error, or $.05 > p > .01$ (probability of the obtained difference happening by sampling error is between .05 and .01).

2. If a difference would happen 1% of the time or less by sampling error but is not large enough so that it reaches the 0.1% level, we state that the difference is significant at the .01 level, or $p \leq .01$ that the difference would happen by sampling error, or $.01 > p > .001$.

3. If a difference would happen 0.1% of the time or less by sampling error, we state that the difference is significant at the .001 level, or $p \leq .001$.

We will have occasion in a later section to examine these various significance levels in greater detail and to show how they are involved in making decisions regarding sampling error.

The Null Hypothesis and Other Hypotheses

We have pursued the simplest approach in testing the null hypothesis. We eventually choose H_0: $\mu_1 - \mu_2 = 0$ or reject it in favor of the alternate hypothesis, H_A: $\mu_1 - \mu_2 \neq 0$. It is a common error to confuse the alternate hypothesis, H_A, with a researcher's *experimental* hypothesis. An important maxim in statistical decision making is that the *rejection of the null hypothesis does not necessarily make an experimental hypothesis true*. For example, a researcher might hypothesize that elementary school pupils who had attended nursery school would get better grades than those who had not attended nursery school, because of the socializing influence of the nursery school setting.

The researcher first assumes the null hypothesis that there is no difference between the academic performance of both groups and then gathers data and runs a t test. If there is a significant difference between the two groups, the researcher can conclude only that $\mu_1 - \mu_2 \neq 0$. It cannot be said, for example, that the children with a nursery school background get better grades because they are more conforming, or more classroom-oriented, or more socially adjusted, on the basis of the statistical test alone. The statistical procedure allows us only to reject the null hypothesis, since such a decision is based on the probability of a difference occurring by sampling error. The researcher cannot go any farther than that and use this approach to prove why a difference exists.

While we are on the subject of null hypotheses, we must note that we do not always assume a null hypothesis H_0: $\mu_1 - \mu_2$ that is equal to zero. Occasionally, we may wish to test our obtained difference, $\overline{X}_1 - \overline{X}_2$, against some other null hypothesis. For example, the usual difference in yields between two varieties of corn might be 17 bushels per acre as reported from different experimental seed plots in Iowa and Nebraska. However, a test of the two varieties under different rainfall and soil conditions in several western states might have produced a sample difference of $\overline{X}_1 - \overline{X}_2 = 26$ bushels per acre. A t test could then be run on this difference to see whether the null hypothesis H_0: $\mu_1 - \mu_2 = 17$ bushels, should be rejected.

Note 9.1

Statistical Significance Versus Practical Significance

When we use the term *significant difference*, our definition of *significant* is just as we have explored in the last few pages—it is simply a statement of an arbitrarily chosen probability level.

However, we sometimes make the association "significant = important." This is unfortunate, because a difference between two means may be declared significant or nonsignificant solely on the basis of sample size. For example, a researcher in a state department of education conducts a survey with a sample of 40,000 fourth-graders. Among other things the researcher reports that the mean mathematics aptitude score is 52.3 for children who regularly eat breakfast versus 52.1 for those who come to school hungry, $t(39,998) = 1.99, p < .05$, a "significant" difference. Clearly, the difference between 52.3 and 52.1 is hardly cause to embark on a statewide school breakfast program. While the p value is the single determinant of significance, it is necessary in any research to look at the size of the difference between the means. We must distinguish, then, between a trivial difference and one that has practical significance.

If other null hypotheses than $\mu_1 - \mu_2 = 0$ are tested, the formula for t needs to be altered to include your hypothesized value of $\mu_1 - \mu_2$ in place of the 0 in formula 9.4. But, it is probably true that most null hypotheses that we test in education and the behavioral sciences are of the $\mu_1 - \mu_2 = 0$ variety.

Assumptions Underlying the t Test

We noted in Chapter 8 that there were certain restrictions or assumptions about the data that were necessary before a Pearson r could be interpreted meaningfully. In a similar fashion, the t test has four restrictions that must be met before the t can be interpreted in the manner described in the preceding sections. These are as follows:

1. The scores must be interval or ratio in nature.
2. The scores must be measures on random samples from the respective populations.
3. The populations from which the samples were drawn must be normally distributed.
4. The populations from which the samples were drawn must have approximately the same variability (homogeneity of variance).

Since these assumptions will be popping up in a number of other contexts, let us look at each one in some detail.

Note 9.2
The Origin of "Student's *t* Distribution"

In the early 1900s an Englishman by the name of W. S. Gossett was using sampling techniques to ensure quality control at a brewery. The typical sampling procedure involved using a normal curve distribution to set up a confidence interval for estimating the population mean, μ. This procedure required that the researcher take large samples in order to have a sample variance that was a reliable estimate of the population variance, σ^2. Presumably, Gossett tired of the tedious effort involved in taking large samples and developed the *t* distribution, which enabled the researcher to estimate μ with much smaller samples. He published his theory in 1908 under the pseudonym "Student," and the distribution he developed is often called "Student's *t* distribution."

Interval or Ratio Data.   Since means and standard deviations are calculated in the *t* test, the data must be at least interval in nature.

Random Samples.   The statistical theory underlying the *t* test rests heavily on an assumption of random sampling, and this assumption must be met.

Normally Distributed Populations.   In most cases, this is a reasonable assumption, since we are fairly certain that the majority of psychological and physiological characteristics are normally distributed. Note that this is *not* the same as saying that the *samples* are normally distributed.

Homogeneity of Variance.   The formula for the standard error of the difference (formula 9.3) for calculating *t* is based on the assumption of equal variances in the two populations. There are statistical techniques available to test for homogeneity based on the samples, and one technique is demonstrated in the SPSS computer solution at the end of the chapter. One rule of thumb might be helpful. If there are approximately the same number of observations in both groups, we can "eyeball" the standard deviations, and, if one is more than twice as large as the other, we should question whether the homogeneity-of-variance assumption has been met.

In summarizing the four assumptions, we are happy to note that the *t* test will give fairly accurate results, even if these assumptions have been violated to a certain degree. The *t* test is extremely resistant to departures from normality and, to a lesser degree, departures from homogeneity of variance. If you are in doubt about whether you can run a *t* test on some data because these assumptions may not have been met, it may be possible to do so simply by requiring a more stringent significance level (e.g., .01 instead of .05).

TESTING FOR SIGNIFICANT DIFFERENCES: THE *t* TEST FOR TWO CORRELATED SAMPLES

The *t* test that was described in previous sections is intended for samples that are *independent* samples or *uncorrelated* samples. But there are times when we would like to see if there is a significant difference between the means of *correlated* samples, and this section describes a *t* test for either *matched samples* or *repeated measurements of the same subject*.

Matched Samples

We noted in the *t* test for *independent* samples that subjects were assigned at *random* to one of two groups or *random* samples were taken from two populations. With matched samples, we do not depend on random assignment to get our samples but construct them carefully to make sure they are equal on any variables that affect what we are measuring. We can do so by matched pairs, split litters, and co-twin controls.

Matched Pairs.   When matched pairs are used, they are usually matched on the basis of some variable that correlates highly with what we are measuring. For example, if we wanted to see if college freshmen who come from metropolitan high schools get better grades in college than those who come from rural schools, we would probably decide to use college entrance exam scores as the matching variable. For example, a person with a high entrance exam score from an urban school would be matched with a person with a high score from a rural school. In this manner, we would feel quite certain that both groups of matched pairs are equal in ability at the start and that any differences in future college grades would be due to the environmental setting from which they came.

Split Litters.   Many animal experiments involve the split-litter method, which resembles the matched-pair method. One member of a litter of kittens, for example, may be placed in an experimental group and another of the same litter placed in the control group. This method would ensure that both groups are alike with respect to certain hereditary and prenatal factors that might influence the variable that we are measuring.

Co-Twin Controls.   The purpose of the co-twin control is very similar to that of the split-litter technique, except that human identical twins are used. In many studies of maturation and development, one child is assigned to a control group and its twin to the experimental group. Any differences between the groups as a result of some experimental procedure would then be attributed to the independent variable, since both groups are similar in hereditary and maturational factors.

Repeated Measures of the Same Subject

One way to ensure that both groups are equal before some experimental procedure is attempted would be to have the same person serve in both groups. For example, if we were to investigate whether a person has greater hand steadiness with the preferred or the nonpreferred hand, we could test each subject under both conditions: once with the preferred hand and once with the nonpreferred hand. At least we do not have to worry about both groups being equal at the start, since both "groups" consist of the same people!

Calculating a Correlated *t* Test: Direct Difference Method

Whether we use matched pairs or repeated measurements, we wind up with one measurement in each condition. These are *correlated* data, since if one member of a pair scores high in one condition the matched partner would have a tendency to score high in the other condition. Obviously, the same would hold true for repeated measures, where a person scoring high in one condition would tend to score high in the other condition.

There are a number of computational methods for calculating a correlated *t* test, but one of the simplest is called the *direct difference* method. Table 9.4 shows an example of the tunnel-vision effect discussed at the beginning of this chapter. Each driver's reaction time to the peripheral lights was measured during a simple visual task and during a complex visual task. The simple task required subjects to point a cursor at a spot of light changing direction once a second. In the complex task, the spot changed direction three times a second. Reaction times are shown in hundredths of seconds in Table 9.4. Since each driver served in both conditions, this is an example of the repeated measures design.

Note that in the direct difference method, we are working only with the differences between the pairs of observations in the difference column (D). The formula for the mean of the differences would be

$$\overline{D} = \frac{\Sigma D}{N} \tag{9.5}$$

where

ΣD = the sum of the differences (D) column

N = the number of pairs

In Table 9.4, the algebraic sum of the D column is 27, so the mean of the differences, $\overline{D}$, is 2.7. As you can see, this is the same as the difference between the means of the reaction times, 39.9 and 37.2.

You calculate the standard deviation of the differences in the usual way, by squaring each difference to obtain the D^2 column and substituting ΣD^2 into the slightly modified version of our ordinary standard deviation formula,

$$s_D = \sqrt{\frac{\Sigma D^2 - \frac{(\Sigma D)^2}{N}}{N-1}} \tag{9.6}$$

Table 9.4
Direct difference method for correlated t test

Subject	Simple	Complex	D	D²
A	37	39	2	4
B	39	45	6	36
C	35	34	−1	1
D	41	43	2	4
E	32	37	5	25
F	35	38	3	9
G	36	35	−1	1
H	39	45	6	36
I	40	42	2	4
J	38	41	3	9
	372	399	27	129
	$\bar{X}_1 = 37.2$	$\bar{X}_2 = 39.9$	$\bar{D} = 2.7$	

Mean of the Differences:

$$\bar{D} = \frac{\Sigma D}{N} = \frac{27}{10} = 2.7$$

Standard Deviation of the Differences:

$$s_D = \sqrt{\frac{\Sigma D^2 - \frac{(\Sigma D)^2}{N}}{N-1}} = \sqrt{\frac{129 - \frac{(27)^2}{10}}{9}}$$

$$= \sqrt{\frac{129 - 72.9}{9}} = \sqrt{6.2333}$$

$$= 2.50$$

Standard Error of the Mean for the Differences:

$$s_{\bar{D}} = \frac{s_D}{\sqrt{N}} = \frac{2.50}{\sqrt{10}} = \frac{2.50}{3.16} = 0.79$$

Correlated t Test:

$$t = \frac{\bar{D}}{s_{\bar{D}}} = \frac{2.7}{0.79} = 3.42$$

There is a significant difference between the means, $t(9) = 3.42$, $p < .01$.

where

ΣD = the sum of the D column
ΣD^2 = the sum of the D^2 column
N = the number of pairs

The standard deviation of the differences, s_D, in Table 9.3 is 2.50.

We next calculate the standard error of the mean for the differences, $s_{\bar{D}}$, using the following formula:

$$s_{\bar{D}} = \frac{s_D}{\sqrt{N}} \qquad (9.7)$$

where

s_D = the standard deviation of the differences
N = the number of pairs

Note that this formula is similar to an earlier one for the standard error of the mean, where a standard deviation is divided by $\sqrt{N}$. In Table 9.4, $s_{\bar{D}}$ is calculated to be 0.79.

Finally, we calculate the correlated t test by

$$t = \frac{\bar{D}}{s_{\bar{D}}} \qquad (9.8)$$

where

$\bar{D}$ = the mean of the differences
$s_{\bar{D}}$ = the standard error of the mean of the differences

For the data of Table 9.4, $t = 3.42$. Checking Table D we see that for 9 degrees of freedom and a two-tailed test, a t of 3.250 is significant at the .01 level. The reaction time to the peripheral lights during the complex task was significantly longer than during the simple task, $t(9) = 3.42$, $p < .01$.

ERRORS IN MAKING DECISIONS: THE TYPE I AND TYPE II ERRORS

On several occasions, both in this chapter and in Chapter 6, we have examined in detail the problem of deciding whether a particular experimental result was due to sampling error or whether the observed difference between the sample means represented a *real* difference in the variables under study. We have noted that if a result could occur *by chance* 50% of the time, or 13%, or 6%, we will still attribute the results to sampling error. And, as was pointed out earlier, statisticians have conventionally used the 5% level as the cutting point; that is, if a certain result happens 5% of the time or less by chance, we will say that it is *not* sampling error but the result is a real one.

These statements should be very familiar to you by now, but let us look closely at the problems that arise when we are confronted with decisions between sampling error and real results. Suppose that we run a study to see if there is any difference in reading proficiency between left-handers and right-handers. As usual, we assume the null hypothesis, H_0: $\mu_1 - \mu_2 = 0$, gather a sample of left- and right-handed schoolchildren, administer a reading proficiency test, and perform the necessary calculations. We now have to decide whether our findings are "significant."

Let us pause a moment to consider the choices confronting us. As usual, we are faced with the two familiar possibilities:

1. There is no difference between left- and right-handers (H_0: $\mu_1 - \mu_2 = 0$ is true), and the obtained difference is due to sampling error.
2. There is indeed a difference between left- and right-handers (H_0: $\mu_1 - \mu_2 = 0$ is *not* true).

If we find that our t value will occur 5% of the time or less just by sampling error, we will very likely choose option 2 and decide that there is a real difference between left- and right-handers, rejecting the null hypothesis. *But we could be wrong!* We just might have been unlucky enough to get one of those rare occurrences that happen 5% of the time or less even when the null hypothesis is true. If there is no difference between the means of the populations from which the samples were drawn, then $\mu_1 - \mu_2 = 0$, and we have made a mistake by calling our difference a significant one instead of sampling error. This mistake is called a *Type I error.* Formally defined, a Type I error is committed *if the null hypothesis is rejected when it actually is true.*

So, what are we to do in order to avoid making a Type I error? In an earlier section, we noted that there are different significance levels, and as cautious, conservative researchers, we might very well demand that our t value be significant at the .01 level, or even the .001 level, in order to be more certain that we do not label as significant a difference that really is only sampling error.

But look what happens when we do this. Suppose we choose option 1 and decide that our finding is due to sampling error—*but it may be a real difference!* That is to say, there may be a difference between the means of the two populations that we have decided to attribute to sampling error. This error is called a *Type II error.* A Type II error is committed *if the null hypothesis is accepted when actually it is false.*

We obviously have a real dilemma here, because the more we try to avoid making a Type I error by demanding greater significance, the greater are the chances of our making a Type II error. And, if we scrupulously avoid the taint of a Type II error by not being quite so strict, the possibility of our making a Type I error is back again. Before looking at ways in which this problem is handled, let us review this complex decision process in the form of a *decision matrix* (shown in Table 9.5) and consider each of the four decision possibilities.

H_0 *Is Rejected When It Is, in Fact, True.*   The upper left square of the matrix illustrates the Type I error, where the researcher decides that the t value is significant

Table 9.5
Decision matrix for rejecting or not rejecting H_0

	Decision on the Basis of Sampling	
	Reject H_0	Accept H_0
H_0 is True in population	Type I error $p = \alpha$	correct
H_0 is False in population	correct $p = 1 - \beta$	Type II error $p = \beta$

and rejects the null hypothesis when it really is true. The probability of making a Type I error is the same as the value of the significance level that the researcher chooses. As noted earlier, the Greek letter alpha, α, is used to indicate significance levels, so α can be .05, .01, .001, etc. Thus, if $\alpha = .05$, for example, we say that the probability of a Type I error occurring is .05. A moment's reflection should show why this is true. Since 5% of the sampling distribution (with $\mu_{diff} = 0$) is in the region of rejection when the researcher chooses $\alpha = .05$, if all differences were labeled as significant, he or she would be wrong 5% of the time (i.e., whenever the difference fell in this region). One thing must be noted: The probability of a Type I error is under our direct control, since we are responsible for setting the significance level.

H_0 *Is Accepted When It Is True.* The upper right square indicates a decision to accept H_0, which was a correct decision, since H_0 is, in fact, true. We must be careful to note that a finding of nonsignificance does not *prove* that the null hypothesis is true. It is evidence, but it is not conclusive proof.

H_0 *Is Accepted When It Is False.* The lower right square of the decision matrix illustrates the Type II error, where the researcher decides to accept the null hypothesis, when, in fact, the null hypothesis is false. The probability of making a Type II error is noted by the Greek letter beta, β. In the next chapter we will examine the characteristics of β, but for now we should note that the relationship between α and β is not a simple one. However, it is true that as we decrease the probability of a Type I error we increase the probability of a Type II error.

H_0 *Is Rejected When It Is False.* The lower left square indicates the correct decision to reject the null hypothesis when it is false. We gave only a passing comment to the other correct decision (accepting H_0 when it was true), but we need to devote more time to the correct rejection of the null hypothesis. The typical researcher is very much concerned with correct rejection of the null hypothesis, since we basically are seeking to establish significant relationships. In other words, if there is a difference between two variables out in the population, we want to find it. Therefore, we want to use a statistical test that is sensitive to these differences. *The ability of a test to reject the null hypothesis when it is false is called the "power" of a test.* Power (defined as $1 - \beta$) is a characteristic of any statistical test; the more power a statistical test has, the more likely it is to detect significant differences if they exist. So, all things being equal, a researcher will choose a statistical test that has the greatest amount of power. We will examine the issue of power in considerable detail in Chapter 10.

Resolving the Sampling Error–Real Difference Dilemma

You have probably gathered by now that there is no easy way of determining whether an observed difference is sampling error or a real difference. But we can ask ourselves if we prefer a Type I error or a Type II error! Our choice of which error to risk is determined by the nature of the subject matter being studied.

On important theoretical issues, such as demonstrating the existence of ESP, we might wish to set our significance levels very low ($\alpha = .01$ or $.001$). We do not want to risk our laboratory or scientific career by stating that we found some weird or bizarre result to be significant when it was really due to sampling error. In this instance we definitely prefer to avoid a Type I error (by reducing our α to .01 or .001) and to risk a Type II error.

If, on the other hand, a researcher is comparing two proven poultry disinfectants for germ-killing ability and poultry farmers are in dire need of some kind of disinfectant, we do not really care very much if we pronounce brand A better than brand B. If we say that one is better than the other, when actually there is no difference, we are making a Type I error, but since some kind of disinfectant is sorely needed, no great problem arises from our error. Either brand A or brand B will do the job. It is clear that considerations other than statistical ones are necessary to make a decision to favor a Type I or Type II error.

Correlated versus Uncorrelated *t* Tests and Type II Errors

If instead of using the direct difference method on the data of Table 9.4, we had mistakenly used the *t* test for random samples, our *t* value would have been 1.79, which is not significant ($p > .05$), rather than 3.42, which is significant at the .01 level. The reason for the larger *t* when we are using the correlated *t* test is that the method has a built-in correction for the amount of correlation between the matching variable and the actual measures. If it turned out that the correlation between the two were actually 0, both the direct difference method and the *t* test for random samples would yield the same value of *t*.

The larger *t* with the correlated *t* test means that you are more likely to reject the null hypothesis and *less likely to make a Type II error*. You are more likely to pick up a difference, if it exists, with a correlated *t* test.

Then why not use a correlated design with its matched pairs all the time? The answer to this question lies in the number of degrees of freedom for the two different approaches. As we saw earlier in the chapter, the degrees of freedom for a t test for independent samples was $df = (N_1 - 1) + (N_2 - 1)$. Note that this is twice as many degrees of freedom as we have in the correlated t test, where $df = N - 1$ and N is the number of pairs. As a result, a somewhat higher t value is needed for significance at a given level with the correlated t test.

Consequently, there should be a substantial correlation between the variable that is used for matching the pairs (the independent variable) and the variable that is used for the measurements to be made (the dependent variable). For example, a researcher studying the reading comprehension of science majors versus humanities majors would not match pairs on the basis of height or weight, since there is no relationship between reading comprehension and these physical measures. As explained in the previous paragraph, using these as a matching variable would only reduce the number of degrees of freedom in the t test.

ONE-TAILED VERSUS TWO-TAILED TESTS

The significance tests that we have discussed so far have all been *two-tailed* tests. This means that we propose a null hypothesis H_0: $\mu_1 = \mu_2$, so, if we decide to reject the hypothesis, it may be that either $\mu_1 > \mu_2$ or $\mu_2 > \mu_1$. In other words, the null hypothesis will be rejected if the t value (or z, or other statistics to be discussed in future chapters) is either to the extreme left of the sampling distribution or to the extreme right. In Figure 9.1 you saw that the region of rejection at the .05 level was to the left of a z of -1.96 or to the right of a z of 1.96. Since both of the "tails" of the sampling distribution are involved in this decision, such an approach is called a *two-tailed* test. The null hypothesis states that $\mu_1 = \mu_2$, and the rejection of it leads us to accept the alternate hypothesis that $\mu_1 \neq \mu_2$. We are *not* stating the *direction* of the difference when we say that $\mu_1 \neq \mu_2$, only that there *is* a difference. If we are using the .05 level of significance, our t value is significant in a two-tailed test if it falls in either the top 2.5% or the bottom 2.5% of the sampling distribution of differences.

The One-Tailed t Test

If an investigator predicts before collecting the data that μ_1 is greater than μ_2, the alternate hypothesis is not $\mu_1 \neq \mu_2$ but $\mu_1 > \mu_2$. Note that this expression not only states that there will be a difference but predicts the direction of the difference as well. Hence it is sometimes called a *directional* hypothesis. Since our interest is in only those $\overline{X}_1 - \overline{X}_2$ differences that are positive, the region of rejection is now confined to the right end of the sampling distribution. This region of rejection is at one end of the sampling distribution only, and we have what is called a *one-tailed test* (as shown in Figure 9.6).

When is an investigator able to predict that the difference, if it exists, will be only in one direction? The answer is not always obvious, but in some cases a difference in the opposite direction would be virtually impossible because of prior in-

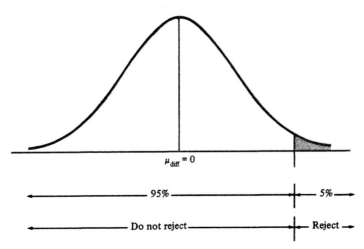

Figure 9.6
Region of rejection for a one-tailed test.

formation regarding physiology, developmental stages, or maturation. For example, if we were investigating the effect of vitamin C on the incidence of common colds, we would certainly have a directional hypothesis and would specify a one-tailed test. The alternate hypothesis would be $\mu_{NoC} > \mu_C$, that is, that those not taking vitamin C would have more colds than those taking the vitamin. It would seem unreasonable to hypothesize that $\mu_C > \mu_{NoC}$, that those taking the vitamin would have more colds! As a result, we are more efficient by specifying $\mu_1 > \mu_2$ as an alternate hypothesis instead of $\mu_1 \neq \mu_2$, since this approach places the region of rejection all in one tail of the sampling distribution of differences.

If a one-tailed approach is used, the t test is computed by *always subtracting the sample mean that was predicted to be the smaller from the sample mean that was predicted to be the larger.* In other words, the one-tailed test makes use of positive $\overline{X}_1 - \overline{X}_2$ differences only. In the two-tailed test it was immaterial whether we subtracted $\overline{X}_1$ from $\overline{X}_2$ or $\overline{X}_2$ from $\overline{X}_1$, but in the one-tailed test we *always* subtract in the direction of our prediction. Of course, if the difference turns out to be negative, then our results are opposite to what we predicted, and we can forget about calculating the t test entirely.

Let us examine some of these concepts through the use of an example. An educational psychologist is interested in the effects of knowledge of results in a classroom setting. She assigns 10 children at random to the knowledge-of-results (KR) group and 10 to the no-knowledge-of-results (NKR) group. In the KR group each child's arithmetic paper is scored and returned immediately after the daily test is completed, while in the NKR group children do not get their tests back until the next day. After a two-week period, a unit exam is given over the same material. The errors for each student are shown in Table 9.6. Is there a significant difference in errors between the two groups?

Table 9.6
Calculating the one-tailed t test for error scores as a function of knowledge of results

KR Group	NKR Group
1	4
1	3
3	1
2	2
4	4
2	7
2	3
1	2
3	1
1	4
$\Sigma X = 20$	$\Sigma X = 31$

$\Sigma X^2 = 50 \qquad\qquad \Sigma X^2 = 125$

$\overline{X}_1 = 2.0 \qquad\qquad \overline{X}_2 = 3.1$

$$s_1 = \sqrt{\dfrac{\Sigma X^2 - \dfrac{(\Sigma X)^2}{N}}{N-1}} \qquad\qquad s_2 = \sqrt{\dfrac{\Sigma X^2 - \dfrac{(\Sigma X)^2}{N}}{N-1}}$$

$$= \sqrt{\dfrac{50 - \dfrac{(20)^2}{10}}{9}} \qquad\qquad = \sqrt{\dfrac{125 - \dfrac{(31)^2}{10}}{9}}$$

$$= \sqrt{\dfrac{10}{9}} = \sqrt{1.1111} \qquad\qquad = \sqrt{\dfrac{28.9}{9}} = \sqrt{3.2111}$$

$$= 1.05 \qquad\qquad\qquad = 1.79$$

$$s_{\text{diff}} = \sqrt{\dfrac{(N_1 - 1)s_1^2 + (N_2 - 1)\,s_2^2}{N_1 + N_2 - 2}\left[\dfrac{1}{N_1} + \dfrac{1}{N_2}\right]}$$

$$= \sqrt{\dfrac{9(1.05)^2 + 9(1.79)^2}{10 + 10 - 2}\left(\dfrac{1}{10} + \dfrac{1}{10}\right)}$$

$$= \sqrt{\dfrac{38.7594}{18}\,(.2)} = \sqrt{.4307}$$

$$= 0.66$$

$$t = \dfrac{\overline{X}_2 - \overline{X}_1}{s_{\text{diff}}} = \dfrac{3.1 - 2.0}{.66} = 1.67$$

Not a significant difference at the .05 level, $t(18) = 1.67$, $p > .05$.

The researcher will likely use a one-tailed test in this situation, since KR has been shown in previous research to aid the learning process. Certainly, we would not expect KR to retard learning! So, the usual null hypothesis would be $\mu_{NKR} = \mu_{KR}$, and the alternate hypothesis will be $\mu_{NKR} > \mu_{KR}$ (i.e., the mean number of errors for the population receiving NKR will be greater than that for the population receiving KR).

The calculations for the one-tailed test are shown in Table 9.6. The procedure is identical to that for the two-tailed tests of Tables 9.2 and 9.3. The only difference is that $\overline{X}_1$ must be subtracted from $\overline{X}_2$ in computing t, since that was the direction hypothesized by the researcher.

After t is calculated, we enter Table D with $df = 18$ and obtain the one-tailed values. The tabled value at the .05 level is 1.73, and our t of 1.67 is smaller, so we conclude that for this sample there is no significant difference in the number of errors between NKR and KR.

It should be noted that a one-tailed t has more *power* than a two-tailed t; that is, with the one-tailed t test, the null hypothesis is more likely to be rejected if it should be rejected. This statement is true, however, *only if the direction of the difference is predicted in advance of collecting the data*. If the researcher on knowledge of results originally wanted to see if there was *any* kind of difference but, after seeing the first three exam papers, proposed a directional hypothesis, this would be an unacceptable foundation for a one-tailed test. A two-tailed test should have been run under those conditions. It is probably safe to conclude that a two-tailed test should be run unless we are willing to retain the null hypothesis even when the results are extreme in the *unexpected* direction. If we are willing to adhere to this vow, we may use a one-tailed test, but, in actual practice, it is a rare research situation where we are willing to relinquish the right to report on a significant result opposite to our expectations.

TESTING HYPOTHESES ABOUT A SINGLE SAMPLE MEAN

Back in Chapter 6 we had occasion to test whether there was a significant difference between the mean of a sample, $\overline{X}$, and some hypothesized population mean, μ. For example, in Sample Problem 1 in Chapter 6, a group of researchers assessed the effect of early childhood intervention on the IQ tested later on in the upper elementary grades. A well-known IQ test with a mean of 100 and a standard deviation of 16 was used to assess intelligence (i.e., $\mu = 100$ and $\sigma = 16$). A group of 40 ten-year-olds from an economically disadvantaged area of a midwestern city was given this IQ test, and a mean of 82 was calculated.

We first calculated the standard error of the mean:

$$\sigma_{\overline{X}} = \frac{\sigma}{\sqrt{N}} = \frac{16}{\sqrt{40}} = \frac{16}{6.3246} = 2.53$$

We then set up a 95% CI about the sample mean:

$$\bar{X} \pm 1.96\sigma_{\bar{X}}$$

$$82 \pm 1.96(2.53)$$

$$82 \pm 4.96$$

$$77.04 \text{ to } 86.96$$

We were then able to test the hypothesis that the population mean IQ, μ, was 90. However, we noted early in Chapter 6 that this technique was limited to situations *where we knew the population* standard deviation, σ. We are now ready to consider situations where we do *not* know σ, and we must make two changes in the method. First, we note that we now will be using the *sample* standard deviation, *s,* in the formula for the standard error of the mean instead of the population standard deviation, σ. This, of course, is a welcome change, since we can test virtually any set of measures without wondering about the population standard deviation, σ. We simply use our obtained sample standard deviation. The formula for the standard error is now

$$s_{\bar{X}} = \frac{s}{\sqrt{N}} \tag{9.9}$$

where

    $s_{\bar{X}}$ = the standard error of the mean**
    s = the standard deviation of our sample
    N = the size of the sample

Second, instead of relying on the familiar normal curve with z values of 1.96 and 2.58 for our confidence intervals, we must use the t distribution and t values from Table D. The procedure can best be illustrated by an example.

Table 9.7 shows the results of a random sample of grade-point averages (GPA) taken from 40 second-semester freshmen at a large university. The sample mean was 2.92 with a standard deviation of 0.60. Notice that we follow the same steps we did in Chapter 6—first calculating the standard error of the mean and then forming the confidence interval.

The only change in procedure is in the confidence interval itself. Since we can no longer assume a normal curve and the z values of 1.96 and 2.58, we must use the t distribution and the t values associated with the size of the sample. The 95% confidence interval would be

95% CI: $\qquad\qquad\qquad\qquad \bar{X} \pm t_{05}\, s_{\bar{X}} \tag{9.10}$

where

    $\bar{X}$ = the sample mean
    t_{05} = the value of t at the .05 level for the associated degrees of freedom
    $s_{\bar{X}}$ = the standard error of the mean calculated from the sample standard deviation

---

**Note that the symbol for the standard error of the mean is $\sigma_{\bar{X}}$ when calculated from the population σ and is $s_{\bar{X}}$ when calculated from the sample standard deviation, *s.*

Table 9.7
Estimating the grade-point average
of university freshmen: Calculating
the standard error of the mean
when σ is unknown

Sample Data:

$\bar{X} = 2.92$ $s = 0.60$ $N = 40$

Standard Error of the Mean:

$$s_{\bar{x}} = \frac{s}{\sqrt{N}} = \frac{0.60}{\sqrt{40}} = \frac{0.60}{6.3246} = .09$$

95% Confidence Interval:

$$\bar{X} \pm t_{05}s_{\bar{x}} = 2.92 \pm 2.021(.09)$$

$$2.92 \pm .18$$

$$2.74 \text{ to } 3.10$$

The 99% confidence interval would be

99% CI: $\bar{X} \pm t_{01}\, s_{\bar{x}}$ (9.11)

where all the terms are as previously defined, except t_{01} would be the value of t at the .01 level for the associated degrees of freedom.

So, the only change as far as computation goes is that we must look up the t value for the degrees of freedom in our sample. For the GPA data of 40 freshmen in Table 9.7, we note that in Table D the t value at the .05 level for $df = 39$ ($df = N - 1 = 40 - 1 = 39$) is 2.021. As you can see, the 95% CI becomes 2.74 to 3.10. If the director of institutional research at this university had hypothesized that the average GPA for the entire freshman class should be 3.00 (i.e., $\mu = 3.00$), we would have no reason to reject the hypothesis, since a mean GPA of 3.00 is in the 2.74 to 3.10 interval.

We constructed confidence intervals for μ on a number of occasions in Chapter 6 but were always limited because we had to know the value of the population standard deviation, σ, in order to calculate the standard error of the mean. But with the t distribution and the formula for the standard error of the mean using the *sample* standard deviation, we are now able to use the confidence interval approach in many practical applications.

SIGNIFICANT DIFFERENCES BETWEEN OTHER STATISTICS

This entire chapter has been devoted to testing the significance of the difference between means. A similar approach is used in testing the significance of a difference between medians, proportions, standard deviations, and other statistics. For example, we might want to know if our local political candidate has any chance to win the election if a sample of voters shows that 48% will vote for her. Since she needs 50% of the vote to win, we ask if 48% is only sampling error (we hope!) or if it is the real population value and our candidate stands to be defeated. A test for the significance of a proportion would help us answer our question.

A number of these significance tests are beyond the intended scope of this introductory textbook, and you are referred to one of the more advanced textbooks listed in the References.

SAMPLE PROBLEM 1

A social psychologist is investigating the development of "generosity" in preschool children and would like to see if girls are more generous than boys at age 4. Each child at a day-care center is given 16 small pieces of candy and is asked to "put some in a sack for your very best friend." The numbers of candies set aside for "friends" by 12 girls and 10 boys follow. Calculate a t test for random samples to see if there is a significant sex difference in generosity.

Girls		Boys	
X	X^2	X	X^2
7	49	2	4
3	9	3	9
6	36	5	25
9	81	3	9
3	9	4	16
8	64	2	4
6	36	2	4
7	49	1	1
5	25	2	4
9	81	3	9
8	64	27	85
7	49		
78	552		

(continued)

SAMPLE PROBLEM 1 (*CONTINUED*)

Calculator Solution

Means:

$$\bar{X}_1 = \frac{78}{12} = 6.5 \qquad\qquad \bar{X}_2 = \frac{27}{10} = 2.7$$

Standard Deviations:

$$s_1 = \sqrt{\frac{\Sigma X^2 - \dfrac{(\Sigma X)^2}{N}}{N-1}} \qquad\qquad s_2 = \sqrt{\frac{\Sigma X^2 - \dfrac{(\Sigma X)^2}{N}}{N-1}}$$

$$= \sqrt{\frac{552 - \dfrac{(78)^2}{12}}{11}} \qquad\qquad = \sqrt{\frac{85 - \dfrac{(27)^2}{10}}{9}}$$

$$= \sqrt{\frac{45}{11}} = \sqrt{4.091} \qquad\qquad = \sqrt{\frac{12.1}{9}} = \sqrt{1.3444}$$

$$= 2.02 \qquad\qquad\qquad\qquad = 1.16$$

Standard Error of the Difference:

$$s_{\text{diff}} = \sqrt{\frac{(N_1-1)s_1^2 + (N_2-1)s_2^2}{N_1 + N_2 - 2}\left[\frac{1}{N_1} + \frac{1}{N_2}\right]}$$

$$= \sqrt{\frac{11(2.02)^2 + 9(1.16)^2}{12 + 10 - 2}\left(\frac{1}{12} + \frac{1}{10}\right)}$$

$$= \sqrt{\frac{56.9948}{20}(.1833)} = \sqrt{0.5224}$$

$$= 0.72$$

$$t = \frac{\bar{X}_1 - \bar{X}_2}{s_{\text{diff}}} = \frac{6.5 - 2.7}{.72} = \frac{3.8}{.72} = 5.28$$

The difference between the means is significant, $t(20) = 5.28$, $p < .001$.

Since our calculated t of 5.28 is greater than the value for the .001 level for 20 degrees of freedom in Table D, we would conclude that the girls set aside significantly more candies than the boys and that the difference in means was significant at the .001 level.

Computer Solution

The SPSS output for a t test for independent samples for the generosity data is shown in Table 9.8. The top box shows the usual descriptive statistics for the two groups (1 = boys, 2 = girls). The boys provided an average of 2.7 candies for friends, while girls set aside an average of 6.5.

The bottom box begins at the left showing the computations for "Equal variances assumed" and "Equal variances not assumed." This matches what we noted earlier, and since we are assuming homogeneity of variance, we will use the top row of results in this box.

We next see "Levene's Test for Equality of Variances" and the F value of 2.693 with its probability ("Sig.") of .116. We will be covering the F test in Chapter 11, but for now we note that the probability, $p = .116$, is greater than the usual significance level of $p = .05$. Thus we have reason to believe that the two variances are indeed equal.

The t test for independent samples follows and shows the t, df, and two-tailed probability. Notice that the probability is listed at .000. This does not mean that the probability is 0, but rather that the probability is less than .001 ($p < .001$).

The t value of 5.252 is slightly less than our calculated value of 5.28, again due to differences in rounding.

Table 9.8
SPSS printout for generosity of preschool girls and boys

T-Test

Group Statistics

	SEX	N	Mean	Std. Deviation	Std. Error Mean
GENEROUS	1	10	2.70	1.16	.37
	2	12	6.50	2.02	.58

Independent Samples Test

	Levene's Test for Equality of Variances		t-test for Equality of Means						
								95% Confidence Interval of the Mean	
	F	Sig.	t	df	Sig. (2-tailed)	Mean Diff.	Std. Error Diff.	Lower	Upper
Equal variances assumed	2.693	.116	−5.252	20	.000	−3.80	.72	−5.31	−2.29
Equal variances not assumed			−5.512	17.971	.000	−3.80	.69	−5.25	−2.35

SAMPLE PROBLEM 2

Eight novice bowlers are dissatisfied with their present bowling averages and decide to take a lesson from a professional bowler. For a month after the lesson they calculate their bowling averages again and compare them with the averages before the lesson. Use a t test for correlated samples to see if there was a significant difference between the bowling averages before the lesson and after the lesson.

Bowler	Before	After	D	D²
A	144	151	7	49
B	126	120	-6	36
C	132	137	5	25
D	143	154	11	121
E	133	132	-1	1
F	128	131	3	9
G	152	149	-3	9
H	126	130	4	16
	1,084	1,104	20	266
	$\bar{X}_1 = 135.5$	$\bar{X}_2 = 138$	$\bar{D} = 2.5$	

Calculator Solution

Mean of the Differences:

$$\bar{D} = \frac{\Sigma D}{N} = \frac{20}{8} = 2.5$$

Standard Deviation of the Differences:

$$s_D = \sqrt{\frac{\Sigma D^2 - \frac{(\Sigma D)^2}{N}}{N-1}} = \sqrt{\frac{266 - \frac{(20)^2}{8}}{7}}$$

$$= \sqrt{\frac{266 - 50}{7}} = \sqrt{30.8571}$$

$$= 5.55$$

Standard Error of the Mean for the Differences:

$$s_{\bar{D}} = \frac{s_D}{\sqrt{N}} = \frac{5.55}{\sqrt{8}} = \frac{5.55}{2.8284} = 1.96$$

Correlated *t* Test:

$$t = \frac{\overline{D}}{s_{\overline{D}}} = \frac{2.5}{1.96} = 1.28$$

Not a significant difference between the means, $t(7) = 1.28$, $p > .05$.

Since our calculated *t* of 1.28 is less than that required for significance at the .05 level for a two-tailed test, we conclude that there was no significant difference in the average bowling scores after the lesson.

Computer Solution

Table 9.9 shows the SPSS output for the correlated *t* test for the before and after bowling averages. The upper block contains the usual descriptive statistics for the before and after averages. The middle block shows the correlation between the before and after averages. The Pearson *r* of .892 indicates a high degree of relationship between the pairs of averages.

The lower block shows the relevant statistics for the difference scores. The mean, standard deviation, standard error, and *t* value are almost identical to the results we obtained with the calculator solution.

Table 9.9
SPSS output for the correlated *t* test on the before and after bowling averages

T-Test

Paired Samples Statistics

		Mean	N	Std. Deviation	Std. Error Mean
Pair 1	AFTER	138.00	8	12.07	4.27
	BEFORE	135.50	8	9.68	3.42

Paired samples correlations

		N	Correlation	Sig.
Pair 1	AFTER & BEFORE	8	.892	.003

Paired Samples Test

		Paired Differences						
		Mean	Std. Deviation	Std. Error Mean	95% Confidence Interval of the Difference		t	df	Sig. (2-tailed)
					Lower	Upper			
Pair 1	AFTER – BEFORE	2.50	5.55	1.96	–2.14	7.14	1.273	7	.244

STUDY QUESTIONS

1. How different must two means be before you know whether or not you have a "real" difference?
2. Under the null hypothesis, the sampling distribution of <u>differences</u> is normally distributed about $\mu_{diff} = 0$ with a standard deviation of $\sqrt{\sigma_{\bar{X}_1}^2 + \sigma_{\bar{X}_2}^2}$. What does this statement mean?
3. A null hypothesis is often stated as $\mu_1 - \mu_2 = 0$. How is this statement related to $\mu_{diff} = 0$ in study question 2?
4. Sketch a sampling distribution of differences with $\mu_{diff} = 0$ and show the regions of rejection and nonrejection.
5. What do we mean when we say a difference is "significant at the .05 level."
6. A difference is labeled "not significant." What does this statement mean?
7. How does the t distribution differ from the normal curve?
8. What is the difference between σ_{diff} and s_{diff}?
9. What is the distinction between statistical significance and practical significance?
10. List the assumptions for the t test.
11. Distinguish between independent samples and correlated samples.
12. Distinguish between a Type I error and a Type II error.
13. Under what conditions would you be willing to settle for one type of error rather than the other?
14. What is the difference between a one-tailed test and a two-tailed test? Which would we be most likely to use?

EXERCISES

1. Bar-press responses are calculated for 15 rats in one experimental group and 17 in another. A researcher finds a t of 2.12 for these data. Using a two-tailed

test, is there a significant difference between the means at the .05 level? At the .01 level?

2. A clinical psychologist conducts an experiment with 12 subjects in an experimental group and 14 subjects in a control group. She calculates the means and standard deviations for a particular behavior in each group and conducts a t test on her data. She finds a t value of 2.80. Using a two-tailed test, is there a significant difference between the means at the .05 level? At the .01 level?

3. A study on facial expression and anxiety was conducted to determine if anxious subjects exhibit more or fewer facial expressions than nonanxious subjects. The means and standard deviations for the number of facial expressions exhibited in response to 25 emotional cues for 15 anxious subjects and 25 nonanxious subjects are shown. Was there a significant difference between the mean number of facial expressions exhibited by each group? (Use a two-tailed test.)

Anxious Subjects   **Nonanxious Subjects**
$N_1 = 15$ $N_2 = 25$
$X_1 = 18.0$ $X_2 = 13.8$
$s_1 = 5.67$ $s_2 = 3.50$

4. Researchers have shown that college students who were firstborns are more prone to Type A behavior than later-born siblings (Phillips, Long, & Bedeian, 1990). The Jenkins Activity Survey (JAS) was used to measure Type A behavior, with higher JAS scores indicative of greater Type A behavior. In a follow-up study, 11 firstborn college students and 13 later-born college students were given the JAS, and the means and standard deviations of their scores are shown. Use a two-tailed test to see if there was a significant difference between the JAS scores of the two groups.

JAS, Firstborns   **JAS, Later-Borns**
$N_1 = 11$ $N_2 = 13$
$X_1 = 7.82$ $X_2 = 7.0$
$s_1 = 3.33$ $s_2 = 3.39$

5. A human resources manager at a large insurance company gave all her sales representatives an extroversion/introversion self-evaluation. She then compared the sales representatives' extroverted/introverted evaluation with their selling success. Shown in the following lists are the sales commissions from the previous year in thousands of dollars for five introverted and seven extroverted sales representatives. Use a two-tailed test to see if there was a significant difference in commission generated by introverted and extroverted sales representatives.

Introverted   **Extroverted**
32   43
51   45
44   66

49	48
36	59
	61
	42

6. In a study of adolescent aggression in inner-city schools, a researcher presented a video segment of a frustrating situation to 14 male 13-year-olds who were from one-parent homes and 12 male 13-year-olds who were from two-parent homes. The subjects then filled out an aggression index that measured the subjects' feelings of aggression related to the frustrating video segment. The aggression scores follow. Was there a significant difference between the aggression felt in males from single-parent homes and the aggression felt in males from two-parent homes? (Use a two-tailed test.)

One Parent	Two Parents
20	21
18	15
16	17
19	16
22	19
14	17
12	15
16	11
16	13
9	11
15	14
13	12
17	
10	

7. Researchers studied the effectiveness of a new medication for high blood pressure. They recorded the systolic and diastolic blood pressure for 12 patients before giving them the medication and again four weeks after daily medication. The data for the systolic blood pressure readings taken before and after use of the medication are shown. Was there a significant difference in systolic blood pressure before and after use of this medication? (Use a two-tailed test.)

Before Medication	After Medication
140	125
163	121
182	131
154	118
162	123
177	134
157	123
167	150
144	134

168	154
181	166
179	132

8. Researchers were interested in blood glucose levels before exercise and after exercise. For 14 subjects, a blood sample was drawn (after the subjects had not eaten for eight hours), and blood glucose levels recorded. The following day, each subject again fasted for eight hours and then ran on a treadmill for half an hour prior to having blood drawn and blood glucose levels recorded. The blood glucose levels (in mg/dl) for the subjects under each condition are listed. Was there a significant difference in blood glucose levels before exercise and after exercise? (Use a two-tailed test.)

Before Exercise	After Exercise
86	141
91	93
102	101
94	118
93	95
85	86
90	88
85	93
94	87
92	97
103	87
87	85
96	93
92	94

9. Research has suggested that attractive defendants in court cases are given less punishment for their crimes than unattractive defendants. Some political science majors at a university conducted their own study in which they provided a written case account of a crime to 20 senior university students. For 10 of the subjects, a picture of an attractive defendant was provided with the written case account, and for the other 10 subjects, a picture of an unattractive defendant was provided with the case account. The subjects were asked to assign punishment by suggesting the number of years the defendant should serve in prison for the crime, with the results shown in the following lists. Was there a significant difference in the suggested years of imprisonment for attractive and unattractive defendants? (Use a two-tailed test.)

Attractive	Unattractive
2	3
3	2
1	5
2	3
2	2

2	3
3	2
4	3
1	4
1	2

10. A child psychologist is investigating recall ability in fifth-graders and would like to see if children recall visual stimuli or auditory stimuli better at age 11. In one group, 12 children are shown pictures of 20 common household items (e.g., bed, chair, television, table), and in another group, 13 children simply listen as these 20 items are read aloud to them. Next, each child is given a blank sheet of paper and asked to write down all of the items shown or told to him or her. The number of items recalled by each child is shown. Was there a significant difference in the number of items recalled in the two conditions? (Use a two-tailed test.)

Visual	Auditory
7	9
9	7
10	8
8	5
13	6
8	9
7	4
9	8
11	7
11	6
6	8
9	5
	9

11. A sample of 25 high school seniors had an average SAT I: Reasoning score of 535 with a standard deviation of 80. According to the SAT manual, the national average is 500. Given the 95% CI, is this result likely? Given the 99% CI, is it likely?

12. A sample of 30 college students at a midwestern private liberal arts college with part-time jobs showed an average number of hours worked per week was 11. A national survey of liberal arts colleges yielded an average work week of 9 hours. Given the 95% CI, is this result likely? Given the 99% CI, is it likely?

COMPUTER EXERCISES FOR APPENDIX 4 DATA BANK

For the following exercises report the t, df, and p values, and a summary statement.

C1. Was there a significant difference in physical symptom scores between men scoring high (above the median) on the BSRI Masculinity scale and those scoring low (below the median)?

C2. Did men scoring high (above the median) on the JAS Speed and Impatience scale report significantly more physical symptoms than those men scoring low (below the median)?

C3. Was there a significant difference between men and women in physical symptoms?

C4. Did women scoring high (above the median) on the JAS Speed and Impatience scale report significantly more symptoms than those women scoring low (below the median)?

CHAPTER 10

Decision Making, Power, and Effect Size

Joan is designing a study on prosocial (helping) behavior for her research paper in social psychology. Previous research has shown a reluctance on the part of people to assist a person who is markedly different from them. Joan will have a confederate approach strangers at a large shopping mall, tell them she lost her billfold, and ask for coins to make a phone call. On half the occasions the confederate will be well-groomed and neatly dressed, but on the other half she will be unkempt and shabbily dressed. The number of people helping the well-groomed confederate will be compared with the number helping the poorly groomed confederate. But how many strangers should be contacted in these two conditions in order to be able to reject the null hypothesis? Should Joan try for 20 of each? 30? 50?

Luis is designing a research study on the relationship between Type A behavior and daily "hassles," that is, the daily annoyances and frustrations everyone experiences from time to time. Other investigators have found that college students who are "Type A" also tend to report more daily hassles. Luis at first planned to use a sample of university students but wondered if his results might be more valid if he used other participants. Should he also include a sample of high school students? Should he also include a sample of working adults? And how would this increased variability affect the possible rejection of the null hypothesis?

Marisa is training her rat to press the lever in a Skinner box, and notices how tiny the food pellets are. She wonders if her lab rats would learn the lever-pressing response faster if they received a larger reinforcement than the single tiny pellet. Marisa would like to know if the amount of reinforcement is important, and she decides to compare a one-pellet reinforcement with a larger number. But how many pellets should be used for the larger reinforcement? Two? Three? Five? How large a difference is needed to reject the null hypothesis?

It is clear from these research examples that there is still more to be considered on the topic of significance testing. We learned in Chapter 9 that our choice of alpha level ($\alpha = .05$ or $.01$) affected the probability of a Type I or Type II error. We now need to consider other factors that are important in the decision process to reject or not reject a null hypothesis.

Our first research example emphasized the need to determine how large a sample size should be used. How many strangers must Joan's well-dressed or shabbily dressed confederate approach? In the second example, the question of homogeneous or heterogeneous samples came up. Should Luis test only university students or include high school students and working adults? And our third example examined the size of the difference between two experimental conditions. Should Marisa compare the reinforcement value of one food pellet with the value of two pellets, or one versus three, or one versus five?

In this chapter we will take up the issues of power and effect size, and how they will help us in decision making. These decisions are important in planning our own research and critiquing the research of others. We will begin by illustrating the Type I and Type II errors discussed in Chapter 9 by using a graphical approach. Before going any further in this chapter, you might consider reviewing the decision matrix and the discussion of Type I and II errors on pages 251–254. A thorough knowledge of these errors is essential in understanding the power and effect-size concepts.

TYPE I AND TYPE II ERRORS REVISITED

Table 10.1 shows the decision matrix we first examined in Chapter 9. As before, we are interested in the upper left (Type I error) and lower right (Type II error) boxes of the decision matrix. The Type I error is again defined as rejecting the null hypothesis when it in fact is true. And the Type II error is failing to reject the null hypothesis when it is in fact false.

It will be easier to understand the Type I and Type II errors if we make two minor alterations in our original explanation in Chapter 9. First, we will use a one-sample case in a one-tailed test in order to simplify our graphical approach. Second, we will consider both a null hypothesis and the alternate hypothesis simultaneously, since this approach will give us a picture of power and effect size that is simpler and easier to understand.

Table 10.1
Decision matrix for rejecting or not rejecting H_0

| | **Decision on the Basis of Sampling** | |
	Reject H_0	**Accept H_0**
H_0 is True in population	Type I error $p = \alpha$	correct
H_0 is False in population	correct $p = 1 - \beta$	Type II error $p = \beta$

Decision Making and Sampling Error

A school psychologist is conducting a study and administers a well-known reading aptitude test to 25 sixth-graders. Her results are as follows:

Sixth-Grade Reading Scores

$$N = 25$$

$$\overline{X} = 106$$

$$s = 16$$

She later remarks to a principal that her mean turned out to be 106. The principal stops short and replies, "I thought the average reading score for that test was 100. Are our kids that far above average?" We, of course, would use different terminology, and state a null hypothesis, H_0: $\mu = 100$ and an alternate hypothesis, H_A: $\mu > 100$.

Evaluating H_0 and H_A

We can evaluate the principal's statement that the population mean $\mu = 100$ in our usual fashion by using a sampling distribution of sample means where $\mu_{\overline{x}} = 100$. We then will locate our sample mean $\overline{X} = 106$ in the sampling distribution. If $\overline{X} = 106$ is in the "Do not reject" region, we could agree with the principal's statement that the population's average reading score should be around 100. This, of course, would be in agreement with the null hypothesis H_0: $\mu = 100$.

On the other hand, if our sample mean $\overline{X} = 106$ is in the "Reject" region, we would have reason to believe that the population mean is greater than 100. Note that we are using a one-tailed test, and the alternate hypothesis is H_A: $\mu > 100$.

Before we can evaluate H_0 and H_A, we need to

1. Calculate the standard error of the mean of the sampling distribution.
2. Find the t value from the t distribution in Table D that marks off the bottom 95% (Do not reject) from the top 5% (Reject) for our particular sample size. We are assuming the traditional .05 significance level.

3. Calculate the t value for our mean $\overline{X} = 106$, and locate it in the sampling distribution.

Calculating the Standard Error of the Mean.

$$s_{\overline{X}} = \frac{s}{\sqrt{N}} = \frac{16}{\sqrt{25}} = \frac{16}{5} = 3.2$$

Determining the Critical t Value from Table D.   In Table D we use the .05 level, one-tailed values. For the degrees of freedom, $df = (N - 1) = (25 - 1) = 24$. The t for 24 df is 1.711.

Calculating a t *for Our Sample Mean,* $\overline{X} = 106$. We need to convert our sample mean to a t value so we can locate it in the t distribution. All we have to do is to modify the usual z score formula, $z = (X - \mu)/\sigma$ (score minus mean divided by standard deviation). For the t distribution the "score" would be the sample mean, $\overline{X}$; the mean would be the mean of the sampling distribution under the null hypothesis, $\mu_{\overline{X}}$; and the standard deviation would be the standard error of the mean, $s_{\overline{X}}$.

$$t = \frac{\overline{X} - \mu_{\overline{X}}}{s_{\overline{X}}} = \frac{106 - 100}{3.2} = 1.88 \qquad (10.1)$$

What If the Null Hypothesis Is True?

We can now sketch our sampling distribution of means under the null hypothesis, locate our sample mean, $\overline{X} = 106$, and draw a conclusion. This sampling distribution is shown in Figure 10.1a. Note that if the null hypothesis were true, 95% of the t values would be less than 1.711. Since our sample $\overline{X} = 106$ has a t value of 1.88, it is in the "Reject" region, since *less* than 5% of the t values, if the null hypothesis is true, are larger than 1.711. As a result, we decide to reject the null hypothesis, H_0: $\mu = 100$, in favor of the alternate hypothesis, H_A: $\mu > 100$, $p < .05$. If the null hypothesis were true, we would be making a Type I error.

   This procedure is shown in Figure 10.1a. However, if we evaluate the null hypothesis as being only *true* we are only half done. What if H_0 is *false*? We must now concentrate on the alternate hypothesis H_A and associated sampling distribution to get a more complete picture of power and Type I and Type II errors.

What If the Null Hypothesis Is False?

To help us visualize what the decision matrix of Table 10.1 is saying, let us look at the second possible condition of the world from which the sample of sixth-graders was drawn. Let us suppose that the population mean is really 103, not 100. The bottom sampling distribution is one representing the alternate hypothesis, H_A: $\mu > 100$. But since $\mu = 103$, this, of course, would result in a sampling distribution with a mean, $\mu_{\overline{X}} = 103$. We are also assuming that the two sampling distributions have the same shape.

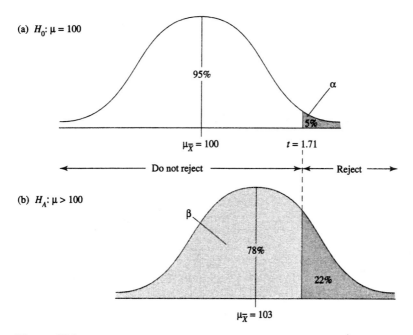

Figure 10.1
Two sampling distributions (a) when the null hypothesis is true, H_0: $\mu = 100$; and (b) when the null hypothesis is false, $\mu = 103$.

Type I and Type II Errors Are Related. We must look at both sampling distributions in Figure 10.1 to fully understand the Type I and Type II errors. If the population mean $\mu = 103$, a large number of samples of $N = 25$ would result in a sampling distribution with a mean of means $\mu_{\bar{x}} = 103$. This sampling distribution is shown in Figure 10.1b. Note the vertical dashed line connecting the two sampling distributions and marking off areas in both distributions.

In significance testing, we assume a null hypothesis; in this case, H_0: $\mu = 100$. In our example of the reading aptitude scores for 25 sixth-graders, the null hypothesis resulted in the sampling distribution of Figure 10.1a. But what if the null hypothesis is false, and $\mu = 103$ instead of 100? We do not know that it is, of course, and our decision is made on the basis of our sample mean and the sampling distribution that accompanies the null hypothesis. This distribution is used to define the region of rejection, since it is the null hypothesis that is being directly tested. Let us look carefully at Figure 10.1a.

We noted earlier that if H_0: $\mu = 100$ is true, we expect to correctly not reject the null hypothesis 95% of the time, and make a Type I error by incorrectly rejecting H_0 5% of the time. We can control the likelihood of a Type I error, of course, by changing our alpha level to $\alpha = .01$ or $.001$ or some other value.

Before we do any changing of alpha, let us see how our choice of the traditional $\alpha = .05$ significance level affects our conclusions when H_0: $\mu = 100$ *is false.*

If we look at the sampling distribution for H_0 in Figure 10.1a, we note the traditional cutoff point at $\alpha = .05$ ($t = 1.711$ in this particular example). We see in the bottom sampling distribution (H_A: $\mu = 103$), that this would result in our correctly rejecting the false null hypothesis in only 22% of our samples. In a whopping 78% of the time we would commit a Type II error ($\beta = .78$), failing to reject H_0 when it should be rejected.

It should be clear which parts of Figure 10.1 illustrate the four cells of the decision matrix of Table 10.1.

If the Null Hypothesis Is True

Correct H_0 Decision.   In Figure 10.1a, the unshaded area lies to the left of $t = 1.71$ under the $H_0 : \mu = 100$ sampling distribution. The probability of making this correct decision to not reject H_0 with $\alpha = .05$ is $p = .95$.

Type I Error.   In Figure 10.1a, the colored area to the right of $t = 1.71$ is the probability under the null hypothesis of making a Type I error. With $\alpha = .05$, this probability of rejecting H_0 when it is true is $p = .05$.

If the Null Hypothesis Is False

Correct H_A Decision.   If $\mu = 103$, the null hypothesis is false and the mean of the sampling distribution under H_A is $\mu_{\bar{x}} = 103$. We then, of course want to reject H_0. The probability of rejecting H_0 in this example is shown in Figure 10.1b in the dark colored H_A distribution. The probability of rejecting H_0 when it is false with a t of 1.71 or greater (in the H_0 distribution) is $p = .22$. In the long run our choice of $\alpha = .05$ would let us find this real difference only 22% of the time.

Type II Error.   Again, if $\mu = 103$, the null hypothesis is false and the mean of the sampling distribution under H_A is $\mu_{\bar{x}} = 103$. H_0 should then be rejected, since H_0 is false. However, many of the sample means will produce t values less than the critical t in the H_0 distribution at $\alpha = .05$. This is shown in light colored area in the bottom distribution. The probability of not rejecting H_0 when it should be rejected (β) is shown in Figure 10.1b as $p = .78$. In this example, in the long run our choice of $\alpha = .05$ would cause us to declare a real effect not significant 78% of the time.

POWER

In Chapter 9 we identified the term *power* as the ability of a test to reject the null hypothesis when it is false. In Table 10.1, this feature is shown in the lower left cell of the decision matrix. We emphasized the importance of this concept in our discussion in Chapter 9. For us social and behavioral scientists, if an important difference between variables exists in the population, we want to find it!

It follows, then, that power is a very important feature of our statistical procedures, and we would want to do everything to increase the amount of power in our analysis. In the next few sections we will examine some of the variables that affect power, and what we can do to increase the power of our analysis. But first we need a more precise definition of power.

The Type II Error and Power

In Table 10.1, the lower right corner shows the Type II error—failing to reject the null hypothesis when it should be rejected. The probability of making a Type II error, as we noted in Chapter 9, was called beta, β. Let us examine the sampling distribution for $\mu = 103$ in Figure 10.1b. Notice that all of the sample means in the light colored area would not be rejected if $\alpha = .05$ in the H_0 sampling distribution. This accounts for 78% of the sample means, so the probability of making a Type II error in this example was $\beta = .78$.

Power is defined as the probability of rejecting H_0 when it should be rejected, and is the complement of β:

$$\text{Power} = 1 - \beta$$

We look again at Figure 10.1b and see that the probability of making the correct decision to reject H_0 is $p = 1 - .78 = .22$. With this particular research design, the power is $p = .22$. In the long run we could expect to find significant differences only 22% of the time.

Clearly, the research situation pictured in Figure 10.1 leaves much to be desired. Power here is only $p = .22$, and we would hope that most research designs would have a better chance of picking up significant differences if, in fact, they do exist.

But what can we do to increase the power of our research design? And what are the variables that affect power? In the sections to follow we will look in detail at three such variables and how we might make use of them to increase the power of our analysis.

Power and the Real Difference between H_0 and H_A

Power increases as the difference between μ under the null hypothesis (μ_{hyp}) and μ under a *real* alternative hypothesis (μ_{real}) increases. Let us say, for example, that the *real* μ in the population is 108. If we carefully compare Figures 10.1 and 10.2, we see that the power has increased from $p = .22$ to .74. With $\mu_{real} = 108$, the sampling distribution has shifted to the right, so that more of the sample means are to the right of the $\alpha = .05$ dashed line.

This line is at the value of t at $\alpha = .05$, and the dark colored area in H_A represents the proportion of time that we would reject the null hypothesis. With the difference between $\mu_{hyp} = 100$ and $\mu_{real} = 108$, the power is now $p = .74$. We are much more likely to reject the null hypothesis and less likely to commit a Type II error than when μ_{real} was only 103.

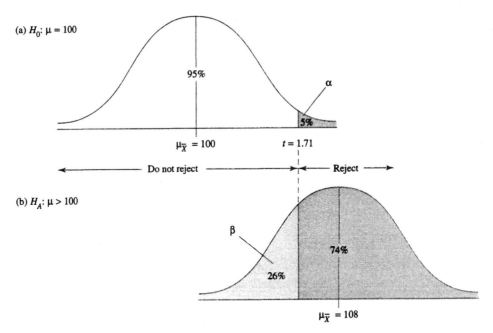

(a) H_0: $\mu = 100$

95%

α

5%

$\mu_{\bar{X}} = 100$ $t = 1.71$

$\longleftarrow$ Do not reject $\longrightarrow$ $\longleftarrow$ Reject $\longrightarrow$

(b) H_A: $\mu > 100$

β

74%

26%

$\mu_{\bar{X}} = 108$

Figure 10.2
Power is increased when the difference between the hypothesized population mean and the real population mean is larger.

In practical terms, we are more likely to find a significant effect when the real difference is larger than when it is smaller. In the research examples at the beginning of the chapter, Marisa wondered if her rats would learn faster with a larger reinforcement. In her study she wanted to compare a one-pellet reinforcement with a larger number, and wondered how many should be used for the larger number. If size of reinforcement really is a factor, Marisa should use four or five pellets for the larger reinforcement rather than just two. With greater power, she is more likely to find a significant difference.

Power and Sample Size

Power increases as the size of the sample increases. Let us suppose that the school psychologist had used a sample of 100 sixth-graders instead of 25 (and found the same $\bar{X}$ and s). Figure 10.3 shows that if the null hypothesis were false, the probability of our making a Type II error (β) is .42, and the power of our analysis is $p = .58$. If we carefully compare Figures 10.1 and 10.3, we see that both sampling distributions have $\mu_{\bar{X}}$ of 100 under H_0 and 103 under H_A.

Then why the difference in power? The answer lies in the amount of overlap of the H_0 and H_A distributions. In Figure 10.1, the sampling distributions are more spread out, while in Figure 10.3 each is more tightly clustered. The reason for the difference in variability is seen in the formula for the standard error of the mean,

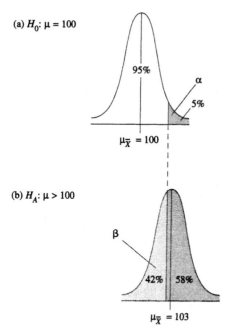

(a) H_0: $\mu = 100$

95%

α

5%

$\mu_{\bar{X}} = 100$

(b) H_A: $\mu > 100$

β

42% 58%

$\mu_{\bar{X}} = 103$

Figure 10.3
Power is increased with a larger sample size.

$s_{\bar{X}} = s/\sqrt{N}$. As N increases, $s_{\bar{X}}$, the standard deviation of the sampling distribution, decreases. There is greater power with less overlapping, since more of the sample means fall to the right of the dashed $\alpha = .05$ line.

Increasing the size of the sample is probably one of the easier ways of increasing the power of an analysis. In the research scenarios at the beginning of the chapter, Joan needed to know how many strangers her confederate should approach in the experiment on helping behavior. Although it might be tempting to recommend as large a sample size as possible, we need to remember the cautions sounded in Note 9.1. We still need to distinguish between a trivial difference and one that has practical significance. A whopping sample size may serve only to find a trivial difference.

Power and the Amount of Variability in a Sample

It follows from the previous section that we are more likely to find a significant difference if we could reduce our value of $s_{\bar{X}}$ in any way we can. The sampling distributions shown in Figure 10.3 had smaller standard deviations and showed less overlap and, thus, more power.

But aside from increasing the sample size of $s_{\bar{X}} = s/\sqrt{N}$ to decrease $s_{\bar{X}}$, the only other way we can decrease $s_{\bar{X}}$ would be to decrease s, the standard deviation of the sample itself. The standard deviation may seem like a fixed value—it just happens to be a particular size as we collect our data. In some cases it may be just that, an accurate estimate of the amount of variation in the variable we are measuring. However, in many of our research designs, we might be able to reduce the variability by using measures (tests, inventories, questionnaires, experimental manipulations, etc.) that are highly reliable and valid. If errors of measurement can be reduced through careful research design, the amount of variability in a sample may be lowered as well. This lowered variability could lead to an increase in power similar to that shown in Figure 10.3 for increased sample size. Much thought is given to sample size when researchers are collecting data, but probably little is devoted to decreasing the variability of the sample.

However, there even may be times when a better research design in terms of practical use actually would *increase* the variability and possibly *reduce* the amount of power. In the research illustration described at the beginning of the chapter, Luis was considering extending his study of Type A behavior and daily hassles to include high school students and working adults, along with his university student group. This diverse sample would undoubtedly allow for more practical applications, but the degree of overlap shown in Figure 10.3 would increase, resulting in less power. If a more heterogeneous sample is deemed essential, however, a larger sample size could offset the increased variability!

Other Factors Influencing Power

We learned in the previous subsection that power is influenced by (1) the distance between the *hypothesized* population mean and the *real* value of the population mean, (2) the size of the sample, and (3) the amount of variability within the sample. However, there are other factors that influence our ability to reject the null hypothesis when it should be rejected. Factors generally providing greater power in the analysis would be correlated data (e.g., the correlated t test), significance level ($\alpha = .05$ instead of .01), and one-tailed tests (as compared to the two-tailed variety). Each of these factors has specific characteristics that may limit its power, and a full discussion of these is beyond the intended scope of this text. An excellent treatment is presented in Minium, King, and Bear (1993).

EFFECT SIZE

The One-Sample Case

We have been investigating the possible difference between a hypothesized μ and the real μ using the null hypothesis approach. This difference between μ_{hyp} and μ_{real} in standard deviation units is called the *effect size*. The formula for the effect size, *d*, is

$$d = \frac{\mu_{real} - \mu_{hyp}}{\sigma} \tag{10.2}$$

where

  d = the symbol for effect size
  μ_{real} = the true mean of the population under consideration
  μ_{hyp} = the mean of some hypothetical population
  σ = the standard deviation of either population, usually estimated by our sample s

In our example of the 25 sixth-grade reading scores shown in Figure 10.1, a mean of 100 was hypothesized (H_0: $\mu = 100$) but the real mean was 103. The effect size, d, using the sample s as an estimate of σ, would be calculated as

$$d = \frac{\mu_{real} - \mu_{hyp}}{\sigma} = \frac{103 - 100}{16} = 0.19$$

In other words the real value, $\mu_{real} = 103$, was only about two-tenths of a standard deviation from our hypothesized $\mu_{hyp} = 100$. However, in our second example shown in Figure 10.2, with $\mu_{real} = 108$, we found the effect size to be

$$d = \frac{108 - 100}{16} = 0.5$$

or, the difference between μ_{hyp} and μ_{real} was equal to half a standard deviation.

The Two-Sample Case

For the two-sample case, such as the t test for the difference between means, the effect size, d, would be

$$d = \frac{(\mu_1 - \mu_2)_{real} - (\mu_1 - \mu_2)_{hyp}}{\sigma} \qquad (10.3)$$

where

  μ_1 = the mean of the population of the first sample
  μ_2 = the mean of the population of the second sample
  σ = the standard deviation of either sample

For the two-sample case, such as the t test for the difference between means, we found in Chapter 9 that the symbol $(\mu_1 - \mu_2)_{hyp}$ is the null hypothesis, which is most often H_0: $\mu_1 - \mu_2 = 0$. So our interest centers on $(\mu_1 - \mu_2)_{real}$ which, of course, is the "real" difference that we are attempting to find.

Calculating Effect Sizes

The previous subsection offered formulas for calculating the effect size, d, for both the one- and two-sample cases. However, the formulas required a knowledge of the population mean or means and the standard deviation. How do we calculate effect sizes if we don't know these population values? Howell (1995) suggests that we can estimate effect sizes three ways: (1) from previous research, (2) from an appraisal of what constitutes an important difference, and (3) from using special conventions (i.e., rule of thumb).

Previous Research.   Other researchers have come up with their own samples, and we can get a rough estimate of population means and standard deviations based on their earlier studies.

What Is an Important Difference?   As we conduct research in our specialty fields, we can usually distinguish between a trivial difference and a meaningful difference. We would want to specify the size of an important difference in advance of collecting the data ("Headache frequency will decrease at least 20% in the relaxation training group").

Special Conventions.   Many researchers assess their own effect sizes using Cohen's (1988) suggested effect sizes as a benchmark for comparison. Cohen proposed the following:

Effect Size

Small	.20
Medium	.50
Large	.80

So, if an investigator found .76 of a standard deviation between μ_{hyp} and μ_{real}, he or she would consider the difference quite large.

Effect Size, Sample Size, and p Value

It should be obvious that effect size tells us more about our data than the ubiquitous p values. To find that a difference between a hypothesized mean reading score and the real mean in the one-sample case was significant, $p < .001$, tells us nothing about *how much* of a difference there was. Similarly, in the two-sample case, a $p < .001$ in the difference between the generosity (number of candies saved for friends) scores of boys and girls, tells us nothing about how large a difference there was.

In fact, p values can be misleading, since they are affected by sample size. In Note 9.1 we saw a researcher using a sample of 40,000 fourth-graders and reporting that the mean mathematics aptitude score is 52.3 for children who regularly eat breakfast versus 52.1 for those who come to school hungry, $t(39,998) = 1.99$, $p < .05$, a "significant" difference.

In contrast, let us suppose that a teacher in one of the elementary schools in that state is doing research for a master's thesis and finds that for the 100 fourth-graders in her building, the mean mathematics aptitude score for those who eat breakfast is 53.6 versus 50.3 for the noneaters, $t(98) = 1.65$, $p > .05$, a "nonsignificant" difference.

The paradox should be obvious—with a combined N of 40,000, a difference in means of only 0.2 of an item is pronounced significant, but a study with only

100 students finds a mean difference of 3.3 items that is declared nonsignificant. In Note 9.1, we noted that 0.2 of an item is hardly cause to embark on a statewide nutritional program, but should we ignore the importance of the 3.3-item difference that was judged nonsignificant?

It should be clear by now that assessing the difference between means should involve both a probability statement and an effect size. And both the probability of rejecting H_0 and the effect size are related to the power of the statistical test being used. Several variables affect the relationship between sample size, effect size, and power. These concepts are beyond the intended scope of this text, and the interested reader is referred to more advanced sources for a treatment of these topics (e.g., Cohen, 1988; Howell, 1995; Minium et al., 1993).

STUDY QUESTIONS

1. What is meant by a Type I error?
2. If the null hypothesis is true, how often will a Type I error occur?
3. What is meant by a Type II error?
4. What are the steps involved in estimating the probability of a Type II error?
5. What is the relationship between a Type II error and power?
6. How does the difference between μ_{hyp} and μ_{real} affect power?
7. How does sample size affect power?
8. How do changes in variability in the samples affect power?
9. Give a definition of effect size.
10. Differentiate between the methods for calculating effect sizes for the one-sample case and the two-sample case.
11. What are the three methods suggested by Howell for determining effect size?

EXERCISES

1. In Figure 10.1, if the researcher had chosen the .01 level ($\alpha = .01$) instead of the .05 level as shown, how would the probability of a Type I error have been affected? How would the probability of a Type II error be affected? Explain your answer.
2. Assume that $\mu = 101$ instead of $\mu = 103$ in Figure 10.1b. How would this change affect the probability of a Type I error? Of a Type II error? Explain your answer.
3. A researcher notes that in some old life insurance tables the average height for college women is 5 feet 4 inches. Let us suppose that the real average height in the population of college women is 5 feet 6 inches. Draw a figure similar to Figure 10.1 with the following characteristics:

   Top figure (like Figure 10.1a): The researcher assumes a null hypothesis of H_0: $\mu = 64$ inches and chooses the .05 significance level.

   Bottom figure (like Figure 10.1b): The *real* average height in the population of college women is $\mu = 66$ inches. The dashed .05 line from the top figure down to the bottom figure bisects the sampling distribution of means so the area to the left of the dashed line (light-colored area) is 14% and to the right (dark-colored area) is 86%. If our researcher had measured the heights of a sample of college women, *and*

a. The null hypothesis were true (H_0: μ = 64 inches), what would be the probability (α) of making a Type I error?

b. The actual value of the population mean, μ, were 66 inches, what would be the probability (β) of making a Type II error?

c. The actual value of the population mean, μ, were 66 inches, what would be the power of the researcher's test?

4. A university admissions counselor finds an average score of 50 on a Spanish language placement exam for a group of incoming freshmen. Let us suppose that the real average score in the population of incoming freshmen is 55. Draw a figure similar to Figure 10.1 with the following characteristics:

Top figure (like Figure 10.1a): The counselor assumes a null hypothesis of H_0: μ = 50 and chooses the .05 significance level.

Bottom figure (like Figure 10.1b): The *real* average placement score in the population is μ = 55. The dashed .05 line from the top figure down to the bottom figure bisects the sampling distribution of means so the area to the left of the dashed line (light-colored area) is 37% and to the right (dark-colored area) is 63%. If the counselor had conducted a study on placement scores with a sample of incoming freshmen, *and*

a. The null hypothesis were true (H_0: μ = 50), what would be the probability (α) of making a Type I error?

b. The actual value of the population mean, μ, were 55, what would be the probability (β) of making a Type II error?

c. The actual value of the population mean, μ, were 55, what would be the power of the researcher's test?

CHAPTER 11

One-Way Analysis of Variance

Subliminal perception has been a fascinating topic for decades, with people claiming that their behavior was affected by messages that they did not "really" see or hear. Recently audiocassette distributors have marketed tapes containing soothing music or the sounds of ocean surf with messages below the threshold of conscious awareness presented over and over. These messages are supposed to help us with such diverse skills as stress relief through deep relaxation, achieving creative success, and strengthening our memory power and learning power.

Since many of these topics are related to academic success, college students have been targeted by advertisers to try this "painless, relaxing way to improve memory and learning skills." However, since the idea that subliminal messages may help us in our conscious, self-aware activities is highly suspect, a number of studies have been conducted to see if this utopian ideal is really possible.

In one such study (Russell, Rowe, & Smouse, 1991) 79 college students in a career development class volunteered to participate in a study to see if they could raise their course grades or semester GPAs. Three conditions were investigated. In the *treatment* condition, students listened to a subliminal audiotape on improving study habits and passing exams. All the students heard was the sound of an ocean surf, with the information on improving study habits presented below the level of conscious awareness. Twenty-eight students were randomly assigned to this condition. In the *placebo* condition the audiotape contained only the surf sounds. Twenty-eight students were randomly assigned to this condition. The *control* condition simply used the course grades and semester GPAs of the 23 students randomly assigned to this condition.

Students in the treatment and placebo conditions listened to the tapes for approximately 50 hours during the 10-week study. Course grades and semester GPAs for the three groups were then compared. Did the treatment group that had the subliminal messages on improving study habits and passing exams have significantly higher course grades or semester GPAs than the placebo or control groups?

The *t* tests described in Chapter 9 have one very serious limitation—they are restricted to tests of the significance of the difference between only *two* groups. Certainly there are many times, as in the preceding example, when we would like to see if there are significant differences among three, four, or even more groups. In these cases we cannot use the ordinary *t* test, because more than two groups are involved.

We *cannot* solve the problem by running a *t* test on two groups at a time. If we have three means, $\overline{X}_1$, $\overline{X}_2$, and $\overline{X}_3$, we cannot use the ordinary *t* test first on $\overline{X}_1$ and $\overline{X}_2$, then on $\overline{X}_1$ and $\overline{X}_3$, and finally on $\overline{X}_2$ and $\overline{X}_3$. The reason this is an invalid procedure is that the probabilities associated with obtaining various *t* values given in Table D are for pairs of means from *random* samples. If we have a number of pairs of means to be compared, we definitely are *not* choosing two of them at random for the *t* test, since, if we have chosen to compare, say, $\overline{X}_1$ with $\overline{X}_2$ first, then our next two choices must necessarily be $\overline{X}_1$ with $\overline{X}_3$ and $\overline{X}_2$ with $\overline{X}_3$. Thus the probability values given in Table D are not applicable.

It is for this reason that we now consider one of the most useful techniques in statistics—the analysis of variance (abbreviated AOV or ANOVA). This technique allows us to compare two or more means to see if there are significant differences between or among them. In the subliminal-messages experiment, there were three means to be evaluated. Russell, Rowe, and Smouse (1991) compared treatment with placebo, treatment with control, and placebo with control. They found no differences in course grade or semester GPA in any of the three comparisons.

The analysis of variance is used in a wide variety of applications and in varying degrees of complexity by researchers in such diverse fields as psychology, agriculture, education, and industrial engineering. It is such an important part of the professional's repertoire that at least superficial acquaintance with ANOVA is essential for anyone in education and the behavioral sciences. Since there are entire textbooks and two-semester courses devoted to ANOVA, we will just barely scratch the surface in applying this statistical tool. But we will become acquainted with the introductory concepts and build a foundation for further course work. In this chapter we will consider the most elementary form of ANOVA—the *simple analysis of variance,* sometimes called the *one-way classification analysis of variance.*

THE CONCEPT OF VARIANCE REVISITED

Before beginning the discussion, it might be a good idea to review briefly the concept of variance. We noted in Chapter 4 that the variance is a measure of variability based on the squared deviations from the mean. The numerator of the formula is

Table 11.1
Calculating an estimate of the population variance

X	$(X - \bar{X})$	$(X - \bar{X})^2$
12	6	36
7	1	1
9	3	9
2	−4	16
10	4	16
7	1	1
1	−5	25
3	−3	9
4	−2	4
5	−1	1
60	0	$\Sigma(X - \bar{X})^2 = 118$

$$\bar{X} = 6$$

$$s^2 = \frac{\Sigma(X - \bar{X})^2}{N - 1} = \frac{118}{9} = 13.11$$

the familiar $\Sigma(X - \bar{X})^2$, which is called the *sum of squares*. You will recall from Chapter 4 that the sum of squares is the result of subtracting the mean from each score to obtain the deviation $(X - \bar{X})$, squaring each deviation $(X - \bar{X})^2$, and finally summing the squared deviations to obtain $\Sigma(X - \bar{X})^2$. In the example of Table 11.1, $\Sigma(X - \bar{X})^2 = 118$.

The denominator of the variance formula is the degrees of freedom, $N - 1$. As you can see from Table 11.1, the variance, s^2, is obtained by division of the sum of squares by the degrees of freedom, or $118/9 = 13.11$. This value is a measure of variability for these 10 scores, and s^2 would be smaller for a group of scores that deviated less from the mean and larger for a group that deviated more.

Note that the sum of squares, $\Sigma(X - \bar{X})^2$, is not itself a measure of variability, since the size of $\Sigma(X - \bar{X})^2$ depends not only on the extent of the deviations from the mean but also on the size of the sample. Thus it is necessary to divide by the degrees of freedom to obtain a sort of average.

SOURCES OF VARIATION

Let us use a hypothetical example to show graphically the basic structure of the one-way classification ANOVA. A researcher wants to know which of four methods of teaching introductory psychology produces the best results: (1) lecture, (2) films and videotapes, (3) discussion groups, or (4) self-study with a programmed text. A total of 200 college students is available for the research project,

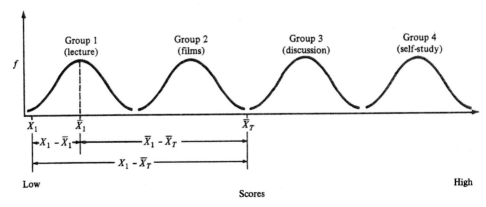

Figure 11.1
Within-groups variability and between-groups variability equals total variability.

and 50 are assigned at random to each of the four groups. After the semester's course work is completed under each of the four different techniques, all students are given a final exam covering basic psychological principles.

To make our graphic analysis easier, let us assume that the 50 scores in each group are normally distributed and that there is no overlapping of any of the groups. This nonoverlapping, of course, would never happen in practice, but it is easier to see the *sources of variation* in this way.

Figure 11.1 shows the four frequency polygons for the final examination scores. Note that the self-study group had the highest scores and the lecture group (this is a hypothetical example!) had the lowest exam scores. Also shown on the polygon is a score (X_1) made by a student in group 1, the mean of group 1 $(\overline{X}_1)$, and the mean of all 200 students, called the total mean $(\overline{X}_T)$. Examining Figure 11.1 carefully, we see that there are really three kinds of variability shown.

Total Variability

We can see that there is variability in the distribution of all 200 scores, which is exemplified by the deviation of a score in group 1 from the total mean, or $X_1 - \overline{X}_T$. This $X_1 - \overline{X}_T$ shown in Figure 11.1 would be the contribution to *total* variability of the single score X_1. There would, of course, be 199 others $(X_2 - \overline{X}_T, X_3 - \overline{X}_T, \text{ etc.})$, and each deviation of a score from the total mean contributes to the *total variability* in the combined distribution.

But note in Figure 11.1 that the deviation of a single score from the total mean, $X_1 - \overline{X}_T$, can be broken down into two separate components. The first component is the deviation of a given score from its group mean, $X_1 - \overline{X}_1$, and the second component is the deviation of the group mean from the total mean, $\overline{X}_1 - \overline{X}_T$. Note that these are additive, both graphically in Figure 11.1 and algebraically, since $(X_1 - \overline{X}_1) + (\overline{X}_1 - \overline{X}_T) = X_1 - \overline{X}_T$.

Variability within Groups

The deviation of a score from its group mean is part of the variability *within groups;* that is, the amount each score in any group deviates from its own mean. The deviation of $X_1 - \overline{X}_1$ in Figure 11.1 would be one part of the variability within group 1, and each of the other 49 scores would contribute its deviation to the variability within group 1. There would be a similar variability in the other three groups.

Variability between Groups

The deviation of a group mean from the total mean contributes to the *variability between groups*. Again looking at Figure 11.1, we see that the deviation of the mean of group 1 from the total mean, $\overline{X}_1 - \overline{X}_T$, is part of the variability between groups. Note that the term *between groups* is used despite the fact that the actual deviation is not between the individual means themselves but between the group mean and the total mean ($\overline{X}_1 - \overline{X}_T$, $\overline{X}_2 - \overline{X}_T$, etc.).

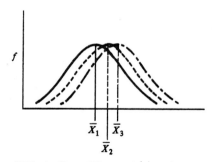

(a) No significant differences between the means

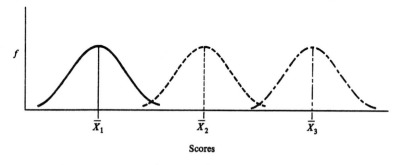

(b) Significant differences between the means

Figure 11.2
Possible relationship between three group means for significant and nonsignificant differences.

Significant Differences between Means

The aim of our analysis, of course, is to determine whether there are significant differences between the group means. *We will do this eventually by comparing the variability between groups with the variability within groups.* We know that in any single distribution of scores there will be variability, so we will always expect to find *variability within groups.*

However, if there are no significant differences between the means of the groups, we expect that there will be very little variability between groups—only the small amount we expect to find by sampling error.

This point is illustrated in Figure 11.2 for three distributions. Note that in Figure 11.2a the three groups differ very little from each other and their means differ only slightly due to sampling error. There is still variability *within each group,* of course, but there is much less *variability between groups* than in Figure 11.2b, where the means of the groups differ markedly. Eventually, we will be able to use the comparison of the *variability between groups* to the *variability within groups* to show whether there are significant differences between the means.

CALCULATING THE SUMS OF SQUARES

Before we can calculate some variances to analyze, we need to develop formulas to calculate the sums of squares, which will be the numerators of the various variance formulas. Remembering that the *total variability* is composed of variability *within groups* and variability *between groups,* we can express this as we did before, in Figure 11.1, as

$$(X - \overline{X}_T) = (X - \overline{X}_1) + (\overline{X}_1 - \overline{X}_T)$$

As we noted before, this equation expresses the contribution to the total variability of *one* score in group 1, and the deviation of this score from the total mean is composed of the deviation of the score from its group mean plus the deviation of the group mean from the total mean.

However, the deviation from the mean must be squared before we can arrive at the sums of squares, so we must square both sides of the preceding expression to obtain

$$(X - \overline{X}_T)^2 = (X - \overline{X}_1)^2 + 2(X - \overline{X}_1)(\overline{X}_1 - \overline{X}_T) + (\overline{X}_1 - \overline{X}_T)^2$$

This equation represents the squared deviation of *one* score in group 1. We now have to sum for *all* of the scores in group 1. Summing both sides of the equation gives

$$\sum^{N_1} (X - \overline{X}_T)^2 = \sum^{N_1}(X - \overline{X}_1)^2 + 2(\overline{X}_1 - \overline{X}_T)\sum^{N_1}(X - \overline{X}_1) + N_1(\overline{X}_1 - \overline{X}_T)^2$$

Note that $\sum^{N_1}$ means that we are summing the various deviations for all the scores in group 1. Note also that in the second term on the right-hand side of the equation, both 2 and $(\bar{X}_1 - \bar{X}_T)$ are constants, so they appear in front of the summation sign, since the sum of a constant times a variable is equal to the constant times the sum of the variable. Note also that in the third term on the right-hand side, we finish up with $N(\bar{X}_1 - \bar{X}_T)^2$, since the sum of a constant is equal to N times the constant.

Examining the second term again, we note that it contains $\overset{N_1}{\Sigma}(X - \bar{X}_1)$. This is nothing more than our $\Sigma(X - \bar{X})$, which we know is equal to 0 for a given group of scores. Thus the entire second term drops out, and we are left with

$$\overset{N_1}{\Sigma}(X - \bar{X}_T)^2 = \overset{N_1}{\Sigma}(X - \bar{X}_1)^2 + N_1(\bar{X}_1 - \bar{X}_T)^2$$

In a verbal description of this formula, along with the graphical representation of Figure 11.1, we would say that the squared deviations of the scores in group 1 from the total mean are made up of the squared deviations of the scores from the mean of group 1 plus the size of group 1 times the squared deviation of the mean of group 1 from the total mean.

There remains one additional step. The formula given is for scores in one group only. We now need to sum over all the groups (k = number of groups), to obtain

	Within-	Between-
Total Sum of	Groups Sum	Groups Sum
Squares	of Squares	of Squares

$$\overset{k\ N_G}{\Sigma\ \Sigma}(X - \bar{X}_T)^2 = \overset{k\ N_G}{\Sigma\ \Sigma}(X - \bar{X}_G)^2 + \overset{k}{\Sigma}N_G\,(\bar{X}_G - \bar{X}_T)^2 \qquad (11.1)$$

Note that the subscript G refers to the number of the group. For example, N_3 refers to the number of scores in group 3, while $\bar{X}_2$ would be the mean of group 2.

Formula 11.1 is one of the most complex formulas we have encountered in this book, but it is probably one of the most important, so let us examine each component in detail. Remember that each is a sum of squares (abbreviated SS), that is, the sum of squared deviations from a mean, $\Sigma(X - \bar{X})^2$.

Total Sum of Squares (SS_T)

$$SS_T = \overset{k\ N_G}{\Sigma\ \Sigma}(X - \bar{X}_T)^2 \qquad (11.2)$$

This term represents the squared deviations of *all* scores from the total mean. The expression $(X - \bar{X}_T)^2$ is the squared deviation of a score from the total mean. $\overset{N_G}{\Sigma}$ indicates that these squared deviations are to be summed for all the scores in each group, and $\overset{k}{\Sigma}$ indicates that the sums of the squared deviations from each group are to be added together finally to give the total sum of the squared deviations.

Within-Groups Sum of Squares (SS_{WG})

$$SS_{WG} = \overset{k\ N_G}{\Sigma\ \Sigma}(X - \bar{X}_G)^2 \qquad (11.3)$$

This term represents the squared deviations of scores from their respective group means. $(X - \overline{X}_G)^2$ is the squared deviation of a score from its group mean. $\sum\limits^{N_G}$ indicates that the squared deviations are to be summed for each group; and $\sum\limits^{k}$ indicates that the sums for each group are to be added together to give the within-groups sum of squares for all groups.

Between-Groups Sum of Squares (SS_{BG})

$$SS_{BG} = \sum\limits^{k} N_G(\overline{X}_G - \overline{X}_T)^2 \tag{11.4}$$

Table 11.2
Calculation of sums of squares: Deviation formulas

Inpatient		Clinic Outpatient		Med Center Outpatient	
3		11		2	
1	$\overline{X}_1 = 2$	6	$\overline{X}_2 = 8$	6	$\overline{X}_3 = 4$
2		5		4	
6		10		12	
		32			

$$\overline{X}_T = \frac{\Sigma X_T}{N_T} = \frac{6 + 32 + 12}{10} = 5$$

SS_T:

$$\sum\limits^{k}\sum\limits^{N_G}(X - \overline{X}_T)^2 = (3 - 5)^2 + (1 - 5)^2 + (2 - 5)^2 = 29$$
$$(11 - 5)^2 + (6 - 5)^2 + (5 - 5)^2 + (10 - 5)^2 = 62$$
$$(2 - 5)^2 + (6 - 5)^2 + (4 - 5)^2 = 11$$
$$SS_T = 29 + 62 + 11 = 102$$

SS_{BG}:

$$\sum\limits^{k} N_G(\overline{X}_G - \overline{X}_T)^2 = N_1(\overline{X}_1 - \overline{X}_T)^2 + N_2(\overline{X}_2 - \overline{X}_T)^2 + N_3(\overline{X}_3 - \overline{X}_T)^2$$
$$SS_{BG} = 27 + 36 + 3 = 66$$

SS_{WG}:

$$\sum\limits^{k}\sum\limits^{N_G}(X - \overline{X}_G)^2 = (3 - 2)^2 + (1 - 2)^2 + (2 - 2)^2 = 2$$
$$(11 - 8)^2 + (6 - 8)^2 + (5 - 8)^2 + (10 - 8)^2 = 26$$
$$(2 - 4)^2 + (6 - 4)^2 + (4 - 4)^2 = 8$$
$$SS_{WG} = 2 + 26 + 8 = 36$$

Summary:

$$SS_T = SS_{BG} + SS_{WG}$$
$$102 = 66 + 36$$

This term represents the squared deviation of each group mean from the total mean. $(\overline{X}_G - \overline{X}_T)^2$ indicates this squared deviation. N_G indicates that each squared deviation is to be multiplied by the size of its group (this is called "weighted by N"); and $\overset{k}{\Sigma}$ indicates that the sums for each group are to be added together to give the weighted squared deviations for all groups.

So we conclude that the sum of squares from the total mean is composed of the sum of squares within the groups plus the sum of squares between groups, or

$$SS_T = SS_{WG} + SS_{BG}$$

Let us see how the formulas that we have developed work with actual data. Table 11.2 shows the number of relapses self-reported by clients in therapy for eating disorders. Three groups are shown. The three clients in the first column came from a private inpatient clinic. The second column shows the number of self-reported relapses for four clients at a storefront walk-in outpatient clinic. The three clients in the third column were treated at a university medical center outpatient clinic. Table 11.2 shows the data for these three groups and the calculation of SS_T, SS_{BG}, and SS_{WG}.

Note that the calculations in Table 11.2 are simply the arithmetic counterpart of the logic of ANOVA developed in the previous sections. The calculation of SS_T is the sum of the squared deviations of each score from the total mean of 5. The SS_{BG} value shows the deviation of each group mean from the total mean, each deviation being squared and multiplied by its sample size N. Finally, the SS_{WG} value shows that within each group the deviation of each score from its mean is squared and the squares are summed for the entire group and these sums are themselves summed over all three groups. Of course, the last statement in Table 11.2 shows that $SS_{BG} + SS_{WG} = SS_T$.

CALCULATING THE VARIANCES

The previous sections dealt with the sums of squares, which we noted earlier are the numerators of the variances we wish to calculate. Before we can calculate these variances, we need to deal now with the denominators of the variances, or the *degrees of freedom*, in order to have a variance of the form $\dfrac{\Sigma(X - \overline{X})^2}{N - 1}$. Just as we found that the total sum of squares could be partitioned into a between-groups and a within-groups sum of squares, we now observe that the total degrees of freedom can be partitioned in the same way.

Total df. The degrees of freedom associated with the entire group of observations is equal to $N_T - 1$, where N_T is the total number of observations. The data of Table 11.2 consisted of 10 observations, so the total $df = 9$.

Between-Groups df.   The degrees of freedom associated with the between-groups component is equal to $k - 1$, where k is the number of groups. For the data of Table 11.2, the *df* for between groups would be 2.

Within-Groups df.   The degrees of freedom within *one* group would be one less than the N of that group. Combining them for all groups would give $(N_1 - 1) + (N_2 - 1) + (N_3 - 1)$ and so on for as many groups as required, which would equal $N_T - k$. For the example in Table 11.2, the within-groups $df = 10 - 3 = 7$.

Note that the degrees of freedom are additive in the same way that the sums of squares were; that is,

$$df_T = df_{BG} + df_{WG}$$

$$N_T - 1 = (k - 1) + (N_T - k)$$

For the data of Table 11.2, $2 + 7 = 9$.

The Mean Squares

We are now ready to calculate the variance estimates associated with the between-groups component and the within-groups component. These variance estimates are called *mean squares*. Mean squares are variance estimates, and they consist of a sum of squares divided by the appropriate degrees of freedom. Since we will eventually want to compare the variance estimate based on the between-groups component with the variance estimate based on the within-groups component, we will focus our attention on the mean square between groups, MS_{BG}, and the mean square within groups, MS_{WG}. The formulas for these variance estimates are

$$MS_{BG} = \frac{SS_{BG}}{k - 1} \tag{11.5}$$

$$MS_{WG} = \frac{SS_{WG}}{N_T - k} \tag{11.6}$$

For the relapse data of Table 11.2, the mean squares would be

$$MS_{BG} = \frac{66}{3 - 1} = 33$$

$$MS_{WG} = \frac{36}{10 - 3} = 5.14$$

VARIANCE ESTIMATES AND THE NULL HYPOTHESIS

Now that we have spent considerable time and energy on the calculation of MS_{WG} and MS_{BG}, just what are they? What do they represent? Since they have a sum of squares in the numerator and a *df* term in the denominator, they certainly must be variance estimates of some sort.

MS_{WG} and MS_{BG} as Variance Estimates

We have already stated that the sums of squares within groups, SS_{WG}, was composed of squared deviations from the various group means. For a *single* group, then, SS_{WG_1} would be the sum of squared deviations from the mean of group 1. And if we calculated

$$MS_{WG_1} = \frac{SS_{WG_1}}{N_1 - 1}$$

we would have the mean square within group 1, *which is an unbiased estimate of the population variance from which group 1 came.* To refer back to Figure 11.1, the lecture group, group 1, is a random sample from a population of available college students, and MS_{WG_1} is an estimate of the variance of that population.

We could also calculate MS_{WG_2} by dividing SS_{WG_2} by $N_2 - 1$. This would be an unbiased estimate of the variance of the population from which group 2 came.

We could do this in a similar manner for MS_{WG_3} and MS_{WG_4} or for as many groups as we had. Each one is an unbiased estimate of the variance of the different populations from which the samples came. *However, under the null hypothesis, these various estimates are all estimating the same thing!* Since the null hypothesis states that $\mu_1 = \mu_2 = \mu_3 = \mu_4$, we assume that the populations from which the various samples have been drawn are identical and that MS_{WG_1}, MS_{WG_2}, MS_{WG_3}, and MS_{WG_4} are just estimates of the same population variance. Since we are rather knowledgeable on the topic of sampling by now, we know that a *mean* of these estimates would give us a very accurate overall estimate of the population variance *if the null hypothesis is true.* So, if we take an average of MS_{WG_1}, MS_{WG_2}, and so on, we wind up with our familiar MS_{WG}, the average unbiased estimate of the variance of the population from which the samples came.

Let us get back to the mean square between groups, MS_{BG}. It can be shown that, if the null hypothesis is true ($\mu_1 = \mu_2 = \mu_3$, etc.), then MS_{BG} is *also an unbiased estimate of the variance of the population from which the samples came.* The mathematical proof for this statement is beyond the scope of this book, but we will accept it on faith.

The Ratio MS_{BG}/MS_{WG}

Since MS_{BG} and MS_{WG} are estimates of the same population variance, we would expect that if the null hypothesis is true the ratio MS_{BG}/MS_{WG} will be equal to 1.0. Of course, we do not expect it to be *exactly* 1.0, since we know that there will be some fluctuations due to sampling error.

However, if the ratio is quite a bit larger than 1.0, we reject the null hypothesis and conclude that there is a real difference between the means of the populations from which the samples were drawn ($\mu_1 \neq \mu_2 \neq \mu_3$, etc.). If the ratio is such that it would happen less than 5% or 1% or 0.1% of the time by sampling error alone, we conclude that there is a significant difference between the means. The statistical procedure for determining whether the ratio MS_{BG}/MS_{WG} is significant is called the *F* test.

THE F TEST

The F test (named after a British statistican, Sir Ronald Fisher) consists of examining the ratio of two variances to see if the departure from 1.0 is sufficiently large so that it is not likely to be due to sampling error. The F test (or F ratio), as indicated in the preceding section, is the ratio

$$F = \frac{MS_{BG}}{MS_{WG}} \tag{11.7}$$

But how large must F be before we reject the null hypothesis? We noted earlier with the t test that the value to be equaled or exceeded in Table D depended upon the degrees of freedom on which the t test had been computed. The F value to be equaled or exceeded depends upon the degrees of freedom also, but *both* the numerator and denominator of the F test determine the degrees of freedom. You will notice in Table E in Appendix 3 a list of various values of F that need to be equaled or exceeded for the given significance levels. As with the t distributions, these values are points that mark off the 5% and 1% points in the sampling distribution of F. These values are determined by the degrees of freedom associated with both the numerator and the denominator of the F ratio. For example, if you have 4 degrees of freedom in the numerator and 20 degrees of freedom in the denominator, you would need an F value of at least 2.87 for the ratio to be significant at the .05 level and 4.43 for it to be significant at the .01 level. For the relapse data shown in Table 11.2 the F value would be

$$F = \frac{MS_{BG}}{MS_{WG}} = \frac{33}{5.14} = 6.42$$

Remembering that the df for MS_{BG} was $k - 1 = 2$ and the df for MS_{WG} was $N_T - k = 7$, we would proceed to Table E and note that for 2 and 7 degrees of freedom F_{05} is 4.74 and F_{01} is 9.55. We would then conclude that $p < .05$ that our F of 6.42 happened by sampling error and would state that there is a significant difference between the mean number of relapses of the three groups.

COMPUTATIONAL FORMULAS

The deviation formulas used in Table 11.2 demonstrate the logic of ANOVA very clearly, but they are rather cumbersome to work with. Subtracting a mean from each score and squaring the deviation is very time-consuming, and for this reason computational formulas have been developed. (You may remember we did the same thing for the standard deviation in Chapter 4.) These formulas for the sums of squares deal with the raw scores rather than the deviations. The *raw score* formula for the total sum of squares is as follows:

$$SS_T = \sum_{}^{N_T} X^2 - N_T \overline{X}_T^2 \tag{11.8}$$

In this formula, $\overset{N_T}{\Sigma} X^2$ indicates that *all* scores are squared and then summed, and $N_T \overline{X}_T^2$ indicates that the total mean is squared and multiplied by the total number of observations. This result is then subtracted from $\overset{N_T}{\Sigma} X^2$.

$$SS_{BG} = N_1 \overline{X}_1^2 + N_2 \overline{X}_2^2 + N_3 \overline{X}_3^2 + \cdots - N_T \overline{X}_T^2 \qquad (11.9)$$

This formula for the between-groups sum of squares indicates that each group mean is squared and then multiplied by the size of that group and that these products are added together for as many groups as there are. The quantity $N_T \overline{X}_T^2$, which is the same value calculated previously in the formula for SS_T, is then subtracted.

$$SS_{WG} = \left(\overset{N_1}{\Sigma} X^2 - N_1 \overline{X}_1^2 \right) + \left(\overset{N_2}{\Sigma} X^2 - N_2 \overline{X}_2^2 \right) + \left(\overset{N_3}{\Sigma} X^2 - N_3 \overline{X}_3^2 \right) + \cdots \qquad (11.10)$$

The formula for the within-groups sum of squares shows that the mean of group 1 is squared, multiplied by the size of group 1, and subtracted from the sum of the squared scores in group 1. This procedure is repeated for as many groups as there are, and the sums of squares for each group are then added together to yield SS_{WG}.

Computational Formulas—An Example

To illustrate the use of the computational formulas, let us consider the data of Table 11.3. An investigator was studying the learning abilities of four species of laboratory animals. She taught 5 squirrels, 6 cats, 3 guinea pigs, and 6 rats a simple maze response and kept track of the errors each animal made. Were there significant differences in the learning abilities of these four species?

In applying the raw score formulas for the sums of squares, we should note the starred items in Table 11.3:

1. *Remember that you cannot simply take an average of the four means to obtain $\overline{X}_T$. You must divide the total ΣX by the total N.

2. **The total ΣX^2 is the sum of the individual ΣX^2 columns.

3. ***Note that the quantities $N_1 \overline{X}_1^2$, $N_2 \overline{X}_2^2$, and so on, have already been calculated in the previous SS_{BG} formula. So, each component is simply the ΣX^2 of each group minus the $N\overline{X}^2$ for that group.

The main interest, of course, is in the F value, and we see that the calculated F is 5.24, which is greater than the tabled value at the 5% level for 3 and 16 degrees of freedom. We would conclude that there are significant differences between the means of the maze errors committed by the different laboratory animals. The total statement is expressed as shown, $F(3, 16) = 5.24$, $p < .05$.

THE ANOVA SUMMARY TABLE

A convenient way of displaying the important segments of the ANOVA calculations of Table 11.3 is shown in Table 11.4. The summary table lists the *source of vari-*

Table 11.3
Using the computational formulas for ANOVA

Squirrels		Cats		Guinea Pigs		Rats	
X	X^2	X	X^2	X	X^2	X	X^2
9	81	17	289	12	144	10	100
9	81	16	256	10	100	8	64
3	9	14	196	14	196	7	49
5	25	15	225	36	440	9	81
6	36	10	100			12	144
32	232	6	36			8	64
		78	1,102			54	502
$\overline{X}_1 = 6.4$		$\overline{X}_2 = 13$		$\overline{X}_3 = 12$		$\overline{X}_4 = 9$	

$$*\overline{X}_T = \frac{\Sigma X_T}{N_T} = \frac{32 + 78 + 36 + 54}{5 + 6 + 3 + 6} = \frac{200}{20} = 10.0$$

$$**\overset{N_T}{\Sigma} X^2 = 232 + 1,102 + 440 + 502 = 2,276$$

Sums of Squares:

$$SS_T = \overset{N_T}{\Sigma} X^2 - N_T \overline{X}_T^2 = 2,276 - 20(10.0)^2$$

$$= 2,276 - 2,000$$

$$SS_T = 276$$

$$SS_{BG} = N_1 \overline{X}_1^2 + N_2 \overline{X}_2^2 + N_3 \overline{X}_3^2 + N_4 \overline{X}_4^2 - N_T \overline{X}_T^2$$

$$= 5(6.4)^2 + 6(13)^2 + 3(12)^2 + 6(9)^2 - 2,000$$

$$= 204.8 + 1,014 + 432 + 486 - 2,000 \qquad \textit{(continued)}$$

ance, degrees of freedom, sums of squares, and mean squares, as well as the F value. This is an efficient way of communicating the results of an ANOVA, and you might expect to see some variation of these summary tables in the professional literature as well as in computer statistical packages.

MULTIPLE COMPARISONS: TESTING FOR DIFFERENCES AMONG PAIRS OF MEANS

After a significant F has been obtained, we are faced with the question of which differences between means are significant. If there are three means, $\overline{X}_1$, $\overline{X}_2$, and $\overline{X}_3$, it is possible that they are all significantly different from each other. On the other hand, maybe $\overline{X}_1$ and $\overline{X}_2$ are about the same, but $\overline{X}_3$ is significantly different from those two. With a little imagination, you can see how these comparisons could become complex with as many as five or six or even more groups to be compared.

Table 11.3 (continued)

$SS_{BG} = 136.8$

$$***SS_{WG} = \left(\overset{N_1}{\Sigma}X^2 - N_1\bar{X}_1^2\right) + \left(\overset{N_2}{\Sigma}X^2 - N_2\bar{X}_2^2\right)$$

$$+ \left(\overset{N_3}{\Sigma}X^2 - N_3\bar{X}_3^2\right) + \left(\overset{N_4}{\Sigma}X^2 - N_4\bar{X}_4^2\right)$$

$$= (232 - 204.8) + (1{,}102 - 1{,}014) + (440 - 432) + (502 - 486)$$

$$= 27.2 + 88 + 8 + 16$$

$SS_{WG} = 139.2$

Check:

$$SS_{BG} + SS_{WG} = SS_T$$
$$136.8 + 139.2 = 276$$

Mean Squares and the F Test:

$$MS_{BG} = \frac{SS_{BG}}{k-1} = \frac{136.8}{3} = 45.6$$

$$MS_{WG} = \frac{SS_{WG}}{N_T - k} = \frac{139.2}{16} = 8.7$$

$$F = \frac{MS_{BG}}{MS_{WG}} = \frac{45.6}{8.7} = 5.24$$

$$F(3, 16) = 5.24, \text{ p} < .05$$

Table 11.4
ANOVA summary table for animal learning experiment

Source of Variance	df	SS	MS	F
Between groups	3	136.8	45.6	5.24[a]
Within groups	16	139.2	8.7	
Total	19	276.0		

[a]$p < .05$

Clearly, what is needed is a technique that will enable us to determine which differences between means are significant and which are not. A number of techniques for multiple comparisons have been developed, and you may run across a reference to Duncan's multiple-range test, the Newman–Keuls procedure, the Scheffé method, Tukey's procedure, and others. Each of these methods has been developed for a particular purpose, and your instructor may have a personal bias for or against a particular technique. We will confine our discussion to Tukey's procedure, at the same time remembering that your instructor or an advanced textbook might prefer another approach. The Tukey procedure may be used in all cases where a significant F was obtained in the ANOVA calculation.

The Tukey Method. Unequal N's

The statistic that will enable us to evaluate differences among pairs of means is called the *studentized range statistic, q,* whose general formula is

$$q = \frac{\overline{X}_L - \overline{X}_S}{\sqrt{\dfrac{MS_{WG}}{2}\left(\dfrac{1}{N_L} + \dfrac{1}{N_S}\right)}} \tag{11.11}$$

where
$\overline{X}_L$ = the larger of the two means
$\overline{X}_S$ = the smaller of the two means
MS_{WG} = the mean square within groups from the ANOVA calculations
N_L = the size of the group with the larger mean
N_S = the size of the group with the smaller mean

If q is large enough, we can reject the hypothesis that the difference between two means is due only to sampling error, and we pronounce the difference as significant. How large does q have to be? Table L in Appendix 3 lists the values for the .05 and .01 significance levels (i.e., for α). If these tabled values are equaled or exceeded by our calculated q, they are significant at the stated level. Table L is entered by using (1) the appropriate value of k, the number of means in the ANOVA, and (2) the df for the MS_{WG}, the number of degrees of freedom in the calculation of MS_{WG}.

Let us use the animal learning data shown in Table 11.5 to help clarify the procedure. Note that each mean is paired with every other mean, and the calculated q is compared with the tabled values from Table L. Since we have four means and $df = 16$ for the MS_{WG}, we enter Table L to find that $q_{05} = 4.05$ and $q_{01} = 5.19$. In Table 11.5 we see that the mean error score for squirrels ($\overline{X} = 6.4$) is significantly less than the mean error score for cats ($\overline{X} = 13$), with a q value of 5.22, $p < .01$. However, we would have to conclude that the rest of the means are not significantly different, $p > .05$.

The Tukey Method. Equal N's

The procedure described in the preceding subsection is greatly simplified if all the groups are of equal size. If $N_1 = N_2 = N_3$, and so on, then formula 11.11 reduces to

$$q = \frac{\overline{X}_L - \overline{X}_S}{\sqrt{\dfrac{MS_{WG}}{N_G}}} \tag{11.12}$$

Table 11.5
The Tukey method for animal learning data (errors)

	Squirrels	Cats	Guinea Pigs	Rats
	$\overline{X} = 6.4$	$\overline{X} = 13$	$\overline{X} = 12$	$\overline{X} = 9$
	$N = 5$	$N = 6$	$N = 3$	$N = 6$

$$MS_{WG} = 8.7$$
$$df = N_T - k = 16$$

Squirrels–Cats:

$$q = \frac{\overline{X}_L - \overline{X}_S}{\sqrt{\dfrac{MS_{WG}}{2}\left(\dfrac{1}{N_L} + \dfrac{1}{N_S}\right)}} = \frac{13 - 6.4}{\sqrt{\dfrac{8.7}{2}\left(\dfrac{1}{6} + \dfrac{1}{5}\right)}} = \frac{6.6}{\sqrt{4.35\,(.367)}}$$

$$= \frac{6.6}{\sqrt{1.596}} = \frac{6.6}{1.26} = 5.24 \qquad \text{Significant, } p < .01$$

Squirrels–Guinea Pigs:

$$q = \frac{12 - 6.4}{\sqrt{\dfrac{8.7}{2}\left(\dfrac{1}{3} + \dfrac{1}{5}\right)}} = \frac{5.6}{\sqrt{4.35\,(.533)}} = \frac{5.6}{\sqrt{2.319}} = \frac{5.6}{1.52} = 3.68$$

Not significant, $p > .05$

Squirrels–Rats:

$$q = \frac{9 - 6.4}{\sqrt{\dfrac{8.7}{2}\left(\dfrac{1}{6} + \dfrac{1}{5}\right)}} = \frac{2.6}{\sqrt{4.35\,(.367)}} = \frac{2.6}{\sqrt{1.596}} = \frac{2.6}{1.26} = 2.06$$

Not significant, $p > .05$

Cats–Guinea Pigs:

$$q = \frac{13 - 12}{\sqrt{\dfrac{8.7}{2}\left(\dfrac{1}{6} + \dfrac{1}{3}\right)}} = \frac{1}{\sqrt{4.35\,(.5)}} = \frac{1}{\sqrt{2.175}} = \frac{1}{1.47} = .68$$

Not significant, $p > .05$

Cats–Rats:

$$q = \frac{13 - 9}{\sqrt{\dfrac{8.7}{2}\left(\dfrac{1}{6} + \dfrac{1}{6}\right)}} = \frac{4}{\sqrt{4.35\,(.333)}} = \frac{4}{\sqrt{1.449}} = \frac{4}{1.20} = 3.33$$

Not significant, $p > .05$

Guinea Pigs–Rats:

$$q = \frac{12 - 9}{\sqrt{\dfrac{8.7}{2}\left(\dfrac{1}{3} + \dfrac{1}{6}\right)}} = \frac{3}{\sqrt{4.35\,(.5)}} = \frac{3}{\sqrt{2.175}} = \frac{3}{1.47} = 2.04$$

Not significant, $p > .05$

303

where N_G is the size of any group and the rest of the terms are as described earlier. When the groups are of equal size, we begin the Tukey procedure by selecting the *largest* difference between means, applying formula 11.12, and evaluating our value of q in Table L. We then repeat the procedure with the next largest difference and continue until our q is no longer significant. Obviously, since the denominator remains the same, once we have a difference between means that is not large enough to yield a significant q, it is pointless to test smaller differences. This procedure is illustrated in the Sample Problem at the end of this chapter.*

It must be emphasized that the Tukey method is only one of many methods for making multiple comparisons, and your instructor may wish to pursue one or more of the other methods mentioned earlier.

ASSUMPTIONS FOR THE ANALYSIS OF VARIANCE

In order for the F test to be a valid procedure for determining the significance of the differences between means, the following assumptions or restrictions must be met. These assumptions are identical to those listed in Chapter 9 for the t test.

1. The scores must be interval or ratio in nature.
2. The scores must be measures on random samples from the respective populations.
3. The populations from which the samples were drawn must be normally distributed.
4. The populations from which the samples were drawn must have approximately the same variability (homogeneity of variance).

CONCLUDING REMARKS

This elementary introduction to the analysis of variance barely touches on the use of a highly popular and versatile statistical tool. Almost any professional journal in education or the behavioral sciences will contain one or more studies where ANOVA has been used for the data analysis. The reasons for its popularity have not been obvious in our examination of the single classification method, which may appear to be nothing more than an extension of the t test for more than two means. One of the unique features of the more complex ANOVA designs is its measurement of an *interaction* effect, the relationship that one variable has to another variable in producing a significant difference. This form of ANOVA will be treated in detail in the next chapter.

---

*It is possible to find a significant F value in your ANOVA computation and not find any q values to be significant. Such an occurrence is quite rare, however.

SAMPLE PROBLEM

An industrial psychologist was investigating three different training methods for speeding up assembly line production. Thirty workers were assigned at random to three groups, and each group was trained in a different method for completing the assemblies. Each worker's performance was then measured in number of units assembled per hour. These measurements are shown in the following table for each of the three different methods. Was there a significant difference in the workers' performance in the three training methods? If so, which differences were significant?

Method A		Method B		Method C	
X	X^2	X	X^2	X	X^2
52	2,704	61	3,721	76	5,776
54	2,916	62	3,844	65	4,225
49	2,401	68	4,624	66	4,356
62	3,844	58	3,364	76	5,776
45	2,025	43	1,849	84	7,056
47	2,209	39	1,521	83	6,889
31	961	41	1,681	78	6,084
35	1,225	50	2,500	66	4,356
41	1,681	50	2,500	73	5,329
40	1,600	53	2,809	62	3,844
456	21,566	525	28,413	729	53,691

Calculator Solution

$$\overline{X}_1 = \frac{456}{10} = 45.6 \qquad \overline{X}_2 = \frac{525}{10} = 52.5 \qquad \overline{X}_3 = \frac{729}{10} = 72.9$$

$$\overline{X}_T = \frac{\Sigma X_T}{N_T} = \frac{456 + 525 + 729}{30} = \frac{1,710}{30} = 57.0$$

$$\overset{N_T}{\Sigma} X^2 = 21,566 + 28,413 + 53,691 = 103,670$$

Sums of Squares:

$$SS_T = \overset{N_T}{\Sigma} X^2 - N_T \overline{X}_T^2 = 103,670 - 30(57)^2$$
$$= 103,670 - 97,470$$
$$SS_T = 6,200$$
$$SS_{BG} = N_1 \overline{X}_1^2 + N_2 \overline{X}_2^2 + N_3 \overline{X}_3^2 - N_T \overline{X}_T^2$$
$$= 10(45.6)^2 + 10(52.5)^2 + 10(72.9)^2 - 97,470$$
$$= 20,793.6 + 27,562.5 + 53,144.1 - 97,470$$

(continued)

SAMPLE PROBLEM (*CONTINUED*)

$$SS_{BG} = 4,030.2$$

$$SS_{WG} = \left(\overset{N_1}{\Sigma} X^2 - N_1 \overline{X}_1^2 \right) + \left(\overset{N_2}{\Sigma} X^2 - N_2 \overline{X}_2^2 \right) + \left(\overset{N_3}{\Sigma} X^2 - N_3 \overline{X}_3^2 \right)$$

$$= (21,566 - 20,793.6) + (28,413 - 27,562.5)$$
$$\quad + (53,691 - 53,144.1)$$
$$= 772.4 + 850.5 + 546.9$$
$$SS_{WG} = 2,169.8$$

Check:

$$SS_{BG} + SS_{WG} = SS_T$$
$$4,030.2 + 2,169.8 = 6,200$$

Mean Squares and the *F* Test:

$$MS_{BG} = \frac{SS_{BG}}{k-1} = \frac{4,030.2}{2} = 2,015.1$$

$$MS_{WG} = \frac{SS_{WG}}{N_T - k} = \frac{2,169.8}{27} = 80.36$$

$$F = \frac{MS_{BG}}{MS_{WG}} = \frac{2,015.1}{80.36} = 25.08$$

Source of Variance	df	SS	MS	F
Between groups	2	4,030.2	2,015.1	25.08[a]
Within groups	27	2,169.8	80.36	
Total	29	6,200.0		

[a]$p < .01.$

Since an *F* value of 25.08 would happen less than 1% of the time by sampling error, we conclude that there is a significant difference between the means of the three training groups.

Tukey's Procedure

Method A	Method B	Method C
$\overline{X}_1 = 45.6$	$\overline{X}_2 = 52.5$	$\overline{X}_3 = 72.9$

$$MS_{WG} = 80.36; \ df = 27; \ k = 3$$

Methods A and C:
$$q = \frac{\overline{X}_L - \overline{X}_S}{\sqrt{\dfrac{MS_{WG}}{N}}} = \frac{72.9 - 45.6}{\sqrt{\dfrac{80.36}{10}}} = \frac{27.3}{\sqrt{8.036}}$$

$$= \frac{27.3}{2.83} = 9.65 \qquad \text{Significant, } p < .01$$

Methods B and C:
$$q = \frac{72.9 - 52.5}{2.83} = \frac{20.4}{2.83} = 7.21$$

Significant, $p < .01$

Methods A and B:
$$q = \frac{52.5 - 45.6}{2.83} = \frac{6.9}{2.83} = 2.44$$

Not significant, $p > .05$

We conclude that method C is superior to methods A and B; however, there appears to be no significant difference between methods A and B. Note that we used formula 11.12 for Tukey's procedure, since there were an equal number of subjects in the three groups.

Computer Solution

Computer output for the three training methods is shown in Table 11.6. The first box shows the descriptive statistics for the three training methods (1, 2, and 3 instead of A, B, and C). Also shown in this box are the standard error and 95% confidence intervals for each mean.

Table 11.6
SPSS output for one-way analysis of variance on assembly line performance for three training methods

One-Way

Descriptives

		N	Mean	Std. Deviation	Std. Error	95% Confidence Interval for Mean Lower Bound	95% Confidence Interval for Mean Upper Bound	Minimum	Maximum
TRAINING METHOD	1	10	45.60	9.26	2.93	38.97	52.23	31	62
	2	10	52.50	9.72	3.07	45.55	59.45	39	68
	3	10	72.90	7.80	2.47	67.32	78.48	62	84
	Total	30	57.00	14.62	2.67	51.54	62.46	31	84

(continued)

SAMPLE PROBLEM *(CONTINUED)*

ANOVA

		Sum of Squares	df	Mean Square	F	Sig.
TRAINING	Between groups	4030.200	2	2015.100	25.075	.000
	Within groups	2169.800	27	80.363		
	Total	6200.000	29			

Post Hoc Tests

Multiple Comparisons

Dependent Variable: ASSEMBLY
Tukey HSD

(I) METHOD	(J) METHOD	Mean Difference (I-J)	Std. Error	Sig.	99.9% Confidence Interval	
					Lower Bound	Upper Bound
1	2	−6.90	4.009	.216	−23.28	9.48
	3	−27.30*	4.009	.000	−43.68	−10.92
2	1	6.90	4.009	.216	−9.48	23.28
	3	−20.40*	4.009	.000	−36.78	−4.02
3	1	27.30*	4.009	.000	10.92	43.68
	2	20.40*	4.009	.000	4.02	36.78

*The mean difference is significant at the .001 level.

The second box shows the ANOVA summary table, with a p value ("Sig." in this table) of .000, which means $p < .001$.

The multiple comparisons are shown in the bottom box labeled "Post Hoc Tests." The term *post hoc* (literally, "after this [thing]") simply means that the comparisons are done after a significant F is obtained. Note that this application of Tukey's procedure does not result in the q statistic as discussed earlier. Instead, the difference between each pair of means is shown in the "Mean Difference" column, and the probabilities of each difference occurring just by chance are given in the "Sig." column. Again, .000 means $p < .001$.

Each difference appears twice, since each mean is positioned both first and second in the subtraction procedure. Whether or not a particular difference reaches significance at the stated level is also obvious when we examine the confidence intervals for each difference. Any interval not containing zero indicates that the listed difference is in the "Reject" region at the specified significance level.

We conclude that there is no difference in the assembly performance between training group A and training group B, since a difference of 6.90 is not significant, $p > .05$ ($p = .216$). However, there is a significant difference between group A and group C, with a difference of 27.30, $p < .001$. There is also a significant difference between group B and group C, with a difference of 20.40, $p < .001$.

STUDY QUESTIONS

1. If you are testing to see if there are significant differences between three means, why is it incorrect to use three separate t tests with $\overline{X}_1$ and $\overline{X}_2$, $\overline{X}_1$ and $\overline{X}_3$, and $\overline{X}_2$ and $\overline{X}_3$?
2. What is meant by the term *sum of squares*?
3. Why is the sum of squares not used as a measure of variability?
4. In your own words describe what is meant by the expression $(X_1 - \overline{X}_1) + (\overline{X}_1 - \overline{X}_T) = (X_1 - \overline{X}_T)$.
5. "We will always expect to find variability *within* groups, but there may not be variability *between* groups." What does this mean?
6. What does MS_{WG} represent? Under the null hypothesis what does MS_{BG} represent?
7. Why should the ratio MS_{BG}/MS_{WG} equal 1.0 under the null hypothesis?
8. What information does an ANOVA summary table contain?
9. Why is Tukey's procedure needed after a significant value of F has been found?
10. What are the assumptions of the one-way analysis of variance?

EXERCISES

1. Language development scores for children in three different age groups are shown. Use the deviation formulas (as in Table 11.2) to calculate SS_T, SS_{BG}, and SS_{WG} for these data.

Age 2	Age 3	Age 4
3	7	7
2	6	8
4	2	10
		11

2. Calculate MS_{BG}, MS_{WG}, and the F test for exercise 1. Is there a significant difference in language development scores of these three age groups?

3. Use the computational formula to calculate SS_T, SS_{BG}, and SS_{WG} on the data in exercise 1, checking your results against the deviation method.

4. Spelling quiz scores for three groups of students are shown. Use the deviation formulas (as in Table 11.2) to calculate SS_T, SS_{BG}, and SS_{WG}.

Group 1	Group 2	Group 3
6	8	6
1	7	8
3	7	11
2	9	11
8	9	9

5. Calculate MS_{BG}, MS_{WG}, and the F ratio for exercise 4. Is there a significant difference between the quiz scores for these three groups?

6. Calculate SS_T, SS_{BG}, and SS_{WG} for exercise 4 using the computational formulas, checking your results against the deviation formulas.

7. A physiological psychologist is measuring the startle reflex latency of rats under three different conditions of noise. She has 9 rats in group 1, 7 rats in group 2, and 8 rats in group 3. How large must her F value be to be significant at the .05 level?

8. A child psychologist is testing problem-solving ability of children in four different age groups. He has 8 children in one group, 6 in a second group, 4 in a third group, and 10 in a fourth group. How large must his F value be to be significant at the .01 level?

9. The researcher in exercise 7 wishes to apply Tukey's procedure to see which means are significantly different. How large must her q value be to be significant at the .05 level?

10. You are running an analysis of variance on data from four groups of subjects with 9 subjects in each group. If you use Tukey's procedure to test for significant differences among the means, how large a q value will you need for significance at the .05 level?

11. In a study to determine whether highly active individuals are more optimistic than less active individuals, 20 college students were administered an optimism and pessimism scale in addition to being asked how often they exercise. Optimism scores for five highly active, eight moderately active, and seven inactive subjects are shown. Was there a significant difference in optimism scores between the three groups? If so, use Tukey's procedure to find which differences were significant.

Inactive	Moderately Active	Highly Active
58	59	62
48	49	48
53	54	63
56	59	47
50	50	55

60	62
46	46
	61

12. A health counselor in a large southern university conducted a private study in which she asked 10 students diagnosed with bulimia nervosa, 7 students diagnosed with anorexia nervosa, and 8 students with no eating disorder to complete a questionnaire. The questionnaire measured anxiety levels, and the anxiety scores for the students in each group are listed. Was there a significant difference in the anxiety scores from the three groups? If so, use Tukey's procedure to find which means were significantly different.

Bulimics	Anorexics	Normal Eaters
13	14	9
12	11	10
14	12	8
15	17	9
14	16	12
13	15	10
12	13	6
15		8
16		
14		

13. A sixth-grade teacher testing the effectiveness of three different teaching methods divided her class into three groups. One group of 10 students watched a video about the solar system. Another group of 10 students was given a pamphlet about the solar system and instructed to read it. A third group of 9 students listened to the teacher talk about the solar system. The following day, all 29 students received a 20-point pop quiz over information they had received about the solar system, and their scores are presented in the following table. Was there a significant difference in scores between the three groups? If so, use Tukey's procedure to find which differences were significant.

Video	Pamphlet	Lecture
18	13	14
19	12	13
20	11	9
20	10	12
19	9	18
18	5	15
20	8	10
18	14	14
16	18	18
17	7	

14. The National Weather Service studied the effect of a high pressure system in a small part of the northern hemisphere and measured the temperature (in Fahrenheit) at three weather stations located 10 miles apart within the high pressure area. Measurements were taken three times a day for three days at equal times in each area, with the results shown. Was there a significant difference in temperature between the three areas? If so, which differences were significant?

Station 1	Station 2	Station 3
34	29	30
32	27	28
30	26	27
37	31	35
34	27	32
29	26	31
34	29	33
34	30	32
28	26	27

COMPUTER EXERCISES FOR APPENDIX 4 DATA BANK

For the following exercises report the results of your analysis in the form of descriptive statistics, an ANOVA summary table, and post hoc tests, similar to Table 11.6.

C1. Divide the sample into approximately equal thirds (highest third, middle third, and lowest third), based on the Speed and Impatience (S&I) scores. The top third would be designated high S&I; the middle third, moderate S&I; and the lowest third, low S&I. Use the one-way ANOVA to see if there were any differences in physical symptoms reported by these three groups. If there is a significant difference, examine the multiple comparisons to see which differences were significant.

C2. Use the same three-way split in S&I to see if there were any differences in the Hard Driving and Competitive (HD&C) scores.

C3. Divide the sample into approximately equal thirds, based on their Self-Monitoring scores, to get high self-monitoring, moderate self-monitoring, and low self-monitoring. Use the one-way ANOVA to see if there were any differences in Masculinity scores among these three groups. If there is a significant difference, examine the multiple comparisons to see which differences were significant.

C4. Use the same three-way split in Self-Monitoring to see if there were any differences in the Femininity scores.

CHAPTER 12

Two-Way Analysis of Variance

Cardiologists and health psychologists have long been interested in the relationship between Type A behavior and coronary heart disease. Hundreds of studies have compared individuals high in Type A behaviors, who are trying to do more and more things in less and less time than their more relaxed counterparts who are low in Type A behaviors.

Many studies have investigated the reactivity of the cardiovascular system of high Type A's. A typical study would look at the systolic blood pressures (the high number) of high and low Type A's, but would find no difference. Even when exercising on a treadmill, the blood pressures of the two groups would remain the same. However, if the exercise were supervised by a trainer who continually emphasized beating the competition and encouraging the participant to do even better, the blood pressures of high Type A's would rise higher and take longer to return to normal than the blood pressures of low Type A's.

In this kind of study researchers would be examining two variables simultaneously instead of just one. The first variable is Type A (high or low), and the second variable is exercise (unsupervised or competitive).

In Chapter 11 we were interested only in *one* variable, and the chapter was devoted entirely to the *one-way* ANOVA. If, for example, we want to see which of three teaching methods (lecture, discussion, or interactive television) is best for teaching freshman English to college students, we can assign freshmen at random to one of three groups. Each group can then learn under its designated instructional method, and we can use final test scores as our criterion measure. We can diagram the results schematically as follows, where the blanks are final exam scores, and $\overline{X}_1$, $\overline{X}_2$, and $\overline{X}_3$ are the group means for the three instructional methods.

Lecture	Discussion	Interactive Television
————	————	————
————	————	————
————	————	————
$\overline{X}_1 =$	$\overline{X}_2 =$	$\overline{X}_3 =$

The null hypothesis would state that $\mu_1 = \mu_2 = \mu_3$ and any difference between $\overline{X}_1$, $\overline{X}_2$, and $\overline{X}_3$ is due to sampling error. This design is called a one-way or single-classification ANOVA because only *one* variable (teaching method) is being tested. In this example, we are comparing three levels (lecture, discussion, and interactive television) of a single variable. We might have 3 or 7 or 15 different levels, but we still are dealing with only one variable, that of teaching method.

However, as in the experiment on Type A behavior and blood pressure, we may sometimes want to investigate the effects of *two* variables simultaneously. We may wish to see if the three teaching methods have different effects with superior students than with average students. We could do such an analysis by conducting two separate experiments—one with superior students and one with average students. This approach, however, would be inefficient, since it would require twice as much effort as a single experiment. Also, unfortunately, we would not be able to get a direct measure of the *interaction effect:* One teaching method might be better for superior students, while another method might work better for average students! In the material to follow we will develop a method for looking at the effects of two variables simultaneously, the two-way ANOVA.

FACTORIAL DESIGNS

The two-way ANOVA that we will be examining is called a factorial design, indicating that we are looking at the effects of two factors (variables) simultaneously. For example, let us suppose that we have 60 superior students (determined by their college entrance exam scores) and 60 average students, and we assign 20 of each at random to each of the three English teaching methods mentioned earlier. Since we have two ability levels (superior and average) and three teaching methods (lecture, discussion, and interactive television), we have a 2 × 3 (say "two by three") factorial design. Factorial designs come in all shapes and sizes (3 × 7, 2 × 4, and so on), depending on how many levels we have for each of the two variables.

The 2 × 3 factorial design for the ability level and teaching method experiment is presented in Table 12.1. Each compartment is called a *cell* and will contain the

Table 12.1
An illustration of a two-factor experiment

	Teaching Method for Freshman English			
	Lecture	Discussion	Interactive Television	
Ability Level Superior				$\overline{X}_{Sup} =$
Average				$\overline{X}_{Ave} =$
	$\overline{X}_L =$	$\overline{X}_D =$	$\overline{X}_{TV} =$	

final exam scores for the 20 students in that cell. For example, the upper left cell would have the final exam scores for the 20 superior students taught under the lecture method. After the data have been tabulated into rows and columns as in Table 12.1, a factorial design is always analyzed in terms of two components: main effects and interaction effects.

Main Effects

Obviously, we are interested in the effects of our variables or factors, and these are called *main* effects. In this example, we are looking at the possible effects of teaching method and ability level.

Let us first consider the variable of *ability level*, indicated by the row means. If we disregard which teaching method is used, we have a mean for 60 superior students ($\overline{X}_{Sup}$) and a mean for 60 average students ($\overline{X}_{Ave}$). Even if there were no *real* difference between the performance of superior and average students, we still would expect a slight difference in the sample means, $\overline{X}_{Sup}$ and $\overline{X}_{Ave}$, due to sampling error, so we will use the null hypothesis that these two sample means are random samples from populations with identical means. Later on, we will develop an F test to see if we can reject the null hypothesis that there is no difference in ability level (i.e., that there is a main effect of ability level).

Similarly, we now consider the variable of teaching method, indicated by the column means. We disregard the ability level of the students and note that we have three means—one for the 40 students in the lecture method ($\overline{X}_L$), one for the 40 in the discussion method ($\overline{X}_D$), and one for the 40 using interactive television ($\overline{X}_{TV}$). Under the null hypothesis there is no real difference in the populations from which the sample means were drawn, and differences between $\overline{X}_L$, $\overline{X}_D$, and $\overline{X}_{TV}$ are simply due to sampling error. Again, an F test is used to see if these differences are large enough to be significant, that is, if there is a main effect of teaching method.

Interaction Effects

An important purpose of the factorial design is to explore possible *interaction effects*. For example, variable A may have a different effect at one level of variable B than it does at another level of variable B. In the Type A and blood pressure example, variable A (induced competition) had a different effect at one level of variable B (high Type A's) than it did at the other level of B (low Type A's). Or in the teaching method example, it might be that average students do better than superior students when using the lecture approach (the superior students might find it boring and not do their best work) while superior students might do better than average students in the discussion group method.

This state of affairs is an interaction effect: One variable is behaving differently at one level of the other variable. When an interaction effect occurs, our interest in any main effects is diminished, since the effect of one main variable is dependent upon the level of the other main variable. In our example, if there were a significant interaction effect and someone asked, "Which teaching method is best for freshman English?" we would answer, "It depends on whether you are working with superior or average students." Conversely, if the question were "which students do better in freshman English?" we would have to say that "it would depend on which teaching method is used."

Graphical Methods to Illustrate Interaction

A graph of the result of a factorial experiment is often helpful in understanding the concept of interaction. Let us first consider an experiment where there is no significant interaction effect.

An Example of a Nonsignificant Interaction. A developmental psychologist is studying differences in reading ability between boys and girls and is also interested in whether these differences change with age. She administers a reading test to students in the fourth, fifth, and sixth grades. This is a 2 × 3 factorial design—two levels of sex (boys and girls) and three levels of grade placement (fourth, fifth, and sixth)—and the reading test scores are tabulated for each cell. The means for each cell, as well as row and column means, are shown in Table 12.2.

After completing our table of means, we construct a graph with the dependent variable (reading scores) on the y-axis and one of the main variables (let us use grade level) on the x-axis. The cell means are plotted for both boys and girls, and the resultant graph is shown in Figure 12.1. Any main effects can easily be seen, so if sex differences are significant we conclude that girls had higher reading scores at all grade levels. Similarly, if there is a significant difference between grade levels, we conclude that reading scores are lowest at the fourth grade and highest at the sixth.

However, our main interest in drawing the graph is to examine any possible interaction effect. We note that there is a separation between the curves for girls and boys, but the separation is the same at all three grades; that is, the curves are parallel. If the curves are parallel, *there is no interaction effect,* since the reading

Table 12.2
Table of means for reading scores of boys and girls in grades 4–6

		Sex		
		Girls	Boys	
Grade	4	$\bar{X} = 29$	$\bar{X} = 19$	$\bar{X}_{R_1} = 24$
	5	$\bar{X} = 40$	$\bar{X} = 30$	$\bar{X}_{R_2} = 35$
	6	$\bar{X} = 42$	$\bar{X} = 32$	$\bar{X}_{R_3} = 37$
		$\bar{X}_{C_1} = 37$	$\bar{X}_{C_2} = 27$	

scores are not affected by the sex of the student more at one grade level than another. An examination of the table of means in Table 12.2 is also helpful. We note that the differences between the column means (girls and boys) is $37 - 27 = 10$ points, and this difference is the same at all grade levels. And this, by definition, means there is no interaction effect.

Example of a Significant Interaction. An educational psychologist was investigating the characteristics of creative children. One of her tests for creativity presented the subject with a number of small circles, and the subject was asked to draw as many things using these circles as possible. The psychologist wanted to know what effect there would be if the students were given examples to start them

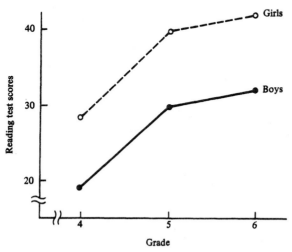

Figure 12.1
Reading test scores. An example of a nonsignificant interaction.

out. She then developed two sets of instructions for the creativity test—one in which the student was shown two examples of drawings from circles and one in which the student was shown no examples at all.

She also wanted to see what effect the two sets of instructions had on "creative" and "noncreative" children. She asked several elementary school teachers to identify which of their children were creative and which were not creative, based strictly on classroom observation.

This design is, of course, a 2 × 2 factorial design. One factor is *instructions* (the two levels are "examples" and "no examples") and the other is *type of student* (the two levels are "creative" and "noncreative"). The elementary school teachers identified 20 creative and 20 noncreative students. Ten of each were assigned at random to the group that was given examples, and 10 of each were also assigned to the group that was not given examples. The creativity test was administered and scored for the number of objects drawn from the circles in 5 minutes. The mean number of objects drawn by each group is shown in Table 12.3 and Figure 12.2.

It is obvious from the column means of Table 12.3 that creative students produced more drawings ($\overline{X}_{C_1} = 9$) than noncreative students ($\overline{X}_{C_2} = 4$). But of greater interest is a possible interaction effect shown in Figure 12.2. When examples were used in the instructions, there was not much difference between creative and noncreative students (who had means of 7 and 5, respectively). However, when no examples were given, creative students produced more drawings while noncreative students were much less productive (with means of 11 and 3, respectively).

Here we have a clear interaction effect. The curves in Figure 12.2 are obviously not parallel. The instructions given had different effects, depending on the type of student. It is possible that the creative students were blocked or inhibited by the examples while the noncreative students were helped by the examples. However, when no examples were given, the noncreative students were definitely handicapped, while the creative students were free to use their inventive abilities to create new forms.

Table 12.3

Number of original drawings by "creative" and "noncreative" students with different instructional sets

		Type of Student		
		Creative	Noncreative	
Instructions	Examples	$\overline{X} = 7$	$\overline{X} = 5$	$\overline{X}_{R_1} = 6$
	No examples	$\overline{X} = 11$	$\overline{X} = 3$	$\overline{X}_{R_2} = 7$
		$\overline{X}_{C_1} = 9$	$\overline{X}_{C_2} = 4$	

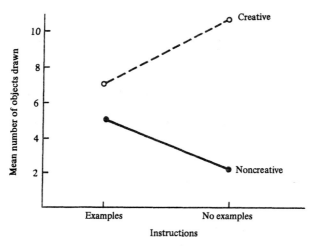

Figure 12.2
Number of objects drawn. An example of a significant interaction.

A Definition of Interaction

Interaction can be defined as a significant departure from a parallel relationship of two or more curves. Even if there is no real interaction between the two variables, we, of course, do not expect to get perfectly parallel curves. The cell means will fluctuate just by sampling error, causing some degree of divergence or convergence from a parallel relationship. However, at some point the deviation from parallelism may be so great that we reject the notion of no interaction and say that we have a significant interaction effect. The sections that follow describe the approach we will use to determine significance.

CALCULATING THE SUMS OF SQUARES

As with the one-way ANOVA, we eventually need to calculate variance estimates of the form $\Sigma(X - \bar{X})^2/(N - 1)$, so we need to find various values of $\Sigma(X - \bar{X})^2$ or sums of squares. We will consider only the computational formulas in this chapter and not develop the deviation formulas discussed in Chapter 11.

The formulas are easier to understand in terms of an example, so let us suppose that the topic of perceptual-motor skills with preferred or nonpreferred hand was investigated by an experimental psychologist. The motor skills performance was measured by pursuit rotor. The apparatus consists of a large disk about the size of a dinner plate that can be made to rotate at different speeds. On the outer edge of this disk is a small target about the size of a dime. The subject attempted to follow this disk with a stylus as it went around. An electronic timer kept track of the time that the stylus was in contact with the disk. This measurement, called "time on target," was recorded to the nearest second. The greater the time on target, the better the performance.

The experimenter was interested in seeing how performance was affected at different pursuit rotor speeds and chose 20, 40, and 60 revolutions per minute (RPM) as the three levels of task difficulty. Since there were two levels of hand used (preferred versus nonpreferred) and three levels of task difficulty (20, 40, and 60 RPM), this was a 2 × 3 factorial design.

Thirty subjects volunteered for the experiment and were assigned at random to *one* of the six combinations of pursuit rotor speed and hand used. Thus there were 5 subjects in each combination. Each subject's time on target during a 20-second trial is shown in Table 12.4. As we have done so many times before, we calculate ΣX, ΣX^2, and $\overline{X}$ for each column. For the first step, we will be using the computational formulas for the one-way ANOVA from Chapter 11, so we also need

the total mean $(\overline{X}_T)$ and the sum of all the squared scores $(\overset{N_T}{\Sigma} X^2)$.

To begin our two-way ANOVA, we first calculate SS_T, SS_{BG}, and SS_{WG} as we did in Chapter 11.

$$SS_T = \overset{N_T}{\Sigma} X^2 - N_T \overline{X}_T^2 = 824 - (30)(4.67)^2$$

$$= 824 - 654.27 = 169.73$$

$$SS_{BG} = N_1 \overline{X}_1^2 + N_2 \overline{X}_2^2 \cdots + N_6 \overline{X}_6^2 - N_T \overline{X}_T^2$$

$$= 5(7)^2 + 5(6)^2 + 5(5)^2 + 5(6)^2 + 5(3)^2 + 5(1)^2 - 654.27$$

Table 12.4
Time on target (seconds) for preferred or nonpreferred hand at three pursuit rotor speeds

	Preferred Hand			Nonpreferred Hand		
	20	40	60	20	40	60
	8	9	6	5	1	2
	7	5	5	5	2	0
	8	7	4	7	4	1
	6	4	5	6	2	1
	6	5	5	7	6	1
ΣX:	35	30	25	30	15	5
ΣX^2:	249	196	127	184	61	7
$\overline{X}$:	7	6	5	6	3	

$$\overline{X} = \frac{35 + 30 + 25 + 30 + 15 + 5}{30} = 4.67$$

$$\overset{N_T}{\Sigma} X^2 = 249 + 196 + 127 + 184 + 61 + 7 = 824$$

$$= 780 - 654.27 = 125.73$$

$$SS_{WG} = SS_T - SS_{BG} = 169.73 - 125.73 = 44.0$$

Note that we calculated SS_{WG} by simply subtracting SS_{BG} from SS_T. We could, of course, have calculated SS_{WG} directly using formula 11.10.

Now that we have our sums of squares separated into the familiar SS_{BG} and SS_{WG}, we need to consider their meaning in a two-way ANOVA. As in the one-way ANOVA, SS_{WG} will be used to calculate a variance estimate, an estimate of the variance of the population from which the samples came. We will have more to say about this estimate later. And what about SS_{BG}? In the one-way ANOVA of Chapter 11, SS_{BG} was used to calculate a variance estimate which, under the null hypothesis, was estimating the same variance as that based on SS_{WG}.

But, in the two-way ANOVA, SS_{BG} reflects *both* the effects of the row variable (speed) and the column variable (hand used), *as well as* the interaction effect if any. This point is easiest to understand if we present the results of Table 12.4 in the form of a table of means. This 2×3 table in Table 12.5 shows 5 subjects in each of the 6 combinations of hand used and pursuit rotor speed. Each of the 6 cells shows the N of 5 in the corner and the mean time on target for the 5 subjects. Note also the row and column means, which indicate performance by a particular row or column. For example, $\overline{X}_{R_2} = 4.5$ is the mean time on target for the 10 subjects at 40 RPM, while $\overline{X}_{C_1} = 6.0$ is the mean for the 15 subjects using preferred hands.

We are now ready to begin calculating the sums of squares that will be used directly in our two-way ANOVA. The formula for the sum of squares for the row variable, SS_R, is

$$SS_R = N_{R_1}\overline{X}_{R_1}^2 + N_{R_2}\overline{X}_{R_2}^2 + N_{R_3}\overline{X}_{R_3}^2 - N_T\overline{X}_T^2 \tag{12.1}$$

Table 12.5
Mean time on target as a function of hand used and pursuit rotor speed

		Hand		
		Preferred	Nonpreferred	
Speed (revolutions per minute)	20	5 $\overline{X} = 7$	5 $\overline{X} = 6$	$\overline{X}_{R_1} = 6.5$
	40	5 $\overline{X} = 6$	5 $\overline{X} = 3$	$\overline{X}_{R_2} = 4.5$
	60	5 $\overline{X} = 5$	5 $\overline{X} = 1$	$\overline{X}_{R_3} = 3.0$
		$\overline{X}_{C_1} = 6.0$	$\overline{X}_{C_2} = 3.33$	$\overline{X}_T = 4.67$

Plugging in the values from Table 12.5, we get

$$SS_R = 10(6.5)^2 + 10(4.5)^2 + 10(3.0)^2 - 30(4.67)^2$$

$$= 422.5 + 202.5 + 90 - 654.27$$

$$= 60.73$$

The formula for the sum of squares for the column variable, SS_C, is

$$SS_C = N_{C_1}\overline{X}_{C_1}^2 + N_{C_2}\overline{X}_{C_2}^2 - N_T\overline{X}_T^2 \tag{12.2}$$

Plugging in the values from Table 12.5, we get

$$SS_C = 15(6.0)^2 + 15(3.33)^2 - 30(4.67)^2$$

$$= 540 + 166.33 - 654.27$$

$$= 52.06$$

The formula for the sum of squares for interaction, $SS_{R \times C}$ (say "rows by columns"), is

$$SS_{R \times C} = SS_{BG} - SS_R - SS_C \tag{12.3}$$

Plugging in the values already obtained, we get

$$SS_{R \times C} = 125.73 - 60.73 - 52.06$$
$$= 12.94$$

CALCULATING THE VARIANCES

The previous section dealt with the calculation of the sums of squares, which are the numerators of the variances we wish to calculate. We noted in Chapter 11 that variances are sums of squares divided by their respective degrees of freedom (df). We are now interested in the total df $(N_T - 1)$ and also in the df associated with the two main variables (rows and columns) and the interaction between the two (rows by columns).

The df for the row variable is one less than the number of rows, or $r - 1$.

$$df_R = r - 1 \tag{12.4}$$

In the example, the row variable is pursuit rotor speed at three levels (20, 40, and 60 RPM), so the df for speed is

$$df_R = 3 - 1 = 2$$

The df for the column variable is one less than the number of columns, or $c - 1$.

$$df_C = c - 1 \tag{12.5}$$

In the example, the column variable is the hand used with two levels (preferred or nonpreferred), so the df for hand used is

$$df_C = 2 - 1 = 1$$

The df for the interaction of the row variable and column variable is one less than the number of levels of the row variable multiplied by one less than the number of levels of the column variable, or $(r - 1)(c - 1)$. The formula for the df for interaction is

$$df_{R \times C} = (r - 1)(c - 1) \tag{12.6}$$

In the example there are three speeds and two hands, so

$$df_{R \times C} = (3 - 1)(2 - 1) = 2$$

In Chapter 11 the formula for the within-groups df was given as $N_T - k$, where k was the number of groups. We use the same approach in the two-way ANOVA except that the number of groups is now the number of cells. Since we have r rows and c columns, the number of groups would be $r \times c$, or rc. Thus the within-groups df would be $N_T - rc$.

$$df_{WG} = N_T - rc \tag{12.7}$$

In the example there were 30 subjects divided among three rows and two columns, so the within-groups df is

$$df_{WG} = 30 - (3)(2) = 24$$

We again expect that the addition of the various degrees of freedom should equal the total df, $N_T - 1$. Using the symbolic notation of the previous paragraphs, we would have $df_T = df_R + df_C + df_{R \times C} + df_{WG}$. Gathering the numbers we just calculated for the pursuit rotor experiment, we have $2 + 1 + 2 + 24 = 29$, which is the same as $N_T - 1 = 30 - 1 = 29$.

The Mean Squares

We can now calculate the variance estimates, or mean squares, by dividing each sum of squares by its appropriate df. We will have four mean squares in a two-way ANOVA, one each for rows, columns, rows by columns, and within groups. The formulas are

$$MS_R = \frac{SS_R}{r - 1} \tag{12.8}$$

$$MS_C = \frac{SS_C}{c - 1} \tag{12.9}$$

$$MS_{R \times C} = \frac{SS_{R \times C}}{(r - 1)(c - 1)} \tag{12.10}$$

$$MS_{WG} = \frac{SS_{WG}}{N_T - rc} \tag{12.11}$$

From the pursuit rotor data, we would calculate the following mean squares.

$$MS_R = \frac{60.73}{2} = 30.365$$

$$MS_C = \frac{52.06}{1} = 52.06$$

$$MS_{R \times C} = \frac{12.94}{(2)(1)} = 6.47$$

$$MS_{WG} = \frac{44}{30 - (3)(2)} = 1.83$$

THE MEANING OF THE VARIANCE ESTIMATES

As in Chapter 11, we stop momentarily after calculating the mean squares in order to reflect on their meaning. They obviously are variance estimates of some sort, since they have a sum of squares in the numerator and degrees of freedom in the denominator. But just what are they estimating?

MS_{WG}.   In the one-way ANOVA of Chapter 11, MS_{WG} was a combined estimate of the variance of the populations from which each sample came. Under the null hypothesis, the population means are identical, so MS_{WG1}, MS_{WG2}, and so on, were estimates of the same population variance, and MS_{WG} was the average of these individual estimates from each group. However, in a two-way ANOVA each cell corresponds to a single "group," and we again could consider MS_{WG} for cell 1, MS_{WG} for cell 2, and so on, as individual estimates of the same population variance. Thus MS_{WG} in a two-way ANOVA is a combined estimate of the variance of the population from which each sample came.

MS_R.   The variance estimate based on the row means is *also* an estimate of the population variance *if the null hypothesis is true*. In other words, if $\mu_{R1} = \mu_{R2} = \mu_{R3}$, and so on, the variance estimate (MS_R) derived from the sample row means ($\overline{X}_{R1}$, $\overline{X}_{R2}$, etc.) is estimating the same population variance as MS_{WG}. We expect, of course, that the sample row means will vary just by sampling error and MS_R will reflect this sampling variation among $\overline{X}_{R1}$, $\overline{X}_{R2}$, and so on. However, if the row variable is exerting a significant effect, the row means will vary more than what would be expected by chance, and MS_R will be larger than the variance estimate, MS_{WG}. With the pursuit rotor data of Table 12.5, we are saying under the null hypothesis that the sample row means of 6.5, 4.5, and 3.0 seconds on target for the various pursuit rotor speeds are different simply because of chance variation.

MS_C.   Using the same logic we applied to MS_R, we note that under the null hypothesis, MS_C is also an estimate of the population variance calculated from the column means. If $\mu_{C_1} = \mu_{C_2} = \mu_{C_3}$, and so on, we expect that the column means ($\bar{X}_{C_1}$, $\bar{X}_{C_2}$, etc.) will vary only by sampling error, and the variance estimate, MS_C, will be an estimate of the same population variance as MS_{WG}. However, if the column variable is exerting a significant effect, the column means will vary more than what would be expected by chance, and MS_C will be larger than the variance estimate, MS_{WG}. In the example, we are saying under the null hypothesis that the sample column means of 6.0 and 3.33 for the preferred and nonpreferred hands are different only because of chance variation.

$MS_{R \times C}$.   Before investigating what the remaining variance estimate, $MS_{R \times C}$, is estimating, let us review the concept of interaction. In Table 12.2 we saw that there was no interaction effect of reading test scores of boys and girls in fourth, fifth, and sixth grades. We stressed that the graph in Figure 12.1 showed *parallel* lines, indicating that the difference between boys and girls was consistent at the three grade levels. Note that, when there is no interaction, we can predict the value of the cell means from the column and row means alone. For example, the girls' mean and boys' mean are 37 and 27, respectively. The total mean would be 32, and these two column means are 5 points on each side of the total mean. Now, looking at the row mean of 24 for fourth-graders, we note that if there is no interaction present at this level the cell means for fourth-grade girls and fourth-grade boys should be 5 points on each side of the row mean for fourth-graders. This would yield means of 29 and 19, respectively, and is exactly what is shown in the fourth-grade cells of Table 12.2. The same calculations could be done, of course, to obtain the means in the remaining cells. In general, we note that for any table of results we have now established what the cell means should be when there is no interaction present. We need only remember that the sample cell means could be expected to deviate from these expected values because of sampling error. The quantity $MS_{R \times C}$ is a variance estimate based on the deviations from these expected values, and under the null hypothesis (no significant interaction) $MS_{R \times C}$ is also an estimate of the variance of the population from which the samples came. And using our usual logic, if the deviations from these expected values are significant (i.e., if the interaction is exerting a significant effect), we note that $MS_{R \times C}$ will be larger than it would if the deviation of the cell means about their expected values were due to chance variation. As a result, the variance estimate of $MS_{R \times C}$ will be larger than the estimate given by MS_{WG}. In the pursuit rotor example of Table 12.5, we are saying under the null hypothesis that the sample cell means of 7, 6, 6, 5, 3, and 1 are deviating from their expected values by an amount due only to chance variation.

THE *F* TESTS

Finally, we are ready to attempt what we set out to do at the beginning of this chapter: to see if one or both of the variables or their interaction in a two-factor experiment has had a significant effect. As with the one-way ANOVA, we will set up a ratio of two variance estimates and see if the resulting F value is significant. Note that the denominator in each case is MS_{WG}, the estimate of the population variance that is *not* affected by the action of the row variable or column variable or by their interaction. The numerator in each case will be a mean square of the row variable or column variable or their interaction. As we noted in the preceding section, these variance estimates are also estimates of the population variance if the null hypothesis is true. However, if the variable is exerting a significant effect, the respective variance estimate will be larger than the estimate given by MS_{WG}, and the F value will be significantly greater than 1. The formula for the row effect is

$$F_R = \frac{MS_R}{MS_{WG}} \qquad (12.12)$$

The formula for the column effect is

$$F_C = \frac{MS_C}{MS_{WG}} \qquad (12.13)$$

The formula for the interaction effect is

$$F_{R \times C} = \frac{MS_{R \times C}}{MS_{WG}} \qquad (12.14)$$

The calculations for the pursuit rotor data are, for the row effect:

$$F_R = \frac{30.365}{1.83} = 16.59$$

for the column effect:

$$F_C = \frac{52.06}{1.83} = 28.45$$

and for the interaction effect:

$$F_{R \times C} = \frac{6.47}{1.83} = 3.54$$

We now summarize the results of all our computational efforts in the typical ANOVA summary table shown in Table 12.6.

Each F value is evaluated by entering Table E with the *df* associated with the numerator and the *df* associated with the denominator. For example, the main effect of speed is tested by the F ratio of MS_R/MS_{WG}, with 2 and 24 *df*, respectively. In Table E we note that for 2 and 24 *df*, our F needs to exceed 3.40 at the 5% level and 5.61 at the 1% level. Since our calculated value of 16.59 exceeds 5.61, we conclude that our F is significant beyond the .01 level. We evaluate the other F values and note their probability levels as shown in Table 12.6.

We are now ready to analyze the results of the pursuit rotor experiment. Our first task is to graph the means shown earlier in Table 12.5, and this graph is

Table 12.6
ANOVA summary table for pursuit rotor data

Source of Variance	df	SS	MS	F
Speed (*R*)	2	60.73	30.36	16.59**
Hand (*C*)	1	52.06	52.06	28.45**
Speed by hand (*R* × *C*)	2	12.94	6.47	3.54*
Within groups	24	44.00	1.83	
Totals	29	169.73		

*Significant, $p < .05$.
**Significant, $p < .01$.

shown in Figure 12.3. We see from the ANOVA summary table that the main effect of pursuit rotor speed is significant, and a glance at Figure 12.3 shows that performance with both preferred and nonpreferred hands decreased as the speed increased from 20 to 60 RPM. The summary table also shows a significant effect of handedness, and the separation of the curves shows better performance for subjects using their preferred hand than subjects using their nonpreferred hand.

Finally, the interaction effect is significant ($p < .05$), which is shown on the graph by the curves diverging as pursuit rotor speed increases. The interaction simply says that at the 20 RPM speed there was not much difference in the performance between preferred and nonpreferred hands. However, as the speed increased, performance of the nonpreferred hand deteriorated more rapidly than performance with the preferred hand. As we noted earlier, a significant interaction effect always modifies our interpretation of the main effects. For example, in re-

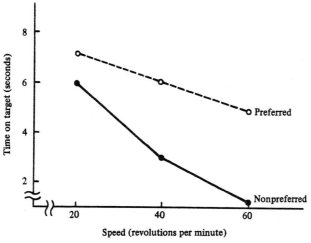

Figure 12.3
Time on target as a function of hand used at three pursuit rotor speeds.

sponse to the question "Does an increase in pursuit rotor speed interfere with performance?" we would answer that the amount of interference depends on whether one is using the preferred or nonpreferred hand.

ASSUMPTIONS FOR THE TWO-WAY ANOVA

The assumptions for the two-way ANOVA are identical to those for the one-way ANOVA described in Chapter 11, except that we are now talking about cells rather than groups.

1. Data must be in interval or ratio form.
2. Subjects must be assigned at random to cells.
3. The populations from which the samples are drawn must be normal.
4. The populations from which the samples are drawn must have equal variances.

In addition to the familiar assumptions listed, the ANOVA procedure described in this chapter assumes *an equal number of observations per cell*. In our pursuit rotor experiment shown in Table 12.5, there were 5 subjects in each of the 6 cells for a total of 30. It is essential for this ANOVA procedure that there be an equal number of subjects in each cell. There are methods for handling ANOVA with unequal numbers in the cells, but the procedures are beyond the scope of this book. If you are interested, consult an advanced statistics textbook for details of the method used.

MULTIPLE COMPARISONS

After a significant F has been obtained with either of the two variables or with their interaction, a logical step is to investigate which differences between means are significant. Referring to the ANOVA summary table of our pursuit rotor results in Table 12.6, we note that there is a significant main effect of hand used. Looking at Table 12.5 and Figure 12.3, we note that the preferred hand was compared with the nonpreferred hand at three different speeds and that the difference between preferred and nonpreferred hand increases as pursuit rotor speed increases. But are the differences at all three speeds significant? There is not much of a difference at 20 RPM, and this difference might not be significant, while the differences at 40 and 60 RPM may indeed be significant. To test for significant differences among these and other pairs of differences, a test for *multiple comparisons* is needed. As was pointed out in the last chapter, tests developed by Scheffé, Duncan, and others can be used, and an advanced statistics text will provide you with the necessary information about these tests.

Note 12.1
Split-Plot Designs?

A casual glance at journal articles, books, and other publications in education and the behavioral sciences shows a wide variety of applications of the analysis of variance—and it is easy to develop the misconception that the analysis of variance is the unique province of these fields. However, much of the theory and application of ANOVA grew out of agricultural and biological research. R. A. Fisher (the F test bears his initial) and his associates at the Rothamsted Experiment Station in England were initially responsible for developing much of the experimental design and analysis used in assessing the effects of soil conditions, types of fertilizer, time of planting, amount of moisture, and a host of other conditions related to agricultural productivity. *Randomized blocks, split-plots, factorial design,* and other such exotic terms were the result of early agricultural and biological research. Gradually, Fisher's applications and ideas were adopted and expanded by researchers in other fields, and present-day research efforts are greatly simplified by the early work of Fisher and the work of subsequent theorists.

CONCLUDING REMARKS

In two rather concentrated chapters we have covered only a small fraction of the possible ANOVA designs. Our interest in an introductory-level statistics textbook is to become familiar with some of the basic concepts underlying this powerful statistical technique. Should you take another statistics course, you will undoubtedly spend much of the time on a variety of ANOVA designs, some of which are mentioned in Note 12.1. When you see how ANOVA can be used to analyze complex relationships among variables, it is easy to understand its wide popularity among researchers.

SAMPLE PROBLEM

A researcher in eating disorders is interested in characteristics of obesity and is studying the amount of effort expended by obese subjects and average-weight subjects to obtain food for a snack. A subject enters the laboratory and is told to fill out an attitude questionnaire. At the table where the subject sits is a bowl of peanuts. For half the subjects the bowl contains shelled peanuts, and for the other half the peanuts are in the shells. The experimenter chooses 20 obese and 20 average-weight subjects from a pool of volunteers and records the number of peanuts each subject eats while filling out the questionnaire. This is a 2 × 2 factorial design (obese and average subjects with

(continued)

SAMPLE PROBLEM (*CONTINUED*)

shelled and unshelled peanuts), with 10 subjects of each weight assigned at random to the shelled or unshelled condition. The results are as follows.

	Obese		Average	
	Shelled	**Unshelled**	**Shelled**	**Unshelled**
	16	4	10	7
	17	2	5	9
	12	2	9	6
	14	0	10	4
	13	1	9	3
	10	3	7	8
	9	2	6	7
	17	1	8	10
	16	1	5	4
	16	4	11	2
ΣX:	140	20	80	60
ΣX^2:	2,036	56	682	424
$\overline{X}$:	14	2	8	6

Calculator Solution

$$\overline{X}_T = \frac{140 + 20 + 80 + 60}{40} = 7.5$$

$$\overset{N_T}{\Sigma} X^2 = 2,036 + 56 + 682 + 424 = 3,198$$

	Shelled Nuts	**Unshelled Nuts**	
Obese	14	10	2	10	8
Average	8	10	6	10	7
	11		4		7.5

Sums of Squares:

$$SS_T = \overset{N_T}{\Sigma} X^2 - N_T \overline{X}_T^2 = 3,198 - 40(7.5)^2 = 3,198 - 2,250 = 948$$

$$SS_{BG} = N_1 \overline{X}_1^2 + N_2 \overline{X}_2^2 + N_3 \overline{X}_3^2 + N_4 \overline{X}_4^2 - N_T \overline{X}_T^2$$

$$= 10(14)^2 + 10(2)^2 + 10(8)^2 + 10(6)^2 - 40(7.5)^2$$

$$= 3,000 - 2,250 = 750$$

$$SS_{WG} = SS_T - SS_{BG} = 948 - 750 = 198$$

$$SS_R = N_{R_1}\overline{X}_{R1}^2 + N_{R_2}\overline{X}_{R2}^2 - N_T\overline{X}_T^2$$

$$= 20(8)^2 + 20(7)^2 - 40(7.5)^2 = 10$$

$$SS_C = N_{C_1}\overline{X}_{C1}^2 + N_{C_2}\overline{X}_{C2}^2 - N_T\overline{X}_T^2$$

$$= 20(11)^2 + 20(4)^2 - 40(7.5)^2 = 490$$

$$SS_{R \times C} = SS_{BG} - SS_R - SS_C = 750 - 10 - 490 = 250$$

Mean Squares and F Tests:

$$MS_R = \frac{SS_R}{r-1} = \frac{10}{1} = 10$$

$$MS_C = \frac{SS_C}{c-1} = \frac{490}{1} = 490$$

$$MS_{R \times C} = \frac{SS_{R \times C}}{(r-1)(c-1)} = \frac{250}{1} = 250$$

$$MS_{WG} = \frac{SS_{WG}}{N_T - rc} = \frac{198}{40-4} = 5.5$$

$$F_R = \frac{MS_R}{MS_{WG}} = \frac{10}{5.5} = 1.82$$

$$F_C = \frac{MS_C}{MS_{WG}} = \frac{490}{5.5} = 89.10$$

$$F_{R \times C} = \frac{MS_{R \times C}}{MS_{WG}} = \frac{250}{5.5} = 45.45$$

ANOVA summary table

Sources of Variance	df	SS	MS	F
Weight (R)	1	10	10	1.82
Nut type (C)	1	490	490	89.10**
Weight by nut type ($R \times C$)	1	250	250	45.45**
Within groups	36	198	5.5	

**Significant, $p < .01$.

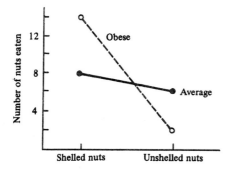

(continued)

SAMPLE PROBLEM (CONTINUED)

We see in the ANOVA summary table a significant F for nut type, and we note from the graph and the table of means that more shelled peanuts were eaten than unshelled peanuts. However, this observation is of minor importance because our main interest is in the interaction effect indicated by a significant F for weight by nut type. As you can see from the graph, when the peanuts were shelled the obese subjects ate more than the average-weight subjects (means of 14 and 8, respectively). However, when the peanuts were not shelled the average-weight subjects ate more than the obese subjects (means of 6 and 2, respectively).

Computer Solution

Computer output for the eating disorder study on snacking is shown in Table 12.7. The first box contains the means and standard errors for the combinations of weight (obese or average) and nut type (shelled or unshelled).

The ANOVA summary table with the usual columns is shown at the bottom. The probability of F is shown in the Sig. column, with .000 indicating $p < .001$. The interaction term is designated as WEIGHT × NUT TYPE. The remaining terms (Model, etc.) require knowledge of statistical concepts beyond the intended scope of this text.

The graph illustrates the significant interaction effect. The number of peanuts eaten by average-weight subjects was not appreciably different whether the peanuts were shelled ($\overline{X} = 8$) or unshelled ($\overline{X} = 6$). However, for the obese subjects, when the peanuts were shelled, the average number eaten ($\overline{X} = 14$) was significantly greater than when the peanuts were not shelled ($\overline{X} = 2$).

Table 12.7

SPSS output for two-way analysis of variance on eating disorders snacking data

ANOVA

Nut Type × Weight

Dependent Variable: PEANUTS

NUT TYPE	WEIGHT	Mean	Std. Error
SHELLED	OBESE	14.00	.742
	AVERAGE	8.00	.742
UNSHELLED	OBESE	2.00	.742
	AVERAGE	6.00	.742

ANOVA[a,b]

			Unique Method				
			Sum of Squares	df	Mean Square	F	Sig.
PEANUTS	Main Effects	(Combined)	500.000	2	250.000	45.455	.000
		WEIGHT	10.000	1	10.000	1.818	.186
		NUT TYPE	490.000	1	490.000	89.091	.000
	2-Way Interactions	WEIGHT × NUT TYPE	250.000	1	250.000	45.455	.000
	Model		750.000	3	250.000	45.455	.000
	Residual		198.000	36	5.500		
	Total		948.000	39	24.308		

a. PEANUTS by WEIGHT, NUT TYPE
b. All effects entered simultaneously

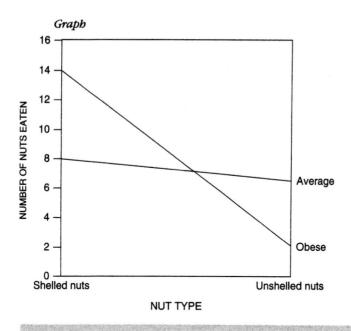

STUDY QUESTIONS

1. Why is the two-way ANOVA considered more efficient than the one-way ANOVA?
2. What is meant by the term *main effect*? What is an *interaction effect*?

3. "When an interaction effect occurs, our interest in any main effects is diminished." Why is this so?
4. A friend of yours suggests that you use a 2 × 3 factorial design in your research paper. Describe what is meant by a "2 × 3 factorial design."
5. Describe the construction of a graph in a two-way ANOVA. How would that graph demonstrate that there was no interaction effect?
6. How would a graph demonstrate that there *was* an interaction effect?
7. How would the relative sizes of MS_R and MS_{WG} indicate whether there was a significant row effect? How about MS_C and MS_{WG}?
8. "If there is a significant interaction, the variance estimate of $MS_{R \times C}$ will be larger than the estimate given by MS_{WG}." What does this statement mean?
9. List the assumptions for the two-way ANOVA, including the size of cells assumption.

EXERCISES

1. The manager of a women's clothing store in a resort area recorded the number of items purchased by the first 15 residents and 15 tourists who entered her store. She did so on a day when there was a "25% off" sale and also on a day when there was no sale. The mean number of items purchased by each group on each day is shown in the table. Draw a graph similar to one in the sample problem. On the basis of the table of means and graph, would you expect to find any significant main effects? Any interaction effect? Give reasons for your answer.

Category

	Residents	Tourists	
Sale	15 $\overline{X} = 1.9$	15 $\overline{X} = 2.7$	$\overline{X} = 2.3$
No sale	15 $\overline{X} = 0.8$	15 $\overline{X} = 2.4$	$\overline{X} = 1.6$
	$\overline{X} = 1.35$	$\overline{X} = 2.55$	

2. In a study on weight training among the elderly, men and women volunteers aged 20–29 and 70–79 bench-pressed their maximum weight after one week of training. There were 14 subjects in each combination of sex and age range. The mean bench press for each group is shown in the table. Using a graph (similar to the one in the sample problem) and the table of means, would you expect to find any significant main effects? Any interaction effects? Give reasons for your answers.

Category

	20–29	70–79	
Male	14 $\overline{X} = 150$	14 $\overline{X} = 55$	$\overline{X} = 102.5$
Female	14 $\overline{X} = 70$	14 $\overline{X} = 20$	$\overline{X} = 45$
	$\overline{X} = 110$	$\overline{X} = 37.5$	

3. Forty data-entry workers in a large company took part in a study to determine whether allowing workers to listen to music on headphones affected work productivity. There were two types of data-entry workers, those whose task involved entering information from a worksheet into a computer (simple), and those whose task involved computation of numbers on the worksheet before entering them into the computer (complex). For each task group, 10 subjects were randomly assigned to the music group and 10 subjects to the no-music group. The mean numbers of errors per minute made by subjects in each group are shown. What effect of music and task complexity were demonstrated in this experiment? Calculate a two-way ANOVA and show a table of means and a graph.

Music		**No Music**	
Complex	*Simple*	*Complex*	*Simple*
3	1	2	0
1	0	0	0
2	0	0	2
4	0	1	1
3	1	2	0
2	2	0	0
1	0	2	0
0	0	0	1
1	1	0	0
2	0	1	0

4. A psychologist studied whether music affected productivity rates of her patients. She gathered 14 depressed patients and 14 nondepressed patients and randomly assigned each to an individual room. Seven of the depressed patients and 7 of the nondepressed patients heard fast music in their room. The other 7 subjects from each group listened to slow music in their room. Each of the subjects was asked to stay in the room for an hour and assemble a series of mini-puzzles. The researchers hypothesized that the two groups of patients listening to fast music would assemble more puzzles than the two groups of patients listening to slow music. The numbers of puzzles assembled by each member of

the four groups are listed. After constructing a table of means and a graph from the data, calculate a two-way ANOVA. Was the researcher correct in her hypothesis? Explain any main effects or interaction effect found.

Depressed Subjects		**Nondepressed Subjects**	
Fast Music	*Slow Music*	*Fast Music*	*Slow Music*
3	2	1	1
2	2	3	2
1	1	2	2
2	1	3	2
3	3	4	3
4	3	3	3
1	1	3	2

5. Twenty mothers of children ages one to two and 20 nonmothers were gathered by researchers and asked to take a 20-minute reading comprehension test. Half of the mothers and half of the nonmothers were assigned randomly to a room where the sound of a crying baby came from an adjoining room. The other half of the mothers and nonmothers were randomly assigned to a room where the vocal expressions of a "happy" baby came from another room. The reading comprehension scores of the mothers and nonmothers in each of the two rooms are shown. What did the experiment show regarding mothers or nonmothers and sounds of babies laughing or crying? Calculate a two-way ANOVA and show a table of means and a graph.

Crying Baby		**Laughing Baby**	
Mothers	*Nonmothers*	*Mothers*	*Nonmothers*
20	24	27	24
18	25	26	28
22	21	28	22
23	26	29	27
19	22	30	26
24	23	24	25
17	19	23	24
21	20	25	23
15	17	22	20
26	20	21	22

6. A researcher in social psychology studied sex differences in an individual's personal space. A male or female confederate stood in a large room while male or female subjects were asked to approach the person and start a conversation. The researcher (by means of a hidden optical system) measured the distance in inches between the subject and the stationary person to see how close they were together when conversation was initiated. Twenty male and 20 female college students were assigned at random to one of four groups—males approaching a male, males approaching a female, females approaching a male, and females ap-

proaching a female. The distances in inches between the approaching subjects and the stationary person are shown in the following list. What did the experiment show regarding the sex of the approaching person and sex of the stationary person? Calculate a two-way ANOVA, and show a table of means and a graph.

	Approaching Male		**Approaching Female**	
Stationary Male	*Stationary Female*	*Stationary Male*	*Stationary Female*
11	16	15	13
14	11	16	11
11	13	14	14
15	12	15	13
16	14	17	14
14	14	15	13
14	15	13	12
13	14	16	14
14	15	15	11
14	14	14	13

7. Researchers for the State Highway Patrol conducted research to determine the best way to ensure that cars do not speed in construction zones. They wanted to know if having the speed-limit sign list the fine for offenders would slow down traffic more than just the speed-limit sign alone. They also wanted to know if having a worker hold the speed-limit sign slowed traffic more than having the speed-limit sign attached to a post. Researchers carried out the four scenarios on four separate summer days at the same time each day. The first ten car speeds for each of the four conditions are shown. The researchers hypothesized that cars would drive slower when the fine is posted and when a worker is holding the sign than when the fine is not posted and a worker is not holding the sign. Construct a table of means and a graph, and calculate a two-way ANOVA to see if the researchers' hypotheses were supported.

Worker Holding Sign		**Sign Posted in Ground**	
Sign + Fine	*Sign Alone*	*Sign + Fine*	*Sign Alone*
30	31	32	40
29	29	31	35
28	30	30	32
29	28	29	37
27	31	32	38
22	35	35	42
35	32	34	40
26	28	39	30
28	33	37	29
27	29	36	27

8. A researcher in sport psychology studied the reaction times of college athletes. The time it took a college swimmer or college track runner to push a button after hearing a gunshot or a buzzer was recorded. The researcher randomly assigned 8 swimmers and 8 track runners to the gunshot condition, and 8 swimmers and 8 track runners to the buzzer condition. He hypothesized that the reaction times of swimmers would be lower in the buzzer condition and the reaction times of track runners would be lower in the gunshot condition. The reaction times in hundredths of seconds are shown for each of the four groups. Complete a two-way ANOVA, including a table of means and a graph to see if his hypothesis was correct. Give reasons for the outcome.

Swimmers		Runners	
Buzzer	Gunshot	Buzzer	Gunshot
40	43	39	37
39	48	42	41
47	57	43	43
38	42	39	38
44	53	44	44
48	61	46	48
41	52	42	43
44	59	40	40

COMPUTER EXERCISES FOR APPENDIX 4 DATA BANK

For the following exercises compose a two-way table of means, the ANOVA summary table, and a graph to show possible interaction effects.

C1. In this exercise we would like to see what effect, if any, the variables of gender and Speed and Impatience have on the reporting of physical symptoms. In computer exercise C1 at the end of Chapter 11, the sample was divided into low, moderate, and high Speed and Impatience (S&I). For this exercise use only the low S&I and high S&I subjects. Further separate these groups into men and women to obtain a 2 × 2 table of gender (men and women) and S&I (low and high). Using the physical symptom scores as your dependent variable, see if there was a main effect of gender or of S&I, or if there is a significant interaction effect between the two.

C2. In this exercise we would like to see what effect the variables of Masculinity and Speed and Impatience have on the reporting of physical symptoms *for men only*. Use only the low S&I and high S&I division for men only. Further separate the groups into high and low Masculinity to obtain a 2 × 2 table of Masculinity (low and high) and S&I (low and high). Using the physical symptom scores as your dependent variable, see if there was a main effect of Masculinity or of S&I, or if there is a significant interaction effect between the two.

C3. In this exercise we would like to see what effect the variables of Femininity and Speed and Impatience have on the reporting of physical symptoms *for women only*. Again use only the low S&I and high S&I subjects. Further separate these groups into low and high Femininity to obtain a 2 × 2 table of Femininity (low and high) and S&I (low and high). Using the physical symptom scores as your dependent variable, see if there was a main effect of Femininity or of S&I, or if there is a significant interaction effect between the two.

CHAPTER 13

Some Nonparametric
Statistical Tests

Health professionals in cardiovascular medicine have stressed the importance of cardiopulmonary resuscitation (CPR) training for everyone. It is believed that such skills may result in the saving of lives when an individual suffers cardiac arrest and a bystander trained in CPR is nearby. However, many people with little or no CPR training may also attempt to aid a victim, and health professionals would like to know how much of an advantage a person trained in CPR would have over one untrained or poorly trained in CPR.

In one study conducted in New York City on 662 cases of cardiac arrest given CPR by bystanders, Gallagher, Lombardi, and Gennis (1995) found that for 305 cardiac arrest victims given CPR by an individual trained in CPR, 14 survived. However, for the 357 victims given CPR by those poorly trained or untrained in CPR, only 5 survived. How do we analyze these data? These are not scores or observations on an interval scale. In fact, these are only nominal ("survived" or "did not survive") data. We cannot test for a difference between means, because there are no means. But before we consider possible solutions, let us look at another example.

In a completely different research area, special education, some investigators in the field of learning disabilities have examined the similarities and differences between students who are low achievers and those classified as having a learning disability. In one study (Ysseldyke, Algozzine, Shinn, & McGue, 1982), a number of the Woodcock-Johnson subtests (e.g., Analogies, Spatial Relations, Picture Vocabulary, Concept Formation) were given to a sample of low-achieving students and learning-disabled students. A number of conclusions can be drawn from the comparisons that were made between the two groups. One such conclusion was that on 15 of the 19 Woodcock-Johnson subtests, the standard deviations for the learning-disabled group were larger. But is 15 out of 19 a significant proportion over what might be expected just by chance alone?

How do we evaluate results such as 14 survivors out of 305 cardiac arrests, or 15 larger standard deviations out of 19 subtests? How can we develop a statistics, something like a t test or an F test, to see if there are significant differences between groups when all we have is the number of cases in each group?

The t test and the F test, described in earlier chapters, are called *parametric* tests; that is, they assume certain conditions about the *parameters* of the populations from which the samples are drawn. We have spent considerable time discussing these conditions, noting, for example, that the populations must be normal and must have equal variances.

These conditions are not ordinarily tested themselves but are assumed to hold, and the meaningfulness that we attach to a particular value of t or F depends on whether these assumptions are valid. In addition, we have also emphasized that the data must be at least interval in nature before the operations necessary to calculate means and standard deviations can be performed and a t or F value obtained.

But what is the researcher to do when he or she knows that a set of data cannot meet these requirements? Even if assured that the normality and homogeneity of variance assumptions are valid, the researcher may frankly admit that the data in question are only nominal or, at best, ordinal in nature. Some measurement purists will go so far as to say that the *majority* of data in education and the behavioral sciences do not reach the precision of an interval scale. We may be able to tell that individual A has more of something than individual B, but we are not sure just *how much* more of it individual A has! Data such as these would be ordinal in nature.

For these reasons, a number of *nonparametric* statistical methods have been developed that allow us to run significance tests on data that do not meet the assumptions of the parametric tests. There is a wide variety of nonparametric tests, but we will be able to include only a small sample of them—just enough to demonstrate their ease of computation and wide applicability. We will consider the appropriate techniques for two general classes of data: independent samples and correlated samples.

NONPARAMETRIC TESTS USING INDEPENDENT SAMPLES

The nonparametric tests to be treated in this section require *independent* samples. This term simply means that the placement of subjects in one category does not affect the occurrence of subjects in another category. If John Doe turns up in one category or if he is assigned at random to a particular group, the selection has no bearing on any other category. In short, our observation of John Doe is independent of any other observation.

The Chi Square: One-Way Classification

Suppose that we flip a coin 20 times and record the frequency of occurrence of heads and tails. We know from the laws of probability that we should expect 10 heads and 10 tails. We also know that because of sampling error, we could easily come up with 9 heads and 11 tails or 12 heads and 8 tails. As we asked ourselves in Note 6.1, at what point do we say that an observed deviation from a 50-50 split is *not* sampling error but is due to some other factor, such as a biased coin? At what point do we say that there is a *significant* deviation between the theoretical 50-50 split and our observed frequency distribution?

A technique that can be used to determine whether there is a significant difference between some *theoretical* or *expected* frequencies and the corresponding *observed* frequencies in two or more categories is the *chi square test* (chi is denoted by the Greek letter χ). The formula for the calculation of chi square is

$$\chi^2 = \Sigma \frac{(O - E)^2}{E} \tag{13.1}$$

where

O = the observed frequency in a given category
E = the expected frequency in a given category

Let us suppose our coin-flipping experiment yielded 12 heads and 8 tails. We would enter our expected frequencies (10-10) and our observed frequencies in a table resembling Table 13.1.

The calculation of χ^2 in a one-way classification is very straightforward. The expected frequency in a category (e.g., "heads") is subtracted from the observed frequency, the difference is squared, and the square is divided by its expected frequency. This is repeated for the remaining categories, and, as the formula for χ^2 indicates, these results are summed for all the categories.

The Chi Square Distribution. How does a calculated χ^2 of 0.8 tell us if our observed results of 12 heads and 8 tails represent a significant deviation from an ex-

Table 13.1
Calculating a χ^2: One-way classification

	Observed	Expected	$(O - E)$	$(O - E)^2$	$(O - E)^2/E$
Heads	12	10	2	4	0.4
Tails	8	10	-2	4	0.4
	20	20			$\chi^2 = 0.8$

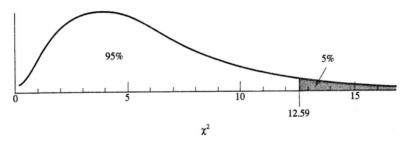

Figure 13.1
Sampling distribution of chi square for 6 *df.*

pected 10-10 split? To answer this question, we again resort to the concept of a sampling distribution.

In the same way that we had a sampling distribution of t or F, we are now concerned with the sampling distribution of chi square. The shape of the chi square sampling distribution depends upon the number of degrees of freedom, and the distribution for $df = 6$ shown in Figure 13.1 illustrates this relationship. As with other sampling distributions, we can mark off the different values that would be equaled or exceeded by sampling error a given percentage of the time. Note in Figure 13.1 that for 6 degrees of freedom χ^2 values of 12.59 or greater happen less than 5% of the time by chance, so we conclude that a χ^2 of 12.59 or greater is significant at the .05 level.

Since the shape of the sampling distribution depends on the number of degrees of freedom, the χ^2 value to be equaled or exceeded a given percentage of the time also depends on the degrees of freedom. Table F in Appendix 3 shows these values for the usual .05, .01, and .001 significance levels. For example, for 1 degree of freedom, we see that our calculated χ^2 must equal or exceed 3.84 to be significant at the .05 level.

The degrees of freedom for a one-way classification χ^2 is $r - 1$, *where* r *is the number of categories.* Since the one-way classification χ^2 is often presented in the tabular form of Table 13.1, r can be thought of as the number of rows. In the coin-flipping experiment of Table 13.1, there are two categories ($r = 2$), so there would obviously be 1 degree of freedom. From Table F we see that a χ^2 of 3.84 or greater is needed for χ^2 to be significant at the .05 level, so we conclude that our χ^2 of 0.8 in the coin-flipping experiment could have happened by sampling error, and that the deviations between the observed frequencies and expected frequencies are not significant.

Another one-way chi square with two categories is shown in Table 13.2. In one of the research examples at the beginning of this chapter, we saw that students with learning disabilities had larger standard deviations on 15 of the 19 subtests of the Woodcock-Johnson. The calculation of the chi square for these results is shown in Table 13.2.

We note that again there is 1 degree of freedom, and from Table F we see that our calculated χ^2 must equal or exceed 3.84 to be significant at the .05 level. Since

Table 13.2
Comparing low-achieving and learning-disabled students on variability

Standard Deviations	Observed	Expected	$(O - E)$	$(O - E)^2$	$(O - E)^2/E$
Larger	15	9.5	5.5	30.25	3.18
Smaller	4	9.5	−5.5	30.25	3.18
	19	19			$\chi^2 = 6.36$

$$\chi^2(1) = 6.36, p < .05$$

our calculated value of 6.36 exceeds 3.84, we conclude that there were significantly more cases where the standard deviation for the students with learning disabilities was larger (15) than smaller (4), $\chi^2(1) = 6.36, p < .05$.

Let us consider another example that involves more than just two categories. A psychology instructor makes out his final grades for 200 students in an introductory psychology class. He is curious to see if his grade distribution resembles the "normal curve" and notes from the college catalog that in a normal distribution of grades 45% of them would be C's, 24% of them would be B's and 24% D's, and 3.5% of them would be A's and 3.5% F's. Table 13.3 shows the chi square table with the instructor's observed grade distribution and the distribution of letter grades that could be expected according to the normal curve model. Note that the professor obtained the expected distribution by multiplying the class size of 200 by the percentage for that letter grade (e.g., 3.5% × 200 = 7 A's).

Note in the data of Table 13.3 that there are 4 degrees of freedom, since $df = r - 1$, where r is the number of categories. From Table F we see that for $df = 4$, a chi square value of 13.28 is needed for χ^2 to be significant at the .01 level, so we conclude that our χ^2 of 18.02 indicates that the professor's grade distribution deviates significantly from a normal distribution.

Table 13.3
Using χ^2 to check "normality" of a grade distribution

Grades	Observed	Expected	$(O - E)$	$(O - E)^2$	$(O - E)^2/E$
A (3.5%)	15	7	8	64	64/7 = 9.14
B (24%)	53	48	5	25	25/48 = 0.52
C (45%)	87	90	−3	9	9/90 = 0.10
D (24%)	33	48	−15	225	225/48 = 4.69
F (3.5%)	12	7	5	25	25/7 = 3.57
	200	200			$\chi^2 = 18.02$

$$\chi^2(4) = 18.02, p < .01$$

The Chi Square: Two-Way Classification

The two-way chi square is a convenient technique for determining the *significance of the difference* between the frequencies of occurrence in two or more categories with two or more groups. For example, we may ask if there is any difference in the number of freshmen, sophomores, juniors, or seniors as to their preference for spectator sports (football, basketball, or baseball). This is called a two-way classification, since we would need two bits of information from the students in our sample—their class and their sports preference.

Another use for a two-way classification chi square would be to see if there are sex differences for some variable. For example, Table 13.4 shows the results of a survey on the feelings of time urgency experienced by 252 students at a midwestern university. The two elements of this two-way classification are sex and time urgency (low, moderate, or high). This type of a two-way table is called a *contingency table,* and each entry is called a *cell.*

Determining the Expected Frequencies.   In the one-way classification, the expected frequencies are determined by some *a priori* hypothesis: a 50-50 split in coin flipping or a normal distribution of grades. However, in the two-way classification, the expected values (sometimes called *independence values*) are calculated from the marginal totals of the contingency table. For example, the total number of students feeling a low sense of time urgency is 89. Since there is a total of 252

Table 13.4
Sex differences in perceived time urgency

		Perceived Time Urgency			
		Low	Moderate	High	Totals
Sex	Men	19 (30.37)	26 (25.60)	41 (30.03)	86
	Women	70 (58.63)	49 (49.40)	47 (57.97)	166
	Totals	89	75	88	252

O	E	$(O - E)$	$\dfrac{(O - E)^2}{E}$
19	30.37	−11.37	4.26
26	25.60	0.40	.01
41	30.03	10.97	4.01
70	58.63	11.37	2.20
49	49.40	−0.40	—
47	57.97	−10.97	2.08
			$\chi^2 = 12.56$

$$\chi^2(2) = 12.56, \; p < .01$$

students, we know that 89/252 or approximately 35.3% of the total group, both men and women, scored low on time urgency.

Now if the null hypothesis were true (i.e., if there were no difference in the number of men and women scoring low on time urgency), we would expect 35.3% of the men and 35.3% of the women to score low on time urgency. Since there are 86 men, we simply multiply 86 by 35.3% to obtain 30. Thus, if there are no sex differences, we would expect 30 men to score low on time urgency. Similarly, 35.3% of 166 yields an expected value of 59. We expect that 59 women would score low on time urgency. These values (to two decimal places) are entered in parentheses for each cell of the contingency table.

A quick and handy way of calculating each of the expected values is to multiply the column total by the row total for each cell and divide by the total N. The expected values for each cell in Table 13.4 would be

$$\frac{89 \times 86}{252} = 30.37 \qquad \frac{75 \times 86}{252} = 25.60 \qquad \frac{88 \times 86}{252} = 30.03$$

$$\frac{89 \times 166}{252} = 58.63 \qquad \frac{75 \times 166}{252} = 49.40 \qquad \frac{88 \times 166}{252} = 57.97$$

After the expected values for each cell have been calculated, the same computational procedures for χ^2 are used as in the one-way classification. The differences between the observed and expected frequencies are found, the differences are squared, the squared difference is divided by its expected value, and the results of all the cells are summed. Notice that the *expected* values in each column or row add up to the same column or row total as the *observed* frequencies. This is an essential requirement for chi square, as we shall see in a later section.

Determining the Degrees of Freedom.   It was easy to see that the *df* for the one-way classification was $r - 1$, because in order for the category frequencies to add up to the total number of cases all the frequencies could vary but one. For example, in the grade distribution data of Table 13.3, there were five categories, and $5 - 1 = 4$ degrees of freedom. That is, four of the category frequencies could take any value, while the fifth, in order for the total to be 200, would be dependent on the first four.

A similar technique is used in the two-way classification, but the number of degrees of freedom depends on both the number of rows *and* the number of columns. For the two-way classification chi square, $df = (r - 1)(c - 1)$, where r is the number of rows and c is the number of columns. For the example in Table 13.4, $df = (2 - 1)(3 - 1) = 2$. In other words, only two cell frequencies are free to vary; after two are given, the remaining frequencies are fixed so that the row and column totals will be correct. You may already have discovered this fact in examining the calculation of the expected values in Table 13.4. You would only have to calculate the expected values for men, low time urgency and men, moderate time urgency, and the rest of the expected values could be obtained by subtraction. Although this is a tempting arithmetically sound shortcut, it might be a good idea to actually calculate several other expected values, in the event that you made a computational error on the first two!

What Does a Significant χ^2 Mean?   In Table F we find that with *df* = 2 a chi square of 9.21 is needed for the difference to be significant at the .01 level. Since chi squares of 9.21 or larger happen by chance less than 1% of the time, we conclude that our χ^2 of 12.56 is significant at the .01 level. Given the data in a contingency table, such as the sex and time urgency tabulation of Table 13.4, what does a significant chi square mean? Besides indicating a significant deviation between observed and expected cell frequencies, it means that we can treat a significant χ^2 as either a *significant difference* between levels of one of the variables or as a *significant relationship* between the two variables.

In Table 13.4, our significant χ^2 tells us that there is a significant difference between men and women in time urgency. We can see that there are proportionately more women who scored low on time urgency than the number that would be expected by chance (70 versus 59) and fewer women who scored high on time urgency than the number that would be expected by chance (47 versus 58).

Another way of describing our significant χ^2 would be to say that there is a significant relationship between the sex of a student and the extent of time urgency. An inspection of the contingency table shows that the relationship is due to the fact that *more* women and *fewer* men than expected by chance scored low on time urgency, while more men and fewer women than expected by chance scored high on time urgency.

Although both of the preceding explanations are used, the *significant difference* approach is the more common.

The 2 × 2 Contingency Table.   When there are two levels of both variables in the two-way classification, the computational effort of calculating the χ^2 value is greatly reduced. The data are tabulated in a 2 × 2 (say "two by two") contingency table with the cell frequencies labeled *A* through *D*, along with the marginal totals and total *N*, as shown:

A	*B*	*A* + *B*
C	*D*	*C* + *D*
A + *C*	*B* + *D*	*N*

The computational formula is

$$\chi^2 = \frac{N(AD - BC)^2}{(A + B)(C + D)(A + C)(B + D)} \qquad (13.2)$$

where
   the letters *A* through *D* refer to the cell frequencies
   N is the total number of observations

$(A + B)$ and $(C + D)$ are row totals

$(A + C)$ and $(B + D)$ are column totals

The degrees of freedom for the χ^2 calculated from this formula is always 1, since in a 2 × 2 table the quantity $(r - 1)(c - 1)$ is, of course, 1.

As an illustration of the 2 × 2 contingency table, let us use the survey mentioned earlier that assessed the number of hours studied per week by students with a Type A personality (hard-driving and competitive) and students with a more laid-back Type B personality. A total of 110 Type A or Type B students reported studying either 0 to 10 hours or 30 hours or more per week, and the results are recorded in Table 13.5.

The χ^2 of 12.81 is significant at the .001 level, so we conclude that there is a significant difference in the number of study hours reported by Type A and Type B students. By inspecting Table 13.5, we see that proportionately more Type A students reported studying more than 30 hours per week, while more Type B's said they studied less than 10 hours per week.

This computational formula for the 2 × 2 table eliminates the separate steps involved in calculating the expected values and performing the arithmetic operations for each step. However, the numbers do get unwieldy at times, and some pocket calculators may not be able to handle the large number of digits.

Assumptions Necessary for Chi Square. Even though a nonparametric statistic does not require assumptions regarding the population, there still are some re-

Table 13.5

Number of weekly study hours reported by Type A and Type B students

		Study Hours per Week		
		0 to 10	30 or more	
	Type A	25 (A)	26 (B)	51 (A + B)
Personality	Type B	48 (C)	11 (D)	59 (C + D)
		73 (A + C)	37 (B + D)	110 (N)

$$\chi^2 = \frac{N(AD - BC)^2}{(A + B)(C + D)(A + C)(B + D)} = \frac{110[25(11) - 48(26)]^2}{(51)(59)(73)(37)}$$

$$= \frac{110(275 - 1{,}248)^2}{8{,}127{,}309} = \frac{110(-973)^2}{8{,}127{,}309} = \frac{104{,}140{,}190}{8{,}127{,}309} = 12.81$$

$$\chi^2(1) = 12.81, \; p < .001$$

strictions regarding its use. The following assumptions are necessary for use of the chi square technique.

1. *The data must be in frequency form.* The entries in the cells indicate *how many* are in a given category and involve only a counting procedure. This is, basically, a technique for nominal data.

2. *The individual observations must be independent of each other.* This means, for example, that you cannot "inflate" χ^2 by asking each of 10 people to guess the suit of a playing card on four successive draws and then claim that you have an N of 40. Since a given person is making four guesses, we could expect that guesses on one occasion might be influenced by the guesses on previous occasions. Clearly, the four observations would be related and not independent of each other.

3. *Sample size must be adequate.* There is general agreement that the chi square value is affected by very small samples, but considerable controversy over just what is meant by "small." Some suggest that you should not attempt to use chi square when your sample size is less than 5 cases per cell. This limitation would mean you would not use a 2 × 2 table if your sample size were less than 20.

   Others are less concerned about whether the chi square is accurate and more concerned about Type I and Type II errors. With very small N's, the chi square is a very low-powered statistic, and the likelihood of a Type II error is increased. There may be a real difference between the observed and expected values, but our chi square statistic did not pick it up. So, for a convenient rule of thumb, we should have sample sizes of at least 5 cases per category for the one-way chi square, and 5 per cell for the two-way.

4. *Distribution basis must be decided on before the data are collected.* In the grade distribution of Table 13.3, our psychology instructor was testing the deviation of his final grade distribution from a normal distribution. You can see that it would be inappropriate for him to "eyeball" his data and choose some kind of a distribution (i.e., rectangular, bimodal, or skewed) to compare with his distribution. Obviously, he could come up with a distribution that would yield nonsignificant or significant results to please his fancy. There must be a logical basis for his choosing the categories before he collects his data.

5. *The sum of the observed frequencies must equal the sum of the expected frequencies.* In order for the chi square formula to "work," the sums of the observed and expected frequencies have to be equal. Tables 13.1 to 13.4 all show the expected and observed sums to be the same. Suppose we rolled a die 60 times and observed the frequency with which a "2" appeared. We could *not* use chi square to see whether there is a significant difference between the 14, for example, observed "2's" and the 10 expected by chance, because 14 and 10 are not the same. What is missing, of course, are the "non-2's." We can indeed run a chi square if we have 14 observed "2's" and 46 "non-2's," with

expected values of 10 and 50, respectively, since now the sum of the observed frequencies is equal to the sum of the expected frequencies.

The Mann–Whitney U Test

The Mann–Whitney test is a very powerful nonparametric technique for determining whether two independent samples have been drawn from the same population. The measurements in both groups must be at least of an ordinal nature. The logic of the method is simple enough: If you have two populations from which you are drawing your two samples, the null hypothesis would state that both populations have the same distribution. That is, if you selected a score from one population, the probability that it would be larger than a score from another population would be $p = .50$. However, if we found that more scores from one population were larger than scores from the other population than would be expected by chance, we would reject the null hypothesis. We would conclude that there was a significant difference between the two populations.

Small Samples. To see how the method works with small samples, let us consider the data of Table 13.6. An interviewer at a state political rally asked four people from community A and five people from community B to rate the efficiency of their local government on a scale from 1 (very inefficient) to 20 (ex-

Table 13.6
Mann–Whitney U test on government efficiency data

Community A	Community B
8	10
11	13
6	16
9	12
	18
$N_1 = 4$	$N_2 = 5$

6	8	9	10	11	12	13	16	18
A	A	A	B	A	B	B	B	B

A precedes B 19 times, $U' = 19$
B precedes A once, $U = 1$

$p = .016 \times 2 = .032$
Significant

tremely efficient). Was there a significant difference in the ratings of the two local governments?

The Mann–Whitney test requires only three bits of information:

1. N_1 = sample size of smaller group.
2. N_2 = sample size of larger group.
3. U = number of times a score in the larger group precedes a score in the smaller group when both groups are ranked together.

As shown in Table 13.6, we take the scores from the columns and rank them from smallest to largest, keeping their identities (A or B) intact. We then simply count the number of times that B (the largest group) precedes A. The only B preceding an A is the B of 10, which precedes an A of 11. Since this is the only B in front of an A, our $U = 1$.

We can check the accuracy of our counting by tabulating *the number of times A precedes B*. We see that the first B (10) is preceded by three A's, the second B (12) by four A's, and the remaining B's each by four A's. The total would be 3 + 4 + 4 + 4 + 4 = 19, and this statistic is denoted U'. This can be a check on the accuracy of our tabulation of U, since there is a relationship between U and U', in that

$$U = N_1 N_2 - U'$$

For the data of Table 13.6,

$$U = (4)(5) - 19$$

$$U = 1$$

It must be remembered that U is *always* smaller than U'. In fact, if we tabulate both, we can tell which value is U because it is the smaller of the two.

Once we have tabulated U, we again resort to a sampling distribution, and the probabilities or critical values are shown in Tables G and H in Appendix 3. Table G is to be used when neither N_1 nor N_2 is larger than 8, and Table H can be used when N_2 (the size of the larger group) is between 9 and 20.

Since the data of Table 13.6 have a small sample size, with $N_2 = 5$, we will use Table G to determine whether our $U = 1$ is statistically significant. The first page of Table G shows a table of $N_2 = 5$, and we go down the left-hand column to a U of 1. With $N_1 = 4$, the probability associated with values this small is $p = .016$. However, the probabilities given in Table G are for a *one-tailed test*. This means that whenever a two-tailed test is used, *these probabilities must be doubled*. Since we did not predict in advance which community would be rated more efficient, we have to make a two-tailed test, and the probability of obtaining a U as small as 1 in a two-tailed test is .016 × 2 = .032. Since this probability is less than the usual .05, we conclude that there is a significant difference between the ratings of the two communities.

Using Table H with Larger Samples.   When N_2 (the larger of the two samples) is between 9 and 20, we cannot use Table G to determine the exact probability of obtaining a value as small as U. With these larger samples, one of the tables from Table H must be used that shows the value of U needed for the difference to be significant at the .001, .01, .025, and .05 levels for a one-tailed test and the .002, .02, .05, and .10 levels for a two-tailed test.

As an example let us consider the data of Table 13.7, where a sample of 7 women drivers and 10 men drivers were assigned safe driving scores based on a complex formula involving accident rate and miles traveled. A higher score indicates a poorer driver. Was there a significant difference between the driving scores of men and women?

Since U is the number of times scores from the larger sample precede scores from the smaller sample, we tabulate the number of times a woman's score (W) is preceded by a man's score (M). We see in Table 13.7 that the women's scores of 22, 27, 32, and 37 are each preceded by one man's score, a woman's score of 52 is preceded by two men's scores, and a woman's score of 67 is preceded by three men's scores. This gives the total of $U = 1 + 1 + 1 + 1 + 2 + 3 = 9$.

As a check on our calculations we tabulate U' and find that a man's score of 17 is preceded by one woman's score, a man's score of 42 is preceded by five

Table 13.7
Mann–Whitney U test on safe driving scores

	Women	Men
	37	17
	52	72
	67	62
	27	75
	32	69
	22	85
	13	42
		77
		71
		81
	$N_1 = 7$	$N_2 = 10$

13	17	22	27	32	37	42	52	62	67	69	71	72	75	77	81	85
W	M	W	W	W	W	M	W	M	W	M	M	M	M	M	M	M

$$U = 1 + 1 + 1 + 1 + 2 + 3 = 9$$

Significant, $p < .02$ (two-tailed test)

women's scores, a man's score of 62 is preceded by six women's scores, and the remaining seven men's scores are each preceded by seven women's scores. This would give a total of $U' = 1 + 5 + 6 + 7 + 7 + 7 + 7 + 7 + 7 + 7 = 61$. Applying the check for accuracy, we obtain

$$U = N_1 N_2 - U'$$
$$U = (7)(10) - 61$$
$$U = 9$$

Keeping in mind that we are running a two-tailed test, we now consult Table H and find the value of U for $N_2 = 10$ and $N_1 = 7$ in the four tables. We note that our value of $U = 9$ is between the tabled U of 5 in the .002 table and the U of 11 in the .02 table. Since our value of 9 is less than the tabled value of 11 in the .02 table, we say that our U is significant between the .02 and the .002 levels. (Note that with the Mann–Whitney test the smaller the value of U the greater the level of significance.) In terms of the experimental data, we conclude that the women's safe driving scores are significantly lower (indicating better drivers) than the men's scores.

The Mann–Whitney test can also be used for samples larger than 20, but space does not permit inclusion of the procedure in this introductory textbook. Other sources (e.g., Daniel, 1978) can provide you with this technique, as well as alternate ways of computing U and U' without going through the laborious (especially if N is large) counting procedure. It should be mentioned again that the Mann–Whitney test is one of the most powerful nonparametric tests, and it is strongly recommended when the assumptions cannot be met for the parametric t test.

The Kruskal–Wallis One-Way Analysis of Variance

The last nonparametric technique for independent samples to be discussed in this chapter is one that is markedly different from the procedures described earlier. Like the parametric analysis of variance, the Kruskal–Wallis test can be used *for more than just two samples*. This test assumes that the data are at least ordinal in nature so they can be converted to ranks.

The procedure requires converting the scores of the individual groups to one *overall* set of ranks. The data of Table 13.8 show the scores for four separate groups ($k = 4$), and their ranks in a single overall series. The smallest score is given a rank of 1, the next smallest a rank of 2, and so on. In Table 13.8, the freshman score of 2 has a rank of 1 and the senior score of 21 has a rank of 28. As with the Spearman method of correlation, from Chapter 7, scores that are tied are given the average ranking. For example, there are two scores of 3, which would be tied for second and third rank, so both scores of 3 are given a rank of 2.5, and the next score is given a rank of 4. Similarly, there are three scores of 8, tied for ranks of 11, 12, and 13, so each score of 8 has a rank of 12, and the next score is given a rank of 14.

The null hypothesis for the Kruskal–Wallis test should be obvious now that we have converted all the scores to ranks. If there were no differences between

Table 13.8
Kruskal–Wallis test on personal concerns inventory

Freshman		Sophomore		Junior		Senior	
Score	Rank	Score	Rank	Score	Rank	Score	Rank
7	9.5	9	14	17	23	21	28
6	7.5	7	9.5	12	18.5	20	27
8	12	6	7.5	19	25.5	18	24
12	18.5	11	17	10	15.5	19	25.5
5	5.5	10	15.5	8	12	16	22
3	2.5	5	5.5	14	20	15	21
8	12	3	2.5				
2	1						
4	4						

$$R_1 = \overline{72.5} \qquad R_2 = \overline{71.5} \qquad R_3 = \overline{114.5} \qquad R_4 = \overline{147.5}$$
$$N_1 = 9 \qquad\qquad N_2 = 7 \qquad\qquad N_3 = 6 \qquad\qquad N_4 = 6$$

$$H = \frac{12}{N(N+1)} \Sigma \frac{R_G^2}{N_G} - 3(N+1)$$

$$= \frac{12}{28(28+1)} \left[\frac{(72.5)^2}{9} + \frac{(71.5)^2}{7} + \frac{(114.5)^2}{6} + \frac{(147.5)^2}{6} \right] - 3(28+1)$$

$$= \frac{12}{812} (584.03 + 730.32 + 2{,}185.04 + 3{,}626.04) - 87$$

$$= 0.0148 \, (7{,}125.43) - 87$$

$$H = 105.46 - 87 = 18.46$$

$\chi^2_{.001}$, $df = 3$, is 16.27
Significant, $p < .001$

the groups, the sums of the ranks for each group would be about the same. That is, if only sampling error were responsible for differences in *scores* among the groups, the *sums of the ranks* for each group would only differ because of sampling error—and we would conclude that the samples had been drawn from the *same* population. On the other hand, if the sums of the ranks for each group differ from each other by more than we would expect by sampling error, we would conclude that these groups were samples from *different* populations, and we would have demonstrated that there is a significant difference between the populations.

The statistic to be evaluated in the Kruskal–Wallis test is *H*, and it is given by

$$H = \frac{12}{N(N+1)} \Sigma \frac{R_G^2}{N_G} - 3(N+1) \qquad (13.3)$$

where

N = the total number of scores
R_G^2 = the squared sum of the ranks in a group
N_G = the number of scores in a group

Although the formula for H looks somewhat imposing, it requires only that after ranking the scores in the manner described, we proceed as follows.

1. Add the ranks for group 1 to obtain R_1.
2. Square this sum of ranks to obtain R_1^2.
3. Divide R_1^2 by N_1, the number of scores in group 1.
4. Since steps 1 to 3 give us R^2/N for the first group only, we repeat these steps for all k groups (k = number of groups).
5. We sum the individual R^2/N for all groups, multiply by $12/N(N+1)$, and subtract the quantity $3(N+1)$.
6. If there are at least five cases in every group, the resultant statistic, H, is distributed as chi square with $df = k - 1$. H is also distributed as chi square if $k = 3$ and there are *more* than five cases in every group. For times when $k = 3$ and there are five cases or fewer in any group, Daniel (1978) has a special table, since the chi square distribution cannot be used.

Table 13.8 shows the results of a "Personal Concerns" questionnaire given to a sample of 28 college students. A personnel dean had predicted earlier that as the students got nearer to receiving their college degrees, they would check more and more items on the questionnaire that dealt with vocational and marital decisions. The sample consisted of 9 freshmen, 7 sophomores, 6 juniors, and 6 seniors. Was there a significant difference between the groups on the number of items checked relating to future decisions?

Since the value of H is greater than the tabled chi square value for $df = 3$ of 16.27, we conclude that our samples are from different populations, with $p < .001$ that such a result would happen by sampling error alone. In terms of the data, the seniors seem to have checked a significantly greater number of items relating to future vocational and marriage plans than have the freshmen and sophomores.

The Problem of Tied Ranks.   When the number of tied ranks becomes quite large, the value of H calculated by the formula is somewhat smaller than it should be. Daniel (1978) presents a correction for tied ranks that we will not consider here, since H is not seriously affected unless the tied ranks are unusually severe. In the data of Table 13.8, for example, 14 of the 28 scores are tied, and the corrected H is 18.52 instead of the 18.46 calculated in Table 13.8. Obviously, this correction did not affect our decision to reject the null hypothesis and conclude that the differences were significant. The Kruskal–Wallis test is a "conservative" test with respect to tied scores; that is, when the correction is made, it tends to make the test even more powerful in its rejection of a false null hypothesis.

In conclusion, we must note that the Kruskal–Wallis test is a reasonable alternative to the one-way analysis of variance when we cannot meet the assumptions of the parametric F test.*

NONPARAMETRIC TESTS USING RELATED SAMPLES

The nonparametric tests in this section are alike in that they all require *correlated data*. As you may remember from Chapter 9, we noted that one type of t test (the direct difference method) used correlated samples. We further noted that correlated data could involve matched samples (split litters, co-twin controls, or matched pairs) or repeated measurements of the same subjects. The nonparametric tests to be described in the following pages are designed for use with such correlated data.

The Sign Test

A very convenient test using matched pairs or repeated measurements is the sign test (so called because plus and minus signs are used to indicate changes). Each pair of measures is considered separately, and, if the second score is *greater* than the first, a minus sign is entered in the *Sign* column. If the second score is *smaller* than the first, a plus sign is entered. If both observations are the same, a 0 is entered. Since we must be able to tell which of the two scores is greater in a given pair, data must be at least ordinal. A typical sign test is shown in Table 13.9.

The example in Table 13.9 shows the results of a study involving the number of negative, self-deprecating statements made by clients during psychotherapy. Tape recordings of the first therapy session for 14 clients at a regional mental health center were studied, and the numbers of negative statements made during therapy were tabulated. Eight sessions later a similar tabulation was made. Was there a significant reduction in the number of negative statements made?

It should be obvious from Table 13.9 that the null hypothesis would state that half the signs would be positive and half would be negative. In other words, if there are no significant differences between the pairs of measurements, about half of the changes should occur in a positive direction and half should be in a negative direction.

The sign test makes use of two bits of information:

1. N is the number of changes. If there are any pairs that show a 0, they are subtracted from the total number of pairs. In the data of Table 13.9, there is one pair with a 0, so $N = 14 - 1 = 13$.

2. x is the frequency of occurrence of the sign that appears less often. There are 10 plus signs and 3 minus signs, so $x = 3$.

---

*As with the parametric F test, there is also a procedure following a Kruskal–Wallis test to see which groups are significantly different. The technique is beyond the scope of this introductory textbook but is described in a text by Daniel (1978).

Table 13.9
Sign test on number of negative statements made
during therapy

Client	First Session	Eighth Session	Sign
A	35	23	+
B	17	17	0
C	14	6	+
D	18	12	+
E	14	10	+
F	36	26	+
G	27	24	+
H	10	14	−
I	16	20	−
J	15	2	+
K	36	13	+
L	25	18	+
M	10	17	−
N	16	14	+

$$N = 13$$
$$x = 3$$

Significant, $p = .046$

When N and x have been determined, we need to consult Table I to determine the probability of obtaining an x as small as our obtained value. Table I can be used for N values as large as 25. With $N = 13$ and $x = 3$, we see that the one-tailed probability of obtaining an x as small as 3 is .046. Since .046 is less than the conventional .05, we state that $p < .05$, and we conclude that there was a significant reduction in the number of negative statements made by clients in the therapy sessions.

We must remember that Table I shows *one-tailed* probabilities, meaning that the researcher is specifying in advance of collecting the data that the change will be in a specific direction. If the researcher is not specifying the direction of the difference, a two-tailed probability is needed, and the values in Table I must be *doubled*. Our researcher in the therapy survey *was* predicting a reduction in the number of negative statements, so she used the one-tailed probabilities in Table I.

The Wilcoxon Matched-Pairs Signed-Ranks Test

The sign test discussed in the previous subsection requires that we merely be able to tell whether one of a pair of scores is greater or less than the other. There may be times when our measuring scale is such that the difference between the two itself can be measured. For example, if pair A has a small difference between the two scores and pair B has a large difference, we would certainly attach more meaning to the larger difference. The sign test, of course, is not sensitive to the magnitude of the differences but only to the *direction* of the differences (plus or minus).

The Wilcoxon test uses the size of each difference. It requires that we determine the size of each difference, rank each difference without regard to its algebraic sign (smallest difference gets a rank of one), and then give each rank the sign of the original difference. Thus, if a rank is associated with a positive difference, it is given a plus sign. If the rank is associated with a negative difference, it is given a minus sign.

If the null hypothesis were true and the differences between paired values were due to sampling error, we would expect about as many small positive differences as small negative differences and about as many large positive differences as large negative differences. We would also expect the sum of the positive ranks to be about the same as the sum of the negative ranks. However, if we found one of these sums to be much smaller than the other, we would suspect that there was a significant difference between the two sets of scores.

Before we examine an example using the Wilcoxon test, we have to agree on how to handle the equivalent pairs and the tied values. If both scores in a single pair are the same, their difference is 0, and such pairs are eliminated from the data analysis, just as with the sign test. That is, N = the number of pairs minus the number of pairs whose difference is 0. In Table 13.10, pairs K and O were eliminated because both differences were 0, so $N = 20 - 2 = 18$.

To handle ties when we are ranking the individual differences, we again use the technique we used in the Spearman rank-difference method of correlation and in the Kruskal–Wallis test: Each tied difference is given the average rank. For example, in Table 13.10, differences of 6 and –6 are tied for fourth and fifth ranks, so each is given a rank of 4.5, and the next score is given a rank of 6. (Remember that in the Wilcoxon test the differences are ranked without regard to sign.)

The data in Table 13.10 show the results of the project of an educational psychologist who was studying the effect that knowledge of results has on the learning process. Forty high school sophomores were used to form 20 pairs that were matched for sex, grade-point average, and manual dexterity. All students were tested on a tracking device, called a pursuit rotor, that tested motor coordination skills. Each member of the experimental group heard a click and saw an indicator light flash every time he or she made an error, while members of the control group had no extra information when they strayed off-target. Was there a significant difference between the number of errors made by the students who had immediate knowledge of results (experimental group) and the number made by those who did not receive additional knowledge of results (control group)?

The paired scores are first listed in columns, as shown in Table 13.10. The differences (D) are then found, the second score being subtracted from the first score in each pair, and the difference, with its algebraic sign, is placed in the D column. These differences are now ranked, *without regard to sign,* and each rank is placed in the appropriate column. As mentioned earlier, zero differences are eliminated

Table 13.10
The Wilcoxon test on knowledge-of-results data

Pair	Control Group	Experimental Group	D	Rank of D	Rank with Less Frequent Sign
A	80	45	35	17	
B	24	62	−38	18	18
C	40	45	− 5	2.5	2.5
D	46	30	16	9	
E	85	56	29	13	
F	52	31	21	11	
G	55	35	20	10	
H	29	36	− 7	6	6
I	77	46	31	14	
J	59	49	10	7	
K	26	26	0	—	
L	46	35	11	8	
M	57	51	6	4.5	
N	46	52	− 6	4.5	4.5
O	69	69	0	—	
P	88	56	32	15	
Q	49	44	5	2.5	
R	49	25	24	12	
S	93	60	33	16	
T	35	39	− 4	1	$T = \dfrac{1}{32.0}$

$$N = 18$$
$$T = 32$$

Significant, $p < .01$

from the analysis and tied differences are given the average of the ranks for which they are tied.

After the ranking is completed, we look at the D column again and note the differences that have the less frequent sign. In Table 13.10, these are the differences with the minus sign, *and the ranks corresponding to these differences* are then placed in the last column on the right. There are only five minus differences in the D column; their ranks are 18, 2.5, 6, 4.5, and 1, and the total of these ranks with the less frequent sign is 32.0. The total of this column is T, the statistic to be evaluated in the Wilcoxon test.

Table J contains the critical values of T necessary for significance at the customary significance levels for values of N up to 25. Since our researcher specified in advance that the knowledge-of-results group would have fewer errors, we use the values for the one-tailed test. We see that for $N = 18$, a T of 33 is significant at the .01 level. Since values smaller than the tabled values of T have a smaller probability of occurrence, our T of 32 is significant beyond the .01 level, and $p < .01$.

We noted earlier that the Wilcoxon test is preferred to the sign test when the magnitude of the differences between paired scores can be measured. If we were to apply the sign test to the data of Table 13.10, with $N = 18$ and $x = 5$, we would see from Table I that the one-tailed probability is .048. This is considerably larger than the probability reported by the Wilcoxon test in Table 13.10, reflecting the fact that the Wilcoxon test is a more powerful test when the magnitude as well as the direction of the differences can be measured.

The Friedman Two-Way Analysis of Variance by Ranks

The Friedman test is a useful nonparametric test when we have *more* than two related samples. If our data are at least ordinal in nature, we can use the Friedman test to test the null hypothesis that our samples have been drawn from the same population. Although this procedure can be used for matched samples, it probably has its greatest application in situations where repeated measurements have been made on the same individual.

The rationale for the analysis is reasonably straightforward. If a table is constructed with the usual columns and rows, the rows correspond to individuals, and the columns are the experimental conditions. In the Friedman test, N is the number of rows, and k is the number of columns. The scores in the different conditions for each individual are entered in the appropriate columns in the row for that individual. Another table is now constructed that shows these scores converted to ranks, and the scores for *each* individual are ranked from 1 to k, where k is the number of conditions. That is, the ranks in each row should go from 1 to k. For example, in Table 13.11, student A has scores of 82, 57, 67, and 60 on four tests ($k = 4$), and these are ranked as 4, 1, 3, and 2 in the table of ranks. Similar rankings have been done for the other nine students.

Under the null hypothesis, the sums of the ranks should be about the same for each column. That is, if there are no differences in the experimental conditions, the ranks should be distributed evenly over the k conditions. However, if one of the conditions, let us say, has consistently lower scores, there will obviously be more ranks of 1 in the column corresponding to that condition, resulting in a smaller sum of the ranks for that column.

Let us consider an example to clarify some of these points. A freshman adviser at a small liberal arts college was curious about the special academic abilities of students who had decided to major in psychology. She wanted to know if beginning freshmen who chose psychology as a major had strong abilities in some special area such as mathematics or the natural sciences. To help answer this question, she chose 10 freshman psychology majors and examined their college entrance examination scores. This particular exam yielded a student's percentile rank in the areas of English, mathematics, social science, and natural science. The data for the 10 students are shown in Table 13.11. The first part of the table shows the percentile ranks in each of the four ability areas, and the second part of the table shows the four per-

Table 13.11
The Friedman analysis of variance on special abilities of psychology majors

	College Entrance Exam Percentile Ranks			
Student	English	Mathematics	Social Science	Natural Science
A	82	57	67	60
B	61	95	79	92
C	88	82	99	70
D	86	98	77	97
E	77	89	72	97
F	99	85	95	98
G	77	46	95	87
H	61	71	79	56
I	10	30	28	19
J	61	34	54	57

	Ranks			
Student	E	M	SS	NS
A	4	1	3	2
B	1	4	2	3
C	3	2	4	1
D	2	4	1	3
E	2	3	1	4
F	4	1	2	3
G	2	1	4	3
H	2	3	4	1
I	1	4	3	2
J	4	1	2	3
	$R_1 = 25$	$R_2 = 24$	$R_3 = 26$	$R_4 = 25$

$$\chi_r^2 = \frac{12}{Nk(k+1)} \Sigma(R_G)^2 - 3N(k+1)$$

$$= \frac{12}{10(4)(4+1)} [(25)^2 + (24)^2 + (26)^2 + (25)^2] - 3(10)(4+1)$$

$$= \frac{12}{200} (625 + 576 + 676 + 625) - 150$$

$$= 0.06 \ (2{,}502) - 150$$

$$\chi_r^2 = 0.12$$

$\chi_{.05}^2$, $df = 3$, is 7.82
Not significant, $p > .05$

Note 13.1

Nonparametric Statistical Tests and How They Grew

Compared to the parametric techniques, which evolved early in the twenti-eth century, nonparametric statistical methods were developed more recently. Frank Wilcoxon (1892–1965), an industrial chemist, proposed the test bearing his name in 1945, which helped to stimulate a variety of researchers in the development of other nonparametric methods. These methods found exten-sive use in education and the behavioral sciences because many rating scales, surveys, and other scaling techniques yielded data that were on an or-dinal scale and did not meet the assumptions of the usual parametric tests. This interest in small-group interactions and measurements of attributes was a primary factor in the immediate popularity of the techniques.

---

centiles ranked for each student. Note that the null hypothesis would state that if there are no differences between the four ability areas the ranks will be distributed in such a way that the sums of the columns are about the same.

The ranks are assigned for each student's scores, with the smallest score being given a rank of 1. If there are tied scores, the familiar procedure of averaging the tied ranks is used. The ranks in the first column are then summed, yielding R_1. The sums are also calculated for the remaining columns. These values of R, along with N (the number of rows) and k (the number of columns) are then substituted into Friedman's formula:

$$\chi_r^2 = \frac{12}{Nk(k+1)} \, \Sigma \, (R_G)^2 - 3N(k+1) \tag{13.4}$$

Note that the sum of ranks for each column is squared, these squares are added, this sum is multiplied by $12/Nk(k+1)$, and, finally, the quantity $3N(k+1)$ is subtracted.

The resulting statistic is χ_r^2 (read "chi square for ranks"), and it is distributed approximately as chi square with $k-1$ degrees of freedom. From Table F we see that, for $df = 3$, a chi square of 7.82 is needed for the difference to be significant at the .05 level. Our $\chi_r^2 = 0.12$ does not come close to being significant, so we must accept the null hypothesis that there are no differences between the conditions. This result does not surprise us, since a glance at the first part of Table 13.11 shows that the ranks for the ability levels are spread out among the 10 students and that there are an approximately equal number of ranks of 1, 2, 3, and 4 in all four conditions. So, we conclude that, at least for this group of students, no abil-ity area seemed to rank consistently high or low among those students choosing a psychology major.

It turns out that the statistic χ_r^2 is distributed as chi square with $df = k-1$ only if the number of columns or the number of rows is not too small. If k is 3 and N is less than 10, or if k is 4 and N is less than 5, you cannot use the usual chi square table to determine significance levels. For these smaller samples, a special table of critical values of χ^2_r is available (Daniel, 1978).

CONCLUDING REMARKS

At the beginning of the chapter we noted that the nonparametric tests were necessary for situations in which (1) the parametric assumptions regarding normality and homogeneity of variance of populations could not be met or (2) data were from a nominal or ordinal scale. We have seen in this chapter a wide variety of statistical tests that are appropriate for just these situations. A convenient way to remember the various nonparametric tests is to study them in tabular form according to the level of measurement (nominal or ordinal) and type of situation (independent samples or related samples). Table 13.12 summarizes these characteristics in a convenient form.

The main weakness of nonparametric tests is that they are less powerful than parametric tests; that is, they are less likely to reject the null hypothesis when it is false. We must remember that when the assumptions of parametric tests can be met, parametric tests should definitely be used, because they are the most powerful tests available. However, if these assumptions cannot be met, we simply do not have any choice in the matter. We are left with nonparametric tests alone, and we must do the best we can.

But this is a rather negative approach, and it has led to the feeling that nonparametric tests are not quite legitimate and should be avoided whenever possible. This feeling is entirely unwarranted because nonparametric tests can be just as powerful as parametric tests if *the size of the samples* is increased. A researcher who had planned initially on using 40 subjects in her project might increase her sample size to 50 if she knew that her data could not meet the assumptions of a parametric test. The precise increases in sample size needed to achieve similar power in nonparametrics are discussed by Daniel (1978).

In some of the tests described in this chapter, there have been restrictions placed on the size of samples that could be used. In an introductory textbook it is just impossible to list all the alternative ways of handling very small samples or samples with an N of more than 25. The text by Daniel (1978) is an excellent re-

Table 13.12
Level of measurement and application for selected nonparametric tests

	Independent Samples	Related Samples
Nominal	Chi square	
Ordinal	Mann–Whitney U test	Sign test
	Kruskal–Wallis ANOVA	Wilcoxon matched-pairs test
		Friedman ANOVA

source for these special situations, and the researcher can find answers to just about any question on statistical analysis by nonparametric procedures.

SAMPLE PROBLEM

In a pilot study that established the link between Reye's (rhymes with "wise") syndrome and aspirin, investigators at the Centers for Disease Control in Atlanta noted that of 29 children contracting the disease, 28 had been given aspirin during the chicken pox or influenza that preceded the disease. For control groups, the researchers also contacted (1) 62 other children who were in the same school or hospital as the children with Reye's syndrome, and (2) 81 children whose parents responded to randomly placed telephone calls. Sixteen of the 62 children in the first control group and 45 of the 81 children in the second control group had been given aspirin during their chicken pox or influenza.

Let us construct a 2 × 3 contingency table and use a two-way chi square to see if there was a significantly larger proportion of children with Reye's syndrome that had been treated with aspirin.

		Group Category		
		Reye's syndrome	School or hospital	Telephone calls
Treatment	Aspirin	15.0 / 28	32.1 / 16	41.9 / 45	89
	No aspirin	14.0 / 1	29.9 / 46	39.1 / 36	83
		29	62	81	172

Calculator Solution

Independence values:

$$\frac{89 \times 29}{172} = 15.0 \qquad \frac{89 \times 62}{172} = 32.1 \qquad \frac{89 \times 81}{172} = 41.9$$

$$\frac{83 \times 29}{172} = 14.0 \qquad \frac{83 \times 62}{172} = 29.9 \qquad \frac{83 \times 81}{172} = 39.1$$

(continued)

SAMPLE PROBLEM *(CONTINUED)*

Chi square:

$$\frac{(13.0)^2}{15} = 11.27 \qquad \frac{(16.1)^2}{32.1} = 8.08 \qquad \frac{(3.1)^2}{41.9} = 0.23$$

$$\frac{(13.0)^2}{14} = 12.07 \qquad \frac{(16.1)^2}{29.9} = 8.67 \qquad \frac{(3.1)^2}{39.1} = 0.25$$

$$\chi^2 = 40.57$$

$$\chi^2(2) = 40.57, \, p < .001$$

With $\chi^2 = 40.57$, $p < .001$, we would conclude that there is a significant difference between the observed and expected frequencies in the contingency table. In inspecting the table, we note that the large chi square value is due to the large proportion of children with Reye's syndrome that had taken aspirin.

Computer Solution

Table 13.13 shows the results of the chi square analysis of the Reye's syndrome data. The first box is the usual summary of valid and missing cases. The second box shows the cross tabulation (usually referred to as a "cross tab") with the 2 × 3 contingency table.

The third box shows the Pearson chi square of 40.494, which varies slightly from the calculator solution of 40.57 because of rounding error. Also shown are the likelihood-ratio and the linear-by-linear-association methods, which are beyond the intended scope of an introductory statistics text.

Table 13.13
SPSS printout for the Reye's syndrome data

Cross Tabs

Case Processing Summary

	Cases					
	Valid		Missing		Total	
	N	Percent	N	Percent	N	Percent
Treatment × Group	172	100.0%	0	.0%	172	100.0%

Treatment × Group Cross Tabulation

Count

		Group			Total
		Reye's	School	Phone	
Treatment					
	Aspirin	28	16	45	89
	No aspirin	1	46	36	83
Total		29	62	81	172

Chi-Square Tests

	Value	df	Asymp. Sig. (2-tailed)
Pearson Chi Square	40.494[a]	2	.000
Likelihood Ratio	47.439	2	.000
Linear-by-Linear Association	4.145	1	.042
N of Valid Cases	172		

a. 0 cells (.0%) have expected count less than 5. The minimum expected count is 13.99.

Graph

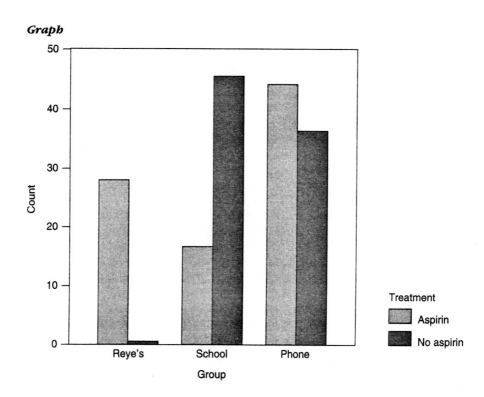

The bar graph is a welcome addition to the usual chi square analysis. The graph clearly shows the source of the significant chi square, with the disproportionate ratio of aspirin to no aspirin in children developing Reye's syndrome.

STUDY QUESTIONS

1. Under what conditions would a nonparametric statistic be used instead of a parametric statistic?
2. What is the difference between *independent* samples and *correlated* samples?
3. Describe how expected frequencies are determined for the one-way chi square.
4. How does sample size affect the use of the one-way chi square?
5. How are expected frequencies calculated for the two-way chi square?
6. How are the degrees of freedom (df) determined for a one-way chi square?
7. Describe how the degrees of freedom for a two-way chi square are calculated.
8. List the assumptions for the chi square.
9. State the null hypothesis for the Mann–Whitney test.
10. In the Kruskal–Wallis test, observations in each category are given an overall rank. Why should the rank sums of each category be the same under the null hypothesis?
11. In what ways are the sign test and the Wilcoxon test alike? How are they different?
12. How would you state the null hypothesis in the Friedman test?
13. What is the main weakness of the nonparametric tests? How might this be overcome?

EXERCISES

1. A speech and hearing clinic reported that in a study of 98 clients there were 87 men and 11 women. Use the one-way chi square to test the null hypothesis that there should be an equal number of men and women.
2. According to the Census Bureau, 12.8% of the population of the United States is over 65. In a study of the 12 midwestern states, researchers found that 8 had more than 12.8% over 65 years of age while 4 states had less than 12.8% over 65. Use the one-way chi square to see if the 8-to-4 split is a significant deviation from the expected 6-to-6 hypothesis.
3. In one of the research scenarios at the beginning of the chapter, a study compared cardiopulmonary resuscitation (CPR) performed by trained and un-

trained persons on 662 victims of cardiac arrest. Use the two-way chi square to see if there was any difference in the outcome of CPR performed by the two groups.

Outcome

		Survived	Did not survive
CPR	Properly done	14	291
	Improperly done	5	352

4. The dean of a small liberal arts college tabulated the number of bachelor's, master's, and doctoral degrees held by men and women faculty. Use the two-way chi square to see if there was a significant difference between men and women in the type of degrees held.

Degree

		Bachelor's	Master's	Doctorate
Sex	Men	5	32	79
	Women	3	31	40

5. In a personal health class, the resting heart rates for 9 men and 7 women were compared. Use the Mann-Whitney U to see if there was a significant difference in the heart rates shown below.

Men	Women
68	65
63	64
85	77
83	78
72	59
71	52
62	75
58	
70	

6. A zoologist was comparing island species with closely related species on the U.S. mainland, and noticed that a bird, the island jay, seemed more inquisitive than its mainland counterpart, the California jay (Haemig, 1984). In one experiment the researcher sounded a novel noise ("squeaking" a balloon), and

when a jay arrived in response to the sound, timed how long the bird or birds remained in the vicinity. The researcher ran this trial 16 times on the island and 10 times on the mainland. The length of time the birds remained near the balloon (in seconds) is shown for the 26 trials. Use the Mann–Whitney test to see if there was a significant difference in the time that the birds spent near the object.

Island		Mainland	
321	110	16	143
370	240	82	75
352	282	40	37
326	298	43	51
400	183	36	20
316	305		
331	300		
376	221		

7. An instructor in business statistics had 8 sophomores, 10 juniors, and 19 seniors in her class and was curious about the relative performance of the three classes. At the end of the term, she compared the course grades (A = 12, A– = 11, B+ = 10, etc.) of the three classes, and the results are as shown. Use the Kruskal–Wallace test to see if there was a significant difference between the classes.

Sophomores	Juniors	Seniors
7	9	12
6	12	12
9	10	6
10	12	11
6	7	6
6	12	9
9	12	12
9	11	6
	7	10
	12	

8. A sample of students at a large university was asked to fill out a questionnaire on fitness, health, and exercise. They also were asked to have their blood pressure, heart rate, and other physiological measures taken. Shown in the following lists are the resting heart rates of students who indicated (1) very little, if any, exercise, (2) a moderate amount of exercise, and (3) a regular exercise routine. Use the Kruskal–Wallis test to see if there was a significant difference in heart rates between the different exercise groups.

Very Little	Moderate	Regular
66	76	84
74	74	60
90	82	70
62	62	74
90	68	72
84	62	64
82	60	48
90	61	
	66	

9. On the first day of class, 10 students in a wellness-fitness course measured their heart rate before exercise and again after stepping up and down on their desk chairs three times, with the results shown. Use the sign test to see if there was a significant increase in heart rate after the stepping exercise.

Student	Before	After
A	73	80
B	70	99
C	69	76
D	76	100
E	76	84
F	96	108
G	61	69
H	62	60
I	62	59
J	84	87

10. An educational psychologist was studying the influence of applied behavioral analysis on nursery school behavior. Children were praised for displaying a positive attitude toward a puppy and were not praised for any negative behavior, such as pinching or pulling its tail. The number of negative behaviors for each of 10 children is listed. The first entry is for a period of a week before the praise period, and the second figure is for the praise period of a week. Use the sign test to see if there was a significant difference in the amount of negative behavior displayed during the two weeks.

Child	Before Praise	During Praise
A	4	1
B	3	2
C	1	1
D	2	1
E	4	3
F	7	2
G	3	2

H	2	1
I	1	2
J	4	2

11. An investigator was studying problem-solving ability under quiet surroundings and noisy surroundings. Twelve subjects were tested under both conditions with the results shown. Use the Wilcoxon method to see if there was a significant difference in performance between the two conditions.

Subject	Quiet	Noisy
A	37	32
B	38	38
C	34	35
D	34	33
E	36	34
F	40	42
G	39	33
H	30	30
I	32	31
J	45	40
K	29	27
L	37	34

12. In a depth perception test, subjects attempted to line up two vertical rods from a distance of 10 feet. A driving school instructor tested 12 students under two conditions. In one condition, they held their heads steady (Fixed) and in the other, they could move their heads from side to side (Moving). The amount of error in millimeters for the two conditions is shown. Use the Wilcoxon method to see if there was a significant difference in errors made in the two conditions.

Student	Fixed	Moving
A	16	8
B	14	10
C	16	15
D	17	16
E	14	10
F	21	13
G	7	10
H	15	9
I	7	9
J	31	17
K	28	15
L	9	8

13. A television sportscaster had 20 viewers call in, ranking their preferences for being a spectator at a World Series game, a Super Bowl, or a heavyweight

championship boxing match. Their rankings follow. Use the Friedman analysis of variance to see if there was a significant difference in preferences for sporting events.

Fan	World Series	Super Bowl	Boxing Match
A	1	2	3
B	1	3	2
C	2	1	3
D	3	1	2
E	1	2	3
F	1	3	2
G	2	1	3
H	1	2	3
I	1	3	2
J	2	1	3
K	1	3	2
L	2	1	3
M	1	2	3
N	1	2	3
O	1	3	2
P	2	1	3
Q	2	3	1
R	1	3	2
S	1	3	2
T	2	1	3

14. A college student adviser was interested in grades received by students in courses in their majors compared with grades in courses in their minors. She also decided to compare these with required courses as well as courses taken as electives. Shown below are the grade-point averages (GPA) for six of her senior advisees. Use the Friedman analysis of variance to see if there was a significant difference between the GPAs in the four different areas.

Student	Major	Minor	Required	Electives
A	3.81	3.21	3.10	3.05
B	3.53	3.50	3.46	3.57
C	3.44	3.09	2.62	3.13
D	2.64	2.43	2.79	2.52
E	3.51	3.48	3.01	3.08
F	3.26	2.83	3.18	3.08

COMPUTER EXERCISES FOR APPENDIX 4 DATA BANK

C1. In computer exercise C1 in Chapter 11, the sample was divided into low, moderate, and high on Speed and Impatience (S&I). For this exercise, divide the sample as before, but construct a 2 × 3 table (men-women × low-moderate-high S&I) showing the number of men and women classified as low, moderate, or high S&I. Calculate a two-way chi square to see if there is a gender difference in speed and impatience.

C2. In computer exercise C1 in Chapter 9, physical symptom scores were compared for men scoring high on the BSRI Masculinity scale and men scoring low on the Masculinity scale. Use the Mann–Whitney U to see if there was a significant difference in symptom scores between these two groups of men. How does this result compare with the t test you computed for C1 in Chapter 9?

C3. In computer exercise C3 in Chapter 11, BSRI Masculinity scores were compared for those scoring low, moderate, and high in Self-Monitoring. Use the Kruskal–Wallis procedure to see if there was a significant difference in masculinity scores between these three groups. How does this result compare with the one-way ANOVA you computed on these same data in exercise C3 in Chapter 11?

REFERENCES

Algozzine, B., Ysseldyke, J. E., and McGue, M. (1995). "Differentiating low-achieving students: Thoughts on setting the record straight." *Learning Disabilities Research and Practice, 10,* 140–144.

Bartz, A. E., and Rose, J. "Type A behavior, sex roles, and physical symptom reporting." Midwestern Psychological Association, May 1989.

Bem, S. L. (1974). "The measurement of psychological androgyny." *Journal of Consulting and Clinical Psychology, 42,* 155–162.

Blaske, D. M. (1984). "Occupational sex-typing by kindergarten and fourth-grade children." *Psychological Reports, 54,* 795–801.

Brandt, K. M. (1996). The effect of booktalks on students' attitudes towards reading. Unpublished master's thesis, Moorhead State University, MN.

Cohen, J. (1988). *Statistical Power Analysis for the Behavioral Sciences,* 3rd. ed. Belmont, CA: Wadsworth.

Cohen, J. (1994). "The earth is round ($p < .05$)." *American Psychologist, 49,* 997–1003.

Daniel, W. (1978). *Applied Nonparametric Statistics.* Boston: Houghton Mifflin.

Duke, J. (1978). "Tables to help students grasp size differences in simple correlations." *Teaching of Psychology, 5,* 219–221.

Estes, T. H. (1971). "A scale to measure attitudes towards reading." *Journal of Reading, 15,* 135–138.

Follman, J. (1984). "Cornucopia of correlations." *American Psychologist, 39,* 701–702.

Fox, J. A., Levin. J., and Harkins, S. (1993). *Elementary Statistics in Behavioral Research.* New York: HarperCollins.

Gallagher, E. J., Lombardi, G., and Gennis, P. (1995). "Effectiveness of bystander cardiopulmonary resuscitation and survival following out-of-hospital cardiac arrest." *Journal of the American Medical Association, 274,* 1922–1925.

Glass, D. C. (1977). *Behavior Patterns, Stress, and Coronary Disease.* Hillsdale, NJ: Erlbaum.

Green, P. J., and Suls, J. (1996). "The effects of caffeine on ambulatory blood pressure, heart rate, and mood in coffee drinkers." *Journal of Behavioral Medicine, 19,* 111–128.

Haemig, P. (1984). Enhanced Exploratory Behavior in Island Jays. Unpublished manuscript, Concordia College.

Howell, D. C. (1995). *Fundamental Statistics for the Behavioral Sciences.* Hillsdale, NJ: Erlbaum.

Jenkins, C. D. Zyzanski, S. J., and Rosenman, R. H. (1971). "Progress toward validation of a computer-scored test for the Type A coronary-prone behavior pattern." *Psychosomatic Medicine, 33,* 193–202.

Minium, E. W., King, B. M., and Bear, G. (1993). *Statistical Reasoning in Psychology and Education.* New York: Wiley.

Nelson, M., and Nilsen, K. (1984). Conformity in the Presence and Absence of a Marked Police Vehicle. Unpublished manuscript, Concordia College.

Rosenthal, R. (1990). "How are we doing in soft psychology?" *American Psychologist, 45,* 775–777.

Russell, T. G., Rowe, W., and Smouse, A. D. (1991). "Subliminal self-help tapes and academic achievement: An evaluation." *Journal of Counseling and Development, 69,* 359–362.

Snyder, M. (1974). "Self-monitoring of expressive behavior." *Journal of Personality and Social Psychology, 30,* 526–537.

Terman, L. M., and Merrill, N. (1960). *Stanford-Binet Intelligence Scale.* Boston: Riverside.

Wahler, H. J. (1983). *Wahler Physical Symptoms Inventory Manual.* Los Angeles: Western Psychological Services.

Ysseldyke, J. E., Algozzine, B., Shinn, M. R., and McGue, M. (1982). "Similarities and differences between low achievers and students classified learning disabled." *Journal of Special Education, 16,* 73–75.

APPENDIX 1

Formulas

Name	Formula	First appears on page
Arithmetic mean (3.1)	$\bar{X} = \dfrac{\Sigma X}{N}$	61
Mean—simple frequency distribution (3.2)	$\bar{X} = \dfrac{\Sigma fX}{N}$	64
Population mean (3.3)	$\mu = \dfrac{\Sigma X}{N}$	72
Combined mean (3.4)	$\bar{X} = \dfrac{N_1\bar{X}_1 + N_2\bar{X}_2 + N_3\bar{X}_3 + \cdots}{N_1 + N_2 + N_3 + \cdots}$	72
Standard deviation— deviation formula (4.1)	$s = \sqrt{\dfrac{\Sigma(X - \bar{X})^2}{N - 1}}$	88
Standard deviation— computational formula (4.2)	$s = \sqrt{\dfrac{\Sigma X^2 - \dfrac{(\Sigma X)^2}{N}}{N - 1}}$	90

Name	Formula	First appears on page
z score—sample (4.3)	$z = \dfrac{X - \overline{X}}{s}$	97
z score—population (4.4)	$z = \dfrac{X - \mu}{\sigma}$	98
Semi-interquartile range (4.5)	$Q = \dfrac{P_{75} - P_{25}}{2}$	102
Standard error of the mean—with population standard deviation (6.1)	$\sigma_{\overline{X}} = \dfrac{\sigma}{\sqrt{N}}$	144
z score—sampling distribution of means (6.2)	$z = \dfrac{\overline{X} - \mu_{\overline{X}}}{\sigma_{\overline{X}}}$	146
95% confidence interval for μ using population σ (6.3)	$\overline{X} \pm 1.96\sigma_{\overline{X}}$	151
99% confidence interval for μ using population σ (6.4)	$\overline{X} \pm 2.58\sigma_{\overline{X}}$	151
Pearson r—z score method (7.1)	$r = \dfrac{\Sigma z_X z_Y}{N}$	170
Pearson r—computational formula (7.2)	$r = \dfrac{N\Sigma XY - \Sigma X \Sigma Y}{\sqrt{N\Sigma X^2 - (\Sigma X)^2}\ \sqrt{N\Sigma Y^2 - (\Sigma Y)^2}}$	172
Standard error of Pearson r (7.3)	$s_r = \dfrac{1}{\sqrt{N - 1}}$	175
Spearman rank-difference correlation coefficient (7.4)	$r_s = 1 - \dfrac{6\Sigma D^2}{N(N^2 - 1)}$	178

Name	Formula	First appears on page
Regression equation (8.1)	$Y' = bX + a$	204
Slope (b) (8.2)	$b = \dfrac{N(\Sigma XY) - (\Sigma X)(\Sigma Y)}{N(\Sigma X^2) - (\Sigma X)^2}$	205
Y intercept (a) (8.3)	$a = \bar{Y} - (b)\bar{X}$	205
Standard error of estimate (8.4)	$s_E = s_Y \sqrt{1 - r^2}$	210
68% confidence interval for Y' (8.5)	$Y' \pm s_E \sqrt{1 + \dfrac{1}{N} + \dfrac{(X - \bar{X})^2}{(N - 1)s_X^2}}$	211
z score—sampling distribution of differences (9.1)	$z = \dfrac{(\bar{X}_1 - \bar{X}_2) - 0}{\sigma_{\text{diff}}}$	235
Standard error of the difference between means—population standard deviation (9.2)	$\sigma_{\text{diff}} = \sqrt{\sigma_{\bar{X}1}^2 + \sigma_{\bar{X}2}^2}$	238
Standard error of the difference between means—sample standard deviation (9.3)	$s_{\text{diff}} = \sqrt{\dfrac{(N_1 - 1)s_1^2 + (N_2 - 1)s_2^2}{N_1 + N_2 - 2}\left[\dfrac{1}{N_1} + \dfrac{1}{N_2}\right]}$	239
t test—independent samples (9.4)	$t = \dfrac{\bar{X}_1 - \bar{X}_2 - 0}{s_{\text{diff}}}$	239
Mean of the differences—direct difference method for correlated t test (9.5)	$\bar{D} = \dfrac{\Sigma D}{N}$	249

Name	Formula	First appears on page
Standard deviation—direct difference method for correlated t test (9.6)	$s_D = \sqrt{\dfrac{\Sigma D^2 - \dfrac{(\Sigma D)^2}{N}}{N-1}}$	249
Standard error—direct difference method for correlated t test (9.7)	$s_{\bar{D}} = \dfrac{s_D}{\sqrt{N}}$	251
t test—correlated samples (9.8)	$t = \dfrac{\bar{D}}{s_{\bar{D}}}$	251
Standard error of the mean—with sample standard deviation (9.9)	$s_{\bar{X}} = \dfrac{s}{\sqrt{N}}$	259
95% confidence interval for μ using sample S (9.10)	$\bar{X} \pm t_{05}s_{\bar{X}}$	259
99% confidence interval for μ using sample S (9.11)	$\bar{X} \pm t_{01}s_{\bar{X}}$	260
t for a single sample mean (10.1)	$t = \dfrac{\bar{X} - \mu_{\bar{X}}}{s_{\bar{X}}}$	276
Effect size—one-sample case (10.2)	$d = \dfrac{\mu_{real} - \mu_{hyp}}{\sigma}$	282
Effect size—two-sample case (10.3)	$d = \dfrac{(\mu_1 - \mu_2)_{real} - (\mu_1 - \mu_2)_{hyp}}{\sigma}$	283
Total sum of squares—deviation formula (11.2)	$SS_T = \sum\limits^{k}\sum\limits^{N_G}(X - \bar{X}_T)^2$	293

Name	Formula	First appears on page
Within-groups sum of squares—deviation formula (11.3)	$SS_{WG} = \overset{kN_G}{\Sigma\Sigma}(X - \overline{X}_G)^2$	293
Between-groups sum of squares—deviation formula (11.4)	$SS_{BG} = \overset{k}{\Sigma}N_G(\overline{X}_G - \overline{X}_T)^2$	294
Mean square between groups (11.5)	$MS_{BG} = \dfrac{SS_{BG}}{k-1}$	296
Mean square within groups (11.6)	$MS_{WG} = \dfrac{SS_{WG}}{N_T - k}$	296
F test (11.7)	$F = \dfrac{MS_{BG}}{MS_{WG}}$	298
Total sum of squares—computational formula (11.8)	$SS_T = \overset{N_T}{\Sigma}X^2 - N_T\overline{X}_T^2$	298
Between-groups sum of squares—computational formula (11.9)	$SS_{BG} = N_1\overline{X}_1^2 + N_2\overline{X}_2^2 + N_3\overline{X}_3^2 \\ + \cdots - N_T\overline{X}_T^2$	299
Within-groups sum of squares—computational formula (11.10)	$SS_{WG} = \left(\overset{N_1}{\Sigma}X^2 - N_1\overline{X}_1^2\right) + \left(\overset{N_2}{\Sigma}X^2 - N_2\overline{X}_2^2\right) \\ + \left(\overset{N_3}{\Sigma}X^2 - N_3\overline{X}_3^2\right) + \cdots$	299
Tukey's method—unequal N's (11.11)	$q = \dfrac{\overline{X}_L - \overline{X}_S}{\sqrt{\dfrac{MS_{WG}}{2}\left(\dfrac{1}{N_L} + \dfrac{1}{N_S}\right)}}$	302

Name	Formula	First appears on page
Tukey's method—equal N's (11.12)	$$q = \dfrac{\overline{X}_L - \overline{X}_S}{\sqrt{\dfrac{MS_{WG}}{N_G}}}$$	302
Sum of squares for row variable (12.1)	$$SS_R = N_{R_1}\overline{X}_{R_1}^2 + N_{R_2}\overline{X}_{R_2}^2 + \cdots - N_T\overline{X}_T^2$$	321
Sum of squares for column variable (12.2)	$$SS_C = N_{C_1}\overline{X}_{C_1}^2 + N_{C_2}\overline{X}_{C_2}^2 + \cdots - N_T\overline{X}_T^2$$	322
Sum of squares for interaction (12.3)	$$SS_{R \times C} = SS_{BG} - SS_R - SS_C$$	322
df for rows (12.4)	$$df_R = r - 1$$	322
df for columns (12.5)	$$df_C = c - 1$$	322
df for interaction (12.6)	$$df_{R \times C} = (r - 1)(c - 1)$$	323
Within-groups df (12.7)	$$df_{WG} = N_T - rc$$	323
Mean square for rows (12.8)	$$MS_R = \dfrac{SS_R}{r - 1}$$	323
Mean square for columns (12.9)	$$MS_C = \dfrac{SS_C}{c - 1}$$	323
Mean square for interaction (12.10)	$$MS_{R \times C} = \dfrac{SS_{R \times C}}{(r - 1)(c - 1)}$$	323
Within-groups mean square (12.11)	$$MS_{WG} = \dfrac{SS_{WG}}{N_T - rc}$$	323
F for row effect (12.12)	$$F_R = \dfrac{MS_R}{MS_{WG}}$$	326
F for column effect (12.13)	$$F_C = \dfrac{MS_C}{MS_{WG}}$$	326

Name	Formula	First appears on page
F for interaction effect (12.14)	$$F_{R \times C} = \frac{MS_{R \times C}}{MS_{WG}}$$	326
Chi square (13.1)	$$\chi^2 = \Sigma \frac{(O - E)^2}{E}$$	343
Chi square—2 × 2 table (13.2)	$$\chi^2 = \frac{N(AD - BC)^2}{(A + B)(C + D)(A + C)(B + D)}$$	348
Kruskal–Wallis test (13.3)	$$H = \frac{12}{N(N + 1)} \Sigma \frac{R_G^2}{N_G} - 3(N + 1)$$	355
Friedman analysis of variance (13.4)	$$\chi_r^2 = \frac{12}{Nk(k + 1)} \Sigma (R_G)^2 - 3N(k + 1)$$	363

APPENDIX 2

Basic Mathematics Refresher

OVERVIEW

Statisticians use a fair amount of mathematics in carrying out their work. However, many of the basic concepts in statistics can be learned with only a working knowledge of a first-year high school algebra course. It would be impractical to present a comprehensive survey of your mathematics training up to high school algebra (and there's little chance that you would have the time or energy to plow through it). So this refresher focuses only on those mathematical skills and ideas used in this book.

CONTENT

Introductory sections on estimation and terms are followed by sections on seven major topics: decimals, fractions, percent, signed numbers and absolute values, exponents and square roots, order of operations, and algebra. Depending on your confidence and preparation, you may reference only a single topic or two or work through the entire review.

FORMAT

Discussions on each major topic start with actual problems you will encounter in your text reading. The skills you'll need to handle those and similar problems in the textbook are summarized in the section titled "You'll Need to Know." The next section, "Here's How," provides instruction on methods for solving the given problems. It's critical that you work out some of the examples and exercises to ensure that you gain the needed mathematical tools and have them readily available. Exercises appear at the end of each section to sharpen your skills. The solutions are available at the end of the Appendix.

Statistics can be a fascinating subject. With a minimum amount of review, your mathematic skills can facilitate, rather than hinder, your studies.

SOME HELPFUL HINTS

If you feel your background in mathematics is weak, don't panic. This textbook is "mathematics friendly." A large number of problems are worked out, each complete with many steps to guide even the mathematically timid right to the solution. A very strong feature of this book is its abundance of helpful hints. A lot of time and effort can be saved by making full use of them.

Two hints are worthy of note.

1. Make a rough guess, that is, estimate your answer before attempting any calculation, and then . . .
2. Check your answer and see how reasonable it appears. This is particularly beneficial in your work in statistics. There are numerous ways to assess the plausibility of your answer. Consider the following examples:
   a. A variance is the sum of squared numbers, so it's always non-negative.
   b. A correlation is never less than −1 nor greater than 1.
   c. The size of a standard deviation can be approximated—it will never be greater than the range.

Although these hints may not be very enlightening at this stage, they are presented here so you are aware that there exist many ways you can evaluate your own answers. You will probably come up with many more on your own, as you become comfortable with statistics!

TERMS

Knowing some of the nomenclature of mathematics will make statistics jargon more meaningful for you and formulas easier to remember.

Operations

Operations represent action in mathematics. Familiar operations include addition, subtraction, multiplication, division, and exponentiation.

Sum

A *sum* is a number found by *adding* two or more numbers. In Chapter 1, you use *summation notation* for problems requiring addition. In Chapter 4, you will calculate the "sum of squared deviations," which implies that you will be doing some adding.

Difference

A *difference* is a number found by *subtracting* one number from another. All of Chapter 9 is concerned with examining the difference between means. This difference can, of course, be found by subtracting one mean from another. (You will study more about means in Chapter 3.) The *deviation* is a related concept. The deviation from the mean is also a difference; the difference between an individual score and the mean score. Suppose the mean score for a class on a test is 75. A score of 83 would yield a deviation of 83 − 75, or 8. You'll use this idea repeatedly in statistics.

Product

A *product* is a number found by *multiplying* two numbers. Each of the numbers being multiplied is referred to as a *factor*. Throughout most of this book, you need to multiply when you encounter the symbol "×" or two numbers written like this 10(17) or (10)(17). Often when variables are used, no symbol is used at all. For example, in Table 3.8, $N_1\overline{X}_1$ means multiply N_1 by $\overline{X}_1$.

Quotient

A *quotient* is a number found by *dividing* two numbers. You will need to divide when you encounter the familiar symbol "÷" or a quotient bar as in the problem $\frac{7.5}{3}$ or 1/4. When a quotient bar is used, remember to divide the bottom number, sometimes called the *divisor*, into the top number. So, in our examples, $\frac{7.5}{3}$ is the same as 7.5 ÷ 3 or 2.5 and 1/4 is the same as 1 ÷ 4 or .25. A *ratio* is used to compare two numbers. It may be expressed in words such as 3 to 5, or as a quotient, such as 3/5. You'll see ratios used in your study of probability and *F*-ratios used to compare numbers in your study of ANOVA in Chapter 11.

Power

The *power*, a^n, is the product of *n* factors of *a*. For example, the *power*, 5^2, is the product of 2 factors of 5. It can be found by multiplying 5 × 5 yielding 25. In this example, 5 is the base and 2 is the exponent. Throughout this book, 2 is the exponent you will see most frequently. Typically, the number, 5^2, is read "5 squared." Hence to "square a number" means to multiply it by itself.

Calculator Hint.   This can be done quite easily. To find 5^2, you can punch the keys

$$\boxed{5} \quad \boxed{\times} \quad \boxed{=}$$

This is handy if you do not have an $\boxed{x^2}$ key on your calculator.

USING THE TERMS

To illustrate how you can use your knowledge of mathematical terms to assist you in understanding statistics, consider the notion of the "sum of squared deviations from the mean" for a list of numbers. Let's start with the deviations. Each deviation can be found by *subtracting* the mean from each number. Now you have a list of deviations. Next, each of the deviations needs to be multiplied by itself, resulting in a list of *squared* deviations. Finally, we can add to find the "sum of the squared deviations." So this rather awesome-sounding phrase and its equally intimidating formula can be understood, remembered, and reduced to subtraction, squaring, and adding.

SUMMARY

Operation	Notation	Literal Meaning
Addition	$a + b$	The sum of a and b
Subtraction	$a - b$	The difference of a and b
Multiplication	$a \times b$	The product of a and b;
	$a \cdot b$	a and b are factors
	$a(b)$	
Division	$a \div b$	The quotient of a and b;
	$\dfrac{a}{b}$	the ratio of a to b; a divided by b
	a/b	
Exponentiation	a^n	The nth power of a; the product of n factors of a; a is the base n is the exponent

DECIMALS

You'll find decimals in nearly every problem in this book, so it's worthwhile to learn how to work with them. Even with the availability of calculators, you'll find a good working knowledge of decimals can be a real time-saver and can improve your accuracy. A sampling of problems similar to some that can be found in the text narrative follows.

Example 1 from Chapter 8, $Y' = 11.1 + 6.57$

Example 2 from Chapter 7, $r = 1 - 0.69$

Example 3 from Chapter 5, $z\sigma = 2.58(2.5)$

Example 4 from Chapter 11, $F = \dfrac{30.365}{1.82}$

You'll Need to Know

- How to add and subtract decimal numbers.
- How to multiply and divide decimal numbers.
- How to round off decimal numbers.

Here's How

Before you start any of the problems, get in the habit of making a rough guess for each answer. This is particularly important if you'll be using a calculator.

Estimates.   Example 1 $\cong 11 + 7 = 18$. Example 2 $\cong 1 - 0.7 = 0.3$. Example 3 will be between $2 \times 2 = 4$ and $3 \times 3 = 9$. Example 4 $\cong 30 \div 2 = 15$.

To Add or Subtract Decimal Numbers.   Line up the decimal points and proceed as you would with whole numbers.

line up
↓

Example 1   11.1   There are an infinite number of trailing zeros.
               6.57   Add as many as you need to perform the operation.
              ─────
              17.67

implied
↓

Example 2   1.00   If no decimal appears, it is assumed to be
             −0.69   behind the last digit. For example, 19 is the
             ─────   same as 19. or 19.0 or 19.00.
              0.31

To Multiply Decimal Numbers.   Carry out the calculations ignoring the decimals. To place the decimal point in your answer, count the total number of digits behind the decimal point for each of the numbers involved in the calculation. That will be the total number of digits behind the decimal point in your answer.

Example 3   2.58   2 digits behind decimal point
                 × 2.5   1 digit behind decimal point
                 ─────
                 1290
                  516
                 ─────
                 6.450   3 digits behind decimal point

To Divide Decimal Numbers.   Terms:

$$\frac{\text{quotient}}{\text{divisor)dividend}}$$

Move the decimal point in the divisor to the right so it's behind the last digit.

1.82.)30.36.5   Move the decimal point in the dividend the same number of places. This is where the decimal will appear in the answer.

```
        16.684
182)3036.5        Divide
    182
    ───
    1216
    1092
    ────
    1245
    1092
    ────
    1530
    1456
    ────
     740
     728
    ────
```

The question of when to terminate this seemingly endless task leads to our next topic.

To Round Off Decimal Numbers.   How many places to leave after the decimal may vary depending on the application. For instance, in the last example, we were calculating a value for an F statistic; such values are commonly reported with 2 decimal places. For more information on how many places to include, consult Note 3.2 in Chapter 3. Regardless of how many places you may choose to have beyond the decimal, the technique for rounding is virtually the same.

• Identify the number of places needed.
• Note the digit to the right of the last place you need. If it is 5 or greater, increase the number to its left by 1. If it's less than 5, leave the number to its left as it is.*

---

*There are other methods championed by some, but this method is adequate for most purposes.

Example 4   Suppose that we want to round our answer to two places.

16.68<u>4</u>   note that this digit is less than 5

answer
rounded to   16.68
two places

Suppose that we had arrived at

16.68<u>7</u>   this digit is greater than 5

so our
answer
rounded to
two places
would have
been   16.69

EXERCISES

1. Find the sum, difference, product, and quotient for each of the following pairs of numbers:
   a. 3.5, 1.39
   b. 1.96, 0.85
   c. 5, 3.5
2. $1.39(3.5) + 7.12 =$
3. $.4861 - .3944 =$
4. $\dfrac{37.5}{15} =$
5. $2.33(2.5) =$
6. $102 + 1.96(0.85) =$
7. $1.11(10) + 6.57 =$
8. $93.5 + \left(\dfrac{8.5 - 6}{3}\right)$

FRACTIONS

Example 1

$$\frac{(O - E)^2}{E} = \frac{64}{7}$$

Solving this problem in Chapter 13 does not require any extensive knowledge of the arithmetic of fractions. This statement also generally holds true for most of the other problems involving fractions in this book. As in the case in the majority of real-life applications, the fraction in our example would be converted to a decimal number with the much appreciated aid of a calculator. Converting fractions to decimals will also be used in your work with probabilities in Chapter 5. Once fractions have been converted to decimals, you need only know how to perform operations with decimals to finish up your calculations. Even so, some of your work in this book can be simplified if you know how to reduce, add, and multiply with fractions.

More examples involving fractions from the text follow.

Example 2

$$r_s = 1 - \frac{2,334}{3,360}$$

Example 3

$$\sqrt{\frac{5.9 + 28.9}{18} \left(\frac{1}{10} + \frac{1}{10} \right)}$$

Example 4

$$\sqrt{\frac{12(3.75) + 10(1.21)}{12 + 10 - 2} \left(\frac{1}{12} + \frac{1}{10} \right)}$$

Example 5

"To check your calculations, take $\frac{1}{4}$ of 14"

You'll Need to Know

• How to convert a fraction to a decimal.

Here's How

To Convert a Fraction to a Decimal.   Divide the numbers *below* the quotient bar *into* the number *above* the quotient bar.

Example 1

$$\frac{64}{7} \text{ is the same as } 64 \div 7.$$

$$\begin{array}{r} 9.1428 \ . \ . \ . \\ 7\overline{)64.} \end{array}$$

You can use the same method discussed in the decimals section to round this nonterminating decimal. So

$$\frac{(O - E)^2}{E} = \frac{64}{7} = 9.14$$

Example 2   2,334/3,360 is the same as 2,334 ÷ 3,360.

$$3,360\overline{)2,334.}\quad\overset{.694\ldots}{}$$

So, $r_s = 1 - .69 = .31$

It's Nice to Know

- How to add fractions.
- How to multiply fractions.

Here's How

To Add or Subtract Fractions.   You need a common denominator. Then, you can add (or subtract) the numerators. With this information in hand, you can save yourself a little work on Example 3 and avoid a common error on Example 4.

Example 3   (1/10 + 1/10)   Since you have a common denominator, you can add the numerators and write

(2/10).   Then convert to a decimal and finish the calculations.

Example 4   (1/12 + 1/10)   There is not a common denominator here, so you cannot add yet.

A convenient approach here, if you're working with a calculator, is to convert each fraction to a decimal.

(0.083 + .100)

To Multiply Fractions

1. Multiply the numerators.
2. Multiply the denominators.
3. Divide.

Example 5 $\frac{1}{4}$ of 14

"of" can be translated as multiplication

$\frac{1}{4} \downarrow \frac{14}{1}$

↑—— any whole number can be written in fractional form in this way

$\frac{1 \cdot 14}{4 \cdot 1} = \frac{14}{4}$ is the same as 14 ÷ 4 or 3.5

EXERCISES

Write your answers using decimal numbers. Round to two decimal places, when necessary.

1. 1/6 =
2. 12/14 =
3. 30/8 =
4. $\dfrac{89 \times 29}{172}$ =
5. 1/4 of 64
6. 1/5 of 64
7. 1/6 + 1/6
8. 1/6 + 1/3
9. 1/3 + 1/5

PERCENTS

You'll find that applications of the notion of percent keep appearing throughout your study of probability and statistics in a variety of forms. The word "per cent" is derived from the Latin "per centum" meaning "for a hundred." Technically, everywhere you read "percent" you could translate it to "hundredths." So, 57% could also be written as 57/100. Therefore, if you take a proportion in decimal form and multiply it by 100, you'll obtain a percent. Similarly, if you want to convert a percent back to a proportion, you need only divide by 100. Advantages of using percents are that the concept is widely understood and it allows for numerous, diverse comparisons to be made. Percents are used in this book in some of the following ways:

Example 1   In Chapter 5, the probability of rolling a "4" in one toss of the die is said to be 1/6. What percentage of the time can we expect to observe a "4" in the long run? That is, convert the proportion 1/6 to a percent.

Example 2   From Chapter 5, if 3.01% of the people in a population have an IQ less than 70, approximately how many with this low IQ would you expect to find in a sample of 15,000? That is, find 3.01% of 15,000.

Example 3   In Chapter 2, while calculating cumulative percentages, you need to determine what percent of sixty 52 represents.

Example 4   If 15 persons constitute the top 2% of all graduates at a college, what is the size of the graduating class?

All of the percent problems you deal with in this text can be transformed into the following:

$$a \text{ is } n \text{ percent of } b$$

$$a = \frac{n}{100} \cdot b$$

part   whole

You'll Need to Know

- How to convert a proportion to a percent.
- How to convert a percent to a proportion.
- How to find the "part" given the percent amount and "whole" amount.
- How to find the percent amount given the "part" and "whole" amounts.
- How to find the "whole" given the "part" and the percent amounts.

Here's How

To Convert a Proportion to a Percent

- Convert the proportion to a decimal.
- Multiply by 100.

    Example 1   1/6 can be converted and rounded off to 0.17
                    .17 × 100 = 17%

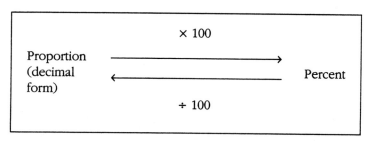

Estimation can also be very helpful in working percent problems. *Before* you do any calculating, guess a "ballpark" figure for your answer.

To Find the "Part" Given the Percent and "Whole"

- Identify the percent amount, n, and the "whole" amount, b, and plug in the equation.
- Solve for a.

Example 2

$$a = \frac{3.01}{100} \cdot 15,000$$

$$= 0.0301 \cdot 15,000$$

$$= 451.5$$

To Find the Percent Amount Given the "Part" and "Whole" Amounts

- Identify the "part," a, and "whole," b, amounts and plug in the equation.
- Solve for n.

Example 3

$$52 = \frac{n}{100} \cdot 60$$

$$52 = n \cdot \frac{60}{100}$$

$$52 = n \cdot 0.6$$

$$\frac{52}{0.6} = n \qquad \text{Divide both sides by 0.6.}$$

$$86.7\% = n$$

To Find the "Whole" Amount Given the "Part" and Percent Amounts

- Identify the "part" and percent amounts and plug them into the equation.
- Solve for b.

Example 4

$$15 = \frac{2}{100} \cdot b$$

$$15 = 0.02 \cdot b$$

$$\frac{15}{.02} = \frac{0.02 \cdot b}{.02} \qquad \text{Divide both sides by 0.02.}$$

$$750 = b$$

Another method for solving percent problems that does not lend itself quite so readily to the word problems is the ratio-proportion method.

$$\frac{a}{b} = \frac{n}{100}$$

Cross multiplying, $100 \cdot a = b \cdot n$, where a, b, and n have the same interpretations as previously discussed.

If you are more comfortable with this method, by all means continue to use it. The important points are

1. To make a rough guess beforehand and later check your answer to see if it is consistent with your guess.
2. To become adept at setting up and solving percent problems.

EXERCISES

Make an estimate before calculating each answer.
1. Express 1/9 as a percent.
2. Express 5/7 as a percent.
3. Express 0.0062 as a percent.
4. Express 0.0301 as a percent.
5. Express 37% as a proportion
6. Express 125% as a proportion.
7. Express 0.5% as a proportion.
8. Express 12.14% as a proportion.
9. Determine 65% of 50.
10. Determine 25% of 120.
11. Determine 80% of 410.
12. Determine 0.3% of 200.
13. What percent of 50 is 13?
14. What percent of 480 is 200?
15. What percent of 10,000 is 2?
16. What percent of 15,000 is 9?
17. If 31 represents 90 percent of the students in the class, what is the total number of students in the class?
18. If 146 represents 15 percent of the gifted persons in a population, how many persons are there in the population?

SIGNED NUMBERS AND ABSOLUTE VALUE

You have, no doubt, been introduced, at one time, to the idea that every number has an opposite. For example, the opposite of 5 is –5. The opposite of –1.2 is 1.2, and so on. In statistics, it will be important to recall how these signed numbers appear on a number line as well as how to perform the basic operations with them. Absolute values will assist us in this discussion, but will also be of interest in their own right in a few statistical applications.

Example 1

X	$X - \overline{X}$	$|X - \overline{X}|$
14	$14 - 12 = 2$	2
12	$12 - 12 = 0$	0
9	$9 - 12 = -3$	3
17	$17 - 12 = 5$	5
8	$8 - 12 = -4$	4

Example 2

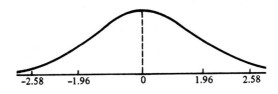

Example 3

$$z = \frac{2 - 6}{2.68} =$$

Example 4

$$\chi^2 = \frac{(|2 - 10| - 1)^2}{2 + 10} =$$

You'll Need to Know

- How to find the absolute value of a number.
- How to locate signed numbers along a number line.
- How to add, subtract, multiply, and divide signed numbers.

Here's How

To Find the Absolute Value. Determine the magnitude of the number without regard to its sign. *Hint:* An absolute value will always be non-negative.

Example 1

$$|2| = 2$$
$$|0| = 0$$
$$|-3| = 3$$

and so on.

To Locate Signed Numbers along a Number Line
- Recall that all negative numbers are to the left of zero and all positive are to the right.

- The absolute value of a number indicates the number of units the point is from zero.

  Example 2

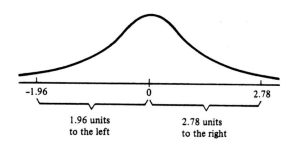

To Subtract Signed Numbers
- Write as addition problems and follow the rules for adding the following signed numbers.

  Example 1 [continued]

  $$14 - 12 = 14 + -12$$
  $$12 - 12 = 12 + -12$$
  $$9 - 12 = 9 + -12$$
  $$17 - 12 = 17 + -12$$
  $$8 - 12 = 8 + -12$$

To Add Signed Numbers
- If the signs are the same, add as always and attach the common sign. For example,

  $$-3 + -4 = -7$$
  $$5 + 6 = 11$$

- If the signs are different, subtract and attach the sign of the number with the larger absolute value.

Example 1 [continued]

$$14 + -12 = 2 \qquad |14| \text{ is the larger}$$

$$12 + -12 = 0$$

$$9 + -12 = -3 \quad |-12| \text{ is the larger}$$

$$17 + -12 = 5$$

$$8 + -12 = -4$$

To Multiply or Divide Signed Numbers

- Proceed as always working with the absolute values.
- To determine the sign of the answer: If both signs are the *same,* the answer is *positive.*

$$\frac{-10}{-2} = 5 \quad \text{or} \quad 4/5 = 0.8$$

- If the signs differ, the answer is *negative.*

$$\frac{-10}{2} = -5 \quad \text{or} \quad \frac{4}{-5} = -0.8$$

Example 3

$$Z = \frac{2 - 6}{2.68} = \frac{2 + -6}{2.68} = \frac{-4}{2.68} = -1.49$$

Example 4

$$\chi^2 = \frac{(|2 + -10| - 1)^2}{12}$$

$$= \frac{(|-8| - 1)^2}{12}$$

$$= \frac{(8 - 1)^2}{12}$$

$$= \frac{(7)^2}{12}$$

$$= \frac{49}{12} = 4.08$$

EXERCISES

1. Find the sum of the following deviations:

$$2, 0, -3, 5, -4$$

2. Find the difference of the chemistry and biology scores for each of the students.

	Chemistry Score	Biology Score	Difference
Student 1	73.5	73.9	
2	74.6	72.1	
3	72.8	71.3	
4	73.4	74.6	
5	72.9	72.9	

3. Multiply $-1.96(0.85) =$

4. Multiply $-2.58(0.36) =$

5. Multiply $-3(-3) =$

6. Multiply $-4(-4) =$

7. $\dfrac{62 - 72}{8} =$

8. $\dfrac{437 - 500}{100} =$

9.

X	$X - 12$	$|X - 12|$
14		
12		
9		
17		
8		

EXPONENTS AND SQUARE ROOTS

The widespread use of calculators has dramatically improved the way exponents and square roots are handled. Students of statistics will appreciate these improvements, since statisticians make frequent use of exponents and square roots.

In addition to learning the definitions, one of your primary tasks here will be to master the proper operation of your calculator. As with all your calculator work, make an estimate before you start. Then check to see if your calculated answer is consistent with your estimate.

Example 1

X	$(X - \bar{X})$	$(X - \bar{X})^2$
6	1	1
8	3	9
2	-3	9

Example 2

$$S = 3.38 \text{ so } S^2 = (3.38)^2 =$$

Example 3

$$S = \sqrt{\frac{30}{8}} = \sqrt{3.75} =$$

You'll Need to Know

- How to "square" a number.
- How to find the square root of a number.

Here's How

To Square a Number

- Multiply it by itself

$$7^2 \text{ is the same as } 7 \cdot 7 \text{ or } 49$$

$$(-4)^2 \text{ is the same as } -4 \cdot -4 \text{ or } 16$$

Hint: Squared numbers are always positive (except for 0^2).

Example 1

$$1^2 = 1 \cdot 1 = 1$$

$$3^2 = 3 \cdot 3 = 9$$

$$(-3)^2 = -3 \cdot -3 = 9$$

Example 2 $(3.38)^2$ can be rounded to 11.42.

Terminology

Radical sign $\sqrt{25}$ Radicand

To Find the Square Root of a Number

- Find the number that multiplied by itself yields the radicand

$$\sqrt{25} \text{ is the same as } \pm5$$

since $5 \cdot 5$ is 25 or $(-5) \cdot (-5)$ is $25^\dagger$

- Or use a calculator with a $\boxed{\sqrt{x}}$ key.

---

†In this book, we will be concerned only with positive square roots.

Example 3

$\sqrt{\dfrac{30}{8}}$ is the same as $\sqrt{3.75}$. Using a calculator $\sqrt{3.75}$ can be rounded to 1.94.

EXERCISES

1. $S = 1.94$. Find S^2.
2. $S = 6.34$. Find S^2.
3. Evaluate $\sqrt{720}$.
4. Evaluate $\sqrt{16/40}$.

ORDER OF OPERATIONS

For a sample problem, let us evaluate the expression

$$69.5 + \dfrac{37.5}{15} =$$

Use your calculator to evaluate (find the number for) this expression. If you first divided 37.5 by 15 to obtain 2.5, and then added this result to 69.5, you would have correctly found the expression equal to 72.

If this isn't the answer you calculated, read on. Many a person will innocently (and incorrectly) add 69.5 to 37.5 and then divide the result (107) by 15. Their (wrong) answer of 7.13 suggests some ambiguity inherent in mathematics notation.

Both parties could argue that their calculations were done without error. How does one determine, then, which answer is the correct one? Mathematicians solved this dilemma by agreeing to perform the operations in a specific order.

You'll Need to Know

• Which order to perform the operations of exponentiation, multiplication, division, addition, and subtraction.

Here's How

To perform the operations in the correct order, work from left to right. First, do all the work inside parentheses, then evaluate all the exponents and square roots, and then carry out all the multiplication and division. Finally, you can perform all addition and subtraction.

Back to Our Sample Problem. We need to add and we need to divide.

$$69.5 + \dfrac{37.5}{15}.$$

SUMMARY

Parentheses	First
Exponents and Square Roots	
Multiplication and Division	
Addition and Subtraction	Last

The established order of operations instructs us to divide first and then add. So, 72 is the correct value for the expression.

TRY THESE EXERCISES

1. $1.11(10) + 6.57 =$

Multiply, to obtain

$$11.1 + 6.57 =$$

Then, add

$$11.1 + 6.57 = 17.67$$

2. $\dfrac{\dfrac{973}{15} - (7.73)(7.47)}{(4.03)(2.24)} =$

Parentheses are implied above and below the quotient bar, so evaluate what you have above and below the bar first, then divide.
Above: Carry out the division and multiplication first

$$64.87 - 57.74$$

Then subtract to obtain 7.13
Below:

$$(4.03)(2.24) = 9.03$$

So, we have:

$$\frac{7.13}{9.03} = 0.74$$

3. $\dfrac{3}{\sqrt{100 - 1}} =$

Be sure and carry out the subtraction under the radical *before* taking the square root.

$$\frac{3}{\sqrt{99}} = 3/9.95 = 0.30$$

4. $\dfrac{1}{10} \sqrt{10(432) - (60)^2}$

Again make sure the work under the radical is done *before* finding the square root. Under the radical use the same order discussed.

Under the radical:
Exponentiation first

$$\frac{1}{10} \sqrt{10(432) - 3{,}600}$$

Then multiplication

$$\frac{1}{10} \sqrt{4{,}320 - 3{,}600}$$

Finally, subtraction

$$\frac{1}{10} \sqrt{720}$$

Now take the square root

$$\frac{1}{10}\,(26.83)$$

Divide

$$2.68$$

FOR MORE PRACTICE

1. $72 + 5\left(\dfrac{-30}{50}\right)$

2. $59.5 + 5\,(1/14)$

3. $1.11(16) + 6.57$

4. $93.5 + \left(\dfrac{8.5 - 6}{3}\right)$

5. $\dfrac{9 - 6}{2.68}$

6. $\dfrac{437 - 500}{100}$

7. $\dfrac{10(17) + 30(20) + 40(23)}{10 + 30 + 40}$

8. $\sqrt{\dfrac{432}{10} - (6)^2}$

9. $15(6.0)^2 + 15(3.33)^2 - 30(4.67)^2$

10. $\dfrac{15(973) - (116)(112)}{\sqrt{15(1{,}140) -\ 116^2}\ \sqrt{15(912) - (112)^2}}$

11. Find S given $S = \dfrac{1}{10} \sqrt{10(10{,}677) - (325)^2}$

12. $S = \sqrt{\dfrac{432}{10} - (6)^2}$

13. $q = \dfrac{9 - 6.4}{\sqrt{\dfrac{8.7}{2}\left(\dfrac{1}{6} + \dfrac{1}{5}\right)}}$

14. $r = \dfrac{10(2,799) - (130)(210)}{\sqrt{10(1,752) - (130)^2} \, \sqrt{10(4,498) - (210)^2}}$

15. $S_E = 0.67 \sqrt{1 - (.53)^2}$

EXERCISE FOR FUN

$$\frac{12}{28(28 + 1)} \left[\frac{(72.5)^2}{9} + \frac{(71.5)^2}{7} + \frac{(114.5)^2}{6} + \frac{(147.5)^2}{6} \right] - 3(28 + 1)$$

ALGEBRA

You should be pleased to find out that you actually will have a chance to put your high school training in algebra to work in statistics!

While studying algebra, you gained some skills in working with symbols. No matter how accomplished you may have become with symbols, you'll find statistics easier and more interesting if you recognize that symbols are used as an efficient way to communicate an idea. When working with symbols, you may find it helpful to translate the ideas into words. Here's an example:

$$\overline{X} = \frac{\Sigma X}{N}$$

Translation:

$\overline{X}$	$=$	Σ	X	$\div$	N
↓	↓	↓	↓	↓	↓

"The mean is the sum of the observations divided by the number of observations."

Not only will the "translations" make the formulas easier to remember and use, but the concepts and similarities among the formulas will become apparent.

Chapter 1 begins with a discussion of one of the most fundamental concepts in statistics: variables. Statisticians use the concept of a variable in very specific ways, but the general notion of variables you are familiar with will be helpful in statistics.

Terms

- A *variable* is a letter used to represent a set of numbers. In statistics, variables are used to denote quantities that may vary, such as test scores, IQ, or weight.

- A *formula* is an equation relating two or more variables. You'll find an entire section of the Appendix devoted entirely to formulas used in statistics. The next examples from the text illustrate some uses of formulas in statistics.

- *Inequalities* are statements involving the *greater than*, >, or *less than*, <, symbols. In elementary statistics, inequalities are used to describe the size of some values, such as $p < .01$, and to define an interval, such as the confidence intervals in Chapter 6.

Example 1   The formula for the combined mean is

$$\overline{X} = \frac{N_1 \overline{X}_1 + N_2 \overline{X}_2 + N_3 \overline{X}_3 + \cdots}{N_1 + N_2 + N_3 + \cdots}$$

Find the combined mean, $\overline{X}$, given

$$N_1 = 10 \qquad N_2 = 30 \qquad N_3 = 40$$

$$\overline{X}_1 = 17 \qquad \overline{X}_2 = 20 \qquad \overline{X}_3 = 23 \qquad \text{[Chapter 3]}$$

Example 2   Given the formula

$$z = \frac{X - \overline{X}}{s}$$

Find X in terms of z, $\overline{X}$, and s.   [Chapter 4]

    Example 3

Suppose that $Y' = 1.11X + 6.57$
What does the graph look like?   [Chapter 8]
What is Y' when X is 10?

You'll Need to Know

- How to perform a substitution, that is, find the value of one variable given specific numerical values for the other variables in a formula.
- How to solve a formula for one of the variables in terms of the others.
- How to recognize a linear equation, identify the slope of its graph, and use the equation to find other points on the line.

Here's How

To Perform a Substitution
- Plug the given numerical values in for each corresponding letter and carry out the calculations.

    Example 1

$$\overline{X} = \frac{10(17) + 30(20) + 40(23)}{10 + 30 + 40}$$

$$= \frac{170 + 600 + 920}{80}$$

$$= \frac{1690}{80}$$

$$= 21.125$$

To Solve a Formula for One Variable in Terms of the Other Variables

- Isolate the variable of interest on one side of the equation by using one or more of the following operations:

  a. Multiply (or divide) both sides by the same nonzero quantity.

  b. Add (or subtract) the same quantity from each side of the equation.

  Example 2

$$z = \frac{X - \overline{X}}{s} \qquad \text{solve for } X$$

$$z(s) = X - \overline{X} \qquad \text{multiply both sides by } s$$

$$z(s) + \overline{X} = X - \overline{X} + \overline{X} \qquad \text{add } \overline{X} \text{ to each side}$$

$$z(s) + \overline{X} = X$$

To Work with a Linear Equation

- The graph of all linear equations is a line.
- Equations that can be written in the form $y = bX + a$, where b is the slope and a is the y-intercept (the place where the line crosses the y-axis), are referred to as linear equations. In our example, $Y' = 1.11X + 6.57$. The graph of all ordered pairs (X, Y'), which satisfies this equation is a straight line with a slope of 1.11 crossing the y-axis at 6.57.
- To find Y' when $X = 10$, just plug 10 in for X in the equation and calculate.

  Example 3

$$Y' = 1.11(10) + 6.57$$

$$Y' = 11.1 + 6.57$$

$$Y' = 17.67$$

So the ordered pair (10, 17.67) represents another point on the line.

EXERCISES

1. Use the combined mean formula given in Example 1 to determine the value of the combined mean when

$N_1 = 42$	$N_2 = 15$	$N_3 = 9$	$N_4 = 14$	
$\overline{X}_1 = 26{,}800$	$\overline{X}_2 = 20{,}480$	$\overline{X}_3 = 36{,}600$	$\overline{X}_4 = 18{,}900$	[Chapter 3]

2. If $r = \dfrac{N\Sigma XY - \Sigma X\Sigma Y}{\sqrt{N\Sigma X^2 - (\Sigma X)^2}\ \sqrt{N\Sigma Y^2 - (\Sigma Y)^2}}$

and

$$\Sigma X = 130 \qquad \Sigma Y = 210$$
$$\Sigma X^2 = 1{,}752 \qquad \Sigma Y^2 = 4{,}498$$
$$\Sigma XY = 2{,}799 \qquad N = 10,\ \text{find}\ r$$

3. If $s_{\text{diff}} = \sqrt{\dfrac{(N_1 - 1)s_1^2 + (N_2 - 1)s_2^2}{N_1 + N_2 - 2}\left[\dfrac{1}{N_1} + \dfrac{1}{N_2}\right]}$

and

$$N_1 = 14$$
$$N_2 = 13$$
$$s_1 = 5.38$$
$$s_2 = 5.70,\ \text{find}\ s_{\text{diff}}$$

4. If $z = \dfrac{X - \mu}{\sigma}$, find X in terms of z, σ, and μ.   [Chapter 5]

5. Show that $N_T - 1 = (k - 1) + (N_T - k)$ [Chapter 11]

6. Given the formula

$$\chi^2 = \dfrac{N(AD - BC)^2}{(A + B)(C + D)(A + C)(B + D)}$$

calculate the value of χ^2 if

$A = 12$

$B = 19$

$C = 28$

$D = 6$

$N = 65$

7. $p < .01$. The actual value of p could be
   a. .15.
   b. .07.
   c. .021.
   d. .003.

8. $p > .10$. The actual value of p could be
   a. .15.
   b. .07.
   c. .021.
   d. .003.

EXERCISE SOLUTIONS

DECIMALS

1.	Sum	Difference	Product	Quotient
a.	4.89	2.11	4.865	2.52
b.	2.81	1.11	1.666	2.31
c.	8.5	1.5	17.5	1.43

2. 11.985
3. 0.0917
4. 2.5
5. 5.825
6. $102 + 1.666 = 103.666$
7. $11.1 + 6.57 = 17.67$
8. $93.5 + \dfrac{2.5}{3} = 93.5 + 0.83 = 94.33$

FRACTIONS

1. 0.17
2. 0.86
3. 3.75
4. $\dfrac{89 \times 29}{172} = \dfrac{2{,}581}{172} = 15.01$
5. $1/4 \cdot 64 = \dfrac{64}{4} = 16$
6. $1/5 \cdot 64 = \dfrac{64}{5} = 12.8$
7. $2/6 = 0.33$
8. $0.17 + 0.33 = 0.5$
9. $0.33 + 0.2 = 0.53$

PERCENTS

1. $0.1111 \times 100 = 11.11\%$
2. $0.7143 \times 100 = 71.43\%$
3. $0.0062 \times 100 = 0.62\%$

4. $0.0301 \times 100 = 3.01\%$

5. $37/100$ or 0.37

6. $125/100$ or 1.25

7. $\dfrac{.5}{100}$ or 0.005

8. $\dfrac{12.14}{100}$ or 0.1214

9. $65/100 \times 50 = .5 \times 65 = 32.5$

10. $25/100 \times 120 = .25 \times 120 = 30$

11. $80/100 \times 410 = .80 \times 410 = 328$

12. $\dfrac{.3}{100} \times 200 = .003 \times 200 = 0.6$

13. $13 = \dfrac{n}{100} \times 50 \qquad n = \dfrac{13}{.5} = 26\%$

14. $200 = \dfrac{n}{100} \times 480 \qquad 200 = 4.8n \qquad N = \dfrac{200}{4.8} = 41.67\%$

15. $2 = \dfrac{n}{100} \times 10,000 \qquad 2 = 100n \qquad n = \dfrac{2}{100} = 0.02\%$

16. $9 = \dfrac{n}{1.00} \times 15,000 \qquad 9 = 150n \qquad n = \dfrac{9}{150} = 0.06\%$

17. $31 = 90/100 \times b \qquad 31 = .9b \qquad b = \dfrac{31}{.9} = 34.44$ students

18. $146 = 15/100 \times b \qquad 146 = .15b \qquad b = \dfrac{146}{.15} = 973.33$ persons

---

SIGNED NUMBERS AND ABSOLUTE VALUES

1. $2 + 0 + (-3) + 5 + (-4) = 0$

2. $73.5 - 73.9 = -0.4$
   $74.6 - 72.1 = 2.5$
   $72.8 - 71.3 = 1.5$
   $73.4 - 74.6 = -1.2$
   $72.9 - 72.9 = 0$

3. -1.666

4. -0.9288

5. 9

6. 16

7. $\dfrac{62 + -72}{8} = \dfrac{-10}{8} = -1.25$

8. $\dfrac{437 + -500}{100} = \dfrac{-63}{100} = -0.63$

9.

X	$X - 12$	$\|X - 12\|$
14	2	2
12	0	0
9	-3	3
17	5	5
8	-4	4

EXPONENTS AND SQUARE ROOTS

1. $S^2 = (1.94)^2 = 3.7636$
2. $S^2 = (6.34)^2 = 40.1956$
3. 26.83
4. $\sqrt{\dfrac{16}{40}} = \sqrt{0.4} = 0.63$

ORDER OF OPERATIONS

1. $72 + \dfrac{-150}{50} = 72 + (-3) = 69$

2. $59.5 + \dfrac{5}{14} = 59.5 + 0.36 = 59.86$

3. $17.76 + 6.57 = 24.33$

4. $93.5 + \dfrac{2.5}{3} = 93.5 + 0.83 = 94.33$

5. $\dfrac{3}{2.68} = 1.12$

6. $\dfrac{-63}{100} = -0.63$

7. $\dfrac{170 + 600 + 920}{80} = \dfrac{1,690}{80} = 21.125$

8. $\sqrt{43.2 - 36} = \sqrt{7.2} = 2.68$

9. $15(36) + 15(11.0889) + -30(21.8089) = 540 + 166.3335 + (-654.267)$
$$= 52.0665$$

10. $\dfrac{14,595 - 12,992}{\sqrt{17,100 - 13,456}\ \sqrt{13,680 - 12,544}} = \dfrac{1,603}{\sqrt{3,644}\ \sqrt{1,136}}$

$\dfrac{1,603}{(60.37)(33.70)} = \dfrac{1,603}{2,034.47} = 0.79$

11. $S = 1/10\sqrt{106,770 - 105,625} = 1/10\sqrt{1,145} = \dfrac{33.84}{10} = 3.38$

12. $S = \sqrt{43.2 - 36} = \sqrt{7.2} = 2.68$

13. $q = \dfrac{2.6}{\sqrt{4.35(0.17 + 0.20)}} = \dfrac{2.6}{\sqrt{4.35(0.37)}}$

$\quad = \dfrac{2.6}{\sqrt{1.61}} = \dfrac{2.6}{1.27} = 2.05$

14. $r = \dfrac{27,990 - 27,300}{\sqrt{17,520 - 16,900}\ \sqrt{44,980 - 44,100}}$

$\quad = \dfrac{690}{\sqrt{620}\ \sqrt{880}} = \dfrac{690}{(24.90)(29.66)} = \dfrac{690}{738.53} = 0.93$

15. $S_E = 0.67\sqrt{1 - 0.28}$
$\quad = 0.67\sqrt{0.72}$
$\quad = 0.67(0.85)$
$\quad = 0.57$

EXERCISE FOR FUN

$$12/812(584.03 + 730.32 + 2,185.04 + 3,626.04) - 87$$
$$= 0.0148(7,125.43) - 87$$
$$= 105.46 - 87$$
$$= 18.46$$

ALGEBRA

1. $\overline{X} = \dfrac{42(26,800) + 15(20,480) + 9(36,600) + 14(18,900)}{42 + 15 + 9 + 14}$

$\quad = \dfrac{1,125,600 + 307,200 + 329,400 + 264,600}{80}$

$\quad = \dfrac{2,026,800}{80} = 25,335$

2. $r = \dfrac{10(2,799) - (130)(210)}{\sqrt{10(1,752) - (130)^2}\ \sqrt{10(4,498) - (210)^2}}$

$\quad = \dfrac{27,990 - 27,300}{\sqrt{17,520 - 16,900}\ \sqrt{44,980 - 44,100}}$

$\quad = \dfrac{690}{\sqrt{620}\ \sqrt{880}} = \dfrac{690}{(24.90)(29.66)}$

$\quad = \dfrac{690}{738.53} = .93$

3. $S_{\text{diff}} = \sqrt{\dfrac{(14 - 1)(5.38)^2 + (13 - 1)(5.70)^2}{14 + 13 - 2} \left(\dfrac{1}{14} + \dfrac{1}{13} \right)}$

$\phantom{S_{\text{diff}}} = \sqrt{\dfrac{376.2772 + 389.88}{25} \,(.0714 + .0769)}$

$\phantom{S_{\text{diff}}} = \sqrt{30.6463(0.1483)}$

$\phantom{S_{\text{diff}}} = \sqrt{4.5448}$

$\phantom{S_{\text{diff}}} = 2.13$

4. $z\sigma = X - \mu$ multiplying both sides by σ

$\mu + z\sigma = X$ adding μ to each side

5. $N_T - 1 = N_T - 1 + (k - k)$ rearranging terms on the right-hand side

6. $\chi^2 = \dfrac{65(12 \cdot 6 - 19 \cdot 28)^2}{(12 + 19)(28 + 6)(12 + 28)(19 + 6)}$

$ = \dfrac{65(-460)^2}{31 \cdot 34 \cdot 40 \cdot 25}$

$ = \dfrac{13,754,000}{(1,054)(1,000)}$

$ = 13.05$

7. d

8. a

APPENDIX 3

Statistical Tables

A. Areas Under the Normal Curve between the Mean and z

B. Values of r for the .05 and .01 Levels of Significance

C. Values of Spearman r_s for the .05 and .01 Levels of Significance

D. Values of t at the .05, .01, and .001 Levels of Significance

E. Values of F at the 5% and 1% Levels of Significance

F. Values of Chi Square at the .05, .01, and .001 Levels of Significance

G. Probabilities Associated with Values as Small as Observed Values of U in the Mann–Whitney U Test

H. Critical Values of U in the Mann–Whitney U Test

I. Probabilities Associated with Values as Small as Observed Values of x in the Binomial Test

J. Critical Values of T in the Wilcoxon Matched-Pairs Signed-Ranks Test

K. Random Numbers

L. Critical Values of the Studentized Range Statistic, q

Table A
Areas under the normal curve between the mean and z

z	Area from Mean to z	z	Area from Mean to z	z	Area from Mean to z
0.00	.0000	0.35	.1368	0.70	.2580
0.01	.0040	0.36	.1406	0.71	.2611
0.02	.0080	0.37	.1443	0.72	.2642
0.03	.0120	0.38	.1480	0.73	.2673
0.04	.0160	0.39	.1517	0.74	.2704
0.05	.0199	0.40	.1554	0.75	.2734
0.06	.0239	0.41	.1591	0.76	.2764
0.07	.0279	0.42	.1628	0.77	.2794
0.08	.0319	0.43	.1664	0.78	.2823
0.09	.0359	0.44	.1700	0.79	.2852
0.10	.0398	0.45	.1736	0.80	.2881
0.11	.0438	0.46	.1772	0.81	.2910
0.12	.0478	0.47	.1808	0.82	.2939
0.13	.0517	0.48	.1844	0.83	.2967
0.14	.0557	0.49	.1879	0.84	.2995
0.15	.0596	0.50	.1915	0.85	.3023
0.16	.0636	0.51	.1950	0.86	.3051
0.17	.0675	0.52	.1985	0.87	.3078
0.18	.0714	0.53	.2019	0.88	.3106
0.19	.0753	0.54	.2054	0.89	.3133
0.20	.0793	0.55	.2088	0.90	.3159
0.21	.0832	0.56	.2123	0.91	.3186
0.22	.0871	0.57	.2157	0.92	.3212
0.23	.0910	0.58	.2190	0.93	.3238
0.24	.0948	0.59	.2224	0.94	.3264
0.25	.0987	0.60	.2257	0.95	.3289
0.26	.1026	0.61	.2291	0.96	.3315
0.27	.1064	0.62	.2324	0.97	.3340
0.28	.1103	0.63	.2357	0.98	.3365
0.29	.1141	0.64	.2389	0.99	.3389
0.30	.1179	0.65	.2422	1.00	.3413
0.31	.1217	0.66	.2454	1.01	.3438
0.32	.1255	0.67	.2486	1.02	.3461
0.33	.1293	0.68	.2517	1.03	.3485
0.34	.1331	0.69	.2549	1.04	.3508

Table A. (continued)

z	Area from Mean to z	z	Area from Mean to z	z	Area from Mean to z
1.05	.3531	1.40	.4192	1.75	.4599
1.06	.3554	1.41	.4207	1.76	.4608
1.07	.3577	1.42	.4222	1.77	.4616
1.08	.3599	1.43	.4236	1.78	.4625
1.09	.3621	1.44	.4251	1.79	.4633
1.10	.3643	1.45	.4265	1.80	.4641
1.11	.3665	1.46	.4279	1.81	.4649
1.12	.3686	1.47	.4292	1.82	.4656
1.13	.3708	1.48	.4306	1.83	.4664
1.14	.3729	1.49	.4319	1.84	.4671
1.15	.3749	1.50	.4332	1.85	.4678
1.16	.3770	1.51	.4345	1.86	.4686
1.17	.3790	1.52	.4357	1.87	.4693
1.18	.3810	1.53	.4370	1.88	.4699
1.19	.3830	1.54	.4382	1.89	.4706
1.20	.3849	1.55	.4394	1.90	.4713
1.21	.3869	1.56	.4406	1.91	.4719
1.22	.3888	1.57	.4418	1.92	.4726
1.23	.3907	1.58	.4429	1.93	.4732
1.24	.3925	1.59	.4441	1.94	.4738
1.25	.3944	1.60	.4452	1.95	.4744
1.26	.3962	1.61	.4463	1.96	.4750
1.27	.3980	1.62	.4474	1.97	.4756
1.28	.3997	1.63	.4484	1.98	.4761
1.29	.4015	1.64	.4495	1.99	.4767
1.30	.4032	1.65	.4505	2.00	.4772
1.31	.4049	1.66	.4515	2.01	.4778
1.32	.4066	1.67	.4525	2.02	.4783
1.33	.4082	1.68	.4535	2.03	.4788
1.34	.4099	1.69	.4545	2.04	.4793
1.35	.4115	1.70	.4554	2.05	.4798
1.36	.4131	1.71	.4564	2.06	.4803
1.37	.4147	1.72	.4573	2.07	.4808
1.38	.4162	1.73	.4582	2.08	.4812
1.39	.4177	1.74	.4591	2.09	.4817

(continued)

Table A. (continued)

z	Area from Mean to z	z	Area from Mean to z	z	Area from Mean to z
2.10	.4821	2.45	.4929	2.80	.4974
2.11	.4826	2.46	.4931	2.81	.4975
2.12	.4830	2.47	.4932	2.82	.4976
2.13	.4834	2.48	.4934	2.83	.4977
2.14	.4838	2.49	.4936	2.84	.4977
2.15	.4842	2.50	.4938	2.85	.4978
2.16	.4846	2.51	.4940	2.86	.4979
2.17	.4850	2.52	.4941	2.87	.4979
2.18	.4854	2.53	.4943	2.88	.4980
2.19	.4857	2.54	.4945	2.89	.4981
2.20	.4861	2.55	.4946	2.90	.4981
2.21	.4864	2.56	.4948	2.91	.4982
2.22	.4868	2.57	.4949	2.92	.4982
2.23	.4871	2.58	.4951	2.93	.4983
2.24	.4875	2.59	.4952	2.94	.4984
2.25	.4878	2.60	.4953	2.95	.4984
2.26	.4881	2.61	.4955	2.96	.4985
2.27	.4884	2.62	.4956	2.97	.4985
2.28	.4887	2.63	.4957	2.98	.4986
2.29	.4890	2.64	.4959	2.99	.4986
2.30	.4893	2.65	.4960	3.00	.4987
2.31	.4896	2.66	.4961	3.01	.4987
2.32	.4898	2.67	.4962	3.02	.4987
2.33	.4901	2.68	.4963	3.03	.4988
2.34	.4904	2.69	.4964	3.04	.4988
2.35	.4906	2.70	.4965	3.05	.4989
2.36	.4909	2.71	.4966	3.06	.4989
2.37	.4911	2.72	.4967	3.07	.4989
2.38	.4913	2.73	.4968	3.08	.4990
2.39	.4916	2.74	.4969	3.09	.4990
2.40	.4918	2.75	.4970	3.10	.4990
2.41	.4920	2.76	.4971	3.11	.4991
2.42	.4922	2.77	.4972	3.12	.4991
2.43	.4925	2.78	.4973	3.13	.4991
2.44	.4927	2.79	.4974	3.14	.4992

Table A. (continued)

z	Area from Mean to z	z	Area from Mean to z
3.15	.4992	3.25	.4994
3.16	.4992	3.26	.4994
3.17	.4992	3.27	.4995
3.18	.4993	3.28	.4995
3.19	.4993	3.29	.4995
3.20	.4993	3.30	.4995
3.21	.4993	3.40	.4997
3.22	.4994	3.50	.4998
3.23	.4994	3.60	.4998
3.24	.4994	3.70	.4999

Table B
Values of r for the .05 and .01 levels of significance

$df(N-2)$	.05	.01	$df(N-2)$	.05	.01
1	.997	1.000	31	.344	.442
2	.950	.990	32	.339	.436
3	.878	.959	33	.334	.430
4	.812	.917	34	.329	.424
5	.755	.875	35	.325	.418
6	.707	.834	36	.320	.413
7	.666	.798	37	.316	.408
8	.632	.765	38	.312	.403
9	.602	.735	39	.308	.398
10	.576	.708	40	.304	.393
11	.553	.684	41	.301	.389
12	.533	.661	42	.297	.384
13	.514	.641	43	.294	.380
14	.497	.623	44	.291	.376
15	.482	.606	45	.288	.372
16	.468	.590	46	.285	.368
17	.456	.575	47	.282	.365
18	.444	.562	48	.279	.361
19	.433	.549	49	.276	.358
20	.423	.537	50	.273	.354
21	.413	.526	60	.250	.325
22	.404	.515	70	.232	.302
23	.396	.505	80	.217	.283
24	.388	.496	90	.205	.267
25	.381	.487	100	.195	.254
26	.374	.479	200	.138	.181
27	.367	.471	300	.113	.148
28	.361	.463	400	.098	.128
29	.355	.456	500	.088	.115
30	.349	.449	1000	.062	.081

Adapted from A. L. Sockloff and J. N. Edney, Some extension of Student's t and Pearson's r central distributions. Technical Report (May 1972), Measurement and Research Center, Temple University, Philadelphia.

Table C
Values of Spearman r_s for the .05 and .01 levels of significance

N	.05	.01	N	.05	.01
6	.886	—	19	.462	.608
7	.786	—	20	.450	.591
8	.738	.881	21	.438	.576
9	.683	.833	22	.428	.562
10	.648	.818	23	.418	.549
11	.623	.794	24	.409	.537
12	.591	.780	25	.400	.526
13	.566	.745	26	.392	.515
14	.545	.716	27	.385	.505
15	.525	.689	28	.377	.496
16	.507	.666	29	.370	.487
17	.490	.645	30	.364	.478
18	.476	.625			

From E. G. Olds, Distribution of sums of squares of rank differences for small numbers of individuals, *Annals of Mathematical Statistics 9:* 133–48 (1938); and E. G. Olds, The 5% significance levels for sums of squares of rank differences and a correction, *Annals of Mathematical Statistics 20:* 117–18 (1949). Copyright 1938 and Copyright 1949 by the Institute of Mathematical Statistics, Hayward, Calif. Reprinted by permission of the publisher.

Table D
Values of *t* at the .05, .01, and .001 levels of significance

	Two-Tailed				One-Tailed		
df	.05	.01	.001	*df*	.05	.01	.001
1	12.706	63.657	636.619	1	6.314	31.821	318.309
2	4.303	9.925	31.599	2	2.920	6.965	22.327
3	3.183	5.841	12.924	3	2.353	4.541	10.215
4	2.777	4.604	8.610	4	2.132	3.747	7.173
5	2.571	4.032	6.869	5	2.015	3.365	5.893
6	2.447	3.707	5.959	6	1.943	3.143	5.208
7	2.365	3.500	5.408	7	1.895	2.998	4.785
8	2.306	3.355	5.041	8	1.860	2.897	4.501
9	2.262	3.250	4.781	9	1.833	2.821	4.297
10	2.228	3.169	4.587	10	1.813	2.764	4.144

(continued)

Adapted from A. L. Sockloff and J. N. Edney, Some extension of Student's *t* and Pearson's *r* central distributions, Technical Report (May 1972), Measurement and Research Center, Temple University, Philadelphia.

Table D (continued)

	Two-Tailed				One-Tailed		
df	.05	.01	.001	df	.05	.01	.001
11	2.201	3.106	4.437	11	1.796	2.718	4.025
12	2.179	3.055	4.318	12	1.782	2.681	3.930
13	2.160	3.012	4.221	13	1.771	2.650	3.852
14	2.145	2.977	4.141	14	1.761	2.625	3.787
15	2.132	2.947	4.073	15	1.753	2.603	3.733
16	2.120	2.921	4.015	16	1.746	2.584	3.686
17	2.110	2.898	3.965	17	1.740	2.567	3.646
18	2.101	2.879	3.922	18	1.734	2.552	3.611
19	2.093	2.861	3.883	19	1.729	2.540	3.579
20	2.086	2.845	3.850	20	1.725	2.528	3.552
21	2.080	2.831	3.819	21	1.721	2.518	3.527
22	2.074	2.819	3.792	22	1.717	2.508	3.505
23	2.069	2.807	3.768	23	1.714	2.500	3.485
24	2.064	2.797	3.745	24	1.711	2.492	3.467
25	2.060	2.787	3.725	25	1.708	2.485	3.450
26	2.056	2.779	3.707	26	1.706	2.479	3.435
27	2.052	2.771	3.690	27	1.703	2.473	3.421
28	2.048	2.763	3.674	28	1.701	2.467	3.408
29	2.045	2.756	3.659	29	1.699	2.462	3.396
30	2.042	2.750	3.646	30	1.697	2.457	3.385
40	2.021	2.705	3.551	40	1.684	2.423	3.307
50	2.009	2.678	3.496	50	1.676	2.403	3.261
60	2.000	2.660	3.460	60	1.671	2.390	3.232
70	1.994	2.648	3.435	70	1.667	2.381	3.211
80	1.990	2.639	3.416	80	1.664	2.374	3.195
90	1.987	2.632	3.402	90	1.662	2.369	3.183
100	1.984	2.626	3.391	100	1.660	2.364	3.174
∞	1.960	2.576	3.292	∞	1.645	2.327	3.091

Table E
Values of *F* at the 5% and 1% levels of significance

df Associated with the Denominator		*df* Associated with the Numerator								
		1	2	3	4	5	6	7	8	9
1	5%	161	200	216	225	230	234	237	239	241
	1%	4052	5000	5403	5625	5764	5859	5928	5982	6022
2	5%	18.5	19.0	19.2	19.2	19.3	19.3	19.4	19.4	19.4
	1%	98.5	99.0	99.2	99.2	99.3	99.3	99.4	99.4	99.4
3	5%	10.1	9.55	9.28	9.12	9.01	8.94	8.89	8.85	8.81
	1%	34.1	30.8	29.5	28.7	28.2	27.9	27.7	27.5	27.3
4	5%	7.71	6.94	6.59	6.39	6.26	6.16	6.09	6.04	6.00
	1%	21.2	18.0	16.7	16.0	15.5	15.2	15.0	14.8	14.7
5	5%	6.61	5.79	5.41	5.19	5.05	4.95	4.88	4.82	4.77
	1%	16.3	13.3	12.1	11.4	11.0	10.7	10.5	10.3	10.2
6	5%	5.99	5.14	4.76	4.53	4.39	4.28	4.21	4.15	4.10
	1%	13.7	10.9	9.78	9.15	8.75	8.47	8.26	8.10	7.98
7	5%	5.59	4.74	4.35	4.12	3.97	3.87	3.79	3.73	3.68
	1%	12.2	9.55	8.45	7.85	7.46	7.19	6.99	6.84	6.72
8	5%	5.32	4.46	4.07	3.84	3.69	3.58	3.50	3.44	3.39
	1%	11.3	8.65	7.59	7.01	6.63	6.37	6.18	6.03	5.91
9	5%	5.12	4.26	3.86	3.63	3.48	3.37	3.29	3.23	3.18
	1%	10.6	8.02	6.99	6.42	6.06	5.80	5.61	5.47	5.35
10	5%	4.96	4.10	3.71	3.48	3.33	3.22	3.14	3.07	3.02
	1%	10.0	7.56	6.55	5.99	5.64	5.39	5.20	5.06	4.94
11	5%	4.84	3.98	3.59	3.36	3.20	3.09	3.01	2.95	2.90
	1%	9.65	7.21	6.22	5.67	5.32	5.07	4.89	4.74	4.63
12	5%	4.75	3.89	3.49	3.26	3.11	3.00	2.91	2.85	2.80
	1%	9.33	6.93	5.95	5.41	5.06	4.82	4.64	4.50	4.39
13	5%	4.67	3.81	3.41	3.18	3.03	2.92	2.83	2.77	2.71
	1%	9.07	6.70	5.74	5.21	4.86	4.62	4.44	4.30	4.19
14	5%	4.60	3.74	3.34	3.11	2.96	2.85	2.76	2.70	2.65
	1%	8.86	6.51	5.56	5.04	4.70	4.46	4.28	4.14	4.03
										(continued)

From M. Merrington and C. M. Thompson, Tables of percentage points of the inverted beta (*F*) distribution. *Biometrika* *33:* 73–88 (1943). Corrected in *Biometrika Tables for Statisticians 2,* Table 5 (1972).

Table E (continued)

df Associated with the Denominator		df Associated with the Numerator								
		1	2	3	4	5	6	7	8	9
15	5%	4.54	3.68	3.29	3.06	2.90	2.79	2.71	2.64	2.59
	1%	8.68	6.36	5.42	4.89	4.56	4.32	4.14	4.00	3.89
16	5%	4.49	3.63	3.24	3.01	2.85	2.74	2.66	2.59	2.54
	1%	8.53	6.23	5.29	4.77	4.44	4.20	4.03	3.89	3.78
17	5%	4.45	3.59	3.20	2.96	2.81	2.70	2.61	2.55	2.49
	1%	8.40	6.11	5.18	4.67	4.34	4.10	3.93	3.79	3.68
18	5%	4.41	3.55	3.16	2.93	2.77	2.66	2.58	2.51	2.46
	1%	8.29	6.01	5.09	4.58	4.25	4.01	3.84	3.71	3.60
19	5%	4.38	3.52	3.13	2.90	2.74	2.63	2.54	2.48	2.42
	1%	8.18	5.93	5.01	4.50	4.17	3.94	3.77	3.63	3.52
20	5%	4.35	3.49	3.10	2.87	2.71	2.60	2.51	2.45	2.39
	1%	8.10	5.85	4.94	4.43	4.10	3.87	3.70	3.56	3.46
21	5%	4.32	3.47	3.07	2.84	2.68	2.57	2.49	2.42	2.37
	1%	8.02	5.78	4.87	4.37	4.04	3.81	3.64	3.51	3.40
22	5%	4.30	3.44	3.05	2.82	2.66	2.55	2.46	2.40	2.34
	1%	7.95	5.72	4.82	4.31	3.99	3.76	3.59	3.45	3.35
23	5%	4.28	3.42	3.03	2.80	2.64	2.53	2.44	2.37	2.32
	1%	7.88	5.66	4.76	4.26	3.94	3.71	3.54	3.41	3.30
24	5%	4.26	3.40	3.01	2.78	2.62	2.51	2.42	2.36	2.30
	1%	7.82	5.61	4.72	4.22	3.90	3.67	3.50	3.36	3.26
25	5%	4.24	3.39	2.99	2.76	2.60	2.49	2.40	2.34	2.28
	1%	7.77	5.57	4.68	4.18	3.86	3.63	3.46	3.32	3.22
26	5%	4.23	3.37	2.98	2.74	2.59	2.47	2.39	2.32	2.27
	1%	7.72	5.53	4.64	4.14	3.82	3.59	3.42	3.29	3.18
27	5%	4.21	3.35	2.96	2.73	2.57	2.46	2.37	2.31	2.25
	1%	7.68	5.49	4.60	4.11	3.78	3.56	3.39	3.26	3.15
28	5%	4.20	3.34	2.95	2.71	2.56	2.45	2.36	2.29	2.24
	1%	7.64	5.45	4.57	4.07	3.75	3.53	3.36	3.23	3.12
29	5%	4.18	3.33	2.93	2.70	2.55	2.43	2.35	2.28	2.22
	1%	7.60	5.42	4.54	4.04	3.73	3.50	3.33	3.20	3.09
30	5%	4.17	3.32	2.92	2.69	2.53	2.42	2.33	2.27	2.21
	1%	7.56	5.39	4.51	4.02	3.70	3.47	3.30	3.17	3.07

Table E (continued)

df Associated with the Denominator		df Associated with the Numerator								
		1	2	3	4	5	6	7	8	9
40	5%	4.08	3.23	2.84	2.61	2.45	2.34	2.25	2.18	2.12
	1%	7.31	5.18	4.31	3.83	3.51	3.29	3.12	2.99	2.89
60	5%	4.00	3.15	2.76	2.53	2.37	2.25	2.17	2.10	2.04
	1%	7.08	4.98	4.13	3.65	3.34	3.12	2.95	2.82	2.72
120	5%	3.92	3.07	2.68	2.45	2.29	2.18	2.09	2.02	1.96
	1%	6.85	4.79	3.95	3.48	3.17	2.96	2.79	2.66	2.56

Table F
Values of chi square at the .05, .01, and .001 levels of significance

df	.05	.01	.001	df	.05	.01	.001
1	3.84	6.64	10.83	16	26.30	32.00	39.29
2	5.99	9.21	13.82	17	27.59	33.41	40.75
3	7.82	11.34	16.27	18	28.87	34.80	42.31
4	9.49	13.28	18.46	19	30.14	36.19	43.82
5	11.07	15.09	20.52	20	31.41	37.57	45.32
6	12.59	16.81	22.46	21	32.67	38.93	46.80
7	14.07	18.48	24.32	22	33.92	40.29	48.27
8	15.51	20.09	26.12	23	35.17	41.64	49.73
9	16.92	21.67	27.88	24	36.42	42.98	51.18
10	18.31	23.21	29.59	25	37.65	44.31	52.62
11	19.68	24.72	31.26	26	38.88	45.64	54.05
12	21.03	26.22	32.91	27	40.11	46.96	55.48
13	22.36	27.69	34.53	28	41.34	48.28	56.89
14	23.68	29.14	36.12	29	42.56	49.59	58.30
15	25.00	30.58	37.70	30	43.77	50.89	59.70

From R. A. Fisher, *Statistical Methods for Research Workers,* 14th ed. (New York, 1970), pp. 112–13. Copyright 1970 by Hafner Press. Reprinted by permission of the publisher.

Table G
Probabilities associated with values as small as observed values of U in the Mann–Whitney U test

$N_2 = 3$

U \ N₁	1	2	3
0	.250	.100	.050
1	.500	.200	.100
2	.750	.400	.200
3		.600	.350
4			.500
5			.650

$N_2 = 4$

U \ N₁	1	2	3	4
0	.200	.067	.028	.014
1	.400	.133	.057	.029
2	.600	.267	.114	.057
3		.400	.200	.100
4		.600	.314	.171
5			.429	.243
6			.571	.343
7				.443
8				.557

$N_2 = 5$

U \ N₁	1	2	3	4	5
0	.167	.047	.018	.008	.004
1	.333	.095	.036	.016	.008
2	.500	.190	.071	.032	.016
3	.667	.286	.125	.056	.028
4		.429	.196	.095	.048
5		.571	.286	.143	.075
6			.393	.206	.111
7			.500	.278	.155
8			.607	.365	.210
9				.452	.274
10				.548	.345
11					.421
12					.500
13					.579

$N_2 = 6$

U \ N₁	1	2	3	4	5	6
0	.143	.036	.012	.005	.002	.001
1	.286	.071	.024	.010	.004	.002
2	.428	.143	.048	.019	.009	.004
3	.571	.214	.083	.033	.015	.008
4		.321	.131	.057	.026	.013
5		.429	.190	.086	.041	.021
6		.571	.274	.129	.063	.032
7			.357	.176	.089	.047
8			.452	.238	.123	.066
9			.548	.305	.165	.090
10				.381	.268	.120
11				.457	.268	.155
12				.545	.331	.197
13					.396	.242
14					.465	.294
15					.535	.350
16						.409
17						.469
18						.531

From H. B. Mann and D. R. Whitney, On a test whether one of two random variables is stochastically larger than the other, *Annals of Mathematical Statistics 18:* 50–60 (1947). Copyright 1947 by the Institute of Mathematical Statistics, Hayward, Calif. Reprinted by permission of the publisher.

Table G (continued)

N_1 U	1	2	3	4	5	6	7
			$N_2 = 7$				
0	.125	.028	.008	.003	.001	.001	.000
1	.250	.056	.017	.006	.003	.001	.001
2	.375	.111	.033	.012	.005	.002	.001
3	.500	.167	.058	.021	.009	.004	.002
4	.625	.250	.092	.036	.015	.007	.003
5		.333	.133	.055	.024	.011	.006
6		.444	.192	.082	.037	.017	.009
7		.556	.258	.115	.053	.026	.013
8			.333	.158	.074	.037	.019
9			.417	.206	.101	.051	.027
10			.500	.264	.134	.069	.036
11			.583	.324	.172	.090	.049
12				.394	.216	.117	.064
13				.464	.265	.147	.082
14				.538	.319	.183	.104
15					.378	.223	.130
16					.438	.267	.159
17					.500	.314	.191
18					.562	.365	.228
19						.418	.267
20						.473	.310
21						.527	.355
22							.402
23							.451
24							.500
25							.549

(continued)

Table G (continued)

N_1 / U	1	2	3	4	5	6	7	8	t	Normal
0	.111	.022	.006	.002	.001	.000	.000	.000	3.308	.001
1	.222	.044	.012	.004	.002	.001	.000	.000	3.203	.001
2	.333	.089	.024	.008	.003	.001	.001	.000	3.098	.001
3	.444	.133	.042	.014	.005	.002	.001	.001	2.993	.001
4	.556	.200	.067	.024	.009	.004	.002	.001	2.888	.002
5		.267	.097	.036	.015	.006	.003	.001	2.783	.003
6		.356	.139	.055	.023	.010	.005	.002	2.678	.004
7		.444	.188	.077	.033	.015	.007	.003	2.573	.005
8		.556	.248	.107	.047	.021	.010	.005	2.468	.007
9			.315	.141	.064	.030	.014	.007	2.363	.009
10			.387	.184	.085	.041	.020	.010	2.258	.012
11			.461	.230	.111	.054	.027	.014	2.153	.016
12			.539	.285	.142	.071	.036	.019	2.048	.020
13				.341	.177	.091	.047	.025	1.943	.026
14				.404	.217	.114	.060	.032	1.838	.033
15				.467	.262	.141	.076	.041	1.733	.041
16				.533	.311	.172	.095	.052	1.628	.052
17					.362	.207	.116	.065	1.523	.064
18					.416	.245	.140	.080	1.418	.078
19					.472	.286	.168	.097	1.313	.094
20					.528	.331	.198	.117	1.208	.113
21						.377	.232	.139	1.102	.135
22						.426	.268	.164	.998	.159
23						.475	.306	.191	.893	.185
24						.525	.347	.221	.788	.215
25							.389	.253	.683	.247
26							.433	.287	.578	.282
27							.478	.323	.473	.318
28							.522	.360	.368	.356
29								.399	.263	.396
30								.439	.158	.437
31								.480	.052	.481
32								.520		

Header spanning: $N_2 = 8$

Table H
Critical values of U in the Mann–Whitney U test

	Critical Values of U for a One-Tailed Test at $\alpha = .001$ or for a Two-Tailed Test at $\alpha = .002$											
N_1 \ N_2	9	10	11	12	13	14	15	16	17	18	19	20
1												
2												
3									0	0	0	0
4		0	0	0	1	1	1	2	2	3	3	3
5	1	1	2	2	3	3	4	5	5	6	7	7
6	2	3	4	4	5	6	7	8	9	10	11	12
7	3	5	6	7	8	9	10	11	13	14	15	16
8	5	6	8	9	11	12	14	15	17	18	20	21
9	7	8	10	12	14	15	17	19	21	23	25	26
10	8	10	12	14	17	19	21	23	25	27	29	32
11	10	12	15	17	20	22	24	27	29	32	34	37
12	12	14	17	20	23	25	28	31	34	37	40	42
13	14	17	20	23	26	29	32	35	38	42	45	48
14	15	19	22	25	29	32	36	39	43	46	50	54
15	17	21	24	28	32	36	40	43	47	51	55	59
16	19	23	27	31	35	39	43	48	52	56	60	65
17	21	25	29	34	38	43	47	52	57	61	66	70
18	23	27	32	37	42	46	51	56	61	66	71	76
19	25	29	34	40	45	50	55	60	66	71	77	82
20	26	32	37	42	48	54	59	65	70	76	82	88

(continued)

From D. Auble, Extended tables for the Mann–Whitney statistic, *Bulletin of the Institute of Educational Research at Indiana University,* Vol. 1, No. 2 (1953). Copyright 1953 by the Institute of Educational Research, Indiana University, Bloomington, Ind. Reprinted by permission of the publisher.

Table H (continued)

Critical Values of *U* for a One-Tailed Test at α = .01 or for a Two-Tailed Test at α = .02

N_1 \ N_2	9	10	11	12	13	14	15	16	17	18	19	20
1												
2					0	0	0	0	0	0	1	1
3	1	1	1	2	2	2	3	3	4	4	4	5
4	3	3	4	5	5	6	7	7	8	9	9	10
5	5	6	7	8	9	10	11	12	13	14	15	16
6	7	8	9	11	12	13	15	16	18	19	20	22
7	9	11	12	14	16	17	19	21	23	24	26	28
8	11	13	15	17	20	22	24	26	28	30	32	34
9	14	16	18	21	23	26	28	31	33	36	38	40
10	16	19	22	24	27	30	33	36	38	41	44	47
11	18	22	25	28	31	34	37	41	44	47	50	53
12	21	24	28	31	35	38	42	46	49	53	56	60
13	23	27	31	35	39	43	47	51	55	59	63	67
14	26	30	34	38	43	47	51	56	60	65	69	73
15	28	33	37	42	47	51	56	61	66	70	75	80
16	31	36	41	46	51	56	61	66	71	76	82	87
17	33	38	44	49	55	60	66	71	77	82	88	93
18	36	41	47	53	59	65	70	76	82	88	94	100
19	38	44	50	56	63	69	75	82	88	94	101	107
20	40	47	53	60	67	73	80	87	93	100	107	114

Table H (continued)

Critical Values of *U* for a One-Tailed Test at $\alpha = .025$ or for a Two-Tailed Test at $\alpha = .05$

N_1 \ N_2	9	10	11	12	13	14	15	16	17	18	19	20
1												
2	0	0	0	1	1	1	1	1	2	2	2	2
3	2	3	3	4	4	5	5	6	6	7	7	8
4	4	5	6	7	8	9	10	11	11	12	13	13
5	7	8	9	11	12	13	14	15	17	18	19	20
6	10	11	13	14	16	17	19	21	22	24	25	27
7	12	14	16	18	20	22	24	26	28	30	32	34
8	15	17	19	22	24	26	29	31	34	36	38	41
9	17	20	23	26	28	31	34	37	39	42	45	48
10	20	23	26	29	33	36	39	42	45	48	52	55
11	23	26	30	33	37	40	44	47	51	55	58	62
12	26	29	33	37	41	45	49	53	57	61	65	69
13	28	33	37	41	45	50	54	59	63	67	72	76
14	31	36	40	45	50	55	59	64	67	74	78	83
15	34	39	44	49	54	59	64	70	75	80	85	90
16	37	42	47	53	59	64	70	75	81	86	92	98
17	39	45	51	57	63	67	75	81	87	93	99	105
18	42	48	55	61	67	74	80	86	93	99	106	112
19	45	52	58	65	72	78	85	92	99	106	113	119
20	48	55	62	69	76	83	90	98	105	112	119	127

(continued)

Table H (continued)

Critical Values of *U* for a One-Tailed Test at α = .05 or for a Two-Tailed Test at α = .10

N_1 \ N_2	9	10	11	12	13	14	15	16	17	18	19	20
1											0	0
2	1	1	1	2	2	2	3	3	3	4	4	4
3	3	4	5	5	6	7	7	8	9	9	10	11
4	6	7	8	9	10	11	12	14	15	16	17	18
5	9	11	12	13	15	16	18	19	20	22	23	25
6	12	14	16	17	19	21	23	25	26	28	30	32
7	15	17	19	21	24	26	28	30	33	35	37	39
8	18	20	23	26	28	31	33	36	39	41	44	47
9	21	24	27	30	33	36	39	42	45	48	51	54
10	24	27	31	34	37	41	44	48	51	55	58	62
11	27	31	34	38	42	46	50	54	57	61	65	69
12	30	34	38	42	47	51	55	60	64	68	72	77
13	33	37	42	47	51	56	61	65	70	75	80	84
14	36	41	46	51	56	61	66	71	77	82	87	92
15	39	44	50	55	61	66	72	77	83	88	94	100
16	42	48	54	60	65	71	77	83	89	95	101	107
17	45	51	57	64	70	77	83	89	96	102	109	115
18	48	55	61	68	75	82	88	95	102	109	116	123
19	51	58	65	72	80	87	94	101	109	116	123	130
20	54	62	69	77	84	92	100	107	115	123	130	138

Table I

Probabilities associated with values as small as observed values of x in the binomial test

N \ x	0	1	2	3	4	5	6	7	8	9	10	11	12	13	14	15
5	031	188	500	812	969	†										
6	016	109	344	656	891	984	†									
7	008	062	227	500	773	938	992	†								
8	004	035	145	363	637	855	965	996	†							
9	002	020	090	254	500	746	910	980	998	†						
10	001	011	055	172	377	623	828	945	989	999	†					
11		006	033	113	274	500	726	887	967	994	†	†				
12		003	019	073	194	387	613	806	927	981	997	†	†			
13		002	011	046	133	291	500	709	867	954	989	998	†	†		
14		001	006	029	090	212	395	605	788	910	971	994	999	†	†	
15			004	018	059	151	304	500	696	849	941	982	996	†	†	†
16			002	011	038	105	227	402	598	773	895	962	989	998	†	†
17			001	006	025	072	166	315	500	685	834	928	975	994	999	†
18			001	004	015	048	119	240	407	593	760	881	952	985	996	999
19				002	010	032	084	180	324	500	676	820	916	968	990	998
20				001	006	021	058	132	252	412	588	748	868	942	979	994
21				001	004	013	039	095	192	332	500	668	808	905	961	987
22					002	008	026	067	143	262	416	584	738	857	933	974
23					001	005	017	047	105	202	339	500	661	798	895	953
24					001	003	011	032	076	154	271	419	581	729	846	924
25						002	007	022	054	115	212	345	500	655	788	885

†$p = 1.0$ or approximately 1.0.

From *Statistical Inference* by Helen M. Walker and Joseph Lev. Copyright 1953 by Holt, Rinehart and Winston, Inc. Reprinted by permission of Holt, Rinehart and Winston, Inc.

Table J
Critical values of T in the Wilcoxon matched-pairs signed-ranks test

	Level of Significance for One-Tailed Test		
	.025	.01	.005
	Level of Significance for Two-Tailed Test		
N	.05	.02	.01
6	1	—	—
7	2	0	—
8	4	2	0
9	6	3	2
10	8	5	3
11	11	7	5
12	14	10	7
13	17	13	10
14	21	16	13
15	25	20	16
16	30	24	19
17	35	28	23
18	40	33	28
19	46	38	32
20	52	43	37
21	59	49	43
22	66	56	49
23	73	62	55
24	81	69	61
25	90	77	68

From F. Wilcoxon and R. Wilcox, *Some Rapid Approximate Statistical Procedures* (New York, 1964), p. 28. Copyright 1964 by the American Cyanamid Co. Reproduced with the permission of the American Cyanamid Company.

Table K
Random numbers

Row	Col. 1	Col. 2	Col. 3	Col. 4	Col. 5	Col. 6	Col. 7	Col. 8
1	6822	2438	0106	4633	7718	8304	1682	7340
2	3450	0233	1029	4771	6063	5993	6711	9744
3	1291	9984	2750	2898	4876	6190	8064	4856
4	1325	0121	8719	0582	4750	6977	4612	5232
5	6388	2888	8376	0993	9817	0837	1685	5104
6	8115	1865	1272	3259	9855	2134	7910	3188
7	8476	7712	3157	2807	7810	5009	8226	8305
8	3251	1440	7117	3223	6307	5784	6939	7690
9	6583	2922	0261	6572	9492	7927	2403	4168
10	0781	0208	6177	2093	6832	1812	1815	9555
11	0658	4550	1168	6332	3211	5496	9302	3844
12	0031	1616	8494	0400	7145	5992	2792	6867
13	7476	3269	4335	8876	3178	8836	8737	1779
14	0662	7734	6573	1328	7929	4282	4215	5172
15	8778	9723	7844	0073	2083	2073	3310	5419
16	8683	4130	9412	5405	2962	8417	2844	5065
17	2791	7163	0447	7880	5890	4947	1164	6649
18	1923	6685	4354	2371	7207	7678	2020	8706
19	4786	5539	1195	5748	5506	3503	2665	7724
20	3963	2539	9704	1352	1694	6886	2413	4226
21	3551	8090	0320	8228	3785	1421	5253	5059
22	8449	3413	0146	2717	7401	9133	1699	1678
23	7352	8759	1968	9140	5507	4418	1123	5315
24	4610	6602	2235	8329	1796	1400	3259	0107
25	3902	5337	1581	0491	1386	9152	7091	8521
26	3675	0897	2274	5108	3034	5587	1528	5906
27	2707	7735	5828	6070	3567	5116	3615	1228
28	8241	5184	7561	3557	1666	0569	2772	1982
29	3786	2014	9881	6136	8161	1697	9318	7660
30	6408	0394	7972	2072	2016	6209	8590	8823
31	2827	7501	4103	7556	8944	1803	7156	7304
32	3339	4375	1932	3034	8661	1761	9007	6303
33	8156	5254	8820	5930	4148	6875	7454	2017
34	8583	8138	2787	1764	1688	2384	6454	2600
35	8108	9992	0300	1368	4018	4470	0008	3393
36	1766	4260	2073	8064	1144	2403	4995	7772
37	7430	3256	2347	6441	9309	7727	1205	0461
38	5898	8041	9097	6056	0229	6189	4472	8019
39	6752	1593	4567	2155	8829	4600	1304	7640
40	0241	2784	5174	5141	1995	0875	0767	6251
41	8850	8884	9330	4334	6304	2512	0440	1887
42	7244	6324	9686	6812	9376	3312	4640	9026
43	8042	5197	3290	7326	2003	9883	8299	5023
44	4218	0135	7539	2597	7018	0433	6531	2939

(continued)

Table K. (continued)

Row	Col. 1	Col. 2	Col. 3	Col. 4	Col. 5	Col. 6	Col. 7	Col. 8
45	3458	4485	4978	3144	1366	8435	0521	0903
46	3891	9023	7321	1278	9386	1336	6954	8907
47	1680	8967	6014	0893	0257	8131	3451	6353
48	2611	2101	0323	2475	6698	4587	5442	4283
49	8360	7630	8811	2224	2973	8797	6676	8174
50	4358	8299	6258	2539	2190	9327	9201	4021
51	0395	8978	6883	2444	3655	7577	8509	4899
52	6790	5826	5792	1046	4727	7391	9394	7021
53	8969	2467	3859	2544	2997	8248	2106	0135
54	5896	8496	6622	5967	3655	9680	2112	6032
55	8002	7938	2765	3436	8823	5754	7806	2841
56	2292	6402	2554	6425	1747	7072	6279	2830
57	0919	6350	6772	9031	0030	5830	9503	7734
58	8537	7884	7592	7604	0915	8140	5837	8572
59	0089	7169	5282	8009	7299	4132	7933	4740
60	6688	7744	3190	6707	7749	6430	2153	5995
61	6334	6469	3550	4146	9548	0502	0682	8916
62	2638	7025	0337	5413	5699	2946	8656	9275
63	9538	4036	8895	0491	1202	0700	5990	0199
64	2038	6178	2720	7068	1558	8459	6732	2541
65	4137	6131	0551	2369	0638	8841	3999	4515
66	5856	9688	6631	9342	9581	9034	3882	3124
67	4050	2017	2270	6798	3420	7698	3600	2915
68	5369	0182	1356	9277	0847	0618	5676	4271
69	9094	5406	5487	0303	3939	9584	4252	2261
70	0495	7272	4093	1135	2115	8234	5872	8034
71	7872	5592	5072	1896	4489	6656	8868	8308
72	5629	4712	9965	2034	1112	6192	8080	6146
73	9274	5813	8090	2056	0514	4724	4752	8574
74	7161	2656	3979	9818	7768	1408	1113	8633
75	4913	7146	7418	0542	3370	7959	3484	6903
76	0532	3563	1677	5598	7058	6182	2621	0432
77	6611	3736	5126	4618	6317	1833	6246	2841
78	5669	4421	2483	3818	2607	3447	5292	9150
79	5432	8075	4138	3454	4284	7103	7141	5672
80	1746	8188	8098	9121	4814	0154	0796	6078
81	0265	2261	9460	2891	1960	7302	2384	3856
82	9121	7380	1454	5630	6662	7089	2302	1372
83	3486	1267	1051	6137	6829	4841	6470	4503
84	1863	6426	3537	4142	8436	9500	0681	6727
85	7461	6114	7845	9090	2454	5188	6421	3127
86	2121	0359	9500	9989	2918	6473	6127	8590
87	7333	7176	5448	2520	1526	3403	0676	0001
88	1580	9562	5706	2664	9115	1528	9664	5837
89	1493	9393	7133	6174	6627	1355	8825	4712

Table K. (continued)

Row	Col. 1	Col. 2	Col. 3	Col. 4	Col. 5	Col. 6	Col. 7	Col. 8
90	9034	7151	9392	1468	8859	6384	1522	1484
91	9963	0638	7952	0607	8018	5974	1056	3796
92	0529	1172	6317	3261	0546	7840	9572	2312
93	1589	0785	3590	0016	0890	7589	0509	6296
94	3251	1605	2716	2452	1511	8114	4451	6875
95	1962	0648	7956	2335	8081	1631	6595	7551
96	0204	6178	0022	3652	8878	5417	2645	5109
97	4314	5945	5004	9983	7048	5392	1336	1179
98	3381	2762	7706	7416	1918	7885	8201	5288
99	3880	0274	9828	4809	0658	2903	2822	1858
100	2413	3557	5132	3174	0703	3857	1779	0244
101	1204	1736	0275	2634	8841	4121	8618	5873
102	7322	0992	1208	4458	9994	8765	6123	8260
103	0308	8887	2051	5115	1080	8167	6113	1206
104	1689	1137	4545	3597	7495	7211	3494	8633
105	2326	2005	6169	8194	6905	3175	5280	2996
106	0130	1066	0686	0006	5670	2023	6926	1332
107	2829	3912	6520	5899	1683	6048	0637	2216
108	5113	5929	0328	1713	9967	3832	7045	8221
109	0428	9595	5931	4526	6838	2915	2375	4134
110	6646	3094	7241	7647	7305	8845	3472	3664
111	4055	4271	0141	3886	5997	4026	0120	7317
112	7970	8412	0399	2148	0754	2704	8129	8816
113	5397	4275	9441	8257	0055	3993	5650	2384
114	4795	7277	5554	7023	3268	8373	1000	0201
115	9918	2718	5963	8544	3697	8417	1622	1064
116	8682	4228	0719	3812	8884	9663	0616	3078
117	3691	1275	9601	7767	2131	9797	0831	9248
118	0513	3404	1699	3715	7641	2976	5725	7349
119	2415	9245	5991	3067	8497	7946	3517	1284
120	1464	1715	1462	8458	4456	1962	4747	2103

Table L
Critical values of the studentized range statistic, q

df for Denominator	a	2	3	4	5	6	7	8	9	10
					k (Number of Means)					
1	.05	18.0	27.0	32.8	37.1	40.4	43.1	45.4	47.4	49.1
	.01	90.0	135	164	186	202	216	227	237	246
2	.05	6.09	8.3	9.8	10.9	11.7	12.4	13.0	13.5	14.0
	.01	14.0	19.0	22.3	24.7	26.6	28.2	29.5	30.7	31.7
3	.05	4.50	5.91	6.82	7.50	8.04	8.48	8.85	9.18	9.46
	.01	8.26	10.6	12.2	13.3	14.2	15.0	15.6	16.2	16.7
4	.05	3.93	5.04	5.76	6.29	6.71	7.05	7.35	7.60	7.83
	.01	6.51	8.12	9.17	9.96	10.6	11.1	11.5	11.9	12.3
5	.05	3.64	4.60	5.22	5.67	6.03	6.33	6.58	6.80	6.99
	.01	5.70	6.97	7.80	8.42	8.91	9.32	9.67	9.97	10.2
6	.05	3.46	4.34	4.90	5.31	5.63	5.89	6.12	6.32	6.49
	.01	5.24	6.33	7.03	7.56	7.97	8.32	8.61	8.87	9.10
7	.05	3.34	4.16	4.69	5.06	5.36	5.61	5.82	6.00	6.16
	.01	4.95	5.92	6.54	7.01	7.37	7.68	7.94	8.17	8.37
8	.05	3.26	4.04	4.53	4.89	5.17	5.40	5.60	5.77	5.92
	.01	4.74	5.63	6.20	6.63	6.96	7.24	7.47	7.68	7.78
9	.05	3.20	3.95	4.42	4.76	5.02	5.24	5.43	5.60	5.74
	.01	4.60	5.43	5.96	6.35	6.66	6.91	7.13	7.32	7.49
10	.05	3.15	3.88	4.33	4.65	4.91	5.12	5.30	5.46	5.60
	.01	4.48	5.27	5.77	6.14	6.43	6.67	6.87	7.05	7.21

Adapted from H. Leon Harter, Tables of range and studentized range, *Annals of Mathematical Statistics 31:* 1122–47 (1960). Copyright 1960 by the Institute of Mathematical Statistics, Hayward, Calif. Reprinted by permission of the publisher.

Table L (continued)

df for Denominator	a	2	3	4	5	6	7	8	9	10
11	.05	3.11	3.82	4.26	4.57	4.82	5.03	5.20	5.35	5.49
	.01	4.39	5.14	5.62	5.97	6.25	6.48	6.67	6.84	6.99
12	.05	3.08	3.77	4.20	4.51	4.75	4.95	5.12	5.27	5.40
	.01	4.32	5.04	5.50	5.84	6.10	6.32	6.51	6.67	6.81
13	.05	3.06	3.73	4.15	4.45	4.69	4.88	5.05	5.19	5.32
	.01	4.26	4.96	5.40	5.73	5.98	6.19	6.37	6.53	6.67
14	.05	3.03	3.70	4.11	4.41	4.64	4.83	4.99	5.13	5.25
	.01	4.21	4.89	5.32	5.63	5.88	6.08	6.26	6.41	6.54
16	.05	3.00	3.65	4.05	4.33	4.56	4.74	4.90	5.03	5.15
	.01	4.13	4.78	5.19	5.49	5.72	5.92	6.08	6.22	6.35
18	.05	2.97	3.61	4.00	4.28	4.49	4.67	4.82	4.96	5.07
	.01	4.07	4.70	5.09	5.38	5.60	5.79	5.94	6.08	6.20
20	.05	2.95	3.58	3.96	4.23	4.45	4.62	4.77	4.90	5.01
	.01	4.02	4.64	5.02	5.29	5.51	5.69	5.84	5.97	6.09
24	.05	2.92	3.53	3.90	4.17	4.37	4.54	4.68	4.81	4.92
	.01	3.96	4.54	4.91	5.17	5.37	5.54	5.69	5.81	5.92
30	.05	2.89	3.49	3.84	4.10	4.30	4.46	4.60	4.72	4.83
	.01	3.89	4.45	4.80	5.05	5.24	5.40	5.54	5.56	5.76
40	.05	2.86	3.44	3.79	4.04	4.23	4.39	4.52	4.63	4.74
	.01	3.82	4.37	4.70	4.93	5.11	5.27	5.39	5.50	5.60
60	.05	2.83	3.40	3.74	3.98	4.16	4.31	4.44	4.55	4.65
	.01	3.76	4.28	4.60	4.82	4.99	5.13	5.25	5.36	5.45
120	.05	2.80	3.36	3.69	3.92	4.10	4.24	4.36	4.48	4.56
	.01	3.70	4.20	4.50	4.71	4.87	5.01	5.12	5.21	5.30
∞	.05	2.77	3.31	3.63	3.86	4.03	4.17	4.29	4.39	4.47
	.01	3.64	4.12	4.40	4.60	4.76	4.88	4.99	5.08	5.16

APPENDIX 4

Computer-Assisted Data Analysis

PERSONALITY VARIABLES IN SELF-REPORTED PHYSICAL SYMPTOMS

The following data are part of a data set that was collected in a study to examine the relationship between certain personality variables and health among college students (Bartz, Rose, & Jagim, 1989).

Students in introductory psychology courses received extra credit towards their final grade for participating in the study. The personality variables were assessed by having students complete a number of personality inventories. The variables and the inventories are listed below.

Sex Roles. Sex role orientation was assessed by the Bem Sex Role Inventory (BSRI; Bem, 1974). Only the scoring protocols yielding Masculinity (BSRIM) and Femininity (BSRIF) scores are reported here.

Self-Monitoring. The Self-Monitoring Inventory (Snyder, 1974) assessed each individual's tendency to monitor and control his or her own social behavior. Those scoring high on self-monitoring are particularly sensitive to cues about the appropriateness of their own social behavior, and adjust their own behavior accordingly.

Physical Symptoms. The Wahler Physical Symptoms Inventory (Wahler, 1983) lists 42 "physical troubles" (e.g., headaches, dizzy spells), and respondents indicate how often they are "bothered" by these troubles on a scale of 0 (almost never) to 5 (nearly every day). Higher scores indicate more symptoms or more frequent symptoms.

Type A Behavior. The college student version (Glass, 1977) of the Jenkins Activity Survey (JAS; Jenkins, Zyzanski, & Rosenman, 1971) assessed the Type A behavior pattern, a sensitivity to deadlines, a sense of time urgency, and the need to accomplish more and more in less time. The three JAS scales yield scores for global Type A, Speed and Impatience (S&I), and Hard Driving and Competitive (HD&C). The higher the score on these scales, the greater the degree of each trait.

The scores on these measures are listed in the following columns, along with the subject's number and sex (1 = male, 2 = female).

SUBNUM	SEX	BSRIM	BSRIF	SELFMON	SYMP	JASA	JASS&I	JASHD&C
1	2	99	107	17	1.93	173	132	80
2	2	92	94	13	0.95	274	98	87
3	2	93	91	14	1.31	178	132	58
4	2	98	105	17	0.62	308	220	119
5	2	102	92	12	1.83	299	245	109
6	2	95	103	13	1.14	249	130	81
7	2	97	93	8	0.98	161	106	76
8	2	101	112	12	1.86	300	199	161
9	2	114	100	10	1.00	293	139	158
10	2	92	108	9	1.83	266	170	51
11	2	100	101	7	1.24	161	236	86
12	2	115	97	10	1.76	140	157	100
13	2	101	94	7	0.55	151	77	106
14	2	88	121	7	1.14	168	148	73
15	2	82	95	12	0.83	259	227	83
16	2	98	102	12	0.36	201	151	95
17	2	78	93	9	0.73	121	152	34
18	2	82	106	10	1.36	253	136	94
19	2	83	113	6	0.71	107	66	74
20	2	91	93	15	0.62	248	159	85
21	2	111	109	10	0.74	351	256	161
22	2	102	113	5	1.74	281	115	145
23	2	112	123	9	0.98	171	78	69
24	2	78	95	9	0.76	122	96	60
25	2	101	77	7	0.71	293	226	100
26	2	113	94	10	1.14	354	171	117
27	2	89	90	5	1.31	277	268	77
28	2	93	95	8	1.05	241	148	80
29	2	92	110	8	0.79	282	204	74
30	2	101	98	10	1.67	214	152	101
31	2	95	111	8	0.29	252	187	113
32	2	106	98	16	1.14	157	95	100
33	1	99	116	14	0.59	309	122	117
34	1	113	100	2	0.86	90	38	92
35	1	99	85	7	0.52	241	114	75

SUBNUM	SEX	BSRIM	BSRIF	SELFMON	SYMP	JASA	JASS&I	JASHD&C
36	1	86	80	9	0.36	156	58	91
37	1	70	103	6	0.26	119	115	74
38	1	107	109	9	0.64	138	125	65
39	1	90	99	5	1.81	95	78	61
40	1	86	80	9	0.31	224	126	70
41	1	85	108	10	1.31	123	98	57
42	1	79	86	12	1.14	233	169	49
43	1	89	76	11	0.57	196	193	60
44	1	116	100	9	0.33	176	190	79
45	1	92	101	11	1.05	162	157	72
46	1	109	97	16	0.62	167	230	65
47	1	80	95	8	0.95	188	161	77
48	1	94	95	10	0.43	161	105	79
49	1	103	90	11	0.69	288	220	109
50	1	106	102	7	0.12	289	142	144
51	1	111	88	11	0.57	278	215	83
52	1	98	105	6	1.40	246	226	123
53	1	98	106	8	0.71	271	138	117
54	1	88	88	10	0.43	203	172	66
55	1	94	83	9	0.69	305	224	77
56	1	109	91	4	0.52	288	216	116
57	1	99	94	16	0.93	273	204	84
58	1	75	105	13	0.79	162	93	59
59	1	108	85	16	0.67	298	251	84
60	1	117	106	6	0.41	177	143	47
61	1	106	101	12	0.45	151	126	115
62	1	90	96	9	0.69	86	119	54
63	1	97	95	4	1.02	232	224	82
64	1	112	101	16	1.64	264	191	78
65	2	81	118	12	1.83	162	110	125
66	1	101	98	10	0.38	191	154	112
67	1	103	87	11	0.52	134	129	71
68	2	88	94	6	1.17	138	80	65
69	2	93	114	13	1.26	146	122	104
70	2	111	93	15	1.50	275	170	96
71	2	61	100	9	0.81	130	141	66
72	2	91	110	5	1.74	156	144	51
73	2	100	91	7	0.55	223	120	97
74	1	115	78	10	0.67	322	100	153
75	2	92	84	13	0.90	251	169	59
76	2	89	95	5	2.45	181	165	50
77	1	85	87	9	0.19	268	218	71
78	2	82	91	12	1.36	203	215	84
79	2	90	96	10	1.40	168	127	67
80	2	115	107	15	0.29	292	152	107
81	1	113	85	13	0.98	311	223	109

(continued)

SUBNUM	SEX	BSRIM	BSRIF	SELFMON	SYMP	JASA	JASS&I	JASHD&C
82	2	101	112	5	0.93	261	127	96
83	2	97	116	3	0.48	170	93	96
84	1	79	92	10	1.33	201	140	59
85	1	97	98	8	0.19	220	116	100
86	2	94	108	11	0.86	164	127	66
87	2	102	99	10	1.76	159	200	50
88	2	116	88	18	2.64	319	229	134
89	2	81	95	7	1.24	159	105	116
90	2	123	103	14	1.43	357	176	179
91	2	58	113	4	1.27	110	85	56
92	2	88	113	4	0.12	145	100	96
93	2	95	87	8	0.86	174	131	49
94	2	97	104	12	1.55	221	156	76
95	2	109	113	9	0.74	174	126	79
96	2	58	107	9	1.59	290	248	93
97	2	84	101	11	1.40	133	114	75
98	2	95	110	13	1.07	171	78	64
99	2	82	103	13	1.43	156	189	68
100	1	117	75	5	0.26	263	145	103
101	2	105	95	10	1.86	298	226	78
102	2	93	118	10	1.62	237	186	115
103	1	106	86	8	0.79	153	132	101
104	2	88	103	5	0.98	280	216	76
105	2	107	115	9	1.36	314	321	87
106	1	87	81	3	0.76	110	115	42
107	2	95	95	13	1.55	160	216	66
108	2	84	103	6	1.14	259	235	80
109	2	115	84	11	2.29	334	205	97
110	2	74	99	7	2.12	231	155	69
111	1	109	85	12	0.67	302	306	94
112	2	121	93	4	1.02	301	236	78
113	1	136	85	12	0.69	361	240	169
114	2	59	144	13	1.59	142	95	64
115	2	116	101	13	0.29	303	207	88
116	2	98	95	13	0.83	335	265	96
117	1	102	86	12	0.62	262	156	105
118	2	121	98	2	1.14	305	231	72
119	1	122	114	12	1.00	159	132	119
120	1	103	105	6	0.48	205	153	101
121	1	95	92	10	0.38	175	194	84
122	2	94	104	10	0.55	239	164	66
123	2	113	74	8	0.67	193	160	78
124	1	94	100	11	0.62	166	150	78
125	1	116	92	8	0.79	350	249	90
126	1	110	91	11	0.93	156	119	81
127	1	125	70	13	0.31	316	261	98

SUBNUM	SEX	BSRIM	BSRIF	SELFMON	SYMP	JASA	JASS&I	JASHD&C
128	1	131	86	14	1.31	373	290	104
129	1	125	90	11	0.21	337	171	109
130	2	98	102	11	0.86	307	235	64
131	1	97	89	8	0.57	251	120	89
132	2	91	84	10	0.81	147	129	62
133	2	95	123	13	1.76	178	150	63
134	1	93	107	13	0.33	127	176	61
135	1	114	86	14	0.57	297	254	75
136	2	98	115	10	0.50	216	202	91
137	2	105	105	8	0.69	245	206	95
138	2	115	96	11	1.19	346	163	119
139	2	69	106	13	0.55	253	192	99
140	2	109	102	12	0.17	335	291	102
141	1	91	95	11	1.24	163	182	69
142	2	88	104	10	0.60	111	105	66
143	2	109	126	10	0.48	147	167	70
144	1	109	85	13	0.05	148	103	70
145	2	91	92	12	0.60	215	201	57
146	2	95	97	12	0.86	186	193	70
147	2	106	92	6	0.34	255	105	146
148	2	100	110	10	0.95	181	126	102
149	2	109	102	14	0.67	162	160	80
150	2	98	118	5	0.67	163	158	104
151	2	68	87	5	0.33	225	150	75
152	1	97	105	12	0.64	264	92	100
153	2	84	105	11	1.26	327	184	131
154	1	96	91	15	0.62	241	210	86
155	1	91	90	6	1.83	241	281	71
156	2	106	88	11	1.38	262	181	69
157	2	101	97	7	1.02	201	159	64
158	1	109	93	11	0.74	210	130	74
159	2	88	77	11	2.02	213	302	58
160	2	91	104	11	0.93	242	161	94
161	2	82	94	15	0.83	189	193	68
162	2	107	107	16	1.10	347	172	122
163	2	105	105	4	1.10	354	236	141
164	2	105	106	8	1.05	303	275	114
165	1	73	87	9	0.83	181	156	59
166	1	99	93	8	0.50	253	278	106
167	2	86	112	12	1.79	115	86	63
168	1	104	91	8	0.62	268	142	103
169	1	96	109	16	1.76	165	234	75
170	1	118	84	12	1.62	340	261	155
171	1	101	97	7	0.83	118	253	106
172	2	105	101	13	0.83	154	80	101
173	2	101	110	11	0.67	101	90	69

(continued)

SUBNUM	SEX	BSRIM	BSRIF	SELFMON	SYMP	JASA	JASS&I	JASHD&C
174	2	101	105	11	2.22	309	250	104
175	2	74	86	10	1.10	131	137	91
176	2	73	106	10	1.88	277	237	86
177	2	59	110	5	1.21	117	179	46
178	2	95	93	10	1.26	152	183	40
179	2	107	111	16	1.62	206	150	99
180	1	109	73	11	0.76	260	171	87
181	1	123	81	3	0.31	305	136	141
182	2	104	94	10	1.36	146	146	44
183	1	96	97	8	0.31	176	153	79
184	2	114	94	8	1.29	266	193	85
185	1	107	59	4	1.05	221	132	86
186	1	98	80	6	1.07	190	143	67
187	1	107	95	18	0.71	175	129	116
188	2	105	114	6	1.33	150	96	107
189	2	113	85	8	1.90	208	206	77
190	2	96	105	16	0.93	246	124	95
191	2	77	107	9	0.88	198	119	73

Answers to Odd-Numbered Exercises

CHAPTER 1

1. (a) N; (b) O; (c) I; (d) O; (e) I; (f) R; (g) N; (h) R

3. (a) $\displaystyle\sum_{i=3}^{5} X_i$ (b) $\displaystyle\sum_{i=1}^{4} Y_i^2$ (c) $\displaystyle\sum_{i=1}^{4} X_i$ (d) $\displaystyle\sum_{i=1}^{N} X_i$

5. (a) Add the numbers from the third value to the sixth value.
   (b) Add together the first seven values.
   (c) Add all the values together.
   (d) Again, add all the values together.

CHAPTER 2

1. (a) 29.5   39.5   34.5   10
   (b) 3.5   5.5   4.5   2
   (c) 6.45   6.95   6.7   0.5
   (d) 75.5   78.5   77   3
   (e) 22.95   23.45   23.2   0.5
   (f) 59.5   89.5   74.5   30
   (g) 99.5   124.5   112   25
   (h) 19.5   39.5   29.5   20
   (i) 44.5   49.5   47   5
   (j) 0.005   0.035   0.02   0.03

3. (a) D; (b) D; (c) D; (d) C; (e) C; (f) C; (g) D; (h) D; (i) C; (j) D

15. (a) Negative; (b) positive; (c) positive; (d) normal; (e) negative; (f) negative

21. (a) 75.5; (b) 71; (c) 58%

23. (a) 5.2; (b) 20%; (c) 4.5 glasses

CHAPTER 3

1. $\overline{X} = 12$
3. $\overline{X} = 10.21$; Median $= 10.5$
5. $\overline{X}_c = \$43,445.67$
7. $\overline{X}_c = 23.38$
9. $\overline{X} = 2.2$; Median $= 2$; positive skewness
11. $\overline{X} = \$672.75$; Median $= \$674.00$. The store did not reach its sales goal.
13. $\overline{X} = 6.24$. Yes, they got free-meal cards.

CHAPTER 4

1. $s = 4.48$
3. Range $= 25,900$. The two extreme scores are not representative, and give a distorted view of the range.
5. $\overline{X} = 27$; $s = 2.45$
7. $\overline{X} = 5.67$; $s = 4.05$
11. English, $z = 0.34$; Mathematics, $z = -0.04$; Reading, $z = 0.45$; Science Reasoning, $z = 0.48$. Best on Science Reasoning and worst on Mathematics.
13. Amy, $z = -0.60$; Cheri, $z = 0.91$; Jen, $z = 0.15$

CHAPTER 5

1. (a) 39.8; (b) 31.86; (c) 88.48; (d) 99.02; (e) 2.5; (f) .49; (g) 95.73; (h) 97.5
3. (a) 1.58%; (b) 8.69%; (c) 203.86; (d) 25.78%; (e) 112.06 to 195.94; (f) 181.39
5. (a) 15.87%; (b) 28.43%; (c) 71.55 or 71.48; (d) 54.12
7. (a) $p = .66$; (b) $p = .034$; (d) 57 to 30; 30 to 57
9. (a) $p = .016$; 2 to 98; 98 to 2
   (b) $p = .087$; 9 to 91; 91 to 9
11. (a) $p = .1587$
    (b) $p = .7157$
13. $p = .02$; $p = .06$
15. $p = .17$; $p = .25$

CHAPTER 6

3. 2.5% + 2.5% = 5.0%
5. (a) 20.18 to 21.82; (b) Not likely; $\mu = 20$ is outside the interval.
7. (a) 195.18 to 208.82; (b) Not likely; $\mu = 210$ is outside the interval.
9. (a) 99.77 to 110.23; (b) Likely, since $\mu = 100$ is inside the interval.

CHAPTER 7

1. (a) +; (b) −; (c) +; (d) 0; (e) 0; (f) −; (g) +
3. $r = .87$
5. $r = .42$
7. $r = .74$
9. $r = .95$
11. Yes. Since $r = .32$ is greater than the tabled value of .254, our obtained r is significant at the .01 level.
13. $r_s = -.96$

CHAPTER 8

1. $b = 2$; $a = 3$
3. a. $Y' = 1.13X - 7.32$
   b. $Y' = 56,492.68$
5. $r^2 = 0.44$
7. a. $Y' = 0.1134X + 0.1311$
   b. $Y' = \$3.53$
9. a. $\overline{X} = 17.4$, $s_x = 4.95$; $\overline{Y} = 7$, $s_y = 2.98$
   b. $r = .80$
   d. $Y' = .49X - 1.53$
   e. 9.25
   f. 9.25 ± 1.84 or 7.41 to 11.09

CHAPTER 9

1. A significant difference is indicated at the .05 level, but not at the .01 level.
3. $s_{\text{diff}} = 1.45$; $t(38) = 2.90$, $p < .01$.
5. $s_{\text{diff}} = 5.37$; $t(10) = -1.79$, $p > .05$.
7. $\overline{D} = 30.25$; $t(11) = -7.02$, $p < .001$.
9. $s_{\text{diff}} = .445$; $t(18) = -1.80$, $p > .05$.
11. 95% CI: 501.98 to 568.02; 99% CI: 490.25 to 579.75

CHAPTER 10

1. If H_0 is true, p of α (Type I error) is decreased. If H_A is true, p of β (Type II error) is increased.
3. a. $p = .05$
   b. $p = .14$
   c. Power $= .86$

CHAPTER 11

1. $SS_T = 92$; $SS_{BG} = 66$; $SS_{WG} = 26$
3. (Same as exercise 1)
5. $MS_{BG} = 35$; $MS_{WG} = 4.67$; $F(2, 12) = 7.50$, $p < .01$
7. $F(2, 21) = 3.47$
9. $q = 3.58$
11. $F(2, 17) = 0.24$, $p > .05$. There were no significant differences between the three groups.
13. $F(2, 26) = 18.21$, $p < .01$. $\bar{X}_1$ and $\bar{X}_2$: $q = 8.45$, $p < .01$; $\bar{X}_1$ and $\bar{X}_3$: $q = 5.09$, $p < .01$; $\bar{X}_2$ and $\bar{X}_3$: $q = 3.13$, $p > .05$

CHAPTER 12

3.

Source	df	SS	MS	F	p
Music	1	3.6	3.6	4.41	$p < .05$
Task	1	8.1	8.1	9.92	$p < .01$
Interaction	1	2.5	2.5	3.06	$p > .05$
Within Groups	36	29.4	0.82		
Total	39	43.6			

5.

Source	df	SS	MS	F	p
Emotion	1	136.9	136.9	15.80	$p < .01$
Motherhood	1	0.1	0.1	0.01	$p > .05$
Interaction	1	16.9	16.9	1.95	$p > .05$
Within Groups	36	312.0	8.67		
Total	39	465.9			

7.

Source	df	SS	MS	F	p
Display	1	240.1	240.1	17.87	$p < .01$
Content	1	40.0	40.0	2.98	$p > .05$
Interaction	1	2.5	2.5	0.19	$p > .05$
Within Groups	36	483.8	13.44		
Total	39	766.4			

CHAPTER 13

1. $\chi^2(1) = 58.94$, $p < .001$
3. $\chi^2(1) = 6.00$, $p < .05$
5. $U = 28$, $p > .05$
7. $H = 6.12$, $p < .05$
9. $N = 10$, $x = 2$, $p = .055$, one-tailed
11. $N = 10$, $T = 7$, $p < .05$, two-tailed
13. $\chi_r^2 = 11.1$, $p < .01$

INDEX